OVERHEARING FILM DIALOGUE

OVERHEARING
FILM
DIALOGUE

SARAH KOZLOFF

UNIVERSITY OF CALIFORNIA PRESS
Berkeley · Los Angeles · London

University of California Press
Berkeley and Los Angeles, California

University of California Press, Ltd.
London, England

Library of Congress Cataloging-in-Publication Data

Kozloff, Sarah.
  Overhearing film dialogue / Sarah Kozloff.
    p.   cm.
  Filmography: p.
  Includes bibliographical references and index.
  ISBN 0-520-22137-0 (cloth : alk. paper)—
  ISBN 0-520-22138-9 (pbk. : alk. paper)
  1. Dialogue in motion pictures.   I. Title.

PN1995.9.D49 K69 2000
791.43′6—dc21
                                    99-046452

Manufactured in the United States of America

08   07   06   05   04   03   02   01   00   99
10   9   8   7   6   5   4   3   2   1

The paper used in this publication meets the minimum
requirements of ANSI/NISO Z39.48-1992 (R 1997)
(*Permanence of Paper*). ⊗

To Lloyd and Bonnie Kozloff
parents extraordinaires

Contents

Acknowledgments

Sabbatical leaves provided by Vassar College were essential to this project; the college also directly underwrote many of the expenses through grants given by the Research Committee.

My greatest intellectual debts are to those who generously gave up their time to read all or parts of the manuscript, providing doses of encouragement at just the point when they were most needed, and enriching it with their suggestions: Peter Antelyes, Elisabeth Arlyck, Leger Grindon, Daniel Kozloff, Lawrence Levi, Jim Steerman, Susan Zlotnick, and two anonymous readers for the University of California Press.

My kind colleagues Michael Pisani (Music), Douglas Glick (Linguistics), Jamie Saeger (English), Denise Walen (Drama), and Robert Brigham (History) shared their expertise on key issues.

I feel lucky to have had the enthusiasm, insights, and painstaking efforts of several Vassar student assistants: Jessica Giannotta (for two years), Maura Keating, Michael Neel, and—during this last year of crucial manuscript preparation—Derek Kane-Meddock.

David Susman and Jasper Long at Vassar's Computer and Information Systems helped me with the illustrations. The staff of the Vassar library not only obtained whatever materials I requested with cheerful alacrity but often anticipated my needs.

My husband, Robert Lechterman, spent hours refining the photos. He also continually refilled the printer's ink cartridge, built a larger bookcase for my videos, took over household duties, and in general provided aid, comfort, licorice, and coffee. In some parallel universe, could I have written this study without him? Or without our boys, who alternately helped out and raised a ruckus right outside my study door? Perhaps, but it would not have been *this* book, which from the beginning has been a labor of love.

Introduction

The Study of Filmic Speech

I'd like to start with a scene from William Wyler's *Wuthering Heights* (1939), a film I admire, even though many would dismiss it as the epitome of Hollywood pretentiousness—an overwrought, unfaithful, "prestige" adaptation of a famous novel. The scene that interests me—nay, haunts me—occurs perhaps a third of the way through the film, when headstrong, frivolous Cathy (Merle Oberon) comes down to the kitchen to tell the servant Ellen that her rich, upper-class neighbor, Edgar Linton, has just proposed to her. What Cathy does not know, but the viewer does, is that Heathcliff (Laurence Olivier), the poor, rough foundling her father adopted years ago, is in the outer passageway listening in on the conversation. The scene proceeds as follows:

Heathcliff opens the door to the kitchen. His hands are bleeding.

HEATHCLIFF: Has he gone?
ELLEN: Heathcliff, your hands—what have you done?
HEATHCLIFF: Linton—is he gone?
ELLEN: What have you done to your hands? Oh, Heathcliff . . . What have you been doing?
HEATHCLIFF: I want to crawl to her feet, whimper to be forgiven, for loving her, for needing her more than my own life, for belonging to her more than my own soul.
CATHY: *(from the other room, off camera)* Ellen . . .
HEATHCLIFF: Don't let her see me, Ellen.
ELLEN: No.

Heathcliff hides in the outer vestibule.

CATHY: Ellen, I wondered whether you were still up.
ELLEN: Has he gone?

All quotations of film dialogue, unless otherwise noted, have been transcribed from the screen. For details of screenwriters, studios, and so on, see the Select Filmography.

1

> CATHY: Ellen, I've got some news for you.
> ELLEN: But the kitchen's no place for that. Let's come into the parlor—
> CATHY: Come here.
> ELLEN: Please, Cathy.
> CATHY: Sit down. Listen. Ellen, can you keep a secret? Ellen, Edgar's asked me to marry him.
> ELLEN: What did you tell him?
> CATHY: I told him I'd give him my answer tomorrow.
> ELLEN: But do you love him, Miss Cathy?
> CATHY: Yes. Of course.
> ELLEN: Why?
> CATHY: Why? That's a silly question, isn't it?
> ELLEN: No, not so silly. Why do you love him?
> CATHY: Because he's handsome and pleasant to be with.
> ELLEN: That's not enough.
> CATHY: Because he'll be rich someday. And I'll be the finest lady in the county.
> ELLEN: Oh. And now tell me how you love him.
> CATHY: I love the ground under his feet, the air above his head, and everything he touches.
> ELLEN: What about Heathcliff?
> CATHY: Oh, Heathcliff. He gets worse everyday. It would degrade me to marry him. I wish he hadn't come back. Oh, it would be heaven to escape from this disorderly, comfortless place.

After these lines Heathcliff silently slips out of the house, a fact communicated to the viewer through the effect of showing a lamp flicker in the breeze of the opened doorway (fig. 1). Alas, Heathcliff has left too soon; he doesn't stay to hear Cathy further reveal her preference:

> ELLEN: Well, if Master Edgar and his charms and money and parties mean heaven to you, what's to keep you from taking your place among the Linton angels?
> CATHY: I don't think I belong in heaven, Ellen. I dreamt once I was there. I dreamt I went to heaven and that heaven didn't seem to be my home and I broke my heart with weeping to come back to Earth. The angels were so angry they flung me out into the middle of the heath on top of Wuthering Heights. And I woke up sobbing with joy. That's it, Ellen—I've no more business marrying Edgar Linton than I have of being in heaven. But Ellen . . . Ellen, what can I do?
> ELLEN: You're thinking of Heathcliff.
> CATHY: Who else? He's sunk so low, he seems to take pleasure in being mean and brutal. And yet, he's more myself than I am. What-

1. *Wuthering Heights.* Ellen notices that Heathcliff has left.

> ever our souls are made of, his and mine are the same. And
> Linton's is as different as frost from fire. My one thought in
> living is Heathcliff. Ellen, I *am* Heathcliff. Everything he's
> suffered, I've suffered. The little happiness he's ever known,
> I've had, too. Oh Ellen, if everything in the world died and
> Heathcliff remained, life would still be full for me.

Cathy has come to know her heart, but it is too late. Hearing only her
slighting remarks, Heathcliff has run out into the storm and quitted
Wuthering Heights. Desperately, Cathy seeks him in the rain, making
herself seriously ill; months later she ends up marrying Linton after all.

What's apt about this scene is its tragic irony. For too many
decades, film viewers have put themselves in the position of Heathcliff: we've been bad eavesdroppers; we've jumped to conclusions;
we haven't listened attentively all the way through. Like Heathcliff,
who walks into the kitchen so smoldering from slights and shame
that moments earlier he's smashed his "dirty hands" through a win-
dowpane, we've listened with preconceptions, with a chip on our

2. *Wuthering Heights.* CATHY: I *am* Heathcliff.

shoulder, and we've only been open to that which confirmed our expectations.

Since the birth of the cinema, we've chanted a mantra: "Film is a Visual Medium." Films must tell their stories visually—editing, deep focus, lighting, camera movement, and nifty special effects are what really count. Dialogue, on the other hand, is just something we have to put up with. John Ford encapsulated these sentiments in a 1964 interview: "When a motion picture is at its best, it is long on action and short on dialogue. When it tells its story and reveals its characters in a series of simple, beautiful, active pictures, and does it with as little talk as possible, then the motion picture medium is being used to its fullest advantage."[1]

Try this experiment: show this scene from *Wuthering Heights* to anyone and ask them what they like best about it, and they are bound to point to the neat trick with the candle flame, a visual effect.

Ask them what they like least about the scene, and they're equally bound to point to the line, "I *am* Heathcliff." For besides serving as a metaphor for faulty eavesdropping, this scene haunts me because it also exemplifies why so many have scorned dialogue for so long—it contains a line of dialogue so outrageously bad that it makes one squirm with discomfort. The sentiment—being such soul mates that one can't tell where one ends and one's lover begins—is so corny that it's embarrassing. The phrasing is too naked, too preposterous.

"I *am* Heathcliff" is easy to scorn. But before we rush to judgment, we might note that the script is by Ben Hecht and Charles MacArthur, a writing team famous for cynicism and wit in plays and films such as *The Front Page* (1928) and *Twentieth Century* (1934). Moreover, the line itself is straight out of Emily Brontë (as is the whole scene), and in the novel, it sounds important, not jarring. Is the phrase itself really so terrible, or is the problem in Merle Oberon's strained performance, with her eyes stretched wide and her phony pause? (According to reports, Wyler was dissatisfied with her playing of the scene and made her do it again and again, until she left the set in tears.)[2] Or is the flaw actually in Wyler's own direction? After all, *someone* decided to emphasize the line through a long pause, a dolly-in, a flash of lightning. Would "I *am* Heathcliff" be palatable if it had been downplayed, thrown away in a sad mumble, by an actress with the skill of Emma Thompson?

Or could the difficulty lie elsewhere altogether, not in the film, but in viewers' expectations? Why is the line's heightened rhetoric so embarrassing to contemporary ears? Isn't this style appropriate, even required, for a gothic melodrama? Why does such a bald expression of love make us squirm?

It is worth admitting, here, at the outset of a defense of film dialogue, that not every line in every film is felicitous. Yet if we allow ourselves to focus too intently on this one bad line, we are repeating Heathcliff's folly. The rest of the scene's dialogue surely merits attention. We might notice that it is through conversation that Cathy actually discovers her own feelings and reveals them to the viewer. We might pause over the complexities of Ellen's strategies—first her attempt to forestall Cathy, then her endeavor to draw her out and lead her to knowledge in an almost Socratic fashion. Cathy's narration of her dream is a key foreshadowing of the story's events, for Cathy does die, but she does not rest quietly in the afterlife, her soul returns to Heathcliff and Wuthering Heights. And as for the dialogue's style, the metaphors concerning frost and fire, heaven and earth are richly evocative. Note, too, that Heathcliff's manner of

speaking—he claims to "belong to her more than [his] own soul"—
exactly matches Cathy's both in substance and in tone. One mark of
these lovers' connection and their separation from everyone else is
that they speak the same impassioned rhetoric. It is the dialogue, not
the flickering flame or Gregg Toland's skillful deep-focus cinematography, that actually gives the scene its substance.

FALLING ON DEAF EARS

Since the late 1970s, when the field of cinema studies "rediscovered"
the sound track, numerous productive studies have been published
on sound technology, film music, sound effects, and sound theory.
With notable exceptions,[3] most of this scholarship has only minimally addressed the most important aspect of film sound—namely,
the dialogue.

Although what the characters say, exactly how they say it, and
how the dialogue is integrated with the rest of the cinematic techniques are crucial to our experience and understanding of every film
since the coming of sound, for the most part analysts incorporate the
information provided by a film's dialogue and overlook the dialogue
as signifier. Canonical textbooks on film aesthetics devote pages and
pages to editing and cinematography but barely mention dialogue.
Visual analysis requires mastery of a recondite vocabulary and
trained attentiveness; dialogue has been perceived as too transpar-
ent, too simple to need study.

Recent historical work on screenwriters has not gone very far toward addressing this neglect. "How to" primers on screenwriting
discuss dialogue superficially; their treatment is invariably prescriptive rather than analytical. Analyses of individual screenplays focus
on the genesis and development of the text (often with the intention
of determining who deserves the credit), rather than on dialogue
technique. Film reviews fall back on vapid clichés—the dialogue is
"witty" or "clumsy"—without specifying the grounds for such evaluations.

The neglect of film dialogue by more recent film scholarship actually reflects the field's long-standing antipathy to speech in film. This
bias is blatant in the writings of early film theorists such as Rudolph
Arnheim, Sergei Eisenstein, and Siegfried Kracauer, who are notori-

ous for championing silent film over sound.* Classical theorists offered numerous and sometimes contradictory reasons for their disdain for film sound and speech: sound would restrict montage; sound would restrict camera movement; silent film had its own poetry precisely because it found visual substitutions for sound; dialogue kept films from crossing national boundaries; dialogue was a distraction from the camera's ability to capture the natural world; dialogue encouraged too much attention to character psychology; dialogue turned film into "canned theater."[4]

Some of the complaints of classical theorists have been assuaged; for instance, improvements in microphones, sound mixing and editing, and the muffling of camera noise swiftly ameliorated the initial difficulties with the transition to sound that had temporarily compromised camera movement and editing. The practical problems with international distribution also have been lessened through workable systems of dubbing and subtitling.

But the fear that incorporating dialogue compromises film as an independent art form by bringing it too close to theater has persisted. "Cinema, at once high art and popular art, is cast as the art of the authentic," explains Susan Sontag. "Theatre, by contrast, means dressing up, pretense, lies. It smacks of aristocratic taste and the class society."[5] Moreover, there has been a widespread embrace of what is called "the specificity thesis," the argument that each artistic medium is distinct, and so to be true to itself and to reach its highest potential, each should capitalize upon its unique characteristics. Noël Carroll has argued, however, that "the specificity thesis" is based on illogical, tautological premises and misconstrues the relationship between narrative arts. Carroll notes that the thesis:

> [A]ppears to envision each art form on the model of a highly specialized tool with a range of determinate functions. A film, play, poem or painting is thought of, it seems, as analogous to something like a Phillips screwdriver. If you wish to turn a screw with a cross-shaped groove on top, use a Phillips screwdriver. If you wish to explore the

---

* There *were* a few early defenders of film speech. Marcel Pagnol, for one, declared: "Any talking film which can be shown silent and remain comprehensible is a very bad talking film" ("The Talking Film," in *Rediscovering French Film*, ed. Mary Lea Bardy [New York: Museum of Modern Art, 1983], 91).

potentials of aesthetically crafted language, use theater. If your topic
is animated action, use film. But I think it is incumbent on us to question whether this underlying metaphor has any applicability when it
comes to art forms. Are art forms highly specialized tools? I think
not. If art forms are like tools at all, then they are more like sticks
than like Phillips screwdrivers. That is, they can be used to do many
things; they have not been designed to perform a specific task. . . . An
artistic medium, including a self-consciously invented one, is such
that many of its potentials remain to be discovered.[6]

Perhaps film *is* adept at many of the goals classical theorists allotted
to it, such as revealing the beauty of the natural world, creating abstract moving images, taking editing to extremes, capturing ma-
chines in motion. Yet Carroll helps us see that being talented in certain areas does not equate with being restricted forever to solely
those objectives.

Although today everyone graciously allows movies to talk,
commonplace attitudes toward dialogue still betray suspicion and
a fierce desire to regulate. Anti-dialogue dicta are not confined to
the era of the transition to sound or to some benighted past; these
prejudices seem to linger like the undead, periodically reappearing
to poison our perception. Witness a 1991 statement by David
Mamet: "Basically, the perfect movie doesn't have any dialogue. So
you should always be striving to make a silent movie."[7] Or note the
definition of dialogue offered in Ephraim Katz's widely used *Film
Encyclopedia* (originally compiled in 1979, with a third edition in
1998):

> **dialogue:** In a film, all spoken lines. Since the cinema is essentially a
> visual medium, dialogue is, or should be, used more sparingly than
> in the theater, supplementing action rather than substituting for it.[8]

However, the wish to separate cinema from the theater and capitalize on its visual expressivity does not really explain these widespread and prolonged efforts to suppress film dialogue. For one
thing, although theater was film's direct competitor in the early
years of the twentieth century, by now film has decisively won the
competition for mass audiences, and the need to distinguish the new
art from its forebear is no longer pressing. For another, in point of
fact, discussions of drama and literature also bear witness to the
same desire to minimize dialogue. "Good dramatic dialogue reveals

but does not explain. The fewer words the character speaks and the more he shows of himself by them, the better the writing," decreed the American playwright Rachel Crothers (1878–1958) in the 1920s.[9] Sam Smiley reprised this stance in a playwrighting manual published in the 1970s:

> What Ernest Hemingway often said about writing fiction applies to dialogue as well: Good writing means erecting an iceberg of words; only a few words are visible; but many more are there under the surface. So it is with dialogue economy in a play. A writer should avoid superfluous words and delete every one that does not carry a burden of meaning. In plays, actors' physical actions can substitute for many words. Although dialogue has to be continually emotive, it should be absolutely economic.[10]

And although twentieth-century playwrights such as Samuel Beckett, Harold Pinter, and Eugène Ionesco have obviously made wordplay their central strategy, other dramatists—specifically Antonin Artaud, the futurists, and the theatricalists—have sought to annihilate the "the theatre of language," believing that pantomime is the essence of theatre.[11] As regards the novel, the so-called "school of virility" in American literature, which enshrined the economic style of Hemingway and demonstrated hostility to expansiveness or eloquence, has been very influential.[12]

If theatrical and literary discourse also reveals the urge to suppress dialogue, and if the prejudices against film dialogue far outlast the memory of the special artistry of silent films and the technical flaws of early sound recording, larger or stronger cultural forces than lags in technology and the rather esoteric issue of aesthetic specificity must be at work.

I believe that the hostility toward cinematic (and theatrical and literary) speech should be seen as just part of the enduring denigration of all speech. Proverbs advise us that "Silence is golden" and "Talk is cheap." Benjamin Franklin counseled: "Speak little, do much."[13] Ambrose Bierce defined "Talk" as: "To commit an indiscretion without temptation, from an impulse without purpose."[14] Søren Kierkegaard once commented: "How ironical that it is by means of speech that man can degrade himself below the level of the dumb creation—for a chatterbox is truly of a lower category than a dumb creature."[15]

In the attacks on speech, certain themes recur:

1. Words can be used to lie, whereas pictures provide more trust-worthy evidence. "One picture is worth ten thousand words."*
2. Words are empty, vacuous. "Actions speak louder than words."
3. Words may be hasty, intemperate, leading the speaker into trouble. "Loose lips sink ships."
4. Showing is superior—more informative, more meaningful, more subtle—than telling.

Although these statements seem seductively reasonable, all four can be refuted or at least qualified. Pictures can also "lie"—they can be doctored, staged, or digitally "enhanced." As for the charge of vacuousness, speech-act theory has taught us that words are hardly empty—they are themselves "actions." Elizabeth Traugott notes:

> One of the most important things to be learned from approaching language in terms of its use is that the familiar opposition between saying something and doing something—between word and deed—is not at all clear-cut. Saying is doing, and utterances are acts, capable of producing enormous and far reaching consequences. For example, the sentence "You are under arrest . . . " can deprive you of your physical freedom.[16]

Physical actions can be as hasty as intemperate words: buying the too-expensive item or grasping the pan before it has cooled are actions one may regret as much as the rash promise or betrayed confidence.

Finally, the belief in the superiority of "showing" over "telling" stems partly from the efficacy of demonstrating some manual skill over merely describing the same in words—a swim instructor who physically demonstrates the motions will get better results than one who just gives verbal commands. However, "showing over telling" has a specific history in aesthetic theory. It reflects the influential and widely echoed argument advanced by the followers of Henry James, such as Percy Lubbock, Joseph Warren Beach, and Ford Madox Ford, in the 1920s and 1930s. Part of modernism's revolt against Victorian

---

* William Safire has traced this phrase's history. It was coined in 1921 by an advertising man, Fred Barnard, who wanted to stress that a photograph of appetizing candy would attract more customers than a verbal description ("Worth a Thousand Words," *New York Times Magazine*, 7 April 1996, 16).

aesthetics, specifically the chatty narrator of Victorian novels, the tenet quickly hardened into an inflexible dogma in literary circles. "Showing," that is, presenting actions without any narrative commentary, is supposed to be more subtle, and to call for more participation by the reader than allowing a narrator to evaluate or summarize. But Wayne Booth has demonstrated in *The Rhetoric of Fiction* that seemingly objective "showing" is just another form of "telling," just another method by which authors guide their readers' responses.[17] Moreover, visuals are not always subtle—note the overly obvious miming of silent film—and words are not necessarily blatant. This argument slights the subtexts of verbal messages, all the subtleties that are common not only in literature and poetry but in everyday social discourse. Engagement is called for whether one is interpreting action or speech, visual images or dialogue.

I suspect that the four charges against words detailed above are to some extent pretexts. The underlying issue stems neither from some essential drawbacks of verbal communication nor from the diverging relationships between words and images/action and the physical world. The fundamental motivation comes from the fact that talkativeness has traditionally been allied with femininity, terse action with masculinity.

Of course, recent scholarship—particularly that linked to the work of Jacques Lacan—has been devoted to pointing out a contrary cultural disposition that identifies the Word, *logos*, as masculine, as the Word of God or the Law of the Father. In this paradigm, women are clearly linked with visual images, with bodies/beauty/silence— in short, with the lack of speech or logic or power. However, these two apparently opposite conceptions are not actually contradictory; they are two sides of the same coin. Walter Ong distinguishes between two kinds of speech: the common *materna lingua* (mother tongue) and the educated, "civilized" *patrius sermo* (father speech).[18] Whenever speech is valued as an important act in a public sphere, it is seen as masculine; when it is held to no account in the casual language of ordinary conversation, it is ascribed to women. The reason that women are silenced and objectified is to deny them access to powerful speech; when women *do* talk, their speech is redefined as inconsequential, nonstop chatter.

I am hardly the first scholar to focus on the association of trivial talkativeness with femininity. In *Literary Fat Ladies: Rhetoric, Gender,*

Property, Patricia Parker has traced the "tradition that portrays women as unflappable talkers" from ancient literature (she cites the biblical admonition: "Let woman learn in silence with all subjection. But I suffer not a woman to teach, not to usurp authority over the man, but to be in silence") to James Joyce's *Ulysses.*[19] In *Gossip,* Patricia Spacks has painstakingly detailed the customary connection of women with this category of speech.[20] Turning from the academic to the popular sphere, maxims also provide abundant evidence of the widespread association of private talk with women:

"Where woman is, silence is not." (France)

"The tongue is the sword of a woman, and she never lets it become rusty." (China)

"The North Sea will sooner be found wanting in water than a woman at a loss for a word." (Jutland)

"Ten measures of speech descended on the world; women took nine and men one." (Babylon)

"Two women and a goose are enough to make as much noise as you would hear at a fair." (Venice)

"Many women, many words; many geese, many turds." (England)

The linkage of talking women with animals is particularly common; in a famous instance in Fritz Lang's *Fury* (1936), the director cuts from a shot of rumormongering women to a shot of clucking hens; this visual metaphor is repeated during the "Pick-a-Little-Talk-a-Little" number in Morton Da Costa's adaptation of *The Music Man* (1962).

Another area in which the correlation of women and excess speech is manifest is in the English language. In *Language: The Social Mirror,* Elaine Chaika writes:

> It has already been noted that English vocabulary reflects a disvaluing of talk for its own sake. Moreover, it was shown that most words that mean "idle talk" in SE [Standard English] also are marked to mean [+ female], and/or [+ young, + trivial]. A person who is gabby, talkative, and gossipy, a nag, a shrew, or a chatterbox, must be a woman.[21]

In actuality, contemporary linguistic research does not support the supposition that the female sex talks the most. Dale Spender flatly states: "There has not been one study which provides evidence that women talk more than men, and there have been numerous studies which indicate that men talk more than women." She explains that the myth of the overtalkative woman has arisen because "women have not been judged on the grounds of whether they talk more than men, but of whether they talk more than silent women. . . . When silence is the desired state for women . . . then any talk in which a woman engages can be too much."[22]

Films that are "talky" come with the connotations "trivial" and "idle" and, ultimately, "female." Visual images and physical activity, which in the history of the cinema came first (as Adam preceded Eve), are associated with masculinity and "naturally" given precedence.

My argument is that dialogue has been continually discredited and undervalued in film because it is associated with femininity. To some it may appear far-fetched to assert that gender stereotypes have unconsciously affected the evaluation of film aesthetics by filmmakers, scholars, and viewers. But many of the "neutral" or "objective" discussions of film aesthetics betray just such an undercurrent. Listen to Alfred Hitchcock, who viewed every issue of his craft in sexual terms:

> Suspense is like a woman. The more left to the imagination, the more the excitement. . . . Movie titles, like women, should be easy to remember without being familiar, intriguing but never obvious. . . .
> A woman of mystery is one who also has a certain maturity and whose actions speak louder than words. Any woman can be one, if she keeps those two points in mind. She should grow up—and shut up.[23]

Kaja Silverman in *The Acoustic Mirror,* Mary Ann Doane in *The Desire to Desire,* and Amy Lawrence in *Echo and Narcissus* have all studied women's roles in American films and noticed how often female characters are silenced or punished for talking. My argument here dovetails with theirs but enters on another level: I believe that all dialogue (regardless of the gender of the speaking character) is associated with femininity, that films that speak "too much" are punished (with criticism from reviewers and academic disdain, and sometimes even low box office receipts). How else can one explain the reflexive, omnipresent pronouncements that dialogue must be "kept in its place"?

Just as Heathcliff is led into grievous error by his preconceptions and poor listening, so film history has been deformed by our lack of respect for dialogue. Many Hollywood directors—Cukor, Wilder, Mankiewicz, Sturges, Capra, Huston, Wyler—who chose to work with more literate scripts have historically been underappreciated. (Several of these have also been castigated as "women's" directors.) Secondly, the importance of screenplays and screenwriters to the final film has been obscured. Moreover, certain films that we now value quite highly were initially dismissed out of hand for their "talkiness"; see, for instance, Penelope Huston's misguided review of *All about Eve* (1950) and *Sunset Boulevard* (1950): "If, as I believe, the first quality of good screen writing is economy, then they are wasteful films, lavishing all that virtuoso writing on material which, in the last analysis, has not the strength to sustain it."[24]

Perhaps the most noteworthy consequence of this anti-dialogue bias is that it has led to misconceptions in our model of how films actually work. Many of the ways in which narrative is communicated, empathy elicited, themes conveyed, visuals interpreted come from the interaction of the words with the visual images. Ignoring the role of the words has led to overestimation of what viewers understand from the visuals or the editing alone.

Even our metaphor regarding the viewing experience needs adjustment. We are accustomed to using the analogy that the filmgoer is a voyeur, surreptitiously spying on the actions of the on-screen characters. What we've often overlooked is that *viewers* are also *listeners*, in fact, they are *eavesdroppers*, listening in on conversations purportedly addressed to others, but conversations that—in reality—are designed to communicate certain information to the audience.

THE NATURE OF FILM DIALOGUE

"Eavesdropping" is a loaded term, implying that the filmgoer is doing something surreptitious, something that gives him or her secret power and/or sexual pleasure. In a paper given at a recent conference, "The Narrative Functions of the Ecouteur," Elisabeth Weis traces the psychoanalytic context of "eavesdropping," noting that Freud placed great stress on the child's overhearing its parents making love, and that he thought such experiences crucial to the child's sexual development. Weis continues,

Psychoanalysts working with patients often hypothesize that the adult eavesdropper recapitulates the primal scene. The listener can identify with either of the people overheard, who represent the aggressive and the submissive parent. Or the listener's identification can be placed with the overhearing child. . . . I would simply suggest here that overhearing is a fundamental experience with profound implications for films. If we consider the film-going experience to be one of watching and overhearing characters who are separated from us, then the entire film-going experience could be defined as eavesdropping as well as voyeurism.[25]

Weis then proceeds to direct attention to films that include scenes of on-screen characters eavesdropping on one another, films such as *Careful, He Might Hear You* (1983), *Stella Dallas* (1937), *Addicted to Love* (1997), and *M*A*S*H* (1970). Weis demonstrates how diegetic eavesdropping raises issues concerning invasion of privacy and of social inclusion versus exclusion, and she examines how the act can lead to the on-screen listener finally recognizing a painful truth or having his or her deepest secrets exposed in public. Weis examines how films offer models of eavesdropping behavior that range from sadistic or pathological to sympathetic, and she examines narrative strategies that sanction the behavior of eavesdroppers, thereby sanctioning that behavior in the audience as well.

There may always be an element of illicit eroticism and mastery involved in sitting in the dark listening as characters enact their most intimate scenes. However, on another level of our consciousness, filmgoers always know that we haven't actually caught these people unawares. Herbert Clark and Thomas Carlson append to speech-act theory a systematic overview of the roles of different participants in conversations. One of their categories deals with "overhearers," such as strangers on a bus, or children listening in on their parents:

Speakers also design their utterances with overhearers in mind. . . . [T]hey realize that the overhearers can nevertheless form conjectures or hypotheses about what they mean. . . . By designing their utterances just right, speakers can lead overhearers to form correct hypotheses, incorrect hypotheses, or even no coherent hypotheses at all. If they know their overhearers, they can even design what they say to fit them in particular. . . . Overhearers are generally not meant to realize how utterances have been designed for them.[26]

Film dialogue has been purposely designed for the viewers to overhear, so that we can draw the best hypotheses, but films disguise the extent to which the words are truly meant for the off-screen listener. Part of the film-going suspension of disbelief is to collaborate in this fiction.

Discarding the fear of the contaminating power of the theater allows film analysts to learn from the work of drama theorists. The best description of how film dialogue works can be gleaned from Jean Chothia's *Forging a Language: A Study of Plays of Eugene O'Neill:*

> Stage dialogue is different from real speech. It operates by duplicity: it is not spontaneous but must appear to be so. It is permanent but must appear to be as ephemeral as the speech it imitates. The actor must seem to speak what in reality he recites. In sharing the convention, the audience in the theatre has a share in the duplicity. We simultaneously accept the illusion of spontaneity and know that it is a pretense. . . . For it is not the hearing of the words by the interlocutor that completes the exchange, as it is in everyday speech, but the witnessing and interpreting of both the utterance and the response by the audience. Much of the particular effect of drama derives from the gap between two ways of hearing, that of the interlocutor on stage and that of the audience, and from the audience's consciousness of the gap. The audience sets each utterance beside each previous utterance made within the limited time span of the play and, in doing so, catches implications beyond those immediately relevant to speaker and interlocutor. . . . If the dramatist is to create an action of significance . . . his dialogue, however natural it may appear, must be most *un*naturally resonant with meaning and implication.[27]

Film dialogue shares with dramatic dialogue these deformations from everyday conversation, this unnatural resonance, this double-layeredness—in short, this dramatic irony. The filmgoers always know *more* than any single character (we know that Heathcliff is hiding in the vestibule, we know that Ellen is aware that Heathcliff is eavesdropping; because of the flashback structure of the film, we even know something of the characters' futures), and we put each speech into the context of all the other information we've been receiving. Because we inevitably have a broader "range of knowledge"[28] about the characters and events, our interpretation of each line of dialogue differs from that of the on-screen conversationalists.

Chothia's description is extremely useful for understanding film speech. Yet film dialogue is distinguished from stage dialogue in two key ways: by the simultaneous signification of camerawork/mise-en-scène/editing that serves to select, emphasize, undercut, distract, reveal, or deform the filmgoer's interpretation; and by the phenomenological absence of the actors from the filmgoers' space and reality, which allows the spectators' cathexis with the characters more free play.*

Film dialogue is distinguished from dialogue in novels by the absence of the literary narrator who could explicitly summarize or interpret the characters' speeches or even render interior views of the characters' minds and emotions. Instead of a narrator sequentially contextualizing the characters' speech, film offers the simultaneous signification of camerawork/mise-en-scène/editing. Moreover, the difference between reading words printed on a page and hearing them spoken aloud by actors is immeasurable.

To further refine our understanding of cinematic dialogue: the interaction between the visual and verbal tracks is always complicated and depends greatly upon the details of each instance. A major goal of this study is to unravel these connections. In general, however, it is a mistake to think of one track as "supplementing" or "adding to" the other. This is why—although I wholeheartedly agree with Michel Chion's analysis—I quarrel with his term "added value." Chion has coined this term to denote the extent to which verbal text affects the interpretation of an image. His discussion is worth quoting at some length:

> An eloquent example that I often draw on in my classes to demonstrate value added by text is a TV broadcast from 1984, a transmission of an air show in England, anchored from a French studio for French audience by our own Léon Zitrone. Visibly thrown by these images coming to him on the wire with no explanation and in no special order, the valiant anchor nevertheless does his job as well as he can. At a certain point, he affirms, "Here are three small airplanes," as we see an image with, yes, three little airplanes against a blue sky, and the outrageous redundancy never fails to provoke laughter.
>
> Zitrone could just as well have said, "The weather is magnificent today," and that's what we would have seen in the image, where there are in fact no clouds. Or: "The first two planes are ahead of the third," and then everyone would have seen *that*. Or else: "Where did the fourth plane go?"—and the fourth airplane's absence, this plane hopping out of Zitrone's hat by the sheer power of the Word, would

---

* To forestall any suspicions that my examples in this book were not drawn from "real" films, I have tried to avoid discussing adaptations of plays. If a few have slipped in—such as *Casablanca* (1942) and *His Girl Friday* (1940)—it's because neglecting these important films entirely would have been just too perverse.

have jumped to our eyes. In short, the anchor could have made fifty other "redundant" comments; but their redundancy is illusory, since in each case these statements would have guided and structured our vision so that we would have seen them "naturally" in the image.[29]

As Chion argues, the announcer's words made the number of airplanes in view important. His statements are neither redundant nor some minor, dispensable "addition," but a fundamental component of the viewer's experience of that moment of the broadcast. "Frankly, my dear, I don't give a damn" is not some supplemental, optional addition to the image of Clark Gable walking out the door at the end of *Gone with the Wind* (1939); these words both explain the reason he is leaving and mete out a measure of revenge. The shots and physical pantomime without these words—with their exact mixture of politeness, affection, anger, and resignation—would not be just less effective, but totally different.

The pantomime has a long-standing international tradition—it has been traced to ancient Rome, the Chinese, Persians, Hebrews, and Egyptians. It was useful for silent film (especially for comedy); it lives on in circus clowns and narrative ballet. Wordless strings of pictures—in stained-glass windows, comic books, photo essays—can also tell simple stories or stories that are already familiar. But dialogue is a necessity for stories and characterizations of more than rudimentary complexity. To the extent that film chooses to be a narrative art form, as opposed to presenting visual poetry or abstraction, it has been and will continue to be dependent upon dialogue as an integral part of its arsenal.

But we must also bear in mind the ways in which film dialogue differs from spontaneous everyday speech. In narrative films, dialogue may strive mightily to imitate natural conversation, but it is always an imitation. It has been scripted, written and rewritten, censored, polished, rehearsed, and performed. Even when lines are improvised on the set, they have been spoken by impersonators, judged, approved, and allowed to remain. Then all dialogue is recorded, edited, mixed, underscored, and played through stereophonic speakers with Dolby sound. The actual hesitations, repetitions, digressions, grunts, interruptions, and mutterings of everyday speech have either been pruned away, or, if not, deliberately included. Less time is devoted to the actual functions of everyday discourse, such as merely establishing social contact (what Roman Jakobson calls "the phatic function") or confirming that a conversational partner is listening attentively. Although one cardinal rule of real conversation is that speakers should not tell each other what the other already knows,[30] film dialogue is often forced to smuggle in information merely for the viewer's benefit. Because the words are in truth directed at the filmgoer, not at the on-screen conversationalists, each word does double duty, works on double layers.

Norman Page has written a valuable study of dialogue in literature. He concludes his analysis of such dialogue's "reality-status" by noting that

> for various reasons it seems overwhelmingly likely that no dialogue in [a] novel or play will consist merely, or even mainly, of an accurate transcript of spontaneous speech. It is important to insist at this point that there is an inevitable gap—wider or narrower at different times, but never disappearing entirely—between speech . . . and even the most "realistic" dialogue in a world of literature.[31]

The same applies to film. This is why, although I have found the work of linguists extremely helpful, I conclude that the cross-disciplinary poaching cannot proceed in the opposite direction; linguists who use film dialogue as accurate case studies of everyday conversation are operating on mistaken assumptions.[32]

SOME POINTS TOWARD
A HISTORICAL PERSPECTIVE

For the most part, this study deals with formal generalizations rather than tracing a history of the development of film dialogue. Yet I do not mean to imply that film dialogue is a static entity or that it exists in a timeless void. Industrial, technological, and social changes have all affected the ways in which films have their characters speak.

First of all, the English language has itself changed enormously over the decades of the sound film. Tom Shachtman argues,

> We have to recognize that English is altering at a phenomenal rate of speed. Comparing successive editions of dictionaries, we find about

10,000 words per decade are added or dropped from the usual college
dictionaries, those which contain the working vocabularies of most
users of our language, somewhere around 100,000 words out of the
entire corpus of more than a million. That is to say, what one generation accepts as its standard is, at least in terms of vocabulary, perhaps
10 to 15 percent altered from what its parents accepted as standard.[33]

If the dialogue of films of the 1930s strikes us now as quaint or unnatural, this may be because of our distance in time from its original
audience and linguistic community.

In recent years, film theory has put new emphasis on the dynamics of film reception. We should keep in mind that while the history
of film production affects movies' use of dialogue, a parallel history
of the audience's reception is equally as important, as Christopher
Faulkner stresses.[34] As a minor instance of the effect of change in reception time, my students always laugh at Edie's line in *On The Waterfront* (1954) claiming that her convent school in Tarrytown is "in
the country." Their amused reaction was certainly not desired or anticipated by the filmmakers; it is a marker of the temporal gap—and
concomitant suburban development—between the world of the
characters and the present day. Similarly, Barbara Klinger points out
that certain lines in Douglas Sirk films spoken by Rock Hudson now
trigger laughter because of contemporary knowledge of Hudson's
homosexuality.[35]

A study focusing on the chronological development of film dialogue would start with the silent era. Speech sometimes literally accompanied silent films—we know that some exhibitors hired lectur-
ers to narrate silent films and local actors to speak lines for the
characters. As the industry moved toward standardization, film producers found it desirable or necessary to include printed dialogue
and expository intertitles. Barry Salt has found dialogue intertitles as
early as 1904;[36] Eileen Bowser records that from 1907 to 1915, producers experimented with finding exactly the right placement and
format for such titles.[37] After 1915, with feature-length films, title
writing became a specialty, and dialogue intertitles were used for
humor, to convey important information and to individuate characters. The critical overvaluation of the few films that tortuously man-
aged to avoid intertitles—for example, F. W. Murnau's *The Last
Laugh* (1924)—should not be taken as indicative of the typical practices of the silent era.

It is well known now that filmmakers experimented with the use of synchronized sound throughout the "silent" era and that numerous sound shorts were produced. Alan Williams has recently theorized that the popularity of *The Jazz Singer* (1927) and its aesthetic breakthrough stemmed, not from its use of sound per se, but from its move away from the direct address of vaudeville-inspired shorts toward the representational style of theater.[38] (In my terms, the shift was so successful because it allowed film audiences to slip into the comfortable role of *overhearers*.)

The transition to sound in the late 1920s was complicated for American studios and theater owners, demanding great outlays of capital and entailing negotiation between competing technologies and corporate strategies.[39] Equally upsetting for the film community was the wrenching ontological shift in the medium caused by the possibilities of sound. Many of the diatribes against sound as a whole and dialogue in particular date to this era—and the suspicions that sound would be the death of the visual artistry of silent film were initially abetted by the limitations of early microphones and recording apparatus, which restricted camera movement and disallowed both postsynchronization and multitrack mixing. From a historical perspective, what is remarkable about the transition to sound is, not that it was bumpy, but that the technical and aesthetic problems were solved so quickly and successfully, so that by the early 1930s the use of dialogue, sound effects, and music betrays none of the restrictions, tinniness, or fumbling of the transition films.

Aside from the legacy of anti-sound prejudice (and the associated critical overestimation of the importance of asynchronous matchings of sound and image), three events during the transition-to-sound years had major consequences for the future development of cinematic speech. First was the importation to Hollywood of East Coast writers, who were suddenly needed to write for the talkies. The newspapermen, playwrights, and vaudevillians who came west in the early 1930s brought with them new sensibilities, new stories, and a fresh approach to language. Pauline Kael has concentrated particularly on the influence of a group of talented cynics (some of whom once clustered at the Algonquin Hotel), including Herman Mankiewicz, Ben Hecht, Dorothy Parker, Charles MacArthur, George S. Kaufman, Nathanael West, S. J. Perelman, Samson Raphelson, Philip Barry, Robert Sherwood, and Sidney Howard. She writes:

Once American films had their voice and the Algonquin group was turned loose on the scripts, the revolting worship of European aristocracy faded so fast that movie stars even stopped bringing home Georgian princes. In the silents, the heroes were often simpletons. In the talkies, the heroes were to be the men who weren't fooled, who were smart and learned their way around. The new heroes of the screen were created in the image of their authors: they were fast-talking newspaper reporters.[40]

Secondly, the addition of sound instantly altered the balance of genres. Film musicals were suddenly possible, as were more literal adaptations of stage plays, which now could retain, not just plot points, but some of the original dramatic dialogue. Verbally based comedies featuring vaudeville performers such as the Marx Brothers and W. C. Fields expanded the contours of film comedy. And genres that had been established during the silent era underwent sea changes because of the new possibilities afforded by sound.

A third event of these years was the adoption of the Production Code, written in 1930 and more stringently enforced after 1934. Although there are numerous and complicated reasons why this formal practice of industry self-censorship was put in place at this time, one of the least discussed is that *verbal transgressions* of prevailing standards were now possible, and such violations were greatly feared. Although much of the Production Code deals with overall plot development, moral attitudes, and viewer conclusions, several of the tenets deal specifically with language. For example:

> *Oaths* should never be used as a comedy element. Where required by the plot, the less offensive oaths may be permitted.
> *Vulgar expressions* come under the same treatment as vulgarity in general. Where women and children are to see the film, vulgar expressions (and oaths) should be cut to the absolute essentials required by the situation.
> The name of *Jesus Christ* should never be used except in reverence.[41]

Censorship has been a major factor influencing cinematic speech. Looking forward in time, the defiance of the Production Code in the late 1950s and the gradual loosening of all restrictions throughout the 1960s prompted something of a seismic upheaval in scripting, allowing the frank treatment of taboo subject matter, the incorporation of street language, and the inclusion of obscenity, while obviating the need for circumlocution or double entendre.

Along with the Production Code, one of the major influences on dialogue throughout the studio years was the star system. The famous advertising slogan for Clarence Brown's *Anna Christie* (1930)— "Garbo Talks!"—is evidence both of the salability of film speech in general, and of the public's interest in hearing its favorite movie stars in particular. Throughout the studio era and continuing into today, scripts have been specifically tailored for their stars' personae and verbal abilities. Lenore Coffee, who wrote for both Bette Davis and Joan Crawford, has volunteered: "The difference was entirely in the dialogue. Bette spits out her words, Joan doesn't. I gave Bette short sentences, short speeches."[42] Production histories are rife with tales of parts being rewritten to accommodate new casting, or of lines being shifted to (or from) the star to enhance his or her stature.

The breakdown of the Hollywood studio system in the 1950s was not in itself a watershed event for film dialogue, because the conventions that were formed during the studio years have long survived that specific industrial organization. While the overall quality of the sound track has been enhanced by technical advances such as magnetic tape and Dolby or THX sound systems, those innovations have been most helpful for the quality of musical scoring and special effects.

However, significant side branches off the main line of dialogue scripting can be identified. The first dates from the late 1960s and early 1970s, when (possibly influenced by the breezy scripting of the French New Wave) American films appeared in which the dialogue was noticeably more colloquial, less careful about rhythm, less polished, more risqué, and marked by an improvisational air. The accompanying acting style was less declamatory, faster, and more throwaway; the recording of lines allowed much more overlapping and a higher degree of inaudibility. This more "realistic," "informal" style of dialogue can be noticed particularly in John Cassavetes's *Faces* (1968), which relies on improvisation,[43] in the films of Robert Altman, who pioneered the use of radio mikes to allow multiple actors to speak at once in films such as *M*A*S*H* (1970), *McCabe and Mrs. Miller* (1971), and *Nashville* (1975);[44] in Hal Ashby's *The Last Detail*

(1973) and *Shampoo* (1975); and in Martin Scorsese's *Mean Streets* (1973) and *Alice Doesn't Live Here Anymore* (1974).

The example of such 1970s films may have contributed to a slight loosening of the careful precision of mainstream films' dialogue over the past twenty years, but actually it has been low-budget independent productions that have been most adventuresome with their dialogue. Partly this stems from independent filmmakers' genuine desire to break new ground, but novel approaches to dialogue have also moved to the fore because they are cheaper and more easily accomplished than extensive special effects or lush production value. Louis Malle's *My Dinner With André* (1982), which confines the film to a dinner-time conversation between two friends, David Mamet's *House of Games* (1987), in which the characters speak in carefully polished cadences approaching blank verse, Gus Van Sant's *My Own Private Idaho* (1991), which literally mixes Shakespeare with prosaic speech, and Julie Dash's *Daughters of the Dust* (1992), in which characters speak in a Gullah dialect, all demonstrate creative manipulation of dialogue. Spike Lee and Quentin Tarantino have made verbal dexterity downright fashionable.

Lower-budget independent films of the 1990s, such as *Before Sunrise* (1994), *Chasing Amy* (1997), and *Grosse Pointe Blank* (1997), commonly allow their dialogue relative prominence. Yet big blockbusters—perhaps because they depend so heavily on earning back their investment with overseas distribution—are less likely to focus on dialogue. As David Kepin notes, "Why bother writing good lines . . . if they will only be mistranslated?"[45]

Erich Auerbach's *Mimesis: The Representation of Reality in Western Literature* sees all of Western literature as a progression towards realism, a halting but unmistakable breakdown of elevated courtly language and subject matter in favor of the serious, respectful treatment of everyday life, told in vernacular language.[46] It is tempting to similarly conclude that the overall progression of film dialogue from 1927 to the present has been a movement toward realism, toward a more colloquial, naturalistic style. Certainly, one could argue that, in general, the films of the 1930s were heavily influenced by theatrical models and reflected the dominance of the white upper class. Nan Withers-Wilson's tracing of the history of voice training in American acting offers relevant evidence:

Throughout the 1920s, 30s and 40s Theatre Speech or Transatlantic was taught in America's professional acting schools. It represented a neutral dialect that borrowed from both Standard British and Standard American pronunciations. . . . Standard American is that variety of American speech that is devoid of regional or ethnic characteristics and does not reveal the geographical or cultural origins of the speaker. . . .

When talking films were introduced in 1927, actors wishing to work in the movies rushed to obtain instruction in this elevated mode of pronunciation. . . . Robert Hobbs' *Teach Yourself Transatlantic* and Edith Skinner's *The Seven Points for Good Speech in Classic Plays* are two texts that provide instruction for the Transatlantic dialect, and it can be readily heard in numerous films from the 1930s and 1940s which include performances by actors such as Bette Davis, Katharine Hepburn and Tyrone Power.[47]

Undeniably, the tide of American culture in manners, dress, and everyday speech over the past seventy years has decisively shifted away from formality, toward individuality and naturalism. This movement has clearly been reflected in the arts: Henry James's and Edith Wharton's upper-class protagonists were supplanted first by Theodore Dreiser's losers, then by John Steinbeck's Oakies and by characters like Richard Wright's Bigger Thomas. Eugene O'Neill introduced lower-class and regional dialects to the stage. Method acting changed the rules for both theater and film, promoting what it claimed was emotional sincerity over eloquence or stagecraft. Many forms of official or unofficial censorship of controversial topics, or references to sex, or obscenity, have been shucked away.

While the progression-toward-realism thesis has a certain validity, it fails to take genre into account. Yes, one can point to the drawing-room dramas of the 1930s, but there were also films like *I Was a Fugitive from a Chain Gang* (1932), which already eschewed "Transatlantic" in favor of lower-class speech patterns. More recently, one can point to the free-wheeling dialogue of *Menace II Society* (1993), but our screens also offer films such as *Remains of the Day* (1993), which are as "elevated" in their language as anything produced in the 1930s. Although *True Romance* (1983), *Full Metal Jacket* (1987), and *Fargo* (1996) contain cursing, street language, or regional dialects, "realistic" in the sense of an accurate transcription of common conversation is the last word I would use to describe them; they are too carefully polished, too rhythmically balanced, too self-consciously artful.* One of the arguments of this study is that genre conventions have been a powerful force in shaping film dialogue, ultimately equally or even more influential than time period.

WHAT IS AT STAKE

This study focuses on English-language narrative cinema, primarily American but including a few British films. I suspect that many of my findings are applicable to all narrative features, but I will not make generalizations about other national cinemas without knowing the language *as well as a native speaker.* Not the least of the deleterious consequences of the traditional disregard of dialogue's importance is that film scholars have cavalierly assumed they could analyze films in languages they don't know.†

Confining my study largely to American films does have the advantage of highlighting the fact that film dialogue is important to American culture. Speech is not some abstract, neutral communicative code: issues of power and dominance, of empathy and intimacy, of class, ethnicity, and gender are automatically engaged every time someone opens his or her mouth. What the characters say, how they say it, and how the filmgoer is influenced are crucial issues.

Much scholarship has been devoted to demonstrating the negative portrayals in American film of women, African-Americans, Hispanics, Asian-Americans, and Native Americans. Most of these analyses have concentrated on the level of plot and characterization. What is often overlooked is how much the speech patterns of the stereotyped character contribute to the viewer's conception of his or her worth; the ways in which dialect, mispronunciation, and inarticulateness have been used to ridicule and stigmatize characters has

---

* The difference between a real-life conversation and those portrayed in films is clearly apparent when one reads linguists' transcriptions of actual talk.

† For a study of dialogue, relying on subtitles would, of course, be intellectually bogus. Subtitles only translate a portion of the spoken text, and only that portion that the subtitler has decided is most important. This filters out emphases that may be unique to the film or to that national cinema. Repetitions, interruptions, slang, curses, antiquated diction, regional accents, of course, are all lost in subtitles. I hope that other scholars will apply my schema to other national cinemas to test its applicability and to discover the unique characteristics of their cinema's dialogue.

often been neglected. Who gets to speak about what? Who is silenced? Who is interrupted? Dialogue is often the first place we should go to understand how film reflects social prejudices. By the same token, if we want to learn more about communities that are different from our own, we might profitably pay attention to the dialogue of films made by minority filmmakers. Mark Winokur argues that the increasing number of films made by African-American filmmakers serve to advance a Bakhtinian polyglossia, allowing into American cinema the voices of audience segments never before heard.[48]

To some extent, films teach viewers how to talk, and thus how to think. When my sons were toddlers, I found myself unaccountably employing the odd endearment "Dollface," a term I could not remember ever hearing or reading. I later realized I had picked it up from *His Girl Friday*'s Walter Burns.

But my own trivial experience is echoed by common practice; film dialogue has often affected off-screen life in substantial ways. Movies have been a medium for language dispersal; linguists believe, for instance, that Hollywood has been instrumental both in contributing to the worldwide dominance of English, and, here at home, in introducing Yiddish expressions to the American public.[49] A more specific instance can be seen in the fact that "[f]or months after *The Day the Earth Stood Still* came out in 1951, grade school kids drove their teachers crazy chanting 'Klaatu barada nikto!,' the words Patricia Neal uses to call off the tinfoil robot Gort, who's hell-bent on atomizing Washington," as Peter Biskind remarks.[50] In the 1960s, rebellious teenagers mocked authority figures by throwing back at them the line of the sadistic prison warden in *Cool Hand Luke* (1967)—"What we've got here is a failure to communicate." Recently, a fund-raiser at Oberlin College quoted *Jerry Maguire*'s "Show me the money" to the *Wall Street Journal*.[51] And surely it is significant that an American president threatened the Congress with a line— "Go ahead, make my day"—from a Dirty Harry movie.

Of all the components of a film, dialogue is the most portable, the easiest for a viewer to extract and make his own. You can't look like the stars, you can't inhabit their world or imitate their actions, but you can mimic their lines. The Internet Movie Database catalogues favorite lines from films and many collections of movie quotes have been published, including several in the format of a reference book of quotations for easy insertion into public presentations. The wisdom of Ovid, Montaigne, and Churchill is being replaced by new cultural touchstones.

––––––––

To return to my opening topic, the prejudices against film dialogue, it is important to realize that no other aspect of film has been subjected to so many prescriptive rules. Cinematography is generally expected to meet certain minimum technical standards, such as being in focus, adequately lit, framing the subject appropriately. Beyond such "visibility" criteria, public discussion does not typically legislate the content of the shots. Yet popular discussion of dialogue goes far beyond minimum "audibility" standards. In the course of my perusal of older and even contemporary screenwriting manuals, film criticism, and theoretical analyses, I've constantly come across dicta such as the following:

Dialogue should be kept to a minimum.

Dialogue should always match the characters' sociological/class background.

Dialogue should be subtle.

Dialogue should never convey expositional information.

Dialogue should never be repetitious.

Dialogue should never be flowery or ostentatious.

Dialogue should never give information that can be conveyed visually.

Dialogue should never be obscure.

Dialogue should never preach.

Dialogue should never be intellectual.

The list goes on and on.

Perhaps these "rules" have been proclaimed so often out of desperation. For my researches have consistently indicated that no matter how loudly they have been shouted, *in actuality they have never been followed by American cinema*. Some of the greatest films, from Ernst Lubitsch's and Preston Sturges's and Howard Hawks's comedies, to Orson Welles's intricate masterpieces, to the Coen brothers' cold satires, offer dialogue that is repetitious, flowery, obscure, "out of character," expositional, intellectual, abundant, even, sometimes, inaudible. Sometimes a short speech offers a surprising zinger; in other cases a long monologue allows for nuance or builds up a head of steam. Everything depends upon the individual movie and its aims. I offer hundreds of examples in the pages that follow.

Which is not to say that all film dialogue is equally valuable, or that films are not sometimes marred by weak dialogue, on the order of "I *am* Heathcliff." But so little serious work has been done on the subject that we do not yet have the tools for determining why one instance of dialogue is brilliantly successful and another leaden-footed. This study is meant to help us make aesthetic evaluations based on informed analysis.

Critics who charge that dialogue is a vehicle for developing character psychology and thus the handmaid of a bourgeois humanistic ideology, are, in large part, correct. But whereas some condemn these ideological ramifications, I judge them a virtue. I believe that there is no more important a topic than *people talking*. Why is the loneliness of losing one's hearing universally feared more than the darkness of losing one's sight? Because talk provides the means for each of us to break out of our singularity and isolation into communion. Talk allows us an imaginative understanding of other worldviews, of other ways of being. Talk is our preeminent means of communicating. As Hannah Arendt has written, "We humanize what is going on in the world and in ourselves only by speaking of it, and in the course of speaking of it we learn to be human."[52]

Film dialogue is a particular kind of imitation of people talking. If we hope to understand either this art form or the broader landscape of American culture, unlike Heathcliff, we need to stay and listen attentively all the way through.

PART I

GENERAL CHARACTERISTICS

ONE

The Functions of Dialogue
in Narrative Film

The first questions to be asked when analyzing a segment of film dialogue may be: "Why are these lines here?" or "What purpose do they serve in the text as a whole?" Such inquiries might imply that one is attempting to uncover the *intentions* of the screenwriters and director, and, indeed, a large degree of overlap might be anticipated between what the filmmakers consciously had in mind and the ultimate effects of dialogue. Some overlap, but not total; for through "accidents" (psychological or practical) and through the unpredictable nuances of performance, filming, editing, scoring, exhibition, reception, and so on, the reverberations of a segment of dialogue may exceed or confound the intentions of its authors. I am interested here, not in the craft of screenwriting,[1] but in the finished film, which takes on a life of its own.

The functions discussed below fall into two groupings. First, those functions I believe to be fundamental because they are centrally involved in the communication of the narrative:

1. anchorage of the diegesis and characters
2. communication of narrative causality
3. enactment of narrative events
4. character revelation
5. adherence to the code of realism
6. control of viewer evaluation and emotions

The second grouping involves functions that go beyond narrative communication into the realms of aesthetic effect, ideological persuasion, and commercial appeal:

7. exploitation of the resources of language
8. thematic messages/authorial commentary/allegory
9. opportunities for "star turns"

Dialogue is commonly employed to serve the ends of this second grouping, but these ends may not be integral to every American film.*

A given instance of dialogue will inevitably fulfill several functions simultaneously. The examples that I offer below are—for demonstration purposes—the least ambiguous I could find. More casual selection would pull out instances of dialogue working in several directions at once.

CREATION OF THE DIEGESIS
AND ANCHORAGE OF IDENTITIES

In Shakespeare's *As You Like It* 2.4, Rosalind, Celia, and Touchstone enter a vacant stage. However, all it takes is Rosalind's assertion, "Well, this is the forest of Arden," for the audience to understand that the travelers have reached their destination; a thicket of noble trees, dappled sun, and birdsong bursts from these seven words.

On the most basic level, dialogue is responsible for "creating" the theatrical diegesis, the fictional world of the narrative. Ericka Fisher-Lichte has pointed out how plays use dialogue to delineate their surroundings:

> If the stage is an empty space that the actor states is a forest and subsequently refers to as a palace, a room, or a dungeon, then this empty space becomes the forest, palace, room, or dungeon in the eyes of the audience. If the actor's words refer to nonexistent objects as if these nevertheless existed, then they do in fact exist for the audience. If, in the actor's words, dusk draws in and the sound of the nightingale and the songs of farmers returning from the fields are to be heard, then all of this can still be seen and heard by the audience.[2]

---

* For better or ill, these categories are my own, derived from a witches' brew of numerous influences. The principal ingredient is narrative theory, particularly the works of Roland Barthes, David Bordwell, Seymour Chatman, and Gérard Genette. I've also profited from the work of drama theorists such as Manfred Pfister and Ericka Fisher-Lichte.

Because of their ability to photograph the physical world, films rarely need to rely upon dialogue to the same extent; why use "verbal" scenery when the camera can take you to any natural setting, or the Hollywood Dream Factory can sumptuously fabricate any locale? The catch is that although the camera can take us anywhere, *identifying* the location is trickier. As Roland Barthes argues, all visual images are polysemous; their meaning must be *anchored* by resort to verbal signs[3] (which is why paintings are given titles, photographs, captions, and tourist postcards, geographical labels). One city skyline, one mountain region, one medieval castle looks very much like another unless its specificity is identified by some means. One popular cinematic strategy is to resort to the language of familiar iconography: the Golden Gate Bridge *means* "San Francisco," the Eiffel Tower, "Paris." Other methods include utilizing superimposed printed captions—"Phoenix, Arizona" in *Psycho* (1960)—or conveniently placed diegetic signs. (Julie Salamon's record of the filming of *Bonfire of the Vanities* [1990] reveals Brian De Palma's insistence upon the size of a street sign reading "Alternate Route Manhattan.")[4]

Yet, in addition to such methods, films use dialogue to identify the diegetic world. That flat farmland could have been anywhere—Oklahoma, Texas, Nebraska—but when Dorothy says, "Toto, I don't think that we're in Kansas anymore," it becomes Kansas. Moreover, this process of verbal identification works, not only for major locations, but for all the characters' movements in time and space throughout a film—the dialogue continually reorients the viewer through what David Bordwell calls "dialogue hooks" (e.g., "Shall we go to lunch?" followed by a long shot of a cafe).[5] For instance, in Dorothy Arzner's *Dance, Girl, Dance* (1940), a reporter calls Elena Harris with the news about Tiger Lily's marriage to Jimmy Harris and the brawl with Judy:

> ELENA: Mr. Harris's marriage has nothing whatever to do with me.
> REPORTER: They're in the Night Court now. Don't you want to make a statement?
> ELENA: I'm not interested. I don't care who's where and I'm not making any statements. *(Slams down the phone, then picks it up again.)* Where in the blazes is the Night Court?

The next shot is a wipe to a courtroom scene, which the viewer "naturally" infers is the Night Court just discussed.

Using dialogue for "re-anchorage" is especially important if a film is departing from linear chronology. In Andrew Davis's *The Fugitive* (1993), the television reporter outside Kimble's apartment notes: "We do know this: that he and his wife Helen were at a fund-raiser at the Four Seasons Hotel earlier this evening, a fund-raiser for the Children's Research Fund." The screen goes white with the bulb of an exploding flash; cut to a large party scene, now identified for us in both time and space.

Exactly where simple anchorage (identifying of existing, but unspecified, time and space) leaves off and literal verbal fabrication of the diegesis (painting in the viewer's imagination a locale that does not physically exist) begins, is difficult to define in film. Production practices always allow for one location to substitute for another: Canadian cities can double for New York, Morocco can be Kafiristan, the Philippines can be Vietnam, the back lot can be anywhere at any point in history. What is important to me here is how implicated the dialogue always is in defining the fictional space. In a real sense, "naming" constitutes "creation." Or, as Tzvetan Todorov puts it, "One cannot verbalize with impunity; to name things is to change them."[6]

Narrative films need not only to identify and create their time and space but also to name the most important elements of that diegesis—the characters. Dialogue, replacing those title cards in silent films that baldly introduced each new person, frequently manages to introduce characters to the viewer via on-screen greetings and meetings. Bordwell has pointed out how often verbal repetition is used to drive home a character's name and identity, so that, for instance, in Michael Curtiz's *Casablanca* (1942), when Captain Renault meets Major Strasser at the airport, Strasser's name is repeated three times.[7]

As an example of dialogue's ability to anchor a narrative, let us take an exchange from an early scene in John Ford's *Stagecoach* (1939). The stagecoach driver has just directed a well-dressed lady passenger to the hotel for a cup of coffee. As she starts toward the hotel porch, she is addressed by another young woman:

> GIRL: Why, Lucy Mallory!
> LUCY: Nancy! How are you, Captain Whitney?
> CAPTAIN WHITNEY: Fine, thanks, Mrs. Mallory.

> NANCY: Why, whatever are you doing in Arizona?
> LUCY: I'm joining Richard in Lordsburg. He's there with his troops.
> CAPTAIN WHITNEY: *(off-screen)* He's a lot nearer than that, Mrs. Mallory. He's been ordered to Dry Fork.
> NANCY: Why, that's the next stop for the stagecoach. You'll be with your husband in a few hours.

This interchange tells us who Lucy is, what state she is in, where she is going, why she is going there, what her husband does, where her husband is, where the stage stops next, and how long it should take until the couple are reunited. A few moments later Nancy again proves her usefulness as narrator-substitute by identifying Hatfield as a "notorious gambler." The Whitneys are not important to the plot (they never appear again), and they are not individualized as rounded characters. They serve to give us this information, and also, by their friendliness and concern, to highlight Lucy's forlorn state.

Bordwell argues that in classical Hollywood film, narrative exposition is concentrated in the beginnings of texts. Certainly, one will find a great deal of identification of characters and anchorage of locations in the opening minutes of a film, when the dialogue is so casually making up for our lack of an omniscient narrator or a detailed dramatic playbill. But it would be a mistake to think that this function is confined to any one section of the text. Witness, from late in *Stagecoach:*

> CURLY: Well, folks, we're coming into East Ferry now.
> BUCK: Lordsburg, next stop.

Movement through space, flashbacks to previous events, ellipses forward in time, and the introduction of new characters will call for dialogue anchorage.

NARRATIVE CAUSALITY

Although it is tempting to use the catch-all category "exposition" to cover both, a theoretical distinction can be drawn between anchorage and the communication of narrative causality, what Roland Barthes calls the "proairetic code."[8] Narratives unfold through a series of events, linked together by succession and causality: "Classical narration communicates what it 'knows' by making the characters haul the causal chain through the film."⁹ Dialogue is the tractor the characters use to haul their heavy load.

The ulterior motive of much of film dialogue is to communicate "why?" and "how?" and "what next?" to the viewer. The "what next" may be a simple anticipation of a plot development, such as takes place during one of Devlin's meetings with Alicia in Alfred Hitchcock's *Notorious* (1946):

> DEVLIN: Look. Why don't you persuade your husband to throw a large shindig so that he can introduce his bride to Rio society, say sometime next week?
> ALICIA: Why?
> DEVLIN: Consider me invited. Then I'll try and find out about that wine cellar business.

This exchange, which sets up the ensuing party and the search of the wine cellar, is filmed in an unflamboyant two-shot of Devlin and Alicia sitting facing forward on a park bench. The party sequence, however, will be remembered as bravura visual filmmaking. From the spectacular crane shot down to the key in Alicia's hand, to the crosscutting of Alex Sebastian's jealous glances, to the repeated shots of the steadily decreasing champagne supply, to the pointed emphasis on the assiduous waiters passing more drinks, the camera movement, framing, and editing make the action unmistakable. Every viewer will recall Devlin's silent investigation of the wine cellar and the excruciating close-ups of the bottle teetering on the shelf's edge. One's memory of the two scenes may imply that all the information was received from self-sufficient visuals. (The screenwriter, Charles Bennett, testifies that Hitchcock had "[n]o interest in dialogue whatsoever.")¹⁰ What may be repressed, however, is how much—even here—the dialogue carries the narrative chain, as the following snippets indicate:

> DEVLIN: He's [Alex's] quite sensitive about you. He's gonna watch us like a hawk. . . .
> DEVLIN: Let's hope the liquor doesn't run out and start him down the cellar for more. . . .
> ALICIA: We'd better hurry. . . . Joseph might have to ask Alex for more wine. He's running out faster than he thought. . . .
> ALICIA: You'd better go out in the garden alone and wait around back of the house for me and I'll show you the wine cellar door. . . .

ALICIA: I'll keep the garden door open and I'll tell you if anything happens. . . .
DEVLIN: We've got to leave things as we found them. Help me find a bottle of wine with the same label as these others. . . .
ALICIA: It isn't really sand, is it?
DEVLIN: Some kind of metal ore. . . .
ALICIA: Someone is coming. It's Alex! He's seen us.
DEVLIN: Wait a minute. I'm going to kiss you.
ALICIA: No! He'd only think we—
DEVLIN: —That's what I want him to think.

We only understand the significance of the shots of the dwindling liquor supply because we've been primed by the dialogue. Similarly, Alex's glances assume narrative importance because we have been informed that they are an obstacle to Devlin's mobility. The viewer sees the black granular material that was hidden in the wine bottle, but we need Devlin to identify it for us. And the climactic action of the scene, the passionate kiss, must—rather incredibly—wait until Devlin has explained, purportedly to Alicia, but really to us, that the kiss is a ruse to allay suspicion. The dialogue paves the way for us to understand the visuals, repeats their information for emphasis, interprets what is shown, and explains what cannot be communicated visually. Together the dialogue and the visual track work to forge each link of the causal chain.

Further evidence of the fact that dialogue is designed to communicate causality *to the viewer* can be drawn from those scenes in which dialogue is omitted because although characters need certain information, the viewers already have it. Famous instances occur in Hitchcock's *North by Northwest* (1959), when the airplane noise drowns out the Professor telling Thornhill all about the mythical George Kaplan, and in Elia Kazan's *On the Waterfront* (1954), when foghorns and music replace Terry's confession to Edie that he participated in her brother's murder. In such cases, films go out of their way not to bore filmgoers by repeating information they already know.

Moreover, dialogue is the preeminent means of communicating to the viewer story events that took place before the time period pictured on screen. It is always through snippets of "accidentally" dropped dialogue that viewers construct a film's "backstory"— Roger Thornhill's earlier failed marriages; Terry Malloy's throwing of the crucial prize fight. Since these background events are never depicted, it is only through the characters' words that filmgoers learn about them.

Expositional dialogue that seems clumsy fails adequately to cloak the fact that this information is for us, not the characters. Generally, there is something forced about the amount of specific detail crammed into presumably incidental conversation, as in Raoul Walsh's *High Sierra* (1941), when Roy Earle, played by Humphrey Bogart, stops at a gas station, and the station attendant practically waylays him with identification of the scenery:

> ATTENDANT: You're looking at the prize of the Sierry's, brother. Mount Whitney, the highest peak in the United States. 14,501 feet above sea level.

Similarly, in the same scene, another car pulls up and the driver introduces himself and his family to Earle and without prompting launches into a capsule backstory:

> PA: Well, I'm going to Los Angeles. I lost my farm back home. But Velma's mother married again and she sort of invited us out.

We do need to know that the action is set in the grandeur of the Sierras and we also need knowledge of the Goodhughs' background. But getting the information across could have been done with a lighter, more indirect touch, as is exemplified by the lines that acquaint us with Roger Thornhill's past in *North by Northwest* :

> ROGER: I've got a job, a secretary, a mother, two-ex-wives, and several bartenders dependent upon me, and I don't intend to disappoint them all by getting myself slightly killed.

David Bordwell argues that one of the hallmarks of Hollywood narrative is that it manufactures a sense of urgency about the unfolding action through the creation of a "deadline," an upcoming point in time by which something important is going to happen— shore leave is going to be over, the airplane is leaving to take the hero to college, the Death Star is going to vaporize the rebel base. Orienting narrative action toward such deadlines lends Hollywood films their characteristic pace and excitement. Because deadlines as entities are nontangible and nonvisual, they have to be communicated verbally one way or another. Dialogue is the simplest tool: it is used to set up the champagne supply crisis in *Notorious;* to communicate the train's arrival time in *High Noon* (1952); to alert us to the dangerously rising levels of carbon dioxide in *Apollo 13* (1995). Another example, this time from *The Wizard of Oz* (1939):

> WICKED WITCH: *(turning over hourglass)* You see that? That's how much longer you've got to be alive. And it isn't long, my pretty, it isn't long! I can't wait forever to get those shoes!

The hourglass is a compelling visual image, and the suspense of Dorothy's rescue by her friends is intensified by the repeated shots of the sand slipping away. But it is the Witch's *dialogue* that links each grain of sand to the supposed remaining seconds of Dorothy's life.

VERBAL EVENTS

Speech-act theory, first promulgated by J. L. Austin and J. R. Searle in the 1960s, has taught us that all conversation can be thought of as events, as *actions.* When one talks, one is *doing something*—promising, informing, questioning, threatening, apologizing. Searle calls these "illocutionary" acts.

In point of fact, Stanislavskian acting theory has long recognized the same phenomenon, and actors have long been taught that in each "beat" of dialogue, a character is performing an action: X is trying to persuade Y to do Z. In James Ivory's *Remains of the Day* (1993), when Mrs. Kenton teases Mr. Stevens about pretty maids, she is trying to spark him into some acknowledgment of his attraction to herself—she is trying to goad him into flirting with her.

From the spectator's perspective, however, some of these speech acts are themselves pivotal links of the narrative chain (what Seymour Chatman would call "kernels");[11] they are major events that would be mentioned in an accurate summary of the story. Some narrative acts are physical—searching a wine cellar, throwing water on a witch, firing a gun—but at times the key narrative event is a verbal act.

As we shall see later, which speech acts assume prominence in which films depends to a large degree on genre conventions. But as a general rule, the most common event is the disclosure of a secret or of crucial information, information vital to the plot, whose revelation poses some risk or jeopardy. These revelations often occur toward the end of the film, and they may ultimately be relinquished only under threat or intimidation. The plot is structured so that the viewer aches for the missing information. A paradigmatic example may be found in Roman Polanski's *Chinatown* (1974), when J. J. Gittes finally forces Evelyn Mulwray into disclosing the secret of the young girl's identity and thus the history of Evelyn's past relationship with her father. Gittes's frustration and brutality increase the impact of the confrontation—he shakes her, yells at her, and slaps her repeatedly—but the key event is *not* his physical action, but Evelyn's verbal act—her reluctant, defiant shout: "She's my daughter *and* my sister!"

The second most important verbal event in Hollywood film is the declaration of love. (Bordwell, Staiger, and Thompson have noted that heterosexual romance was the major or secondary plot line in 95 percent of their sampling of pre-1960 American films.)[12] Just as the revelation of the secret helps solve the mystery/crime plot, the declaration of love "solves" the romance plot. The declaration indicates that the private, secret feeling can no longer be kept hidden; by verbalizing the emotion, the speaker implies commitment and puts the bond into the social realm. As Bonnie tells Geoff in Hawks's *Only Angels Have Wings* (1939), "I'm hard to get—all you've got to do is ask." For the lovers, but especially for the viewers, the words must be spoken: we wait with bated breath (inwardly screaming, "Tell her—you fool!") for Devlin's long-awaited admission of love to Alicia in *Notorious,* for the marriage proposal at the end of *Gigi* (1958), for the avowal under the umbrella that closes *Little Women* (1994). Moreover, these words speak louder than the action, the embrace that customarily follows; a kiss may connote sexual desire, but a declaration implies commitment.[13] Eschewing a verbal declaration can only be compensated for by extravagant physical actions—such as sailing a ship down Fifth Avenue in Robert Zemeckis's *Romancing the Stone* (1984)—which also make a public spectacle of the lover's devotion.

Other common verbal events are those that transpire in courtrooms, such as closing arguments, witnesses breaking down on the stand, and verdicts. Alternatively, key speech acts draw on the power of religion, such as the prayer in *It's a Wonderful Life* (1946), the granting of absolution in *I Confess* (1953), or the exorcism in *The Exorcist* (1973).

James Cameron's *The Terminator* (1984) is undeniably an "action-oriented" film, with exciting chase scenes, explosions, and shootings. Yet even here many of the key events are verbal, such as Sarah Connor's inadvertent betrayal of her location when the Terminator impersonates her mother on the phone, or Reese's declaration of a lifetime of devotion to a woman he hasn't yet met: "I came across time for you, Sarah. I love you. I always have." Verbal events are a major component of every Hollywood film.

CHARACTER REVELATION

"A character's personality in a film is seldom something given in a single shot," writes Richard Dyer. "Rather it has to be built up, by film-makers and audience alike, across the whole film. A character is a construct from the very many different signs deployed by a film."[14] Even those who seek to keep dialogue "in its place" acknowledge its usefulness in characterization. "Great dialogue flashes the light on characters as lightning illumines the dark earth—in flashes," Rachel Crothers says. "It conveys so much in a few words that the actor holds a great instrument in his hand, and with it can make the audience know the depths of his being."[15]

On the most mundane level, dialogue helps us distinguish one person from another.[16] Just as Dickens differentiates his multiple characters by assigning them idiosyncratic phrases and dialects, so cinematic figures may be given a distinctive verbal mannerism partly just to be funny and partly to help spectators keep them straight. Thus, the girlfriend Kit in *Pretty Woman* (1990) speaks with a broad New York accent, and the deputy sheriff in *Lonely Are the Brave* (1962) echoes every command with a rising inflection, and tacks on a "riiight."

But the more significant use of dialogue is to make characters substantial, to hint at their inner life. As Norman Page remarks: "It is probably no exaggeration to say that the speech of any individual is as unique (though not as unchangeable) as his fingerprints."[17] Each time a character opens his mouth, filmgoers learn more about him— is his accent "upper class" or "hillbilly"? Is he or she polite? brusque? thoughtful? quick? lazy? Does the voice carry calm resonant authority (Alec Guinness as Obi Wan Kenobi) or a brittle nervousness (Anthony Daniels as C-3PO)? As will be discussed in a later chapter, the character's psychology is partially determined once the actor is cast—that actor's natural vocal qualities, combined with his or her vocal skills, greatly influence the viewer's perception of the character's personality.

But over and above what we can discern from the way a character speaks, dialogue lines are explicitly designed to reveal character. When Samuel Gerard (Tommy Lee Jones) and his team arrive at the site of the bus/train wreck in *The Fugitive,* they are stopped by a uniformed policeman.

> GERARD: Hi. Who's in charge?
> COP: Sheriff Rawlins.
> GERARD: Rawlins.
> COP: Just follow the TV lights.

"Just follow the TV lights." Even before we meet Rawlins we know he's a vainglorious blowhard, more interested in publicity than in doing his job.

To stick with this text for a moment: Dr. Richard Kimble (Harrison Ford) is *The Fugitive*'s central focus. However, being primarily engaged in a solitary flight and investigation, Kimble talks relatively little, so we are forced to judge him by his actions—his courage in saving the injured guard; his resourcefulness in assuming disguises; his intelligence in tracking down the one-armed murderer through the records of the hospital that adjusted his artificial limb. But it is interesting that *The Fugitive* also finds it necessary to supplement what we *see* Kimble doing with dialogue scenes of Gerard interviewing Kimble's associates, during which the associates speak of Kimble's innocence, self-reliance, and brilliance.

The motif of having secondary characters comment upon a central figure hardly originated with *The Fugitive.* Orson Welles's *Citizen Kane* (1941) may be inimitable, but the pattern of slightly baffled admirers commenting on an enigmatic central character is part and parcel of the Hollywood star system because such comments keep our attention focused on the central figure and reinforce his or her special qualities, exalted status, or air of mystery. Secondary characters spend a lot of words talking *about* Margo Channing (Bette Davis), Scarlett O'Hara (Vivien Leigh), Shane (Alan Ladd), Hank Quinlan

(Orson Welles), Atticus Finch (Gregory Peck), Tristan Ludlow (Brad Pitt). Through their comments we learn about the protagonists' past history, community standing, notorious personality, and so on.

Of course, dialogue is also employed for self-revelation. At one point in *Casablanca*, Rick is invited over to Major Strasser's table, where he learns that the Gestapo major has been keeping a dossier on him. Rick borrows the notebook, glances at it, and quips, "Are my eyes really brown?" Such a statement shows his refusal to be intimidated and his satirical view of Germanic efficiency. This is important in the context of a conversation in which the major is warning Rick not to involve himself in the pursuit of the resistance leader Victor Lazlo, and Rick seems to be agreeing not to interfere. Only Rick's irreverence shows that he is uncowed.

Admittedly, dialogue used for character revelation can be trite or obvious. The flaw here stems, however, not from the fact that dialogue has been used, but from the fact that the conception of the character's psychology is shallow. Sidney Lumet has written,

> In the early days of television when the "kitchen sink" school of realism held sway, we always reached a point where we "explained" the character. Around two-thirds of the way through, someone articulated the psychological truth that made the character the person he was. Chayefsky and I used to call this the "rubber-ducky" school of drama: "Someone once took his rubber ducky away from him, and that's why he's a deranged killer."[18]

And yet, in Hitchcock's *Shadow of a Doubt* (1943)—written by Thorton Wilder—dialogue is successfully used to take us right into the mind of a deranged killer. Uncle Charlie's (Joseph Cotten's) dinner table speech is placed at the time in the plot when viewers know that he is the "Merry Widow Murderer," but we have no clue as to motive, no understanding of why this charming man is a merciless serial killer.

CHARLES: Women keep busy in towns like this. The cities it's different. The cities are full of women, middle-aged widows, husbands dead, husbands who've spent their lives making fortunes, working and working. Then they die and leave their money to their wives. Their silly wives. And what do the wives do, these useless women? You see them in the hotels, the best hotels, every day by the thousands. Drinking the money, eating

> the money, losing the money at bridge, playing all day and all night. Smelling of money. Proud of their jewelry but of nothing else. Horrible, faded, fat greedy women.
>
> CHARLIE: But they're alive. They're human beings!
>
> CHARLES: Are they? Are they, Charlie? Are they human? Or are they fat, wheezing animals? Hmm? And what happens to animals when they get too fat and too old?

The speech reveals a misogyny intense enough to justify murdering vulnerable widows as the putting down of "fat, wheezing animals."

Most scenes reveal character neither in one-line quips ("Follow the TV lights") nor in extended long turns like Uncle Charlie's. It is more common for conversations to combine a character's self-revelations with the insights of his dialogue partner. An early scene in Sydney Pollack's *Tootsie* (1982) between Michael (Dustin Hoffman), an out-of-work actor, and his exasperated agent George (Pollack) begins with Michael rudely bursting into George's office, angry that he has not been sent to audition for a plum role. George tries to reason with him but gradually loses his temper:

> GEORGE: They can't all be idiots, Michael. You argue with everyone. You've got one of the worst reputations in town, Michael. No one will hire you.
>
> MICHAEL: Are you saying that nobody in New York will work with me?
>
> GEORGE: Oh no, that's too limiting. Nobody in Hollywood wants to work with you either. I can't even send you up for a commercial. You played a tomato for 30 seconds, they went a half a day over schedule 'cause you wouldn't sit down.
>
> MICHAEL: Yes, it wasn't logical.
>
> GEORGE: (*shouting*) You were a tomato! A tomato doesn't have logic! A tomato can't move!
>
> MICHAEL: That's what *I* said. So if he can't move, how's he gonna sit down, George. I was a stand-up tomato.

Note that this confrontation does more than paint a thorough portrait of just what a (clever) pain-in-the-ass Michael is. It reveals the relationship between the two characters. George starts by trying to be diplomatic, even kind, and finally gets fed up, and Michael leaves determined to prove George and everybody else wrong. Dialogue serves as character revelation because it navigates the relationship between two people.[19] As Elizabeth Traugott and Mary Louise Pratt note, "Like international relations, interpersonal ones are defined, maintained, and modified chiefly through language."[20]

ADHERENCE TO EXPECTATIONS
CONCERNING REALISM

We know that "realism" is a cultural construct, that when a text is referred to as "realistic," one is actually saying that it adheres to a complex code of what a culture at a given time agrees to accept as plausible, everyday, authentic. These conventions change through history—what strikes one generation as incredibly realistic may strike another as highly mannered. Although mainstream American filmmaking rarely has documentary or even neorealist ambitions, our movies have traditionally aimed toward a surface plausibility. Most American films work hard to encourage the suspension of disbelief; they sustain the illusion that the viewer is observing the action as a fly on the wall. Furthermore, just as some films may deliberately emphasize character portrayals, others choose to emphasize their realistic flavor. The distinctive sound of certain films of the 1970s discussed previously—*McCabe and Mrs. Miller, Alice Doesn't Live Here Anymore*—comes from these texts' emphasis on furthering the spectator's belief in their casualness, as if the camera and sound recording apparatus had haphazardly caught life in the act.

But a proportion of dialogue in every film serves primarily as a representation of ordinary conversational activities, or "verbal wallpaper." Recall all those moments of ordering food in restaurants or interchanges with servants and functionaries. In film after film, a principal character will walk into a restaurant or workplace and exchange greetings with extras we never see again. One might argue that these exchanges exist to show that the character is well-liked, but they primarily function to replicate everyday encounters. The same is true of background pages in hospitals and airports, of echoed commands in submarine films, of party chatter, reporters' shouted questions, and crowd murmurs.

Sometimes a film will foreground everyday banalities. In *The Fugitive,* while Kimble is being transported on the prison bus, we hear a conversation between the guards and the driver about being hungry and tired. The line "Twenty miles from Minard" is pure anchorage, but the rest serves a different function.

BLACK COP: I'm tired.
WHITE COP: Twenty miles from Minard. We should be there in about forty minutes. Yea, I'll be glad to get rid of this load. Let Mackenzie take care of 'em.
BLACK COP: Always got somthin'good to eat there man, I'm starving.
WHITE COP: Awww, me too. Had enough of that prison junk.
BLACK COP: Awww, man.
BUS DRIVER: Old Eddie here, he don't care, his old lady's got him on a diet. Right, Ed?

This conversation has no intrinsic meaning to the narrative, other than to serve as a representation of what prison guards might really talk about on a boring ride. It is intercut, however, with shots of two prisoners silently readying their escape attempt, while Richard Kimble notices their plans. The juxtaposition of this dialogue with this mimed action communicates to the viewer that the guards are distracted by their chatting from paying full attention to their impending peril.

In describing something as realistic, we are often judging that it is an accurate representation of a cultural milieu. I was reminded of realism's pseudo-anthropological ambitions while watching what may initially appear to be the least realistic of films—Steven Spielberg's *E. T.* (1982). The film balances its fantastic sci-fi plot with a careful portrayal of a middle-class Californian family. Thus, the first morning that Elliot has E. T. in his room, he shows the alien his "stuff," including a Coke can, toy plastic figures, an aquarium, a plastic shark on a stick, and a Planter's Peanut bank (fig. 3).

ELLIOT: Come on. It's all right. Come on. Come on. Come on. Come on. Come on. Come on. Do you talk? You know . . . talk. Me human. Boy. Elliot. Ell-i-ot. Elliot. Coke, see. We drink it. It's, uh, it's a drink. You know, food. These are toys. These are little men. This is Greedo. And then this is Hammerhead. See, this is Walrusman. And then this is Snaggletooth. And this is Lando Calrissian. See. And this is Boba Fett. And look, they can even have wars. Look at this. (*Makes war noises as he manipulates the plastic figures fighting each other.*) And look, fish. Fish eat the fish food and the shark eats the fish. But nobody eats the shark. See, this is Pez. Candy. See, you eat it. You put the candy in here and then when you lift up the head, candy comes out and you can eat it. You want some? This is a peanut, you eat it. But you can't eat this one, 'cause this is fake. This is money. See, we put the money in the peanut. You see, bank. See. And then, this is a car.

3. *E. T.* Elliot showing the alien his stuff.

> This is what we get around in. See, car. (*E. T. starts to chew on the Matchbox car.*) Hey! Hey! Wait a second. No. You don't eat 'em. Are you hungry? I'm hungry. Stay. Stay. I'll be right here.

This speech does not advance the plot; instead (in casual, boy-appropriate diction), it skewers the commercialism of Elliot's culture, the movie toys, the Coke, the Peanut bank, the emphasis on money and cars, fighting, and a Darwinian food chain. These values will be counterpoised by the loyalty and love Elliot experiences through his relationship with E. T.

CONTROL OF VIEWER'S EVALUATION/EMOTIONS

As with every element of a film, dialogue is useful in guiding the responses of the spectator. Often dialogue is a tool for controlling pacing; it may, for instance, distract the filmgoer, or set us up for some visual surprise. In other cases, dialogue is used to elongate a moment, to stretch out a suspenseful climax. This is clearly the case in Don Siegel's *Dirty Harry* (1971). Once Detective Callahan has the drop on his prey, he toys with both the criminal and the viewer:

> HARRY: Uh-huh, I know what you're thinkin'. Did he fire six shots or only five? Well to tell you the truth in all this excitement I've kinda lost track myself. But being this is a .44 Magnum, the most powerful handgun in the world, and would blow your head clean off, you've got to ask yourself one question: "Do I feel lucky?" Well, do ya, punk?

Such a speech works not only to reveal Harry's disgust and sadism, and not only to inform us of the possibility that he is out of ammunition, but also—crucially—to force a suspenseful pause in the stream of physical action.

In addition to controlling the viewer's sense of pace, sometimes dialogue is used merely to draw our attention to someone or something. Mary Devereaux points out that in *His Girl Friday*, Walter's line, "Do you always carry an umbrella, Bruce?" forces us to see that the hyper-cautious Bruce is indeed equipped with raingear;[21] similarly, "That plane's dustin'crops where there ain't no crops" turns the audience's attention to the airplane in *North by Northwest*.

Moreover, dialogue guides our interpretation of what we are seeing. Early in William Wyler's *Mrs. Miniver* (1942), the stationmaster, Mr. Ballard, invites Mrs. Miniver into his office to see the rose he has cultivated and wants to name after her. We are shown one brief close-up of the rose; the focus is placed instead on the characters' response to the flower:

> MRS. MINIVER: Oh, Mr. Ballard!
> MR. BALLARD: It's my masterpiece.
> MRS. MINIVER: How lovely!
> MR. BALLARD: You like it ma'am?
> MRS. MINIVER: I think it's the most beautiful rose I've ever seen. The shape . . .
> MR. BALLARD: And the scent.
> MRS. MINIVER: Oh, divine. And the color. I adore red roses.

It is through the dialogue that we "smell" the rose and learn that it is red (the film is in black and white).* Moreover, it is through the dialogue that we learn of the rose's magnificence. The camera is per-

---

* I don't know what color this rose actually is. In Wyler's *Jezebel* (1938), great dialogue stress is placed on Julie's wearing a red dress to the ball but in actuality the dress was black velvet.

fectly capable of showing us a pretty flower, but it is not able to compare that flower to all others.

Another case where dialogue explicitly works on the viewer's emotional state occurs in Ridley Scott's *Alien* (1979). Two-thirds of the way through the film, Captain Dallas is trying to chase the loathsome creature through the space ship's air ducts with a flame-thrower. A female crew member, Lambert, is coaching Dallas over a walkie-talkie as she watches a motion detector. We see shots of the motion detector's screen showing two dots converging; we see shots of Dallas frantically peering through the dark around him. We *hear* Lambert, increasingly agitated, then hysterically screaming: "Oh God, it's moving right towards you! . . . Move! Get out of there! [Inaudible] Move, Dallas! Move, Dallas! Move Dallas! Get out!" Such lines are not particularly informative. Their main function is to frighten the viewer, to increase the scene's tension. In this case, dialogue is accomplishing the task often taken by evocative extradiegetic music—it's working straight on the viewer's guts. This is manifestly also the purpose of "rabble-rousing" lines—all those variants of "Take *that*, you bastard!" with which the hero finally creams the villain and elicits audience cheers, in movies such as *Jaws* (1975), *Die Hard* (1988), and *Independence Day* (1996).

Certainly one can find American films—Brian De Palma's *Mission: Impossible* (1996) is one example—that are ruthlessly "functional" in their dialogue, where dialogue is used as little as possible, only as absolutely required for narrative communicability, and where one could go through the script assigning each line to the above six categories with hardly a scrap of a phrase left over unaccounted for. However, in other cases, dialogue is clearly being utilized more expansively, for additional, and perhaps more nuanced, aims.

EXPLOITATION OF THE RESOURCES OF LANGUAGE

This category is subdivided into four sections. The unifying concept is that the cinematic text defies the strictures of only using language minimally and has chosen to include, perhaps even to revel in, "unnecessary" verbal embroidery.*

Firstly, language is often used poetically. Rouben Mamoulian's *Love Me Tonight* (1932) foregrounds rhyming dialogue, and Abraham Polonsky's *Force of Evil* (1948) approaches blank verse. David Mamet's screenplays are famous for the way in which the dialogue falls into a heavily patterned rhythm. Joe Mantegna compares Mamet's lines to "poetry written in iambic pentameter."[22] And as Anne Dean comments,

> Even [Mamet's] celebrated use of "obscene" language is subjected to close scrutiny. "A line's got to scan," he says. "I'm very concerned with the metric scansion of everything I write, including the rhythmic emphasis of the word 'fucking.' In rehearsal, I've been known to be caught counting the beats on my fingers."[23]

Mamet may represent an extreme, but most scripts will occasionally smuggle in instances when a turn of phrase is offered for its intrinsic appeal. Take the Wizard's challenge to the Tin Man and the Scarecrow when they come to ask him for help:

WIZARD: Step forward, Tin Man. You dare to come to me for a heart, do you? You clinking clanking, clattering collection of collagenous junk? . . . And you, Scarecrow, have the effrontery to ask for a brain, you billowing bale of bovine fodder?

The Wizard's ostentatious alliteration adds to his majesty. In Josef von Sternberg's *Morocco* (1930), Marlene Dietrich as Amy Jolly talks

---

* I have in mind here something analogous to Roman Jakobson's "poetic function," which he defines as "focus on the message for its own sake" ("Closing Statement: Linguistics and Poetics," in id., *Style in Language,* ed. Thomas A. Sebeok [Cambridge, Mass.: Technology Press of Massachusetts Institute of Technology; New York: John Wiley & Sons, 1960], 356.) One could make other connections between my schema and Jakobson's famous six factors in verbal communication:

addresser/context/message/contact/code/addressee,

and his six corresponding functions:

emotive/referential/poetic/phatic/metalingual/conative.

For instance, in self-revelation by characters, the emotive function dominates; in exhortations to the audience, the conative function comes to the fore. However, I cannot claim a tight homology with Jakobson; his schema is designed neither for those who are "overhearing" a communicative exchange nor for exchanges that are part of a carefully designed narrative edifice.

about a Foreign Legion of Women: "But we have no uniforms, no flags. And no medals when we are brave. No wound stripes when we are hurt." This is an lovely extended metaphor, and the structuring of parallel clauses adds to the effect. In a like manner, Terence Mann's climactic speech at the end of Phil Alden Robinson's *Field of Dreams* (1989) about the importance of baseball moves from one poetic image to another: American history has moved by "like an army of steamrollers," but the fans at Ray's Iowa field will be "innocent as children"; they'll be dipped "in magic waters" and "[t]he memories will be so thick they'll have to brush them away from their faces." James Earl Jones's delivery makes the speech unforgettable.

Or a poetic touch may be limited to a single phrase. In *The Fugitive*, speaking of Kimble's foolhardy dive from a great height into the reservoir, Gerard casually tosses off that Kimble "Did a Peter Pan." Such a little comment, but it resonates when one realizes that, like Peter Pan, Kimble is fleeing from grown-up authority figures and fighting an evil one-armed man.

Not only do screenwriters write poetically; fairly often they literally insert poetry into their films. *The Ghost and Mrs. Muir* (1947) recites Keats's "Ode to a Nightingale"; *All I Desire* (1953) includes a performance of Browning; *Sophie's Choice* (1982) highlights Emily Dickinson; *Four Weddings and a Funeral* (1994) showcases W. H. Auden; *Sense and Sensibility* (1995) quotes Shakespearean sonnets. *Peter Pan* is read aloud in *E. T.*, and the Bible is read aloud in *How Green Was My Valley* (1941). The quoted passages highlight emotional moments with their familiarity and special eloquence.

Secondly, many films use their dialogue for jokes and humor.* Even the most intense thriller includes lighter, humorous moments to change the mood, or to relax the viewer before the next frenetic sequence. James Bond's ironic savoir faire illustrates both his bravery and unflappability.[24] Action heroes such as Mel Gibson in the *Lethal Weapon* films, or Bruce Willis in the *Die Hard* series, and Eddie Murphy in the *Beverly Hills Cop* movies not only get to perform heroically, they also get to mouth off constantly. The jokes themselves

---

* Timothy Paul Garrand subdivides humorous dialogue into discreet categories, which he labels "epigrams," "non sequiturs," "misunderstandings," "understatements," "sarcasm," and "wordplay" ("The Comedy Screenwriting of Preston Sturges: An Analysis of Seven Paramount Auteurist Screenplays" [Diss., University of Southern California, 1984], 243).

have a hard, aggressive edge; the heroes' dismissive "deadly wit" is another means of illustrating their power.[25]

In sound comedies, dialogue moves to the fore as the comic engine of the text. Here is a small sampling:

From Leo McCarey's *Duck Soup* (1933):

> FIREFLY: I suggest that we give him ten years in Leavenworth or eleven years in Twelveworth.
> CHICOLINI: I'll tell you what I'll do. I'll take five and ten in Woolworth.

From Mark Sandrich's *The Gay Divorcée* (1934):

> TONETTI: Your wife is safe with Tonetti—he prefers spaghetti.

From Stanley Donen's *Singin' in the Rain* (1952):

> DON: Hey Cos—do something—call me a cab!
> COSMO: Okay. You're a cab.

From Jim Abrahams, David Zucker, and Jerry Zucker's *Airplane!* (1980):

> DOCTOR: Can you fly this plane and land it?
> TED: Surely you can't be serious.
> DOCTOR: I am serious. And don't call me Shirley.

Note that dialogue humor can cut two ways. It can be offered as the deliberate joking of a witty character—Groucho Marx, 007. On the other hand, many of the lines that make us laugh stem from our position of superior knowledge over a character. We don't laugh with Lena Lamont in *Singin' in the Rain*, we laugh *at* her when she says, "What's wrong with the way I talk? What'sa big idea—am I dumb or somethin'?"

This leads us to what I see as the third major use of the resources of language: irony. Although it is possible to convey irony solely through visual images, language greatly expands film's ironic capabilities. Irony is created by the divergence between two levels of knowledge, between, for instance, what the characters know and what the audience knows. In many films, because we are "omnisciently" privileged to observe more than any single character, we are often in the position of seeing through their self-deceits or deliberate falsehoods. In Wyler's *Roman Holiday* (1953), Anna doesn't want Joe Bradley to know that she is a runaway princess, while Joe doesn't want her to know that he has recognized her and is documenting her day for a newspaper scoop. The characters thus mislead or outright lie to one another constantly. In our position of superior knowledge, we constantly "see through" the surface statements to the truth—Anna talks about the "anniversary of her father's job," and we understand she is referring to a celebration of his coronation; Joe tells Anna that he is in the fertilizer business and we recognize that he is giving her a load of bull. Our interpretation of every line is changed because of our superior knowledge.

Similarly, in Joseph Mankiewicz's *All about Eve*, Margo responds to Karen's apology for the stranded car:

> MARGO: Don't give it a thought. One of Destiny's many pranks. After all, you didn't personally drain the gas tank yourself.

However, the words reverberate because the audience knows that Karen did exactly that.

Finally, another, slightly rarer function of on-screen dialogue is to tell stories verbally.* For the most part, on-screen verbal storytelling might be categorized under narrative causality as discussed above. That is, a character will tell a story to explain some key gap in the plot, as in Hitchcock's *Rebecca* (1940) when Maxim de Winter finally explains Rebecca's death. However, with some frequency, films lapse into storytelling that is basically tangential to the plot, although relevant to the film's subtexts.

In Steven Spielberg's *Jaws*, the "action" of the film pauses as the men sit around the *Orca*'s cabin table. Captain Quint (Robert Ryan) tells a harrowing story of the sinking of the USS *Indianapolis* during World War II, when he and eleven hundred other sailors were cast adrift in shark-infested seas. Certainly, the relatively quiet scene of sharing stories around the table is structurally important to the film; by bonding the men together and by allowing the audience to unwind, it sets us up for the heart-stopping attack to come. Quint's

---

* I am excluding here voice-over storytelling, which I have examined in another study.

story might have been motivated by concerns for character revelation, in that it "explains" his fixed hatred of sharks, a hatred so intense that, like Captain Ahab, he is willing to die as long as he kills his nemesis. But both goals—change of tempo and character revelation—could have been accomplished by other means. The story is included because it is compelling *as a story*, because of the intrinsic gratifications of storytelling.

In addition, every filmgoer must recall Bernstein's story in *Citizen Kane* about seeing the girl on the ferry:

> BERNSTEIN: You're pretty young, Mr.—Mr. Thompson. A fellow will remember a lot of things you wouldn't think he'd remember. You take me. One day, back in 1896, I was crossing over to Jersey on the ferry and as we pulled out there was another ferry pulling in—and on it there was a girl waiting to get off. A white dress she had on—and she was carrying a white parasol—and I only saw her for one second. She didn't see me at all—but I'll bet a month hasn't gone by since that I haven't thought of that girl.

Bernstein's past romantic life is totally tangential to the film—we learn nothing whatsoever on the subject. Yet this story captures such a delicate moment of the personal experience: a second that reverberates through a lifetime. It also relates to the Rosebud theme, in that it points to the lingering importance to someone of a moment that may seem trivial to others.

By including poetic effects, jokes, irony, or storytelling, films defy the strictures against cinematic speech, and bring into the medium the vast resources of an older Muse.

THEMATIC MESSAGES / AUTHORIAL COMMENTARY / ALLEGORY AND INTERPRETATION

In the history of criticism of film dialogue, no other function of dialogue has been criticized so much. Possibly, this is because "preachy" passages tend to date quickly if their topic is of the moment, or because such passages have frequently been poorly written, couched in vague generalities so as to offend as few as possible. But I suspect that this aversion is at least partially prompted by the fact that overt moralizing breaks the illusion that viewers are merely overhearing characters talking to one another; it makes plain that the dialogue is addressed to the audience. This both violates the suspension of disbelief and "catches" the viewer in the act of eavesdropping.

This widespread aversion, however, hasn't stopped the prevalence of dialogue such as the following speech given by Jefferson Smith on the Senate floor in Frank Capra's *Mr. Smith Goes to Washington* (1939):

JEFFERSON SMITH: And it seemed like a pretty good idea—getting boys from all over the country, boys of all nationalities and ways of living—getting them together. Let them find out what makes different people tick the way they do. Because I wouldn't give ya two cents for all your fancy rules if behind them they didn't have a little bit of plain, ordinary, everyday kindness and a little lookin' out for the other fella too. That's pretty important, all that. It's just the blood and bone and sinew of this democracy that some great men handed down to the human race, that's all! But of course, if you've got to build a dam where that boy's camp ought to be, to get some graft or pay off some political army or something, well that's a different thing. Oh no.

Lest one think that this use of dialogue is confined to Capra, consider Ted Kramer's response on the witness stand during the custody trial in Robert Benton's *Kramer vs. Kramer* (1979):

TED KRAMER: My wife used to always say to me, "Why can't a woman have the same ambitions as a man?" *(to Johanna)* I think you're right. And maybe I've learned that much. But, by the same token, I'd like to know what law is it that says a woman is a better parent simply by virtue of her sex? You know, I've had a lot of time to think about what is it that makes somebody a good parent: you know it has to do with constancy; it has to do with—with—with patience; it has to do with listening to 'em; it has to do with pretending to listen to 'em, when you can't even listen anymore. It has to do with love like—like—like—like she was saying. And I don't know where it's written that says that a woman has—has a corner on that

> market that—that a man has any less of those emotions
> than—than—than a woman does.

In each case, the speech is spoken by the hero or an authority figure in a setting (the U.S. Senate, family court, criminal court) that calls for honesty and that "realistically" allows for substantive reflection on serious issues. The viewer recognizes such statements as the moral of the text because of their value-laden content and because of their relation to the film as a whole: *Kramer vs. Kramer* is indeed devoted to showing the father's fitness as a parent and to condemning a system that would deprive him of his son. In addition, such "authorial commentary" tends to fall in the film's last quarter, when the thematic stakes have been made abundantly clear, and may be expressed in a single, long climactic speech.

Which brings us to the point that, as a general rule, dialogue in a film's last scenes carries particular thematic burdens, either reinforcing the film's ostensible moral or resisting closure. "In resolutions, narratives can attempt ideological solutions to the contradictions that fuel them. But the traces of conflict and contradiction may remain," Jackie Byars argues. She continues by quoting Rachel Blau DuPlessis: "Subtexts and repressed discourses can throw up one last flare of meaning."[26] "Flare" is a visual image; our perspective here suggests that these repressed discourses may break through and find *voice* in some last closing line(s) . . . as in the highly disturbing end of *Psycho* (1960), where the mother's voice subverts the tidy explanations just offered by the psychiatrist about the causes and meaning of Norman's insanity.

In the case of films motivated by propagandistic goals, character dialogue will even directly exhort the viewer to action. At the end of Hitchcock's *Foreign Correspondent*, filmed in 1940, the hero warns of the Nazi threat and urges the viewer to join in the fight:

JOHNNY JONES: I can't read the rest of the speech I had because the lights have gone out so I'll just have to talk off the cuff. All that noise you hear isn't static, it's death coming to London. Yes, they're coming here now, you can hear the bombs falling on the streets and the homes. It's as if the lights were all out everywhere, except in America. Keep those lights burning. Cover them with steel, ring them

> with guns. Build a canopy of battleships and bombing
> planes around them. Hello America! Hang on to your
> lights. They're the only lights left in the world.

Thematic messages are fairly bald, and the character, of course, is aware of what he or she is saying and what it means—the character has assumed the mantle of conscious spokesperson for the ideals ratified by the rest of the movie. An alternate method of conveying social/moral/political themes is by the use of allegory. M. H. Abrams defines allegory as "a narrative fiction in which the agents and action, and sometimes the setting as well, are contrived to make coherent sense on the 'literal,' or primary, level of signification, and at the same time to signify a second, correlated order of agents, concepts, and events."[27] Many films offer such dual levels of signification—their stories cohere as self-contained narratives, while at the same time the viewer is guided to read an allegory of political or social events. In such cases, as with ironical dialogue, the viewer brings to the dialogue a level of knowledge and interpretation superior to that of the characters; the broader, thematic significance of their words is unavailable to the characters. Allegorical dialogue, however, is less overt than ironical dialogue, because instead of entailing a concrete lie or misunderstanding, the viewer's recognition of the doubled meaning depends upon a systematized interpretation of the total text, an ability to draw the connections between the on-screen diegesis, characters, and events and the wider political/social/moral significance.

For example, only if one is alert to the fact that Abraham Polonsky's *Force of Evil* (1948) is an allegory about the evils of capitalism will one catch all the overtones of the dialogue.

SAM MORSE: It's a normal operation. "776" will hit tomorrow because Taylor makes it hit. Tomorrow night every [numbers] bank in the city is broken. Then we step in and lend money to those we want while we let the rest go to the wall. We're normal financiers.

Force of Evil is not the only film with a comprehensive allegorical subtext; consider *High Noon* (1952) and *Johnny Guitar* (1954) with their anti-McCarthyism parables, or *Invasion of the Body Snatchers*

(1956) with its—disputed[28]—anti-Communism. In films like these, almost as with Spenser's *The Faërie Queene,* a viewer who "misses" the allegorical significance may be said to have missed half the text.

However, more commonly, American films offer what might be called "allegory-lite," that is, an intermittent or vague constellation of references between the fictional diegesis and a second, or wider, significance. Frequently, one recognizes a double-layering only in certain scenes. For instance, to return to Mrs. Miniver and her rose: the rose, which Mr. Ballard explicitly names after her, is a surrogate for the character. The reason that we have more glamour close-ups of Greer Garson than of the flower during this interchange is that the loveliness so stressed is really *her* loveliness. The viewer is led to appreciate her beauty by Mr. Ballard's admiration, the stress on her namesake's transcendence, and the visual evidence of Garson's appealing looks. To the extent that Mrs. Miniver is herself a symbol of traditional British refinement under attack by the Nazis, and to the extent that the rose is often a symbol of England, the seemingly banal dialogue serves to hammer home to the viewer that culture's refinement and worth.

OPPORTUNITIES FOR STAR TURNS

Clearly, this final category is primarily pertinent to a certain category of films, those designed as showcases for stars with unique histrionic talents. In such cases, dialogue sequences may be included to keep our attention focused upon that star, and to give the star a chance to "show off." Such sequences may involve a longer "turn" where the star gets to speak without interruption.

Take the opening of Franklin Schaffner's *Patton* (1970), in which George C. Scott mounts a flag-draped stage and delivers a speech to an unseen audience. The camera stays focused on Scott throughout—there are no cutaways to the troops—and he delivers a speech astounding in its mixture of patriotism, crudity, and cruelty. Scott gives a riveting reading, mostly bombastic, but at times tinged with cynical resignation. The speech is important to the character study of General Patton, but it is mostly a tour de force for Scott.

A comic example can be seen in Chris Columbus's *Mrs. Doubtfire* (1993), when Robin Williams is being interviewed by a court officer adjudicating his children's custody arrangements. Williams tells her that his profession is to dub voices of cartoon characters; her blank look is an excuse for Williams to go off on a riff of thirteen impressions, ranging from Ronald Reagan to Porky Pig. These impressions have nothing whatsoever to do with the narrative—they exist solely to give Williams a chance to do his shtick.

In general, "star turns" can be identified by their length, by the fact that the speeches call for a wider or out of the ordinary range of emotional expression, and showcase vocal skill. As James Naremore notes:

> [F]ilms often call attention to performing skill by means of long speeches: notice Edward G. Robinson's lightning-fast recitation of actuarial statistics in *Double Indemnity* (1944), Brando's famous soliloquy about being a "contender" in *On the Waterfront* (1954), or James Woods's frantic, dizzy talk on the telephone at the beginning of *Salvador* (1986).[29]

All Naremore's examples in this passage, and in another where he discusses James Earl Jones, Olivier, Gielgud, and Welles highlighting their verbal skills, are of male actors. I, too, can only think of examples featuring male performers. It is not that female performers don't have distinctive voices—think of Jean Arthur or Judy Holliday—or consummate verbal skill. But they have been less likely to be given the stage to talk for an extended period, to take a verbal star turn. Naremore reports that vocal power has traditionally been considered an "important sign of 'phallic' performing skill."[30] Perhaps bucking the prejudices against film dialogue may be dared for a male star, but is less likely to be done for actresses, who, particularly in recent years, have generally ranked lower in box office power and salaries.

The preceding discussion has shown how integral dialogue is to the creation of the narrative—how it anchors and identifies the place, time, and participants; how it establishes and conveys causal relationships; how it enacts major events. We have studied how it is used to create and reveal character; to influence audience reactions to these fictional personages; to illuminate the characters' changing interrelationships. I have shown how dialogue communicates thematic or authorial commentary through irony, allegory, embedded

storytelling. Moreover, I have demonstrated how filmic speech contributes to the viewing experience through eloquence or humor, how
it controls pacing, mood, emotion, and interpretation.

One of the benefits of this exercise in classification is that it en-
ables us to notice parts of films, or entire texts, that don't fall into
these categories, that are "transgressive" to a greater or lesser degree. Some movies present only one-dimensional characters and
never use dialogue to deepen their psychological portraits. Some
films delay anchoring their time and space or clarifying relationships
between characters in order to purposefully disorient a viewer.
Moreover, some dialogue practices escape my schema altogether.
Philosophical discussion for its own sake is atypical in American
film—although it may be the meat of a film such as Eric Rohmer's
Ma nuit chez Maude (1970)—American films do not spend much time
in conversation discussing non-plot-related issues. What is precisely
so fresh and interesting about Tarantino's *Reservoir Dogs* (1992) and
Pulp Fiction (1994) are the digressive conversations: the discussion of
tipping in the former and the long conversation about the erotic
meanings of a foot massage in the latter.

I trust this chapter serves as further defense of film dialogue, as if
this evidence of all the things that dialogue does for a filmic text will
finally refute the anti-dialogue critics such as Sergei Eisenstein, V. I.
Pudovkin, Rudolf Arnheim, Paul Rotha, and Siegfried Kracauer. But
even if they could read this, I doubt they would be swayed. Silent
films, after all, used intertitles to anchor time and place, to explain
narrative causality, and to provide authorial commentary; they sub-
stituted embraces for verbal love declarations; revealed character
through gesture and expression; relied on slapstick as opposed to
verbal jokes. In other words, showing that dialogue fulfills my nine
functions does not prove that dialogue is the *only* means of accomplishing these ends; nor, for that matter, have I even attempted to
prove that these ends are requisite for a narrative film.

Perhaps it is pointless to say to devotees of string quartets that
they are missing the contributions of bassoons and French horns and
piccolos, because such instruments do not belong in string quartets.
One can claim that brass and woodwind instruments are essential to
Beethoven's symphonies (and that Sousa's marches are literally unthinkable without them). You can reasonably argue that the full sym-
phony orchestra has a broader tonal range than a string quartet and

that it has more varied means at its disposal for affecting its audience. Without denigrating the continued importance of the string section, you can seek to understand the roles played by the added instruments.

You *can* say to devotees of string quartets that the music they enshrine is not the only music that can or should be played.

TWO

Structural and Stylistic Variables

What variables are manipulated in the writing of film dialogue, and what are the ramifications—narrative, aesthetic, ideological—of these choices? In other words, what factors account for the distinct "flavors" of film dialogue? What, precisely, makes the dialogue of *Casablanca* so different from that of *Citizen Kane?*

The variables discussed below are obviously not of the same genus. Some concern the habits of individual speakers, others the interaction between characters; some relate to the structure of scenes, others to the style of sentences. All, however, concentrate on the dialogue as a verbal text, as opposed to its performance by actors and integration with other cinematic elements (which are the subjects of the next chapter).

We shall neither be able to understand how dialogue differs from real-life conversation nor get much further than characterizing scripts with loose adjectives—"witty," "clumsy," "boring," "clever"—until we delineate the formal parameters constituent of film dialogue. My hope is that the categories disentangled below will give us these tools.

THE QUANTITY OF DIALOGUE

The question of "quantity" is complicated, because it encompasses at least two distinct issues: first, the use of scenes or sequences devoid of character speech, and second, when characters *are* talking, how much does each say in one gulp? In linguistic terms, how long a "turn" does each take? No necessary correlation exists between these two parameters. A film that includes long stretches of silent pantomime may, in the next scene, also allow its characters to be loquacious. Moreover, a film that generally restricts its characters to short statements may include relatively few silent sequences.

Scenes totally bereft of dialogue are rarer in American sound cinema than one might imagine. Establishing shots of locations *are* wordless, but these take up minimal screen time. More often than not, exciting physical action is punctuated with talk: swashbucklers taunt their opponents throughout duels; dogfights are accompanied by radio communications; battlefields echo with calls and commands. Dialogue serves important functions in such physical conflicts (here, and throughout the rest of this study, I use "function" narrowly, to refer to the concepts outlined in the previous chapter), such as demonstrating that the hero is uncowed by the danger, explaining to the viewer what is going on, naturalistically illustrating confusion and chaos. Actually, sustained stretches of silent action can be found: I've noticed that montage sequences compressing time, chase scenes, dances, and lovemaking are particularly likely to be presented with no speech whatsoever. Here the narrative action is self-explanatory and the visual spectacle self-sufficient. The cessation of speech during such sequences is rarely noticeable because it is compensated for by the musical score.

More interesting to me are those less common occasions where silence is noticeable, where the fact that no one speaks becomes crucial to the viewer's experience. As Michel Chion remarks: "It was necessary to have sounds and voices so that the *interruption* of them could probe more deeply into this thing called silence."[1] The opening sequence of Howard Hawks's *Rio Bravo* (1959) shows Dude slinking into the saloon, his degradation having reached the point where he'd consider digging a coin out of the spittoon to be able to buy a drink. Neither Dude nor his taunter speaks; all of their interactions are pantomimed. The silence rivets our attention, and it also mirrors how Dude's alcoholism has removed him from normal human communion. Similarly, the robbery at the beginning of Blake Edwards's *The Pink Panther* (1964) surprises and engages us with its prolonged silence, making us anxious as to whether the burglar will succeed, wondering if and when alarms will sound. "When nothing is said for a long time we can grow tense ... or uneasy," notes Jack Shadoian; the viewer waits expectantly for the echoing quiet to be shattered.[2]

Michel Chion points out that the absence of dialogue is often stressed by adding sound effects, and even mixing these at a higher level, or with a hint of reverberation, so that they create a sense of isolation or emptiness.[3] This is certainly true of the wrenching scene in Rouben Mamoulian's *Applause* (1929) where Kitty sits alone in her apartment waiting to die after drinking poison and the noticeably loud off-screen traffic noise reminds us of the busy, oblivious world outside. And Elisabeth Weis draws our attention to the carefully orchestrated use of silence in Alfred Hitchcock's *The Birds* (1963). Hitchcock once commented:

> For the final scene, in which Rod Taylor opens the door of the house for the first time and finds the birds assembled there, as far as the eye can see, I asked for a silence, but not just any kind of silence. I wanted an electronic silence, a sort of monotonous low hum that might suggest the sound of the sea in the distance. It was a strange, artificial sound, which in the language of the birds might be saying, "We're not ready to attack you yet, but we're getting ready."[4]

In these and other films, silence is being used to great effect.

Although *Movie-Maker* magazine counsels filmmakers to "maximiz[e] the number of completely wordless scenes,"[5] critics more commonly have addressed the second aspect of "quantity," the length of characters' speeches. "It has to be said that the dialogue scenes of talking pictures should be written as though each were a first-rate cable for every word of which the writer has to pay out of his own pocket," argues Sidney Howard.[6] Hank Poster, who advises novices on how to solve "the dilemma of dialogue," counsels: "How long should your dialogue be? Generally, one to three sentences in length—with crisp, clear meaning. The shorter you make your speeches, the better your film will be."[7]

Such attitudes are not restricted to how-to manuals. In his auteurist study of Howard Hawks, Gerald Mast claims: "Perhaps more than any other single element, it is the sparseness of Hawks's dialogue that gives his world its aroma, flavor, and texture."[8] But I'm not sure that Hawks's films *are* chary of dialogue. His adventure films spend much more time in dialogue scenes than in silent action, and his comedies, such as *Bringing Up Baby* (1938), *His Girl Friday* (1940), *Ball of Fire* (1941), and *Gentleman Prefer Blondes* (1953) are wall-to-wall dialogue—that's their glory. What might be true is that

Hawks's characters tend not to take long turns. But is this so? Actually, many of Hawks's characters speak at length: Feathers and Stumpy in *Rio Bravo;* General Sternwood in the opening of *The Big Sleep* (1946); Colonel Applegate during the dinner party in *Bringing Up Baby.* In trying to account for Mast's impression, the best I can come up with is that Hawks's male protagonists tend to be tight-lipped, or at least, they seem taciturn in relation to the people around them. Geoff Carter in *Only Angels Have Wings* and Tom Dunson in *Red River* (1948) set the paradigm. Mast himself argues that "Hawks's use of dialogue owes its allegiance not to cinematic virtue but to the view of humans and human psychology that underlies his narratives. Hawks's characters don't tell everything they know. . . . [Hawks comments:] 'The men I like are not very talkative.' "[9] Not surprisingly, spare dialogue is thus again associated with masculine terseness and prowess. (Am I the only one to detect connotations of knives and phalluses when John Fawell insists, for example, that film scripts must use "hard, simple language," with each line "polished cleanly"?)[10]

Critical aversion to talkative characters has obscured the prevalence and artistry of long turns. If one arbitrarily defines a long turn as a speech of more than a hundred words, they can be found in every genre and in every time period. Cinematic long turns are so common and so artistically compelling that they are collected in several anthologies for acting students to memorize for practice or audition material.[11]*

Long turns are so prevalent because they're so useful in fulfilling the functions analyzed above. They may certainly be "realistic"—people rarely speak in pithy epigrams. They allow for the explanation of a complicated argument or the description of a past narrative event. They contribute greatly to character revelation. They keep our attention focused on a star performance.

I shall offer only one example here: General Jack D. Ripper's (Sterling Hayden's) conversation with Mandrake (Peter Sellers) in Stanley Kubrick's *Dr. Strangelove* (1962) at the point in the plot when the viewer starts to understand the depths of Ripper's madness and the

* Warning! Many selections in anthologies of film quotations contain discrepancies from the film's final dialogue, leading me to believe that they are based on shooting scripts.

peril of bombers having been sent to attack the Soviet Union. (This is all one "turn," because Mandrake's sole comment is more a confirmation that he is listening than an independent move.)

> RIPPER: Mandrake, I suppose it never occurred to you that while we're chatting here so enjoyably, the decision is being made by the President and the Joint Chiefs in the War Room at the Pentagon. And when they realize there is no possibility of recalling the wing there will be only one course of action open . . . total commitment. Mandrake, do you recall what Clemenceau once said about war?
> MANDRAKE: No, I don't think I do sir, no.
> RIPPER: He said war was too important to be left to the generals. When he said that fifty years ago he might have been right. But today war is too important to be left to politicians. They have neither the time, the training, nor the inclination for strategic thought. (*Ripper removes the cigar from his mouth, takes a breath, and proceeds with the cigar in his hand.*) I can no longer sit back and allow communist infiltration, communist indoctrination, communist subversion, and the international communist conspiracy to sap and impurify all of our precious bodily fluids.

Consider how Ripper's remarks are structured. He begins on a note the viewer finds odd and ironic, the suggestion that under these dire circumstances, Mandrake and he are merely "chatting so enjoyably." But he quickly regains apparent reasonableness, showing foresight as to the actions of others and demonstrating his historical perspective with a quotation from Clemenceau. He then switches into skillful self-justifying oratory, building to a crescendo with repeated chimes on the word "communist"; the rhetoric seems lullingly familiar (and must have been more so at the time of the film's initial release in 1963). However, the crescendo culminates in a totally surprising, totally wacko assertion about a conspiracy to sap and impurify—not "the national soul" or "the democratic way of life"—but "all of our precious bodily fluids." Kubrick and Terry Southern, like other screenwriters who favor long turns, skillfully employ what Sam Smiley calls "end position emphasis":[12] they save the shock for the end of a long speech, where it can reverberate.

Unless long turns are shared, they are also markers of one character dominating the conversation, an indication, as with General Ripper and Uncle Charlie, that a character is dominating the exchange.

Short turns, on the other hand, may be associated with swifter pacing, although our sense of pace is determined, not only by how long the turns may be, but also, obviously, by how quickly the actors' speak—John Wayne draws a short line out very slowly, while Eddie Murphy races through a long turn, creating a feeling of breakneck speed. It is the *combination* of short turns with swift delivery that creates a staccato effect, as in the following example, an interchange between Eddie Mars (John Ridgely) and Philip Marlowe (Humphrey Bogart) in Hawks's *The Big Sleep:*

EDDIE MARS: Convenient the door being open when you didn't have a key, eh?

MARLOWE: Yeah, wasn't it? By the way, how did you happen to have one?

MARS: It any of your business?

MARLOWE: I could make it my business.

MARS: I could make your business mine.

MARLOWE: Oh, you wouldn't like it. The pay's too small.

The combination of the narrative situation of a face-off between two antagonists, the actors' swift, snarling delivery, and the short, alternating turns, creates the impression of accelerated pace.

In addition to controlling pace, pithiness may be used for characterization, revealing a character to be reticent or guarded. In Don Siegel's *Escape from Alcatraz* (1979), Frank Morris, played by Clint Eastwood, is asked about his birthday by a fellow inmate. Frank answers that he doesn't know his birthdate. Charley exclaims, "Jeez, what kind of childhood 'd you have?" Frank's one-word reply tells us everything we need to know: "Short."

Brevity may, in many situations when time presses, be the most realistic option. And although it may seem paradoxical, spare writing can also serve the function (discussed above) of "exploiting the resources of language." After all, many verbal forms—haiku, sonnets, limericks—draw their power from extreme condensation. Playwrights like Oscar Wilde and Noël Coward (who is credited with starting a vogue for brief speeches)[13] are famous not for long soliloquies but for clever quips, and Emily Dickinson, Dorothy Parker, and Harold Pinter all exploit extremes of terseness. Many of the most memorable lines from Hollywood films ("Fasten your seatbelts—it's going to be a bumpy night") are short, not because screenwriters want to avoid dialogue or don't value language, but because they know how to utilize condensation artistically.

The above discussion boils down to unsurprising conclusions: films do use silence, but more often they use dialogue; sometimes characters speak briefly, sometimes at length. Contrary to the tide of opinion, all of these permutations are legitimate and valuable, depending upon the context.

HOW MANY PARTICIPANTS?

Given that a scene presents conversation, three alternatives exist: monologue (a character talking out loud with no one else present),[14] duologue (two characters speaking to each other), and polylogue (more than two characters talking).

Cinematic monologues were inherited from theatrical practice. Novels, of course, have no need for such devices, because they may either use a narrator to delve into the character's mind or directly incorporate stream of consciousness. In the theater, monologues are advantageous because they allow audiences access to a central character's feelings or reasoning through a decision that must be made.[15] Cinematic voice-over narration or internal subjective sound can fulfill the same function, but employing those techniques merely for one scene or one revelation would be awkward. I have found most film monologues allotted to male "loner" characters, men who would not plausibly bare their souls in conversation with on-screen confidantes. Sarah Connor's monologue into the tape recorder as she rides off into the desert at the end of James Cameron's *The Terminator* (1984) is the exception that proves the rule, because her horrendous experiences and her prescient knowledge of the future have detached her from the rest of society, literally and figuratively.

Talking aloud to oneself is considered strange in real life. Although monologues are accepted on stage as a convention, expectations of realism make them more problematic in film. Thus special situations must be created in order to provide a convincing motivation. Talking to animals is particularly common (Jack Burns speaks to his horse in *Lonely Are the Brave;* Tom confides to the family dog in *The River Wild* [1994]), as is speaking to oneself in a mirror (Travis Bickle in *Taxi Driver* [1976]). Robert Altman made an unusual choice in allowing Philip Marlowe in *The Long Goodbye* (1973) and John Mc-Cabe in *McCabe and Mrs. Miller* (1971) simply to walk around talking to themselves out loud; their monologues remind one of elderly men muttering, and the overtones of isolation, frailty, and perhaps impotence are appropriate for such anti-heroes.

In John Ford films, the heroes typically talk to the dead. Graveside soliloquies—in each case, by a taciturn older male figure talking to a departed woman or younger man—are a repeated device. Let us look at the monologue in *Young Mr. Lincoln* (1939), when Lincoln (Henry Fonda) visits Ann Rutledge's grave.

> LINCOLN: Well, Ann, I'm still up a tree. Just can't seem to make up my mind what to do. Maybe I ought to go into the law—take my chances. I admit I got kinda a taste for something different than this in my mouth. Still, I don't know. I feel such a fool, settin' myself up as knowin' so much. Course I know what you'd say, I've been hearing it every day over and over again: "Go on Abe, make somethin' of yourself. You got friends, show em what you got in ya." Oh, yes, I know what you'd say, but I don't know. Ann, I'll tell ya what I'll do. I'll let the stick decide. If it falls back toward me then I stay here as I always have. If it falls forward toward you then it's, well, it's the law. Here goes Ann. Well Ann, you win, it's the law. Wonder if I coulda tipped it your way just a little.

This example illustrates the special quality of all monologues—the way they connote an absolute honesty: "Wonder if I coulda tipped it your way just a little." Because "no one" is there to hear, the viewer infers that there is no need to lie, or even to include the typical face-saving shadings and equivocations of social speech. Monologues thus assume the guise of a clear window into the soul. They constitute what John Ellis would call "poignant moments"—occasions where the audience feels it has been given privileged access to the character's innermost feelings.[16]

Polylogues, *au contraire*, illustrate the characters in their social setting; the stress is on the interaction of the group. Sometimes such scenes are used to portray a group reaching a consensus that turns the plot, as when in musicals a bunch of kids decide to put on a show, or in Westerns, when townspeople congeal into a lynch mob. Most often, dialogue in polylogues is used to create the atmosphere of a select subculture, showing the language and mindset that this group has in common, as in the gang-of-guys scenes in John Badham's *Saturday Night Fever* (1977) or the Algonquin lunches of Alan Rudolph's *Mrs. Parker and the Vicious Circle* (1994). Especially in films from the 1970s onward, which use complicated multitrack mixing, portions of polylogues may be inaudible, or overlapping, or drowned out by laughter—the individual lines are less important than the group flavor. In *The Fugitive*, Samuel Gerard works with a cohort of young associates; all their scenes lapse into a chaos of voices, noises, laughter, and in-jokes. The sound design of these scenes serves as a notable contrast to the scenes focused on Kimble; the noisy camaraderie throws the fugitive's solitary silence into relief.

However, not all scenes with three or more characters in them stress group solidarity. The scene in *His Girl Friday* when Walter Burns takes Hildy and Bruce out for lunch shows us three distinct personalities, each pursuing his or her own aims. Or, for another example of conflict—of individual needs and verbal styles—study the confrontation in *Citizen Kane* between Kane, Emily, Boss Jim Getty, and Susan Alexander at Susan's apartment. Nor do all polylogues descend into naturalistic verbal chaos; many are more formal occasions when narrative information must be conveyed.

Actually, American films offer an abundance of what I'd like to call "pseudo-polylogues," that is, several characters are physically present, but secondary figures attend more as witnesses, or bystanders, to the transaction of the scene's key business between two principals. The witnesses may be thrown a line or two for the sake of realism or variety, but their importance to the conversation is to bodily augment one side or another, to make the conversation official, or to respond to it.

Duologues are the most fundamental structure of screen speech, because they are a dramatic necessity. Two characters in conversation provide more "action," more suspense, more give-and-take than monologues, because new information or emotional shadings can be exchanged, questioned, reacted to. On the other hand, in true polylogues, too much is going on; there are too many speakers, too many agendas, too much distraction to routinely handle important narrative functions (e.g., explaining narrative causality, revealing character psychology). Duologues between hero and associate, between lovers, between antagonists, are the engines that drive film narratives forward.

Related to the question of the number of participants is the issue of foreground and background dialogue. Scenes taking place in public locales may include background dialogue mixed at a lower volume than the primary conversation. The background dialogue is present in the service of plausibility (when you are talking to someone in a restaurant or hallway, does everyone else in the world really fall silent?). However, just as Flaubert pointedly intermixes the sound of the agricultural fair with Rudolphe's seduction of Emma in *Madame Bovary*, so filmmakers selectively raise and lower the volume of background dialogue to counterpoint the primary discussion. Hitchcock does exactly this in the auction scene in *North by Northwest*, when the auctioneer's patter is selectively raised to comment upon Eve as "a lovely piece," "in excellent condition," and to draw the audience's attention to the statue containing microfilm.

CONVERSATIONAL INTERACTION

How much time one character spends hogging the floor is only one of a host of verbal variables indicating the flux of relationships between cinematic characters. Linguists have untangled the unconscious rules governing our everyday conversations and the ramifications of breaking these rules. Applying their insights to film dialogue scenes tells us whether characters are on the same wavelength, whether one is in a superior position, whether they are polite, whether they are even listening to each other. In other words, much of what we intuit about character psychology and motivation comes from our instinctive analysis of their behavior as conversational partners. Moreover, how the characters speak to one another has consequences for the third party to the conversation, the eavesdropper in the darkened theater.

For communication to be successful, the participants must approach a conversation with enough shared background and assumptions to provide a workable context for the words exchanged. Most dialogue features "normal" give-and-take: the speakers appear to be listening to one another, understanding one another, and responding appropriately. However, so-called "elliptical" dialogue implies a special closeness amongst the characters; they speak to each other in a shorthand fashion, they understand mysterious prior references, and their minds are moving in the same direction at the same speed. The viewer is put in an inferior position, shut out from the closeness, trying to catch up. Screenwriters regularly quicken the pace by starting a scene in the middle of a conversation, thus forcing the viewer hurriedly to infer the elided moments.

On the other hand, movies can put the spectator in a superior position, listening to characters who are having difficulties understanding one another. "Dialogues of the deaf" refers to the criss-crossing of two monologues, with both speakers pursuing their own trains of thought.[17] Although such moments are extremely rare in actual conversation, they are used to great effect in comedies, demonstrating each character's obliviousness of the other. (See the scene in George Cukor's *Adam's Rib* [1949] when Kip is trying to seduce Amanda while she is obviously thinking only of her husband.) Or characters may be literally deaf. In *The Palm Beach Story* (1942), Preston Sturges has great fun with the hard-of-hearing Wienie King:

WIENIE KING: How much rent do you owe?
GERRY: Well, that isn't really your business.
WIENIE KING: I can't hear you, you're mumbling.
GERRY: I said, it isn't really your business.
WIENIE KING: I'm in the sausage business.

More often characters misunderstand one another because they lack some information or because they are operating under false assumptions. As we shall see, this often has tragic consequences in melodramas. In comedies, however, this is a stock device for furthering lovers' quarrels or elaborating a plot based on mistaken identity. In Mark Sandrich's *Top Hat* (1935), once Dale (Ginger Rogers) mistakenly concludes that Jerry (Fred Astaire) is married to Madge, she misinterprets everything said to her.

Another variable of characters' conversation is turn-taking negotiation. In real-life conversation, negotiating who gets to speak when is a delicate procedure, enacted subconsciously hundreds of times a day. In examining fictional conversations, one sees how often the mechanics of turn-taking negotiation are meaningful.

Sometimes, for instance, a character will invite or demand a response by posing a question. Dennis Aig notices that questions create the suspense of waiting for the answer.[18] This quality is particularly salient in courtroom cross-examinations and in interrogation scenes where everything seems to hinge upon the reply—recall how Szell torments Babe in John Schlesinger's *Marathon Man* (1976) for an answer to "Is it safe?" Yet questions can also imply tentativeness, a need for reassurance; linguists have highlighted the prevalence of "tag questions"—little ending phrases that turn a statement into a question—by those who are insecure.[19] Tentativeness and the need for reassurance are both blatant in Mike Nichols's *The Graduate* (1967) when Dustin Hoffman says: "Mrs. Robinson, you're trying to seduce me. Aren't you?"

"Toppers," on the other hand, are diametrically opposed to questions, in that the latter invite/command the next speaker to take the floor, whereas the former would deny the next speaker his turn. Aig rather narrowly defines a "topper" as "a line which caps off the punch line of a joke. It is really a second punch line."[20] I think of toppers as retorts that attempt to close off a conversational topic by their finality or nastiness. Toppers are particularly conspicuous when they are paired—that is, when one character thinks he has effectively shut down conversation, only to be topped by an even more withering riposte. A classic example can be heard in Bob Fosse's *Cabaret* (1972), when both Sally and Brian are upset by the influence on their lives of the wealthy Maximillian. Brian shouts in anger, "Screw Maximillian!" Sally thinks that she will devastate Brian when she answers: "I do." But Brian tops her with his more surprising, "So do I." Because toppers have such an air of finality, they are often used as the last lines of a scene.

Breaking into another character's speech, making his or her turn stop and yours start, can have a variety of meanings. What Deborah Tannen calls "chiming in" can indicate that characters are exactly on the same wavelength, that they are quite simpatico; in such cases completing someone else's sentence can be a totally friendly contribution.[21] Or it can imply mockery, as when Hildy finishes Walter Burns's habitual speeches for him in *His Girl Friday*. One case of breaking into speech that obviously qualifies as aggressive *interrupting* can be seen in the train wreck scene from *The Fugitive* when Sheriff Rawlins breaks into Gerard's plans:

> GERARD: Uh, with all due respect, uh, Sheriff Rawlins, I'd like to rec-
> ommend check points on a fifteen-mile radius at I-57, I-24,
> and over here on route 13 east of Chestn—
> RAWLINS: Whoa, whoa, whoa, whoa, whoa, whoa, whoa, whoa. Wait
> a minute, the prisoners are all dead. The only thing check
> points are going to do is get a lot of good people frantic
> around here and flood my office with calls.

Rawlins's verbal behavior substantiates the viewer's low opinion of him and leads us to cheer when Gerard gets fed up with this loud-mouth and takes over the investigation.

Overlapping speech may merely indicate that numerous conversations are happily going on simultaneously in a noisy, crowded locale. However, when a small group of characters engaged in one conversation all speak at the same time, the viewer may assume that no one is listening and that everybody is so emotionally involved in their own agendas that they are unwilling to cede the floor (as in Susan Alexander's apartment in *Citizen Kane*). Generally, because the viewers' ability to hear distinctly is compromised, overlapping dialogue is used for realistic texture or comic confusion, not for an important narrative function.

An interesting exception can be found in *M*A*S*H*, where every time the Colonel tries to give Radar an order, Radar acknowledges and repeats the order by speaking over his commander, thereby proving his superior abilities and undermining the Colonel's authority. Robert Self has deciphered the following exchange:

> COLONEL: Radar, get a hold of Major Burns and tell him that we're
> going to have to hold a couple of surgeons over from the
> day shift to the night shift. Get General Hammond down
> there in Seoul; tell him we gotta have two new surgeons
> right away!
> RADAR: (*simultaneously*) I guess I'd better call Major Burns and tell
> him to put another day shift in our night shift. I'll put in a
> call to General Hammond in Seoul. I hope he sends us those
> two new surgeons; we're sure going to need em!

As Self analyses,

> The dialogue summarizes the effects that large numbers of newly ar-
> riving wounded have on the MASH unit; in turn it becomes the
> cause motivating the arrival in the next scene of Duke and Hawkeye—

except that these words so crucial to the viewer's understanding of the initial situation in the story—that set in motion the whole cause-effect narrative logic—are spoken by both characters simultaneously and are incomprehensible. . . . Laughter at what becomes part of the comic business in the film . . . occurs at the expense of clarity in the development of the story.[22]

In such a case overlapping speech is transgressive, not only of the rules of politeness, but of the conventional functioning of film speech; this double transgressiveness makes it all the more effective as a mockery of the chain of command/chain of narration.

The ultimate violation of the rules of decorum regarding turn-taking occurs when one character physically prevents another from talking. Physically silencing someone is an explicit act of dominance, whether it is done by threats, or by putting a hand over another's mouth, or with a kiss.

At the furthest extreme lies those characters who never take a turn at speaking because they are mute. Because they appear with surprising frequency in Hollywood cinema, mute characters have attracted the interest of numerous critics.[23] I hypothesize that ultimately they reflect the lingering influence of a major ancestor of narrative film, stage melodrama, which, as Peter Brooks explicates, also foregrounds the mute role.[24] At any rate, *not speaking* counts as a form of conversational interaction, but it is a form fraught with tension. A character who does not, or cannot, speak cranks up the viewer's anticipation; as is true of scenes that are markedly silent, the viewer waits with impatience for the silence to be broken. And indeed, while some characters remain mute throughout a film, many more dramatically break into speech before the end—Helen Keller in *The Miracle Worker* (1962), Madison in *Splash* (1984), Travis in *Paris, Texas* (1984), Ada in *The Piano* (1993). Bridging the gap from silence into sound is repeatedly thematized by American films, as if the medium compulsively needs to repeat the transition of the mid 1920s.

Narrowing our focus now down to the performance of individual speakers, let us concentrate on the issue of a character's verbal competence, the degree to which he or she shows dexterity or eloquence. Given the general distrust of language, and the overall anti-intellectual tenor of American culture, it should be no surprise that American films offer evidence of a deep distrust of verbal proficiency: articulate, polished speakers—Waldo Lydecker in *Laura* (1944), Harry Lime in *The Third Man* (1949), Hannibal Lecter in *Silence of the Lambs* (1991)—are almost always villains.

"The trick is to use a relatively small and simple vocabulary," counsels the screenwriter/director/professor Edward Dmytryk. "Most scripts do very well with a pool of no more then a few thousand words, the majority of them mono-syllabic and of Anglo-Saxon derivation. After all, the goal is to *reach* the viewer, not to confuse him."[25] Such preconceptions explain why in general film vocabulary is limited and sentences tend to be short. Even during long turns, sentences are restricted to a single independent clause. (Look back at the excerpts from *Shadow of a Doubt*, or *Young Mr. Lincoln*, or *Dr. Strangelove*.) The use of complex subordination, as in the following excerpt from *Citizen Kane*, is atypical:

> KANE: The trouble is you don't realize you're talking to two people. As Charles Foster Kane, who owns eighty-two thousand, three hundred and sixty-four shares of Public Transit Preferred—you see, I do have a general idea of my holdings—I sympathize with you. Charles Foster Kane is a scoundrel, his paper should be run out of town, a committee should be formed to boycott him. You may, if you can form such a committee, put me down for a contribution of one thousand dollars.

Kane's use of embedded clauses conveys his intelligence and pretensions, and seems particularly suited to Welles's theatrical and histrionic talents.

Although most American film characters aren't allotted great verbal dexterity, neither are they tongue-tied or grunting. Extremes of verbal awkwardness are thus also used as special signifiers—either of the pressure of emotions or of character traits. Stuttering, for instance, in film as in life, is taken as a sign of nervousness (as in many Woody Allen films).

Drama theorists have long noted that moments of stammering infelicity are used as guarantors of sincerity. "When one of Mamet's characters has something of importance to say," writes Anne Dean, "his or her abortive attempts at eloquence can paradoxically speak volumes."[26] For filmic examples, look back at Ted Kramer's manifesto of fatherly love on the witness stand, or consider Charlie's declaration of love to Carrie in Mike Newell's *Four Weddings and a Funeral* (1994):

CHARLIE: Umm, Look. Sorry. Sorry. Uh, I just um. Um, well. This is a really stupid question, and uh, particularly in view of our recent shopping excursion, but, uh, I just wondered, if by any chance—umm, uh, I mean obviously not because I am just some kid who's only slept with nine people—but, I—I just wondered. Uh, I really feel—umm uh, in short. Uh, to recap in a slightly clearer version: uh in the words of David Cassidy, in fact, umm while he was still with the Partridge Family, uh—I think I love you. And uh I—I—I just wondered whether by any chance you wouldn't like to . . . umm . . . uh . . . uh . . . No. No. No. Of course not. Umm, I'm an idiot. He's not. Excellent. Excellent. Fantastic. I'm so sorry. Lovely to see you. Sorry to disturb. Better get on. . . . Fuck.

The combination of Hugh Grant's wincing, stumbling delivery and the incoherence of the prose guarantees to the viewer that this declaration is heartfelt.

Awkwardness and grammatical mistakes are also employed as Freudian "slips of the tongue." Will Moore notes that Molière

puts his characters systematically, so to speak, into corners, situations where their speech, intending to be intelligent, is in fact instinctive, where they say more than they mean, or where they are not conscious of what they are saying. Does not comedy largely consist of this use of language against the intention of the user but obeying the intention of the dramatist? . . . Comic drama elicits the utterance of what in most of us is buried, suppressed, unutterable.[27]

Film characters also slip under strain. A perfect example can be seen in *Stagecoach* when Peacock votes to turn back from the journey:

PEACOCK: I'd like to go on, brother. I want to reach the bosom of my dear family in Kansas City, Kansas, as quickly as possible, but I may never reach that bosom if we go on. So, under the circumstances . . . you understand, brother, I think it best we go back with the bosoms . . . [cough] . . . I mean the soldiers.

OTHER LANGUAGES, DIALECTS, AND JARGON

Although I have restricted this study to American films (and a few British examples), nearly all of the films examined include some reference, whether substantive or tiny, to languages other than English. This linguistic diversity could be ascribed to generic plot conventions: Westerns frequently need to encompass Native American languages or Spanish; war films may have German or French or Japanese characters; historical epics may take place in foreign lands. However, the fact that even domestic comedies and dramas often include one or more characters whose native language is not English indicates the pressure of other forces besides genre or setting. Perhaps the presence of many immigrants in the Hollywood filmmaking community created a situation where linguistic diversity was seen as the norm? Perhaps the desire to cast foreign-born actors necessitated the creation of foreign-born characters?* Perhaps the desire to add cosmopolitan élan to a popular medium? Perhaps the need to include references that might appeal to immigrant audiences or eventual foreign viewers?[28] In recent decades, as minority filmmakers have had more access to mainstream film production, movies have appeared that deliberately highlight linguistic diversity and the problems of translation (I'm thinking of Ang Lee's 1993 *The Wedding Banquet*). More theoretically, a Bakhtinian perspective suggests that movies, like novels, display the pressure of *polyglossia*, of national languages jostling up against each other.

Given the pressure on filmic speech to help carry the narrative forward, the presence of non-English speaking characters creates a conundrum. Naturally, the most realistic strategy would be to have such characters speak freely in their native languages, but strict realism always loses out to the other demands on film speech. Thus, the foreign dialogue is generally minimized, and its import is nearly always made clear by context, cognates, or pantomime, or by having a bilingual character handily present to provide a translation.[29] When a film such as Darnell Martin's *I Like It Like That* (1994) chooses to include sentences in Spanish and makes fewer concessions than usual to English-speaking monoglots, it makes a state-

---

* Foreign accents seem to have been thought of as interchangeable: Garbo's Swedish accent marked her as *non-American*, so she could be French in *Camille* (1935) and Russian in *Ninotchka* (1939).

ment about its preferred viewers (and about the role of language in American culture).

But perhaps the most prevalent tactic is to recast the foreign language into English, either after an audio fade—as happens in *The Hunt for Red October* (1990)—or from the very beginning. Typically, this English will be spiced with some of the accent and idioms of the original language to foreground the fact that the characters are foreign, but even so, these magical translations, this "self-dubbing," has been seen as a manifestation of Hollywood's cultural insensitivity. Robert Stam and Ella Shohat comment on what they term "the linguistics of domination": "Hollywood proposed to tell not only its own stories but also those of other nations, and not only to Americans but also to the other nations themselves, and always in English. In Cecil B. de Mille epics, both the ancient Egyptians and the Israelites, not to mention God, speak English."[30] Shohat and Stam argue that Hollywood has "ventriloquized the world."

Yet allowing foreign characters to speak their own languages is not automatically preferable. In David Lean's *Bridge on the River Kwai* (1957), the brutal Japanese commandant of the prisoner of war camp, who (rather unrealistically) speaks perfect English, is a major character, and the audience is encouraged to develop some measure of understanding for his predicament. However, in Michael Cimino's *The Deer Hunter* (1978), when the protagonists are captured and tormented by a group of Viet Cong, the latter's dialogue is left totally untranslated. The foreign dialogue serves primarily as a marker of Otherness, and the fact that we, like the American characters, don't understand anything that the Vietnamese characters are wildly "jabbering" further vilifies them.

One other method is occasionally used to translate foreign dialogue: printed subtitles. Subtitles are most likely to be found in more contemporary films with extended but discrete scenes of narrative relevance transpiring in another language. Alan Pakula's *Sophie's Choice* (1982), for example, uses subtitles for all the German dialogue spoken during the flashback scenes that dramatize Sophie's experiences at Auschwitz. Subtitles allow foreign languages their integrity and unique expressiveness, while still preserving the dialogue's narrative functions for American filmgoers.

Dialects, as opposed to national languages, pose fewer intelligibility problems but are still ideologically potent. As Elaine Chaika points out in *Language: The Social Mirror,* everybody speaks a dialect ("standard dialect" is itself just another arbitrary version of English) and such linguistic subgroups are "inextricably bound up with one's identity. Speech is likely to be the most reliable determiner of social class or ethnic group."[31] Recognizable, clichéd dialects are used on-screen to sketch in a character's past and cultural heritage, to locate each person in terms of his or her financial standing, education level, geographical background, or ethnic group.

Thus, screen dialects lead directly into the problems of stereotyping. Hollywood cannot be charged with inventing this ill (vaudeville and radio skits are even more blatant in their racial and ethnic caricatures), but the film industry has exacerbated negative stereotypes, and instead of being sensitive to the accuracy of nonstandard dialects, movies have historically exploited them to represent characters as silly, quaint, or stupid. Criticism of this bigotry is not a new phenomenon; as early as 1946, Lewis Herman castigated screenwriters for their handling of immigrants' speech: "Then there is another group of writers who resort to a catholic but injudicious use of a bastardized pidgin English adaptable to all nationalities. . . . All their foreign characters, regardless of their national origin, say 'I go now,' or 'Me no want him,' or 'Yah! I be good fella.' "[32]

The baby talk given to Native American characters, the ornate Oriental style of Charlie Chan and other Asian characters, and the broad imitation of black vernacular allotted to Uncle Tom and Mammy characters in countless American films (Butterfly McQueen was once forced to say: "Who dat say who dat when you say dat")[33] demonstrate the filmmakers' cavalier—if not bigoted—approach to cultural identity and linguistic diversity.

(I would like to believe that contemporary filmmakers are more enlightened and held to higher standards of accuracy and sensitivity now, but I'm not convinced. Only one thing is certain: in order to win brownie points for realism, publicity materials frequently stress that actors have spent months or years working with dialogue coaches to perfect an accent.)

Films capitalize on dialects to immediately telegraph individual characterizations—Rita in *West Side Story* (1961) is Puerto Rican, Jim Malone in *The Untouchables* (1987) is Irish, Stella in *Stella Dallas* (1937) is working-class, Tess Carlyle in *Guarding Tess* (1994) is upper-class. Moreover, dialects are manipulated in the service of realism—

if we are in the South, one would expect at least some attempt at Southern accents.* Commonly, films will create a certain linguistic community, a norm, and then employ departures from it for special effect. Thus dialects are frequently used to highlight a character's separation from his fellows: I'm thinking of *Norma Rae* (1979), where Rob Liebman's New York Jewish accent makes him a fish out of water in a small Southern town, or *"Crocodile" Dundee* (1986), where Paul Hogan's Australian idiom sets him apart in New York City.

But when we look only at dialects' ideological ramifications or contributions to realistic texture, what may be overlooked is how dialects "exploit the resources of language"; how they lend a distinctive color to the sound track. As a Northeastern, white, middle-aged viewer I am conscious of a special enjoyment of fresh sounds and rhythms when watching *She's Gotta Have It* (1986), *The Big Easy* (1987), and *Clueless* (1995). Regardless of their accuracy, dialect markers can serve the "poetic" function described in the previous chapter. In the story in *Citizen Kane* quoted earlier, the phrase "A white dress she had on" both stresses Bernstein's Jewish extraction and surprises us into imaginatively seeing the dress's whiteness. By the same token, in Ford's *How Green Was My Valley* (1941), Beth Morgan greets Bronwyn, her future daughter-in-law: "There is lovely you are." The uncommon syntax signifies "Welshness" to an American audience, but, more important, it serves what the Russian formalist critic Victor Shklovsky's identifies as the fundamental strategy of art, the effect of "making strange."[34] The phrase's freshness makes us appreciate Beth's feelings, and Bronwyn's loveliness.

Related to dialects are jargons, terminology particular to certain professions or cultural subgroups, which are also used on-screen for characterizations and in the service of realism. For example, in John Huston's *The Maltese Falcon* (1941), when the cops come to tell Spade that Thursby has been shot, he initially reacts angrily:

SPADE: Sorry I got up on my hind legs, boys, but you fellas tryin' to rope me made me nervous. Miles gettin' bumped off upset me

---

* American film scholars have paid next to no attention to regional accents among characters, but it is interesting to note this issue has assumed significant proportions among those who study French film, perhaps because regional accents have traditionally assumed major importance in French culture. Michel Marie, Sylvia Grendon, and Christopher Faulkner have focused on how regional accents and class markers contribute to the meaning of classic films by Renoir and Pagnol.

and then you birds crackin' foxy, but it's all right now, now that I know what it's all about.

"Hind legs," "rope me," "bumped off," "birds," and "crackin' foxy" are not standard, mid-Atlantic English, but neither do such expressions belong to a distinct regional dialect. Instead, they are meant to imitate the argot of a certain profession, that of the urban, street-wise private eye. (Note that here most of the expressions refer, one way or another, to animals, which fits the urban jungle atmosphere of the film as a whole.) Specific jargons assume great prominence in certain genres, as we shall see later.

STYLISTIC VARIABLES: REPETITION, RHYTHM, AND SURPRISE

Linguists such as Ronald Wardhaugh and Deborah Tannen have stressed how much repetition is a part of ordinary conversation, both deliberately, to clear up any misunderstandings, and subconsciously, as if each speaker's choice of vocabulary is subtly influenced by the words already uttered.[35] Repetition in film dialogue may at times exist to mimic normal conversational habit, but primarily it stems from aesthetic motivations. Roman Jakobson has argued that the distinguishing feature of poetry (as opposed to ordinary language) is the higher degree of patterning and repetition.[36] The artistry of film scripts can be traced to their recurrent patterns.

Repetition in film dialogue can occur immediately or as interweaving. In *The Fugitive,* when Gerard first surveys the train crash, he murmurs: "My, my, my, my, my, what a mess." The repetitions of "my," each with a slightly different intonation, serve to emphasize the extent to which Gerard is impressed by the destruction.[37] In Gus Van Sant's *Good Will Hunting* (1997), the psychiatrist Sean comforts Will concerning the physical abuse Will suffered as a child, saying, "It's not your fault"; but then Sean repeats the phrase verbatim half a dozen times, and with each repetition he penetrates further through Will's defenses and pain. Films more commonly include scattered but persistent references to a key word: *On the Waterfront* hinges on the word "bum" and Terry's desperate struggle to escape that label; similarly, the Coen brothers' *Miller's Crossing* (1990) continually has characters repeat the word "ethics," until it is plain that the film is concentrating on defining ethical action.

Many screenwriters deliberately coin a line or exchange of lines that recurs intermittently throughout the film. These refrains are highly noticeable, they are usually attached to one character as a leitmotif, and they gather meaning from their recapitulation throughout the text. As John Fawell observes, "The most memorable lines in the film are simple ones that are repeated, as a line of poetry might be, or a phrase in a musical score, and which through this repetition achieve a dramatic resonance that is central to the meaning of the film."[38] Examples abound:

From *Bringing Up Baby* (1938), David's fruitless attempt to salvage a business meeting that is constantly sabotaged: "I'll be with you in a minute, Mr. Peabody."

From *Gone with the Wind* (1939), Scarlett's method of dealing with troubles: "I'll think about it tomorrow."

From *Casablanca* (1942), Renault's lackadaisical police work: "Round up the usual suspects." Rick's attempt at living unfettered: "I stick my neck out for nobody." And Rick's infatuation with Ilsa: "Here's looking at you, kid."

From *My Darling Clementine* (1946), Wyatt Earp's complaint about Tombstone's lawlessness: "What kind of a town is this?"

From *The Searchers* (1956), Ethan's habitual claim of invincibility and foreknowledge: "That'll be the day."

From *Butch Cassidy and the Sundance Kid* (1969), Butch's bafflement at a posse that is pursuing them relentlessly: "Who *are* those guys?"

From *The Godfather* (1972), Don Corleone's business methodology: "I'll make him an offer he can't refuse."

From *E. T.* (1982), the alien's attempt to make contact with his ship: "E. T. phone home."

From *Field of Dreams* (1989), the enigmatic assertion, "If you build it, he will come."

From *Philadelphia* (1993), Joe Miller's strategic feigning of ignorance: "Explain it to me like I was a six-year-old."

In each case, the viewer's familiarity with the line makes each appearance more significant, so that the repeated lines take on resonance and power. Often a change in the relationship between characters is solidified by character X repeating something Y has said earlier; in *The Godfather,* when Michael Corleone talks about an offer that can't be refused, we know that he has completely internalized the mafioso culture that he initially resisted; in *Philadelphia,* when the jury foreman asks other jurors to "explain it to me like I was a six-year-old," we know that he has adopted Joe Miller's perspective on the case. "Adopting another's dialogue" is a way to signal connection. Viewers regularly take these tag lines out of movies and make them their own, for similar reasons.

In addition, film may use repetition both more subtly and more integrally, through repeated phrasings or sentence construction. Repetition is endemic in *Casablanca.* Not only do Renault and Rick get tag lines, even minor characters repeat themselves verbatim: Sacha's constant avowals of love for Yvonne; the pickpocket's misleading warning to his prey about "Vultures, vultures everywhere." Even incidental dialogue is highly repetitious, with phrases repeated again and again.

SAM: Boss. (*no answer*) Boss!
RICK: Yeah?
SAM: Boss, ain't you going to bed?
RICK: Not right now.
SAM: Ain't you planning on going to bed in the near future?
RICK: No.
SAM: You ever going to bed?
RICK: No.
SAM: Well, I ain't sleepy either.

The repetition of "going to bed" becomes comic, setting Rick and Sam up almost as a vaudeville duo, helping to illustrate the bond between the two.

So thoroughgoing is the penchant for patterning in *Casablanca* that if characters aren't repeating the same words, they use parallel phrasing:

RICK: *Who* are *you* really? And *what* were *you* before? *What did you* do and *what did you* think?
RICK: *Maybe not to*day, *maybe not to*morrow, but soon and for the rest of your life. . . . Where I'm going you can't follow. What I've got to do you can't be any part of. [My emphasis]

John Fawell comments on the "musicality" of film scripts. Much of this effect comes from the careful orchestration of the rhythm of the characters' speeches, both inside each turn and in the jockeying back and forth between conversational partners.* This rhythmic quality is particularly marked in *Casablanca*, but you can also hear it in most of the dialogue of classical Hollywood cinema, both on the level of individual phrases and on the level of the scenes, which begin slowly, rise through various verbal thrusts and parries, and end with a final resounding clincher.

The final stylistic topic to mention is the issue of "surprise," which I would define as employing an unusual or unexpected turn of phrase for a special effect. (Of course this is part and parcel of my function "exploiting the resources of language.") In *Dr. Strangelove*, for instance, General Buck Turgidson remarks: "Mr. President, I'm not saying we wouldn't get our hair mussed. But I do say, no more than 10 to 20 million killed, tops. Depending on the breaks." The absolute incongruity between the possible death toll and "hair mussing" makes us catch our breath. Or the placement of a single expletive can be used for singular shock value and emphasis, most memorably in "Frankly, my dear, I don't give a damn," where the refinement of the slightly antiquated "Frankly, my dear" contrasts sharply with "damn" at the sentence's end.

The patterning in *Citizen Kane* clearly differs from that of *Casablanca*. Characters rarely repeat themselves or turn a poetic phrase. Actually, Leland as an old man falls into repetition—for instance, he twice asks for a cigar, but Thompson, the reporter, and the viewer, find this an example of dotage, not poetry. There is less emphasis on balanced phrasing: when Kane in his political speech makes an elaborate play on the words "hope" and "prayer"—claiming that he "has something more than a hope, and Boss Jim Gettys something less than a prayer" of being elected—the smug oratory is somewhat distasteful. Yet certain key words are repeated throughout the film: "Rosebud"

---

* A more specialized use of rhythm can be found in the border between speech and song in musicals, when the actors fall into a definite patter. Recall *Singin' in the Rain*, "Moses supposes his toeses are roses, but Moses supposes erroneously," or *The Wizard of Oz*: "Lions and tigers and bears, oh my!"

is the most emphasized of these, of course, but there is also a great deal of stress on the words "love" and "promises," and on each character's name, with an elaborate accentuation of "Charles Foster Kane." And there is a continual, uncommon reliance on both questions and commands.

Numerous other differences separate the two films. *Casablanca* proceeds via a series of duologues (Rick and Ugarte, Rick and Renault, Ilsa and Lazlo, Ilsa and Rick) with a smattering of very tidy polylogues (e.g., Rick/Major Strasser/Renault). Most conversational turns are quite short; this custom is broken only for very important moments, such as Ilsa's recounting of her previous marriage or Rick's climactic good-bye speeches at the airport. In *Casablanca*, everyone is an artificially polite conversationalist, never interrupting or overlapping with someone else; this emphasizes Rick's singular rudeness in cutting Ilsa off when she first tries to tell him why she deserted him in Paris. As befits the international setting, the cafe is a hub of linguistic diversity; the characters speak with a variety of accents, and the war is echoed in the conflict between the German and French songs in the cafe—but all the characters, although of assorted nationalities, speak English. Similarly, all the major characters speak with facility and polish; Renault, Lazlo, and Ferrari (all "foreigners") use constructions that are rather more ornate than the plain-speaking "American" Rick. Class is never raised as an issue, but several of the minor characters who are supposed to be speaking English as a second language make "funny" mistakes ("What watch?" or "Such much?"). The film leaves us with a "tag line"—"Louis, this is the start of a beautiful friendship"—that takes away the sting of the broken romance. There are no extended scenes of silent action.

Citizen Kane, on the other hand, includes numerous polylogues where everyone is talking at once: in the projection room, in the Colorado cabin, taking over *The Inquirer,* at Susan's apartment. These polylogues are quite chaotic, with much of the dialogue overlapping or close to inaudible, indicating the strength of the emotions involved. Background dialogue is cleverly used to comment upon foreground action, as when little Charlie shouts, "Union forever," when his mother is planning to send him away. The length of conversational turns varies greatly; Bernstein, Leland, and especially Kane often speak for a long paragraph, and as mentioned earlier, complex ideas are expressed through complex sentence structure.

Characters overlap with and interrupt each other constantly, sometimes benignly, more often out of attempts to dominate. Class issues are overtly raised by the dialogue: Kane, Emily, Leland speak an upper-class, educated dialect; Kane's brutish father and Susan Alexander both make grammatical and pronunciation mistakes, indicating their lower-class origins. The film ends, not with a tag line, but with a wordless sequence of utmost importance, the almost unnoticed burning of the sled.

The difference between the two films is not between artificiality versus realism—both are artificial—nor between reliance on dialogue versus reliance on images—both give great weight to their dialogue. The difference is between decorum, clarity, humor, and poetry, on the one hand, and transgression, variety, and intricacy, on the other. The overall impressions we have of these films—*Casablanca* as "classic Hollywood," *Citizen Kane* as "prescient modernism"—are thus reconfirmed by an analysis of their dialogue patterns. Or perhaps it was their dialogue that originally created these impressions, only we weren't really listening?

THREE

Integration

Chapter 2 concentrated on dialogue in isolation, pretending that one could divorce it from the rest of the movie. But words in a script become transfigured when they are spoken by an actor, filmed by the camera, edited together, underscored with music. This chapter's goal is more complex: to study how dialogue works in conjunction with the other cinematic signifiers, to understand how spoken words create meaning in *film*.

In basic textbooks of film aesthetics, such as Louis Giannetti's *Understanding Movies,* or David Bordwell and Kristin Thompson's *Film Art,* many of the illustrations used to highlight variables of cinematography have been drawn from dialogue scenes, yet the speech simultaneous with those images is rarely referred to and virtually never quoted. The implication thus conveyed is that the underlying cinematic "grammar" remains the same regardless of the presence (or absence) of dialogue. However, I wonder if most of our knowledge about visual choices hasn't subconsciously taken dialogue into consideration all along: when we see a character with a shadow dramatically bifurcating his or her face, do we read *tortured spirit* from the visuals alone, or did we learn about the character's self-division from surrounding dialogue?

Some cinematic elements don't interact directly with dialogue: for example, choosing to shoot in color as opposed to black and white affects lighting and art direction, but except when color for some reason is at issue in the story, the selection of film stock does not overtly affect speech. The pages that follow examine the four signifiers I judge as most closely intertwined with dialogue: performance, shot content and scale, editing, and sound design.

PERFORMANCE

As Edward Sapir notes, we do not have an adequate vocabulary to describe voices. And yet,

> If we were to make an inventory of voices, we would find that no two of them are quite alike. And all the time we feel that there is something about the individual's voice that is indicative of his personality. We may even go so far as to surmise that the voice is in some way a symbolic index of the total personality.[1]

Or, as Jean Renoir has put it, "Is not the human voice the best means of conveying the personality of a human being?"[2]

The casting of an actor assigns dialogue-as-written to a person, a body, a voice. Different voices—with all their physical individuality and all their markers of age, gender, ethnicity, experience—will give dialogue different nuances. Consider the contrast between Walter Brennan's querulous tones and Orson Welles's resonant bass, or the disparity between the light breathiness of Marilyn Monroe and Cher's nasal alto. The voices of famous movie actors are instantly recognizable, and intimately interwoven with viewers' conceptions of their personae. Writing about Ingrid Bergman in *Notorious*, Amy Lawrence points out that "in this film, the woman's voice is presented with such fervor, approaching reverence, that it becomes almost an auto-fetish, the voice of the star as a new source of cinematic spectacle. . . . The voice is an integral part of the star system."[3] Roland Barthes refers to the unique "grain of the voice" of each individual, how this "grain" is molded by the body of the speaker and how it ineluctably carries sensual overtones. He finds the closeness of cinematic sound blissful.[4]

The best way to see how dialogue changes with casting would be an experiment that put the same lines in several mouths. In actuality, this is exactly what casting sessions do, but ordinary filmgoers are not privy to such experiments. As part of the mammoth publicity for *Gone with the Wind*, however, ninety contenders were tested for the part of Scarlett O'Hara, and some of these screen tests have circulated.[5] It is fascinating to hear the same dialogue spoken by Jean Arthur, Joan Bennett, Paulette Goddard, Susan Hayward—the words are identical and yet also subtly altered. Remakes also provide a venue to study how different actors, different voices affect the same written words. Furthermore, any comparison between a "final shooting script" and the dialogue that is actually on the screen inevitably reveals that in memorizing and speaking the lines, nearly every actor changes the wording. Lines are improvised, cut, repeated, stammered, swallowed, paraphrased; changes may be minor or major, but the results represent the unique alchemy of *that* script in the mouth, mind, and heart of *that* actor.

Miscasting can destroy the effectiveness of a film's dialogue. I have no doubt that Kevin Costner is abundantly talented, and he is well suited to contemporary stories such as *Bull Durham* (1988) and *A Perfect World* (1993), where his lines are couched in a contemporary idiom and his light, casual delivery works well. But Costner is miscast in historical epics—even though he handles the physical action gracefully—because his flat Midwestern accent and thin voice cannot build up the required resonance and power. For instance, toward the end of De Palma's *The Untouchables* (1987), Eliot Ness is supposed to realize how he has himself been corrupted by his fight against the Mob. David Mamet's script reaches for both biblical echoes and a rhythmic cadence:

> NESS: I have forsworn myself. I have broken every law I swore to defend. I have become what I beheld and I am content that I have done right.

Costner's voice does not give these lines the impact that they could have.

Casting in American films takes voice into account, not only in defining the leading parts, but in creating a blend of different tones on the sound track. Elizabeth Kendall reveals, regarding Gregory La Cava's *Stage Door* (1937):

> The casting of the secondary characters was done by ear. La Cava and [the scriptwriter Morrie] Ryskind hung around the studio cafeteria listening to the voices of the RKO starlets. "Try to get a voice," La Cava would say to Ryskind. He meant a distinctive voice, and they put together a symphony of them: the wistful, screwy tones of the young Lucille Ball; the ironic drawl of the even younger Eve Arden; and the Texas twang of the extremely young Ann Miller.[6]

"Try to get a voice" said La Cava, and his casting criterion has been followed by numerous other directors: think about *The Wizard of Oz*, where Judy Garland's slightly low, tremulous tones are bracketed by the Witch's soprano cackle, the Scarecrow's reediness, the Tin Man's melodious tenor, and the Lion's nasal and guttural explosiveness. *The Fugitive* (1993) purposely surrounds Harrison Ford's relatively flat, unaccented voice with contrast; Jeroen Krabbe, playing the villain, Charles Nichols, has a foreign accent, and Tommy Lee Jones's extravagant vocal performance is tinged by a Southern drawl. If one just listens to a scene, practically any scene, you will hear the interweaving of different instruments, as distinct as the characters in *Peter and the Wolf*.

A certain violin may naturally have a certain tone, but obviously it can be played with all different kinds of expression. Actors put on accents as needed; they deliberately use their voices to give lines special emphasis and meaning. Coppola's *The Conversation* (1974) provides an object lesson in the significance of *how* something is said, for the plot hinges on two diametrically opposed line readings: "He'd *kill* us if he had the chance" versus "He'd kill *us* if he had the chance." J. L. Styan, writing about *The Elements of Drama*, summarizes,

> Words that possess any degree of feeling lose some of their force if spoken without intonation. The movement of the voice is as restless and as meaningful as the movement of the emotions, and is inseparable from them. . . . The text is a tune to be sung. The most inexperienced actor knows how infinite in number are the tunes applicable to the smallest phrase, and all of us have amused ourselves at one time or another by playing variations on the pitch, power and pace of our own voices.[7]

"Pitch, power, and pace" are the specific factors, variously labeled, that are most commonly analyzed when considering vocal performances.

To begin with "pace," the actor faces choices concerning overall speed, pauses, and rhythm. A given velocity does not automatically come with set connotations—context is everything. In *His Girl Friday*, as Mary Devereaux points out, the slowness of Bruce's delivery is a tool of character revelation; it shows that he is slow and ponderous, unlike the lightning-fast Walter and Hildy.[8] (The same dynamic is re-played in *Broadcast News* [1987], with the slower and befuddled Tom deliberately placed in contrast to Jane's and Aaron's quick speech patterns.) On the other hand, slowness can be indicative of laid-back confidence, an expression that there is no need to hurry. Surely one of the reasons that Dirty Harry's "Do you feel lucky?" taunt is so memorable is that it is spoken so leisurely, demonstrating his total command, not only over his own anger and frustration, but over a life-and-death situation. And quick speech doesn't have to indicate intelligence; it can signify nervousness or insecurity, as if the charac-ter were racing to get through the words.

A pause in the middle of a character's turn creates anticipation. For a heartbeat or longer, the viewer waits, wondering what the per-son is going to say, and considering why it is unusually hard for him or her to get the words out. As Styan remarks:

> The pause is planned by the author and prepared by the actor for the sake solely of the audience. It is unhelpful to think of it as an imita-tion of a mental reaction as in life, although it is true that in realistic drama the actor will find a realistic excuse for it. The dramatic pause is essentially a means of implanting a dramatic impression and schooling the audience to hear and see what the author wants.[9]

George C. Scott as General Turgidson in *Dr. Strangelove* pauses dra-matically before proposing to the president that the United States follow up the mistake of initially sending out the bombers by or-chestrating an all-out attack. Grace Kelly as Lisa Freemont in *Rear Window* (1954) allows a long beat to pass when she says that she won't be back to visit Jeff . . . until tomorrow night.

"Intonation" is defined as the rise and fall of pitch during speech. Some actors (Arnold Schwarzenegger) recite their lines in a mono-tone, others (Elizabeth Taylor) vary their pitch tremendously. Even pitch may be associated with unflappability—nothing makes this person excited (which is why monotones seem fitting for machine-men like the Terminator).

The last major vocal parameter to consider is volume. Actors can affect the meaning of the dialogue by how loudly or softly they utter the words. Both whispering and shouting are tools for emphasis. At the climax of *Casablanca*, Ilsa whispers to Rick, "When I said I would never leave you." At the end of Stanley Kubrick's *Paths of Glory*

(1957), Colonel Dax, played by Kirk Douglas, who throughout the action has held himself in check and been deferential to his corrupt commanding officers, loses his temper:

> DAX: *(quietly)* I apologize, sir, for not telling you sooner that you're a degenerate, sadistic old man, *(screaming)* AND YOU CAN GO TO HELL BEFORE I APOLOGIZE TO YOU NOW OR EVER AGAIN.

Pace, intonation, and volume ultimately combine as the means of conveying emotion. When performed, dialogue not only conveys semantic meaning but also the emotional state of the speaker, even the beat-by-beat fluctuation of his or her feelings. Actors are extremely skilled at conveying such nuances, and viewers are very proficient in recognizing these emotional states. Psychological research indicates that "[t]he ability to judge emotions through vocal features develops earlier than the ability to judge emotions through facial expressions and body movements and may even be innate."[10]

Along with their voices, of course, performers use their faces and bodies. Psychologists and linguists have studied what we all intuitively learn from everyday life, that words and voice are not the only factors in determining the meaning of a statement. As Ronald Wardhaugh observes:

> What you say may be "unsaid" by how you actually convey your words in the non-verbal "envelope" that accompanies them. . . . the verbal part of any conversation is, of course, extremely important. . . . [But] you will form certain impressions of events that are happening alongside the talking; how the various participants are using their bodies; how they are gesturing; where their eyes are focused; and so on.[11]

Obviously, films—as opposed to purely aural media, such as radio dramas or books-on-tape—convey performances enriched by all the signifiers of nonverbal communication.

Facial expressions tell us how to interpret speech, which can be ambiguous in so many ways. In *Dirty Harry*, Detective Callahan seemingly insults his new Chicano partner with a derogatory comment about "spics," but his gesture—a little wink to a third detective—belies the literal content of his words. In *It's a Wonderful Life* (1946), when Mary (Donna Reed) and George Bailey (Jimmy Stewart) share a telephone receiver to talk to Mary's absent boyfriend, their conversation consists of polite responses, but their faces and bodies show that this unusual physical proximity is driving them mad with desire and leading them to betray the absent boyfriend. How actors stand or sit or hold their bodies contributes mightily; in *Sense and Sensibility* (1995), Colonel Brandon (Alan Rickman) is distraught when he tells Elinor that if she doesn't give him some task to help the dying Marianne, he will go mad; his words attain extra force from the fact that he is leaning against the wall as if on the verge of collapse.

Combining gestures, or "stage business," with dialogue adds another dimension. As James Naremore writes, "An important principle of realist acting, borrowed from theater, is to devise situations in which the characters *talk about one thing while doing something else*."[12] Coupling the dialogue with ordinary activities works in the interest of realism—one does not usually stop every activity, plant one's feet, and address one's conversational partner. But the actions also emphasize or play in counterpoint with the dialogue; for instance, Brigid O'Shaunessey's toying with objects in the apartment shows how nervous she is as she lies to Philip Marlowe in *The Maltese Falcon*, just as Terry Malloy's absent-minded trying on Edie's glove in *On the Waterfront* shows his interest in her. In *Short Cuts* (1993), Robert Altman undercuts the potential eroticism of a scene in which a woman is giving phone sex to a male client by showing her simultaneously diapering her toddler.

In short, words on a page are only the beginning of film dialogue. The job of the actor is to bring these words to life, and the job of the director is to help the actor shape his or her performance; together they choose from among the myriad aural and gestural possibilities just those that enhance the desired meaning and undertones. Together, they transmute dialogue-as-written into something rich and strange.

SHOT CONTENT AND SCALE

And we haven't even added the camera yet. Although by now the plethora of factors that influence film dialogue should be apparent, the question "what is the camera showing while we hear the dialogue" has been the only issue to receive sustained scholarly attention. As mentioned earlier, this critical tradition stems from the coming of sound, when theorists such as Sergei Eisenstein feared that sound would spoil the visual poetry of silent cinema and restrict montage. The recourse was to champion asynchronous sound—that is, keeping the visual track from showing the sound's source. Capturing the face of a person talking was felt to be the height of inartistic redundancy. Eisenstein's dictum was taken up and repeated by other theorists, and there now exists a small library devoted to the issue of asynchronicity versus synchronicity and off-screen versus on-screen sound.[13]

Advocates of asynchronous sound favor such intriguing phenomena as voice-over narration, or aural flashbacks, which can be wedded to visuals in complicated ways. (Michel Chion has done the best job of disentangling the plethora of variables: on-screen, off-screen, nondiegetic, ambient, internal, etc., that can be used to categorize varieties of film sound.)[14] But this study is concentrating only on inter-character diegetic *dialogue*—sidestepping those less central strategies—and the dominant method of filming dialogue scenes has always been to weld together the verbal and visual tracks.

Contemporary theorists continue to discuss Hollywood's penchant for filming speakers in a critical light, arguing that this match works in the service of bourgeois ideology. In Rick Altman's words, "pointing the camera at the speaker disguises the source of the words, dissembling the work of production and technology."[15] Similarly, Mary Ann Doane argues: "The rhetoric of sound is the result of a technique whose ideological aim is to conceal the tremendous amount of work necessary to convey an effect of spontaneity and naturalness. What is repressed in this operation is the sound which would signal the existence of the apparatus."[16] In *The Acoustic Mirror*, Kaja Silverman continues the attack on synchronization from a feminist standpoint, as Amy Lawrence deftly summarizes: "Silverman argues that camouflaging the work that goes into sound/image production masks the medium's material heterogeneity not simply in order to guarantee the cohesiveness of any subject but specifically to shore up male subjectivity."[17]

Although "hiding the existence of the apparatus" may indeed be a secondary *effect*, I would look elsewhere for the *cause* of the dominance of synchronous speech in American film. One place to look is the nature of human perception. Joseph Anderson argues that because of the evolutionary process of human sense perception, humans have an innate interest in matching sight and sound; he cites scientific experiments that demonstrate that the attraction to synchronization is inborn in babies.[18]

Secondly, linguistics teaches us that the words used in conversation are often ambiguous. They are not fully comprehensible in isolation; they must be contextualized for listeners to understand them. Everyday conversational encounters are thus structured as intricate feedback loops between participants, so that questions can be posed to clear up ambiguities, and nods, grunts, and eye contact subconsciously noted to ensure or verify comprehension.[19] However, when watching a film, we viewers are denied ordinary feedback procedures. Filmmakers thus may feel the need to ensure that we have extra opportunity to understand and amalgamate the verbal information. Cutting us off from the actor's face and body—the "non-verbal envelope" discussed by Ronald Wardhaugh—would withhold from us the information that reaffirms (or complicates and undercuts) the spoken words.

Finally, the speech/speaker match also reflects a strong cultural preference. In American everyday life, although we may just shout out from the living room some incidental information to someone in the kitchen ("The bread is in the freezer!"), we don't conduct the important conversations of our lives with co-workers, friends, or lovers separated in different rooms or with our backs turned. We come together spatially to make eye contact possible, to be able to "read" the other's expressions and gestures. This privileging of face-to-face conversation for discussions deemed important is deeply ingrained; consider how often one demands of children, "Look at me when I'm talking to you," or how bad news must be conveyed in person, not over the phone; even in this day of phone, fax, Internet, and express mail, business people fly thousands of miles to negotiate deals face-to-face. In American culture, eye contact with the listener is a guarantor of sincerity, equality, connection.

The contemporary anti-synchronization argument is in line with a major school of film theory, which, following Brecht and other Marxist critics, charges that Hollywood conventions reinforce the social/economic/political status quo by hiding the artificiality, constructedness, and ideological ramifications of filmmaking choices behind excuses about naturalism.* (Murray Smith provides a valuable summary and critique of this theoretical argument.)[20] Thus, for me to counter the attack on synchronization by resorting to the authority of sense psychology, linguistics, or cultural practice may merely strengthen the case of those who condemn the practice—"See, she's arguing that synchronization is 'natural.' " Actually, I do believe that the strong pull toward synchronization may come from the extent to which it satisfies such deep-seated expectations, but I also realize that it is linked both to historical factors, such as the initial fascination with the coming of sound, or the influence of the theater; and to commercial factors, such as the star system, which is invested in promoting these glamorous faces. But the ultimate basis on which I would defend synchronization is textual (artistic, if you will), in that I find watching characters while they talk endlessly enriching because it allows viewers to study and compare so many simultaneous signifiers: the actors' words, their voices, their intonations; their facial expressions, the look in their eyes, their body posture, their gestures, their costuming; the setting and its use of light and art direction. The simultaneous presentation of all this information allows for a tight anchoring of the spectator's identification with the character, but it also permits the viewer to pick up subtle discrepancies and undertones. In *The Wild Bunch* (1969) when Pike says, "If they move, kill 'em," viewers need to see his face (fig. 4) to know whether or not he's joking (he's not). In *North by Northwest*, when Roger Thornhill shows up in Eve's hotel room after the attempted murder by crop-dusting plane, we need to see their mixture of emotions—Roger's anger and suspicion, Eve's relief, guilt, and nervousness—conveyed by their little movements and facial expressions as they converse. As Richard Dyer argues, we are inclined to trust what people betray about their innermost feelings while speaking more than the literal semantics of their words.[21] Incidental dialogue (verbal wallpaper) included merely for realistic effect need not be wedded to shots of the speaker(s), but dialogue that reveals character or enacts a significant narrative event calls for the viewer

---

* These arguments correspond with similar critiques of continuity editing (which is charged with hiding the constructed nature of the scene); of "normal" lens perspective (for implying that the world is all for the pleasure and mastery of the viewer), and of naturalistic acting (which tries to deny that the actor is an impersonator). In essence, the argument is against "illusionism."

4. *The Wild Bunch.* PIKE: If they move, kill 'em.

being able to "read" it thoroughly, and thus for shots of the speaker's face and figure.

The two major alternatives to matching dialogue with shots of the speaker are (a) reaction shots, and (b) shots of the subject of the discussion.

Reaction shots break up the monotony of focusing exclusively on the one who is talking. Moreover, often the importance of a bit of dialogue lies, not in the intentions or feelings of the speaker, but in the reaction of the listener. In the climax of Max Ophuls's *Letter from an Unknown Woman* (1948), Lisa goes to see Stefan to confess her years of devotion. He doesn't recognize her and commences an obviously well-rehearsed pattern of seduction, pouring drinks, ordering a late-night repast, gushing insincere compliments. The camera focuses not on Stefan talking, but on Lisa listening, realizing that he doesn't recognize her, understanding—finally—that her idol has become a shallow roué. In this scene, the camera is offering an unusual number of reaction shots, but the opposite strategy, no reaction shots at all, is equally effective. One of the reasons why *Citizen Kane* still appears so iconoclastic is because it eschews reaction shots. Keeping Thompson anonymous, unseen, means that the camera stays focused on Susan, or Bernstein, or Leland, relentlessly pinning them under its gaze.

"Shots of the subject of the discussion"—in filmmaking parlance they are called "cutaways"—are slightly less prevalent. Occasionally, such shots are included in a system of point-of-view editing: characters see a place, person, or thing, which they discuss, and their conversation is allowed to run over a shot or shots allowing the viewer to see the object too. In the conversation from *Mrs. Miniver* quoted in chapter 1, William Wyler shows us the rose. In *The Wizard of Oz*, we are offered several close-ups of the ruby slippers. In *Rear Window*, the camera shows the neighbors' apartments as Jeff and Lisa remark on their activities off-camera.

One of the distinguishing characteristics of cinema since the French New Wave has been increased freedom in time and place, the use of images to capture not only what is happening in a given scene but the memories or hypotheses or daydreams of the characters. Since the early 1960s, dialogue has been less likely to be matched to the on-screen speaker; one finds many more shots of the subjects of discussion, even if they are far removed in time and space, even if their reality status is in doubt. See, for instance, Olivier Stone's *JFK* (1991), in which the image-track continually "acts out" the spoken verbal hypotheses concerning the Kennedy assassination.

The final, and in American narrative cinema, the rarest, possibility is to lay dialogue over shots that show neither speaker, listener, nor subject of the conversation. The relationship between the words and the image in such cases is oblique or thematic, and at such moments the viewer strongly senses a narrating presence commenting upon the action. In *The Godfather*, Francis Ford Coppola intercuts the scene of the baptismal mass of Michael Corleone's nephew with shots of Corleone hit men preparing to shoot the family's enemies. The priest's Latin and English liturgy plays over the entire sequence. One effect of the continuous dialogue is to enforce our sense of simultaneity— these events are happening *now,* all over the city, while the Corleone family is in church. But the more important result of combining the religious service with the preparations for the murders is to comment ironically on the depth of Michael Corleone's religious hypocrisy and embrace of evil.

Early sound theorists privileged nonsynchronous sound partly because they believed that such pairings opened up the possibility of complex contradictions and ironies between word and image. This kind of irony is easy to discern in *The Godfather* sequence cited above. But I believe that the nuances of performance, captured by shots of "talking heads," are potentially just as multilayered: consider the scene in *Psycho* when Norman brings Marion supper. In *Hitchcock: The Murderous Gaze*, William Rothman offers a brilliant analysis of

5.   *Shadow of a Doubt.* Extreme close-up of Uncle Charlie during dinner speech.

Norman's shy little mannerisms, evasions, suppressed rage, and superiority, of Marion's initial snobbery, then reassessment, of the use of the stuffed birds as props, of Hitchcock's intricate framings and reframings.[22] As in earlier discussions, my point is that both artistic choices—asynchronous and synchronous pairings—are equally legitimate.

The issue of the content of the shot also makes us consider questions of composition. Each variety of shot scale will have ramifications.The extreme close-up of Uncle Charlie in *Shadow of a Doubt* intensifies our sense of revelation of his innermost feelings, especially because the camera moves in closer during his speech and he gazes directly into the lens (fig. 5). Over-the-shoulder compositions, on the other hand, are so common because they make the viewer conscious of the fact that this is a conversation between two people. The listener may or may not contribute all those little "ums" and nods that are a part of real conversations, but just the shadowy presence of his or her shoulder and head subliminally makes the viewer conscious

6. *Bringing Up Baby.* SUSAN: You've torn your coat.

of the dialogic nature of the exchange. Medium shots show several characters at the same time and situate them clearly in their physical surroundings; comedy is traditionally played fairly wide to capture the timing of the characters as they interact. (Look at the restaurant scene in *Bringing Up Baby* where Hawks keeps his camera at roughly knee-or waist-level [fig. 6] so that we can watch the slapstick action with olives, hats, purses, and torn clothes.)During the rendezvous at the restaurant with a fish tank in *Mission: Impossible,* shots using a dramatic Dutch angle show Ethan's dawning perception that his CIA superior suspects that Ethan is the traitor responsible for his colleagues' assassination (fig. 7).

Long shots in which the entire length of an actor's body is seen are slightly less common for dialogue exchanges because of their neglect of facial expressions. However, an extreme long shot works well for the last moments of *Casablanca,* when the camera pulls up and away and we hear, "Louis, I think this is the beginning of a beautiful friendship." Another effective extreme long shot is found in *Alien,*

7. *Mission: Impossible.* ETHAN: This whole operation was a mole hunt.

after the crew have awakened from their dormant sleep, when Ripley repeatedly tries to contact Earth. We hear her voice filtered, as if through a radio: "This is Commercial Towing Vehicle Nostromo [inaudible] Registration No. 180924609. Calling Antarctica Traffic Control, do you read me? Over." The accompanying shot is from outside the spaceship showing it suspended in the dark void of space. This extreme long shot stresses the vastness of space and the loneliness of the unanswered call.

EDITING

Filmmaking manuals offer numerous studies of the shot-by-shot breakdowns of typical dialogue scenes. Karel Reisz and Gavin Miller describe the standard pattern:

> Frequently dialogue scenes are shot something like this: (1) two characters are shown talking to each other in medium or long shot to establish the situation; (2) the camera tracks in towards the characters or we cut to a closer two-shot in the same line of vision as shot (1); (3) finally, we are shown a series of alternating close shots of the two players—usually over the opposite character's shoulder—either speaking lines or reacting. At the main point of interest, close-ups may be used and the camera generally eases away from the actors at the end of the scene.[23]

The editing generally proceeds unobtrusively,* partly because the cuts and the dialogue are staggered. "One of the most common options is to edit dialogue scenes in ways that 'cut against' natural speech rhythms," Bordwell and Thompson note. "By cutting 'against' the rhythm of his lines, the editing smoothes over the changes of shot and emphasizes the words and facial expressions."[24] Allowing the speech of one partner to overlap to the cut of the other also works to unify the two setups in time and space. Even though they were shot at different times, perhaps even on different days, overlapping the dialogue from one speaker to the next ties the two shots together.[25] Similarly, dialogue is also cut to flow smoothly over transitions from one scene to the next—in contemporary movies, it is common for the last line of the previous scene to flow over the establishing shot of the next.

One of the major debates in film aesthetics has been between advocates of "long takes," such as André Bazin, and advocates of editing, such as Eisenstein, Pudovkin, and Rotha. Long takes, used in association with a mobile camera and deep focus, were much more in vogue in the 1940s and 1950s than in earlier or later decades. (Barry Salt contrasts the 1930s average shot lengths of 9 or 10 seconds to 18 seconds in William Wyler's *The Letter* [1940] and 19 in Vincente Minnelli's *The Clock* [1945].)[26] Phillip Lopate, for one, is nostalgic for the days of long takes, when, he claims, you could listen to extended dialogue, your sympathies could sway back and forth between participants, and your eye would be "given the time to travel from one character's face to another's and then to the objects and scenery behind or beside them."[27]

Long takes can certainly be employed to great effect. Consider, for example, a segment at the end of Wyler's *Roman Holiday* (1953). Although she is in love with Joe Bradley (Gregory Peck), Anna (Audrey Hepburn), the runaway princess in disguise, has returned to her royal responsibilities, believing that she will never see Joe again. But at the next day's formal news conference, Joe appears, and reveals his own secrets—that he is a reporter, that he recognized Anna and

---

* Of course, some directors depart from invisibility. Toward the end of *Strange Days* (1995), for example, there is a scene in which the villain must explain all his earlier misdeeds. Kathryn Bigelow tries to jazz up the long expositional passages through numerous jump cuts.

planned to write a scoop about her, but that having fallen in love himself, he now refuses to capitalize on their day together. Departing from traditional custom, Anna descends from the dais to meet some of the representatives of the press. Viewers know that she has done this solely for a last chance of contact with Joe. Wyler refuses to foreshorten the event: we wait with Joe through a long take, dolly shot as Anna slowly moves down a receiving line, shaking hands with each reporter and exchanging a polite remark.*

Most of the dialogue here is verbal wallpaper and some of it is barely audible; it doesn't really matter who these reporters are, al-

8–17. *Roman Holiday*

8.   Long shot of dais.

   PRINCESS: I would now like to meet some of the ladies and gentlemen of the press.

   Princess starts to descend.

---

* The transcription is only approximate, owing both to the linguistic diversity featured and the fact that the technical demands of the dolly shot precluded close miking of the speakers.

9. Mid-shot of Princess as she begins descending the stairs. She halts, until attendants get the hint not to follow her.

10. Long shot of Princess finishing her descent.

11.   Tracking shot of receiving line. The camera pulls back as the princess moves down the line.

JOURNALIST: Hitchcock, *Chicago Daily News.*
PRINCESS: I'm so happy to see you.
JOURNALIST: Canziani, de *La Suisse.*
JOURNALIST: Klinger, *Deutsche Presse Agentur.*
PRINCESS: Freut mich sehr.

12. Tracking shot continues.

JOURNALIST: Maurice Montabré, *Le Figaro.*
JOURNALIST: Ciske Halema, *De Linie,* Amsterdam.
PRINCESS: Dag Mevrouw.
JOURNALIST: Jacques Ferrier, *Ici Paris.*
PRINCESS: Enchantée.
JOURNALIST: Gross, *Davar,* Tel Aviv.
JOURNALIST: Cortes Cabamillas, *ABC,* Madrid.
PRINCESS: Encantada.
JOURNALIST: Lampert, *New York Herald Tribune.*
PRINCESS: Good afternoon.
IRVING: Irving Radovich, *Sierra Photo Service.*
PRINCESS: How do you do?
RADOVICH: May I present your highness with some commemorative
photos of your visit to Rome?

13.   Close-up of photo showing Princess hitting secret service man with a violin.

14.   Close-up of Princess (reaction shot).

PRINCESS: Thank you so very much.

She turns to look at Joe. Pause.

15.   Close-up of Joe Bradley.

16.   Return to tracking shot.

        JOE: Joe Bradley, *American News Service.*
   PRINCESS: So happy, Mr. Bradley.
JOURNALIST: Mario [inaudible], *La Vanguardia de Barcelona.*

17.

JOURNALIST: Steven Howser, *The London Exchange Telegraph.*
  PRINCESS: Good afternoon.
JOURNALIST: Gardisio, *L'Agence Presse.*

though we are impressed again by Anna's international importance and by her regal command of languages and etiquette. It does matter, terribly, that Anna get to meet Joe, and learn his true identity. Thus, the climax of the sequence is Joe's self-nomination—"Joe Bradley, American News Service"—because these words reveal the secret that he has kept throughout the film. Anna's reply, "So happy, Mr. Bradley," works not only as an appropriate public response but as a signal both of her acceptance of his ruse and of her happiness at having experienced their fleeting romance.

Moreover, this dialogue works in tandem with the slow progress of the tracking shot, during which the viewer is led into feeling for the central characters. We empathetically imagine Joe and Anna's impatience for contact with each other, barely controlled by the rigid constraints of the propriety of this situation. Anna's interactions with Irving and with Joe *are* broken down into close-ups, making a brief pause, and then she passes Joe, moving out of his life, and the pain is intensified by the fact that the earlier tracking shot and the greeting/handshaking pattern resume as she slowly moves away. The inexorable constraint of the shot—the camera is locked into a steady, linear progression—matches the way the characters are constrained by the formal setting from speaking their hearts. The slow pace is reflected in the fact that these eight shots consume 155 seconds, an average of 18 seconds per shot.

A contrasting example of the contemporary style of swift editing can be drawn from *The Fugitive,* at the point when Gerard, the U.S. marshal, realizes that Kimble, a convicted murderer, has escaped the train wreck. Gerard's instructions to the assembled law enforcement personnel are intercut with shots of "the subject of the discussion"— that is, Kimble escaping. Kimble is not visible to the characters, only to the viewer; one feels a narrating hand yoking together the two antagonists. Gerard speaks eighty-four words in 41 seconds; the sixteen cuts lead to an average length (for this small excerpt) of 2.5 seconds per shot.

18–25. *THE FUGITIVE*

18.   Medium shot, Gerard in a circle of officers.

GERARD: Listen up, ladies and gentlemen. Our fugitive has been on the run for ninety minutes. Average foot speed over uneven ground . . .

19.   Medium shot.

   GERARD: . . . barring injury is four miles an hour. That gives us a ra-
   dius of six miles.

20.   Kimble running though wooded embankment.

   GERARD: What I . . .

   *As the camera continues cross-cutting between close-ups of Gerard and long-
   shots of Kimble running in the dark woods, Gerard continues:*

            . . . want out of each and every one of you is a hard target
            search of every gas station, residence, warehouse, farmhouse,
            henhouse, outhouse, or doghouse in that area.

21.   Medium shot, Gerard.

   GERARD: Checkpoints go up at fifteen miles.

22.   Kimble, slow-motion, falling on ground of leaves.

23. Close-up, Gerard.

    GERARD: Your fugitive's name is Dr. Richard Kimble.

24. Kimble getting up and running in slow motion toward camera.

25. Close-up, Gerard.

GERARD: Go get him.

Gerard's speech is quite showy. Through the editing, his words literally surround Kimble, intensifying our sense that he is being pursued. Kimble's frantic motion is contrasted with Gerard's firm stasis, his loneliness with Gerard's encirclement by colleagues, his silent flight with Gerard's authoritative speech.

Needless to say, dialogue is equally amenable to both styles of shooting, long take or quick cutting.

THE SOUND TRACK

The film sound track is commonly divided into three subsets—musical scoring, sound effects, and dialogue.

Film music has been the focus of numerous thorough studies tracing its historical development and its formal properties. What concerns us here is a smaller topic, the ways in which music interacts with the film's dialogue. To begin with the rather unique case of musicals: musical numbers could be thought of as extensions of the dialogue, set pieces where the incipient patterning, repetition, and artistry of all film speech is allowed to surface. After all, Harold Hill, the fake professor in *The Music Man* (1962), claims that "Singing is just sustained talking," and many musical numbers highlight this connection, with lengthy lead-ins of rhythmic dialogue. Other numbers, such as those performed by Rex Harrison in *My Fair Lady* (1964), remain "talky" throughout. Even when performers burst into full-throated melody, duets can be overtly dialogic: "Let's Call the Whole Thing Off" from *Shall We Dance* (1937) and "People Will Say We're in Love" from *Oklahoma!* (1956) are conversations, or arguments, set to music. Other songs, such as "Somewhere Over the Rainbow," play the role of monologues in allowing us privileged access to the character's heart.

More generally, musical scoring serves to enhance films by creating atmosphere, commenting on the action, heightening emotion, smoothing transitions, providing local color, and so on. Traditional Hollywood practice, however, has always decreed that background scoring should be subordinated to the speaking voice. Claudia Gorbman discovered that this hierarchy became inscribed in technology in the 1930s:

> In the United States, the practice of lowering the volume of music behind the dialogue, rather than eliminating it, was already *de rigueur.* A machine nicknamed the "up-and-downer," developed as early as 1934, had as its purpose to regulate music automatically. When dialogue signals entered the soundtrack, the up-and-downer reduced the music signal.[28]

Many dialogue scenes are played either devoid of music or with "inaudible" low background scoring—the better to hear the words. However, at crucial emotional moments either a new musical phrase may start or the music that has been playing may suddenly cease; the issue is not the presence or absence of music per se, but a noticeable change. Such changes emphasize that line of dialogue or signal a shift in the scene's emotional tenor. Many of the quotations used throughout this study are underscored by just such slight musical shifts; it may have been the music that subconsciously led me to select these passages as particularly salient.

Music is frequently called upon to support dialogue scenes between love interests. Leonard Bernstein's score suddenly starts playing at the end of the park scene in *On the Waterfront*, when Edie tells Terry that if she had been his teacher, she would have treated him with kindness. In the train dining car in *North by Northwest*, the music modulates into a lush love theme when Eve Kendell invites Roger to her stateroom. When Fiona confesses to Charlie that she has loved him unrequitedly for years in *Four Weddings and a Funeral,* the pathos of the admission is heightened by the introduction of a sad woodwind melody.

As for sound effects, the films that generally attract the most attention and win Academy Awards for sound or sound editing are those with the loudest and most smashing/crashing sound effects, films such as *Terminator 2* (1991) where the sound makes a spectacle of itself.[29] Such effects are foregrounded in action and chase sequences, where they take over where dialogue leaves off, providing aural satisfaction.

But sound effects are, like music, usually subordinated to dialogue. "Sound effects and backgrounds are only enhancements to the movie," the supervising sound editor Norvel Crutcher told an interviewer. "The dialogue—that's what we go to the movies for. You don't walk away saying, 'There were great door closes in that movie.' "[30] Sound effects are used unobtrusively underneath speech to create naturalistic noises such as footsteps, door openings, and dish rattling or to enhance the realism of off-screen space through traffic sounds, dogs barking, or crowd noise.

Sometimes, of course, sound effects are highlighted because they serve a narrative function such as indicating the arrival of a character on horseback or by car, or the approach of some menacing threat. On occasion, sound effects will even interact symbolically with character speech: in *How Green Was My Valley,* when the minister Mr. Gruffyd talks to the paralyzed Huw Morgan about being able to walk again, church bells sound in the distance. In *Blade Runner* (1982), when the examiner subjects the replicant Leon to a test of his emotions, we suddenly hear a loud rhythmic thudding noise—is it the overhead fan made more audible? Is it Leon's heart, beating with fear of being caught?

In terms of dialogue per se, recording, editing, and mixing the actors' speech are complex processes that are highly dependent upon technological capabilities and industry standards. (Different national cinemas have different practices regarding acceptable dialogue sound, as is made clear by the use of post-dubbing in Italian cinema.) A handy layman's summary of American conventions is provided by Stephen Handzo in *Film Sound: Theory and Practice,* which details how much is contingent upon the exact choice of microphone, how difficult location shooting can be, how looping of unsatisfactory lines is accomplished, how many tracks are used in a final mix.[31] Orchestration of these technical variables allows for special manipulations of film dialogue, such as the "filtering effect" of telephone or radio talk, or the carefully designed voices of aliens, robots, God, and the Devil. Orson Welles, with his background in radio (and the assistance of his production mixer, Bailey Fesler, and his rerecording engineer, James Stewart), did a brilliant job of designing the soundtrack of *Citizen Kane,* from adding reverberation to the sequences in Xanadu, the Thatcher Memorial Library, and the campaign hall to starting scenes with a startling sound effect.[32] Although chapter 2 didn't stray into this territory, radically different sound designs constitute one of the key contrasts between the dialogue of *Casablanca* and that of *Citizen Kane.*

The most salient characteristic of the sound of American film dialogue is the privileging of "intelligibility," the subordination of all other considerations to ensuring that the spectator can hear the words fully and well. As Michel Chion notes: "[I]n voice recording what is sought is not so much acoustical fidelity to original timbre, as the guarantee of effortless intelligibility of the words spoken."[33] This privileging of intelligibility has ramifications—it hides the noisy messiness of the actual world (sound technicians are always referring to "cleaning up" their tracks); it relegates sound effects and music to inferior positions; and, most important, it foregrounds character psychology and narrative comprehension. Chion regrets the dominance of intelligibility; he prefers what he calls "emanation speech" (what I term "verbal wallpaper")—speech that may be inaudible, decentered, and that serves no narrative function. I find his argument misanthropic.

Along the same lines, Rick Altman contends that in choosing to favor intelligibility over acoustic fidelity (particularly in abandoning the quest for a match between shot perspective and sound perspective), Hollywood cast aside "the everyday life model in favor of a code of reality provided by the theater."[34] Altman carries his discussion further:

> Now, in order to achieve the continuous close-up sound quality characteristic of Hollywood's standard practice, the microphone must be

brought quite close to the speaker, cutting out unwanted set noises while—and this is the important concern for the present argument— also radically reducing the level of reverberation.

But what is sound without reverberation? On the one hand, to be sure, it is close-up sound, sound spoken by someone close to me, but it is also sound spoken *toward* me rather than away from me. Sound with low reverb is sound that I am meant to hear, sound that is pronounced *for me*. Like the perspective image, therefore, the continuous-level, low-reverb sound track comforts the audience with the notion that the banquet is indeed meant for them. The choice of the reverbless sound thus appears to justify an otherwise suspect urge towards eavesdropping, for it identifies the sound we want to hear as sound that is made for us.[35]

The conclusion Altman reaches through a technological analysis just reconfirms the argument advanced in my Introduction: the defining characteristic of film dialogue is that *it is never realistic; it is always designed "for us."* Altman implies a critique of the ideology of conventional film practice, but who—or what—else would the sound be designed for?

Two more points regarding sound perspective. Altman helps us realize that sound levels staying fairly uniform throughout keeps the visual track's unpredictable mobility—its dizzying changes of shot scale and location—from disturbing viewers. Certainly, this is true of the edited sequence from *The Fugitive* studied above, where Gerard's speech—mixed at a consistent volume—knits together the shots of Kimble fleeing.

Finally, within the dominant code of intelligibility, one finds marked moments when filmmakers will decide to foreground the spatial characteristics of sound, when they call attention to what has been termed "point of audition." Just as filmmakers will periodically stress to viewers that we are now seeing through a character's visual "point of view," so manipulations of sound recording can imply that we are now hearing the dialogue from a specific place, through the ears of a character-surrogate. This becomes noticeable mostly because of some departure from total intelligibility—that is, the sound is muffled, or far away, or, most strikingly, we know that characters are speaking, but we cannot hear them. "Point of audition" sound is very effective for enhancing character identification—in Bob Fosse's *All That Jazz* (1979), when Joe Gideon is having a heart attack during a play rehearsal, we see all the actors hamming it up, but we are situated with him in some realm of pain, fear, and *silence;* in Spielberg's *Saving Private Ryan* (1998), we share with the soldiers terrifying moments of post-explosion sound concussion.

––––––––

If the preceding discussion has done its job, the main thing it will have proven is that this study is woefully inadequate. My printed quotations of film dialogue are like shadow pictures—they lose the original's color and rotundity, its warmth and movement.

A second lesson of this analysis of "integration" is that film dialogue is not solely the province of screenwriters. Screenwriters (although shamefully underappreciated) are only partially responsible; casting directors, actors, directors, cameramen, editors, composers, sound recordists, mixers, and editors are all involved in shaping dialogue.

I'd like to conclude this chapter, and the first half of this book, by taking a more detailed look at two sequences, the final minutes of *Mrs. Miniver* (William Wyler, 1942) and *So Proudly We Hail!* (Mark Sandrich, 1943), in hopes of illustrating how attention to dialogue functions, variables, and integration can be combined and applied.

In so many ways these sequences are amazingly similar; both World War II films, made within a year of each other, conclude with a male authority figure giving a three-minute-long (roughly 400-word) speech that overtly seeks to raise the morale and stiffen the resolve of the movie-going public. Specifically, both hope to convince the audience that the war is not just for soldiers, that it is a "people's war," a war that civilians must wage. And yet the effects of these two endings are completely distinct. Despite its "dated" message, and its concatenation of Christianity, nationalism, and militarism, which is certainly open to question, the Wyler excerpt brings tears to my eyes, while Sandrich's must be seen as a failure. The difference lies not, as so many earlier prejudices would claim, in the quantity of words used, nor in the function the speeches are serving—their nakedly propagandistic intent—but in the way the speeches have been written, acted, and filmed.

So Proudly We Hail! was written by Allan Scott, who had previously worked with Sandrich on several musicals, although his script was meddled with by the Office of War Information, which may be

26–30. *So Proudly We Hail!*

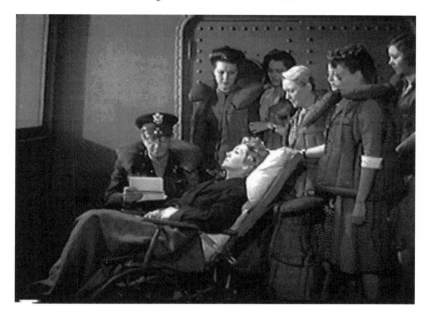

26.   Doctor begins reading to Davey.

responsible for some of the film's awkward moments.[36] The film follows the experiences of a group of nurses who suffer through the defeats at Bataan and Corregidor, heroically striving to help the wounded through desperate circumstances. In the last scene, they are on shipboard, being evacuated to the United States. The lead character, Lieutenant Davidson, or "Davey" (Claudette Colbert), is in a state of catatonia out of grief over the news that her soldier husband, John (George Reeve), has been killed. On ship, a doctor attempts to bring Davey round by reading her a letter that has just caught up with her.

DOCTOR: My darling, I'm writing this from Mindanao. We leave in the morning for an unknown destination. I write with no so-called premonitions. As a matter of fact, I'm writing this in a pleasant little bar on the outskirts. I've ordered two daiquiris—one for you and one for me.
I miss you. I miss you all the time. It was such a short time, wasn't it? And yet, I remember every second of it, from the

27.   Doctor checks to see if Davey is listening.

28.   Davey remains catatonic.

29.   John's voice and image take over letter reading.

moment you washed my back (and I could use a good bath
right now), 'til your face faded from view in the darkness
when I left. I think about you all the time and wish things
were different.

Things will be different. I know that now because there is
good in this war, much as I hate it. This is not just a war of
soldiers—you weren't soldiers in the strict sense, you were
just kids from all walks of life. All kinds of people. There's
something new in this war, something good. You could see
it, this new thing even in their tired hungry faces as they took
courage one from another.

This is not a people's war because civilians also get killed,
this is the people's war because they have taken it over now
and they are going to win it and end it with a purpose. To
live like men with dignity and freedom. This is the good I've
found. There's a small voice whispering around the earth,
and the people are beginning to talk across their boundaries.
This voice will grow in volume until it thunders all over
the world. It's what you said and what José said and what
Rosemary felt and Olivia. It's the raids that made Kansas cry.
It says this is our war now and this time it'll be our peace.

I'm proud. Proud to have known you, proud to have
received your love. Already I've had a complete, rich life in
three short months. I'm enclosing a deed to that little farm

I told you about. It's now in your name. I'll wait for you there, or if you're there first, wait for me.

Thank you, thank you my darling for my life. Thank you for everything.

Your devoted—and this is the first time I've ever written it—your devoted husband,

John.

This passage does not feature sterling prose. Particularly in the third and fourth paragraphs it relies upon maddeningly vague wording such as, "this," "it," "something," "new thing," "what." But the stylistic weakness is dwarfed by the clumsiness of the device of using a personal love letter for such mixed dual functions, as the means both of curing Davey (for she does wake up, and it is she who pronounces the signature "John"), and of conveying an inspirational message to the viewer. "Hiding" the thematic message in a love letter doesn't work very well; it just betrays an uneasiness about sending the message to begin with.

This speech is also in conflict with the facet of the film that gives it great interest and appeal—its unusual focus on women as soldiers in a fighting arena. This letter explicitly denies the nurses the prestige of their valorous actions and commissions and turns them back into civilians, "just scared kids." Instead of keeping up the good fight, Davey is supposed to go home to the farm and wait. Thus this coda strives to reverse all the feminist implications of the story so far.

The accompanying visuals (figs. 26–29)—ten shots alternating among seven setups—consist of the following: shots of the doctor speaking; cutaways to the other nurses, who are awkwardly gathered around her chair, crying; and close-ups of Davey's listening face. Davey's frozen face is not very expressive, even with a dramatic lighting effect, but visual interest is added to this close-up by the fact that someone decided to gradually superimpose John's face on the side of the screen, and to allow his voice to fade in over, and then supplant, the voice of the reading doctor. Presumably, the idea is to take the letter away from the anonymous doctor and to show how John lives on in Davey's heart (or in heaven?), but the technique recalls the superimpositions used to show characters' thoughts in early silent films and feels dated. The heaven motif is echoed in the lines about "waiting for me" and in the film's final image, a shot aimed off the ship's deck into the sky, of sunlight breaking through

30. The last shot.

clouds. Off-screen music attempts to heighten the sequence: starting with pseudo-Polynesian-island effects, then with a sad solo violin, then with fuller, more orchestrated violins, and concluding with a rousing fanfare. But the scoring is not musically integrated; it baldly reaches for different emotions in succession. The overall effect of this sequence is of clumsiness and hokiness.

Mrs. Miniver was written by a team of scriptwriters, including Arthur Wimperis, George Froeschel, James Hilton, and Claudine West. It presents the story of an upper-class British country family and how its comfortable life is turned upside down by the Battle of Britain. In a bombing raid, Carole, the wife of the Minivers' son, Vin, is killed. The film concludes with a scene in the local church, where the vicar, a character who has been part of the movie throughout, seeks to comfort and inspire his charges. Wyler reportedly put great stress on this ending, according to Axel Madsen: "After Pearl Harbor, Wyler felt the vicar's sermon in a bombed-out church at the end of the film was too tame and, together with Wilcoxon [the actor], he rewrote some of it and reshot it."[37]

VICAR: I will read to you from Psalm Number 91.

> I will say of the LORD, He is my refuge and my fortress:
>   my God, in him will I trust.
>   Surely he shall deliver thee from the snare of the fowler,
> and from the noisome pestilence.
>   Thou shalt not be afraid for the terror by night, nor for
> the arrow that flieth by day;
>   Nor for the pestilence that walketh in darkness, nor for
> the destruction that wasteth at noonday.
>   He shall cover thee with his feathers, and under his wing
> shalt thou trust: his truth shall be thy shield and buckler.

> We, in this quiet corner of England, have suffered the loss of
> friends very dear to us. Some close to this church. George West,
> choir boy. James Ballard, stationmaster and bell ringer, and the
> proud winner, only an hour before his death, of the Beldon cup,
> for his beautiful Miniver rose. And our hearts go out in sympa-
> thy for the two families who share the cruel loss of a young girl
> who was married at this altar, only two weeks ago.
>   The homes of many of us have been destroyed and lives of
> young and old have been taken. There's scarcely a household
> that hasn't been struck to the heart.
>   And why? Surely you must have asked yourselves this
> question. Why, in all conscience, should these be the ones to
> suffer? Children. Old people. A young girl at the height of her
> loveliness. Why these? Are these our soldiers? Are these our
> fighters? Why should they be sacrificed?
>   I shall tell you why. Because this is not only a war of sol-
> diers in uniform, it is a war of the people, of all the people,
> and it must be fought not only on the battlefield but in the
> cities and the villages, in the factories and on the farms, in the
> home and in the heart of every man, woman and child who
> loves freedom.
>   Well, we have buried our dead. But we shall not forget them,
> instead they will inspire us with an unbreakable determina-
> tion to free ourselves and those who come after us, from the
> tyranny and terror that threaten to strike us down. This is the
> people's war. It is our war. We are the fighters. Fight it then!
> Fight it with all that is in us. And may God defend the right.

The writing here, as befits the narrative situation, is much more
formal and more artistically wrought. The biblical quotation sets a
majestic tone, and reverberates backward into the film to the scenes
of "terror by night" viewers have just witnessed. The vicar follows

31.　The Minivers entering the church.

32.　Camera reveals damage to church.

33.   The vicar begins his sermon.

34.   Mid-shot of priest at pulpit.

35. The empty seat among the choirboys.

36. Vin Miniver moves next to Lady Beldon.

37. Mr. and Mrs. Miniver sing "Onward Christian Soldiers."

38. The last shot.

the psalm with rhetorical questions ("Are these our soldiers?"), balanced phrases ("in the cities and the villages"), alliteration ("tyranny
and terror"), and careful repetition. Indeed, Madsen recounts: "The
sermon so impressed President Roosevelt that he had the text
reprinted in leaflets in many languages, dropped over German-held
territories and broadcast over Voice of America. *P.M.* and *Look* magazine reprinted the text *in toto*." However effective the speech may be
in print, the words take on added power on the screen because they
are delivered with authority and resonance by the British actor Henry
Wilcoxon (who had earlier won fame in Hollywood by playing Marc
Anthony and Richard the Lion-Hearted for Cecil B. De Mille).

Here, as in *So Proudly*, this final speech is called upon to simultaneously fulfill multiple functions. But the difference is that the sub-
sidiary functions in *Mrs. Miniver* are less far-fetched: first, this sequence gives viewers narrative information that they had not known
before—chiefly that Mr. Ballard was also killed by the bombing—
and secondly, the sermon affects the on-screen characters by stiffen-
ing their resolve and by prompting Vin to move to comfort Lady Beldon, Carole's snobbish upper-class grandmother, with whom he had
previously been at odds.

Most striking is the way Wyler's direction works in tandem with
the dialogue (figs. 31–38). To begin with, there is the setting, a church
that has been so damaged by bombs that sandbags are everywhere,
the rear altar has been replaced by structural wooden beams, and the
roof has an enormous hole in it. Wyler frames his shots to reveal all
this damage to us gradually as the scene progresses, just as the sermon gradually reveals the loss of additional townspeople. While the
visual background and art direction of *So Proudly* are nondescript,
the mise-en-scène of the church amplifies the force of the vicar's
words. Moreover, Wyler cuts frequently throughout the speech (25
cuts alternating between 13 setups), now showing the vicar speaking, now showing the empty space among the choirboys where
George West is missing, now focusing on different members of the
Miniver family whose reaction to a given phrase is most important.
There is no music whatsoever under the vicar's sermon, but when he
concludes, the congregation sings "Onward Christian Soldiers." The
last shot of the film is, as in *So Proudly*, a shot of the sky, but here the
shot is layered—visually and thematically—by being framed through
the hole in the church roof, and by the perfectly timed appearance
there of a formation of British bombers, streaking toward the fight.

One might conclude from examining these two sequences that Wyler is a better director than Sandrich, that one set of screenwriters did a better job than the other, and certainly that Metro-Goldwyn-Mayer poured more money and care into the production of *Mrs. Miniver* than Paramount did into *So Proudly.* But my point is that the type of dialogue that so many critics have scorned the most—a very long speech, marked by formal/artistic language, that explicitly tries to "send a message"—can be brilliantly effective, depending upon the way in which it is integrated into the text.

PART II

DIALOGUE AND GENRE

In 1955, Harvey Purvis published a humorous piece in *Films in Review* entitled "Sure Fire Dialogue." The article consists of a verbal tour through twenty-two film genres:

MYSTERIES: And just where were *you* when all this was taking place, Jamieson? . . . You mean to seriously suggest that the dead man stabbed himself and then proceeded to wipe the dagger clean of blood stains? No, no, Sergeant Dugan, I'm afraid you'll have to do better than that . . . I see. Then that makes you sole heir to this vast estate . . . Whoever he is, our killer is bother clever and cunning . . . You made your first mistake Herr Krundschmidt, alias Dr. Peabody, when you failed to diagnose correctly a simple case of asphidio-calymide poisoning.

SAFARIS: What? A white woman in this part of Mogombiland? She must be mad! . . . Yes, B'wana . . . I agree to lead this safari on one condition . . . Men say much taboo, B'wana. Men say no go on . . . Here come the black devils now . . . And the old women and young warriors will laugh at the mighty chief who trembled in fear of the white man's bang-bang stick.

MUSICALS: Look, kid, why don't you go back home? Know what your chances are? For every star, two thousand are starving . . . This song seems to have been written just for you . . . Sure, the kid's great, but she isn't a NAME . . . That's it! That's it! That's the number we need for the second act . . . I'm going back to Smith Falls where folks may not be sophisticated, but at least they're real human beings . . . Why does everything happen to me? Opening night, a full house, and my leading lady walks out. All right, Freddie, get the little Bronson kid . . . You can *do* it Sally. Now go out there

> and wow them . . . Do you hear that Mr. Weyburn?
> They're bringing the house down. And you said she
> couldn't dance.[1]

What Purvis has so adroitly demonstrated here is that American film genres evince (clichéd) verbal patterns.

Such conventions are identifiable on the level of subject matter— in mysteries characters talk about the crime committed, in safari films about the safari, in musicals, about the show that is being produced—but also in terms of style. Note Purvis's use of longer, more elaborate phrases in mysteries, the "native" baby talk in safaris, the slangy informality in musicals. It is unthinkable that the presumably aristocratic detective in mysteries would say "wow," "kid" or "white man's bang bang stick." It is equally implausible that the stage manager in musicals would build up to the speech act of "triumphant accusation" that climaxes a Sherlock Holmes film.

Genre theory is a rich vein in American film scholarship, and it has made great strides in delineating the underlying themes of the various major American film genres, their narrative conventions, and their patterns of "iconography," of cinematography, costume, setting, or props. What such theory has mostly avoided, however, is any systematic discussion of dialogue.

One genre that has already attracted significant discussion of its dialogue is science fiction, and the reason for this attention is revealing—dialogue in sci-fi has been judged to be particularly bad. Susan Sontag observes:

> The dialogue of most science fiction films, which is of a monumental but often touching banality, makes them wonderfully, unintentionally funny. Lines like "Come quickly, there's a monster in my bathtub," "We must do something about this," "Wait, Professor. There's someone on the telephone," "But that's incredible," and old American stand-by, "I hope it works!" are hilarious in the context of picturesque and deafening holocaust.[2]

In *Screening Space*, Vivian Sobchack further explicates this genre's trouble with words, arguing that the heavy reliance on scientific or pseudo-scientific jargon is stultifying, and that language is inadequate to capture the sense of "other-worldness" or the miraculous that is so essential to the genre.[3] I speculate that the difficulty stems either from prioritizing spectacle and special effects and paying less attention to their scripts or from failing to imagine how characters might react to fantastic events other than in the language of the present day. The sci-fi films that have the most intriguing dialogue—*2001* (1968), in which the characters all speak with a flat coldness; *A Clockwork Orange* (1971), which adopts Anthony Burgess' made-up dialect; and *Blade Runner* (1982), which uses neologisms, marked silence, and poetic diction—have their characters speak in ways that depart markedly from contemporary usage. Grateful as I am for Sontag's and Sobchack's lengthy, sensitive discussions of at least one genre's dialogue dynamics, I can't help but regret that this attention was motivated by a desire to understand the dialogue's inadequacy, not its strengths.

In this second half of the book, I survey the patterns of dialogue in four other major American genres: Westerns, screwball comedies, gangster films, and melodramas. I use the categories identified in the first part of this study—the dialogue functions, the variables concerning style and structure, and the strategies of integration with other cinematic elements—to analyze what is characteristic about the use of dialogue in each case. Investigating each genre's approach to "talk" ends up revealing more about its thematic resonances, and more about how each situates viewers in our role as eavesdroppers.

What accounts for these verbal genre conventions? Partially, they are motivated by the subject matter. Screenwriters are always concerned that dialogue be appropriate to characters' social backgrounds, and thus "realistic,"—or in Steve Neale's terms, marked by "cultural verisimilitude."[4] Accordingly, cinematic rural cowboys speak differently than cinematic urban gangsters. Partially, films are clearly copying preexisting expectations created by other forms of representation; stories, novels, autobiographies, plays, and even silent films have overlapped with sound film genres and helped to delimit the types of speech that Hollywood employs. And partially, I believe, dialogue patterns are related to the underlying gender dynamics of each genre: whether the genre is primarily addressed to male or female viewers and how each genre treats its male and female characters are crucial factors in its use of language.

Once speech conventions were set by financially and critically successful films in the early sound era, such conventions assumed a life of their own, in that later filmmakers and filmgoers have unconsciously internalized these patterns of speech as most appropriate for these types of stories. Thus these verbal patterns became part of our expectations of "generic verisimilitude." Of course, not every film follows the rules, just as not every film slavishly duplicates its genre's visual conventions. But by taking a broad overview, general proclivities can be identified.

We know that genres change and even mutate through time; as Steve Neale argues, genres may be dominated by repetition, but they are also marked by an interplay of difference, variation, and change.[5] Over the course of film history, the verbal proclivities identified here have been stretched or subverted, but I believe that they are still constituent of viewers' unconscious anticipations of genre films, of our "horizons of expectations."

There is a large body of scholarly literature devoted to the problems of genre definition, pointing out the inconsistent and illogical ways in which we often conceive of and talk about film genres, and the fact that the parameters of genres alter, not only with the unrolling of film history, but also with the changing temporal, theoretical, and ideological perspectives of observers.[6] Sometimes the critiques are so persuasive and biting that one imagines just giving up on genre theory altogether, but despite its flaws and uncertainties, I find this methodology too productive and too intriguing to abandon. Possibly, the dialogue patterns that I uncover here may be of some help in this vexatious problem of determining which features of a genre are seen as defining, or in illustrating how films become cross-generic hybrids. Again, dialogue, so taken for granted, may turn out to be crucial.

FOUR

Verbal Frontiers

Dialogue in the Western

If you have to tell a story with words, you're in trouble.
You'd better try and find another story. One of the things
that makes Westerns work is that they're told by images.

John Sturges, interview in *American Cinema,
Part 4: The Western* (1994)

Sturges is mistaken, I think; Westerns, like all American sound films,
rely heavily on their dialogue to communicate their narratives,
sketch in their characters, and so on. Yes, Westerns do place great
emphasis on their mise-en-scènes—those glorious mountains and
deserts and plains—and yes, they commonly include wordless action sequences of chases on horseback, wagons crossing a river, or
pitched gun battles. But the majestic landscape is the background for
a human drama, not stories of sagebrush or rabbits, and these action
sequences are always bracketed and contextualized by dialogue
scenes.

Nevertheless, the question of dialogue here is exceptionally complicated, because this genre in particular acts out a paradoxical
love/hate relationship with language, which turns out to be integral
to the genre's meaning. "Westerns distrust language," Jane Tompkins writes. "Time and again they set up situations whose message is
that words are weak and misleading, only actions count; words are
immaterial, only objects are real. But the next thing you know, someone is using language brilliantly."[1]

As is well known, the Western, as a genre, predates the invention
of the cinema. Some historians trace its origins back to the novels of
James Fenimore Cooper, and later to the dime novels glorifying

cowboys and outlaws. From the *Great Train Robbery* (1902) to the epic scale of *The Covered Wagon* (1923), Westerns were a staple of the silent era, and they made the transition to sound with *The Virginian* (1929). The standard story of the evolution of the genre sees the 1930s and 1940s, as the era of classic Westerns, while in the later 1950s, particularly in the films of Anthony Mann, the Western turned darker and more psychological.[2] During the 1960s and 1970s, films such as *Ride the High Country* (1962) and *The Wild Bunch* (1969) were self-consciously both nostalgic and revisionist. In the 1980s and 1990s, although periodically an isolated film would appear—*Silverado* (1985), *Dances with Wolves* (1990), *Unforgiven* (1992)—Westerns have no longer been produced in sufficient quantities to sustain the genre as a major facet of contemporary culture.

Various typologies of subcategories of the Western have been offered. Subject matter (e.g., "railroad," "outlaw," "Indian," "cavalry," "marshal") can be seen as defining. Alternatively, Westerns can be sorted either in terms of budget and prestige (e.g., epics, "B" pictures, and serials) or by their interweaving of other genres (e.g., comic Westerns, such as *Blazing Saddles;* musical Westerns, such as *Seven Brides for Seven Brothers*). However, the most intriguing system of classification has been developed by Will Wright, who identifies what he sees as the "classical plot," and then defines a "transition theme," a "vengeance variation" and a "professional plot," based upon the films' underlying structural patterns, particularly the hero's relationship with society as a whole.[3]

As Will Wright, Robert Warshow, John Cawelti, and others have pointed out, one of the genre's central concentrations is on the status and character of its mythic creation, the Western hero. This hero is endowed with both exalted skills and an acute sense of his own honor and moral code. Moreover, this hero literally *embodies* the clashes between civilization and savagery, East versus West, law versus chaos, community versus individualism, weakness versus power that seethe through Westerns. He balances on the knife edge of these contradictions, separated from both sides, from the helpless townspeople or settlers, on the one hand, and from the lawless outlaws or Indians, on the other. John Cawelti states that these heroes "are above all 'men in the middle,' that is, they possess many qualities and skills of the savages but are fundamentally committed to the townspeople."[4] Will Wright argues that different variations of the genre resolve the hero's instability in distinct ways—he may give up his exalted status (and his "savage" side) to join the townspeople, as in *The Westerner* (1940), where Cole Hardin becomes totally domesticated; or, despite his love for a woman or respect for Eastern values, he may choose to remain outside of society, as in *Ride Lonesome* (1959), where Ben Brigade gives up Mrs. Steele to his rival and literally remains in the wilderness. Either way, through the greater part of the film, the hero (or group of heroes) keep some distance from society, community, family, and marriage.*

Often the Western hero's loneliness is expressed visually— through all those shots of riders alone in the vastness of the Western landscape. But just as often, Westerns use dialogue to meditate on the hero's choices. Take, for instance, John Sturges's own *The Magnificent Seven* (1960), which features numerous discussions of the gunfighters' choice and dilemma, including the following, a highly wrought set piece that, in its singsong poetry, penetrates to the heart of the myth of the Western hero.

> CHICO: Your gun has got you everything you have. Isn't that true? Hmmm? Well, isn't it true?
>
> VIN: *(bitterly)* Yeah, sure, everything. After a while you can call bartenders and faro dealers by their first name. Maybe two hundred of 'em; rented rooms you live in—five hundred; meals you eat in hash houses—a thousand. Home? None. Wife? None. Kids? None. Prospects? Zero. Suppose I left anything out?
>
> CHRIS: Yeah. Places you're tied down to? None. People with a hold on you? None. Men you step aside for? None.
>
> LEE: Insults swallowed? None. Enemies? None.
>
> CHRIS: *(slight surprise)* No enemies?
>
> LEE: *(softly)* Alive.

Westerns continually offer images of the hero's solitude, but this discussion of the costs and benefits of his rootless lifestyle provides

---

* Some Westerns give the hero company on his precarious knife edge—that is, the hero is presented as part of an elite *group* of men, all of whom have special skills and share the same exalted status. Wright labels such films the "professional" variation and points to *The Professionals* (1966), *El Dorado* (1967), and *The Wild Bunch* (1969) as examples. While these films allow for more male camaraderie, they do not essentially change the sense of isolation inherent in the characterization of the Western hero.

39. *The Magnificent Seven.* Vin counting his ledger.

the viewer with somewhat surprising specifics about rented rooms and hash houses. Moreover, the manner in which each gunslinger picks up the same rhetorical trope illustrates their bond, and their equality, yet the spin that each puts on his contribution differentiates them—Vin evinces regret (fig. 39); Chris, pride, independence, and self-sufficiency; Lee, bravado (which we later learn is false). The rhythm of the sentences, with the repeated, definitive "None," has the power and finality of a moral ledger on Judgment Day.

However, any aficionado of Westerns could make an important addition to Vin's ledger: "Conversation? None." In popular perception, taciturnity is a prerequisite for the Western hero—it is part and parcel of his separateness, his loneliness, his superiority. "[T]he laconic style is commonly associated with the Western hero, particularly in the twentieth century when movie stars like Gary Cooper, John Wayne, James Stewart and Henry Fonda have vied for the prize as the Western hero who can say the fewest words with the least expression," Cawelti notes.[5] This general perception oversimplifies and ignores significant variation: Cooper is tight-lipped in *Man of the West* (1958) but he plays a masterful verbal trickster in *The Westerner* (1940). Stewart withholds vital information in *The Man from Laramie* (1955) but positively babbles in *Destry Rides Again* (1939) and *Two Rode Together* (1961). As Wyatt Earp in *My Darling Clementine* (1946), Fonda talks at length only to his brother's grave; however, in *Fort Apache* (1948), he goes off on tangents about military tacticians. John Wayne, who, as the number one box-office star from 1950 to 1965, may have done more than anyone else to popularize the stereotypical close-mouthed hero of the Western, often fits the mold, but Wayne himself is quite garrulous in *True Grit* (1969). Cawelti might have included Clint Eastwood in his list, for Eastwood's marked silence has a menacing air in *Hang 'Em High* (1968) and in Sergio Leone's spaghetti Westerns. Yet in *Unforgiven* (1992), Eastwood waxes on in ornate phrases about his dear departed wife. Not surprisingly, these actors' dialogue styles vary with different characterizations, narratives, screenwriters, and directors.

And yet the impression that the Western hero must be taciturn is so much a part of the cinematic record, and so embraced by general cultural expectations, that it overwhelms any evidence to the contrary. What accounts for this steadfast impression? Historians and linguists argue that cowboys, were not, in actuality, particularly quiet; on the contrary, tall-tale telling and verbal play were more characteristic of Western speech.* Nor are cowboys particularly taciturn in early fictional accounts such as Cooper's Leatherstocking tales. The rule that the cowboy must be silent is a twentieth-century invention.

Jane Tompkins seeks to explain the association of fictional Westerners with terseness, and her discussion echoes our earlier findings. Westerners believe in doing, not talking. "Language is gratuitous at best; at worst it is deceptive." The Westerner must be silent to enhance his status as a masculine archetype, to prove and enforce his superiority over women. "For a man to speak of his inner feelings not only admits parity with the person he is talking to, but it jeopardizes his status as potent being, for talk dissipates presence, takes away the mystery of an ineffable self which silence preserves. . . . Silence is a sign of mastery, and goes along with a gun in the hand. . . . In Westerns, silence, sexual potency, and integrity go together."[6] Ed Buscombe concurs: "Terseness is a tradition in the Western, in which loquaciousness is often associated with effeminacy."[7]

---

* "Contrary to their laconic image, cowboys love to talk. They're just choosy about who they talk to. Conversations and story-telling offered a welcome relief from often solitary ranch labors," Richard W. Statta says in *The Cowboy Encyclopedia* (Santa Barbara, Calif.: ABC–Clio, 1994), 192. "On the seething frontier, everything went—the turbulence of life in general was inevitably reflected in language. There was an enormous appetite for words, an admiration for words: a man who could bring out a salty phrase or an apt comparison would smash the cracker-barrels," the language historian Frederic Cassidy argues ("Language on the American Frontier," in *The Frontier in Perspective*, ed. Walker Wyman and Clifton Kroeber [Madison: University of Wisconsin Press, 1957], 203).

Tompkins supports her argument by reference to a scene in Hawks's *Red River* (1948) that is so blatant in its association of loquaciousness with femininity as to be worth quoting in full. Tess Millay has caught up with Matthew Garth in an Abilene hotel. She is very distressed because she knows that Tom Dunson has vowed to kill Matt for assuming control of his cattle herd.

> TESS: He's, he's . . . he's camped two or three miles outside of town. He says he'll be here just after sun-up. He says he's going to kill you. What's the matter? Is something . . . ? Oh . . . oh, I must look like I'm in mourning. I didn't mean it that way . . . I . . . or I wouldn't . . . No, no, Matthew, I know you've only a few hours, but, but listen for just a minute, that's all, and, and . . . then I won't talk about it anymore, just a minute. He, he hasn't changed his mind, Matthew.
>
> MATTHEW: I didn't think he would.
>
> TESS: We saw the railroad and I thought . . . I thought it might make a difference, but it didn't. Nothing would. He's . . . he's like something you can't move. Even *I've* gotten to believe it's got to happen, you meeting him. I was gonna ask you to run, but . . . no I'm not, I'm not, it, it wouldn't do any good. You're too much like him. Oh, stop me, Matthew, stop me . . .

Matthew covers her mouth with his hand.

> TESS: (*whispering*) God bless you, Matthew.
>
> MATTHEW: (*kisses Tess*)

Under stress, Tess resorts to blabbering and stammering. She speaks nearly a hundred and fifty words, while Matt speaks five. There is no point in discussing Dunson's plans; Matt is so wise he already knows them, and he also knows that what Tess really needs (to calm her down about this situation, and in general), is for him to take charge of her, to silence her, and to bed her.

As the most macho man in town, the Western hero must be perceived, by other characters, and by the viewer, as the least talkative. This doesn't mean that Westerns really avoid dialogue; they *can't*— like every narrative film, they need to explain why these people are in these situations, what is at stake, when the deadline elapses, who is evil, and who is good. But Westerns deliberately create an imbalance; they shift as many of the dialogue functions as possible away from the hero to other characters, and in a classic case of ingratitude, the films go on to condemn these secondary characters for their talkativeness. (Tess is the one, above, who communicates to the viewer that Dunson is unwavering in his wrath, that the duel is now inevitable, and so on.) The shift is enacted because the hero's comparative silence will only be noticeable if everyone else talks too much. Many women are portrayed as chatterboxes—Calamity Jane in *The Plainsman* (1936), Emma in *Johnny Guitar* (1954), Mattie in *True Grit* (1969)—but it is not only women who can't keep their tongues still. Inferior men also talk too much. This is true of the professional men, the doctors, lawyers, and newspapermen, who are talkers rather than men of action and whose dialogue frequently imparts important plot information. This is certainly true of cowards, punks, and would-be challengers, such as Hunt Bromley in *The Gunfighter* (1950); the punks shoot off their mouths, they brag and posture to cover up their inadequacies. Conversely, the most fearsome antagonists, such as Frank Miller in *High Noon* and Scar in *The Searchers,* match the Westerner's terseness.

But the most common talkative foil for the Western hero is his "sidekick," a desexualized old-timer who speaks for the hero so that he doesn't have to. The sidekick appears as early as the silent film; he reappears memorably as Buck in *Stagecoach,* Groot in *Red River,* Stumpy in *Rio Bravo,* Bull in *El Dorado,* and so on. The actor George Hayes, who was cast as a sidekick in some 150 Westerns, was revealingly nicknamed "Gabby." In Anthony Mann's *The Far Country* (1955), the gabbiness of Walter Brennan's Ben becomes a major plot point, because he inadvertently lets slip Jeff's plan to leave the mining town, causing them to be ambushed by the bad guys.

The lesson that the filmgoer is to learn from many Westerns is that talk is futile, only action will avail. As Will Kane says to Amy in *High Noon,* "If you don't know I can't tell you." Several of the films mentioned above as offering exceptionally talkative heroes actually enact this parable: for instance, *Destry Rides Again* offers an unusual story about a young deputy who initially tries to resolve problems through reasoning and storytelling. After his friend is shot in the back, however, he realizes that the time for talking is over; he must strap on his guns to defeat the villains.

However, as soon as one buys into the claim that the Western devalues language, a major paradox appears: of all American film genres, it is the Western that repeatedly, insistently stresses the sanctity of words, the importance of verbal promises. Western heroes are heroes, not only because of their speed with a gun, but because of their moral integrity. "The Westerner is the last gentleman, and the movies which over and over again tell his story are probably the last art form in which the concept of honor retains its strength," Robert Warshow observes.[8] Time and time again, their plots revolve around the sanctity of "keeping one's word." In Michael Curtiz's *The Comancheros* (1961), John Wayne, as a Texas Ranger named Jake Cutter, finds himself in a difficult position—he feels gratitude to his prisoner, Paul Regret, who has just saved a ranch house from an Indian attack, but Cutter is still determined to deliver Regret to the authorities.

> JAKE: [I] can't let [you] run. [I] swore an oath when they put that badge on [me].
> REGRET: And that's important to you?
> JAKE: I said I swore an oath.
> REGRET: Words.
> JAKE: Mon sewer. Words are what men live by. Words they say and mean. You musta had a real careless upbringing.

The issue of being honor-bound by one's word comes up again and again and again in Westerns. In Ford's *Fort Apache*, Captain York is aghast that Colonel Thursday has tricked Cochise into returning to American soil. He protests,

> YORK: Colonel Thursday, I gave my word to Cochise. No man is gonna to make a liar outta me, sir.

In Richard Brooks's *The Professionals*, Rico holds Bill to his promise to rescue the wife of Grant, a rich businessman.

> RICO: Our word. We gave our word to bring the woman back.
> BILL: Our word to Grant ain't worth a plug nickel.
> RICO: You gave your word to *me*.

In *Red River*, Dunson holds the cowhands to their pledge to finish the cattle drive. In *Ride the High Country*, Steve Judd insists that his group keep faith with the bankers who have employed them. No matter how circumstances change, pledging oneself verbally is viewed as a moral action in Westerns, and the guarantee of the hero's integrity is his keeping of his troth. "Words are what men live by. Words they say and mean."

Additional evidence of the Western's deadly seriousness about language is the weight given to insults and slurs upon one's honor. In other genres, a villain trying to taunt a hero is liable to be met with disdainful laughter or a sassy retort—can you imagine Indiana Jones, James Bond, or Captain Kirk being mortally offended by a slur? But in the cinematic West, everyone is deeply offended by insults. Antagonists taunt the heroes of Westerns constantly, and if gunplay is averted, it is by the narrowest of margins. In Owen Wister's original novel *The Virginian*, considered the popularizer of the Western formula, the first altercation between the hero and Trampas arises from the latter calling the former a "son of a bitch." The motif is repeated in the film *Shane* when Calloway provokes Shane: "New sod-buster, huh? Thought I smelled pigs."

So we are left with several paradoxes: the heroes of Westerns are taciturn—except when they are loquacious; words in Westerns are seen as baseless—except when they are valued beyond measure; Westerns don't rely on dialogue—but they manifestly do.

Even those Westerns that do use a consistently taciturn hero foreground dialogue, for taciturnity is not an absence of speech (the hero is not a mute or a mime), but a particular *style* of speech, a style I'll call "compressed." The abruptness, condensation and power of the Westerner's "plain speaking" is the triumph of good scriptwriting. Philip French even argues that the stylized laconic dialogue of Westerns is "in fact the only consistently satisfactory period speech that the movies—or for that matter contemporary dramatic literature— have found."[9]

For example, in the cafe scene in John Ford's *The Man Who Shot Liberty Valance* (1962), Lee Marvin, playing the outlaw Liberty Valance, deliberately trips Ransom Stoddard (Jimmy Stewart), which leads into a tense confrontation between Valance and Tom Doniphon (John Wayne). Valance indicates that he is supported by two of his gang, but Tom calmly retorts to him, "My boy Pompey, by the kitchen door." The camera shows us Pompey (Woody Strode) now holding a rifle on Liberty's back. The viewer understands Doniphon's verbless phrase to mean something along the order of: "I'm way ahead of you, Valance. You and your cronies can't hold a candle to me and my loyal servant (who is a Negro, and thus I may condescend to him by calling him a 'boy' and implying that he belongs to me). Pompey reflects my prowess; he is so cool that he has quietly gotten the drop on you. You were relying on having me outnumbered, but if you start trouble we'll blow you away." But Doniphon doesn't say this—he just says, "My boy Pompey, by the kitchen door." The additional meaning(s) are completely clear to the viewer from the context and the shots, the editing of the spatial relationships, and Wayne's half-smiling delivery of this short phrase. The viewer fills in the gaps of the understatement—the viewer catches all the inferences.

Compressed dialogue is usually not subtle or ambiguous; I presume that every viewer of *Liberty Valance* gets the same information from that phrase. But in its terseness, it conveys the impression that these are men of action, and it enhances the viewer's feeling of intimacy with the characters, and involvement with the ongoing narrative. As with the use of elliptical phrases in everyday conversation (discussed earlier), in a sense it flatters us by implying that we are such intimates to this world that we don't need things spelled out for us.

The use of verbal understatement in Westerns can be striking and effective—look back, for instance, at the short phrases and "bitten off" quality of the ledger sequence in *The Magnificent Seven* quoted above. Or study the end of *The Wild Bunch* when Pike decides that he is disgusted with himself and the life he leads and that the only noble option left is to try to save Angel from Mapache, even though such a plan is decidedly suicidal. All Pike says to his gang is, "Let's go," and all that is answered is, "Why not?" The extreme close-ups, the editing, the music, and the nuances of performance make these lines intelligible to the viewer.

Far from their neglecting dialogue, speech is a much-emphasized signifier of cultural background in Westerns. Robert Lyons's thorough analysis shows how important dialogue is to *My Darling Clementine*.

> The conflict Doc Holliday embodies between East and West set him
> at the center of a spectrum of characters in the film who represent,
> in different ways, the social values of Eastern and Western America.
> . . . The differences are signaled verbally, and the spectrum ranges
> from the barbaric monosyllables of the Clantons to the fulsome rhet-

oric of the actor Thorndyke. . . . Against these extremes, Wyatt and
Clementine bring East and West into shared communication and
shared admiration. She speaks with articulateness and formality, he
with laconic casualness.[10]

This presentation of a spectrum of verbal styles is not unique to this
movie. Ford highlights the clash in dialogue styles again and
again—the contrast between Ransom Stoddard and Tom Doniphon
in *Liberty Valance* is manifestly a collision between Eastern and Western speech, as is the contrast between Thursday and York in *Fort
Apache*. In *High Noon*, Grace Kelly as the sheriff's Quaker bride not
only looks the picture of ladylike decorum, she speaks with a clear,
formal precision that differs markedly from the speech of all the
other characters. In *Angel and the Bad Man* (1947), Penny's Quaker re-
ligiosity and pacifism are overtly stressed by her use of "thee" and
"thou."

"Eastern," ornate language is frequently deliberately interpolated
into Westerns for contrast. Westerns include a surprising amount of
quoted poetry, surprising, that is, until one realizes that the poetry is
serving as representative of high culture, the culture that is out of
place on the frontier. One could cite Thorndyke's "To Be or Not to
Be" soliloquy in *My Darling Clementine,* or the prominence given to
Poe's "El Dorado" in Hawks's film. The rich poetry of the King
James version of the Bible enters into Westerns recurrently, both for
its moral/religious perspective and for its literary power—for example, *Tombstone* (1993) features Ringo quoting from Revelation: "Be-
hold the pale horse. The man who sat on him was Death. And Hell
followed with him." Performances of melodramas, political oratory,
and elaborate sermons crop up with regularity. The way the "Eastern" rhetoric is handled obviously varies from film to film, so that
the genre as a whole conveys a complex amalgam of admiration and
mockery, the same ambivalence expressed toward all markers of
"civilization."

Thus dialogue is used in Westerns to thematize the antinomies between West and East. But dialogue also stresses issues of ethnic and
cultural identity. Characters with accents are abundant in Westerns.
These accents might be ascribed to realism, since the historical West
was a place of great linguistic diversity. But thematically, the stress
on regional and foreign accents foregrounds the unsettled, transient

nature of the frontier, its distance from "civilization." Southern accents stress to the audience that Miss Cameron in *The Big Trail* (1930) and Torrey in *Shane* are in exile from their defeated homeland, trailing associations of gentility and noble lost causes. European accents further emphasize the West as the American melting pot—one finds Swedes, such as the Jorgensons in *The Searchers*, and Irish, such as Mollie Monahan in *Union Pacific* (1939). The melange of backgrounds highlights that the characters all come from disparate backgrounds and pasts.

The "savage" side is represented verbally by the genre's stress on Spanish and Native American languages. Many Westerns are set in Mexico or the Southwest, and snippets of Spanish are used for cheap local color, but conversations of narrative importance are all in English. Mexican characters are made to speak a highly infantilized, Frito Bandito English—witness Chris, at the halfway station in *Stagecoach*, who tells Lucy Mallory: "Si señora. Leetle . . . what you call it . . . skirmish . . . with the Apaches last night. Soldiers take Captain Mallory to Lordsburg. . . . I think . . . he get . . . hurt, maybe." Treatment of Native American languages in Westerns runs along the same lines. Although there were more than two thousand separate Indian languages, Hollywood often did not bother to get any of them right. Indian characters were given unintelligible grunts or wild screams to utter; they said "Ugh" a lot. "In one serial of the mid-1930s (*Scouts to the Rescue*) the Indians were given a language by running their normal English dialogue backwards," John Price notes. "By keeping them relatively motionless when they spoke, the picture could be printed in reverse and a perfect lipsync maintained."[11] When Indian characters *were* given English dialogue, they often spoke either a halting baby talk, or, contrarily, pontificated with wise aphorisms. As Virginia Wexman states: "The clumsy locutions and halting syntax that characterize the utterances of non-English-speaking groups such as Indians and Mexicans are seen as aspects of their primitivism."[12]

(In more recent films, Native Americans may speak their own language, and their words may or may not be translated for the audience via subtitles. In *Ulzana's Raid* [1973], the narrative import is clear enough from the context, and the incomprehensible speech serves to stress to the audience the Apaches' separateness and otherness. *Dances with Wolves* [1990] is an unusual text in that it makes the difficulties in White/Indian communication one of its major topics;

this film also respected Native American culture and language enough to have its white actors spend months actually learning to speak Lakota, and then to subtitle these exchanges for the audience.)

One of the more fascinating aspects of the heteroglossia of Westerns is the fact that the hero is generally the only white character who can cross verbal boundaries. In *The Big Trail* (1930), Bret Coleman palavers with the Pawnee; in *The Plainsman* (1936), Wild Bill Hickok can speak Cheyenne; in *Hondo* (1953), Hondo Lane can speak Apache. (It comes as a shock, and it is played for laughs when Butch and Sundance have difficulties robbing banks in Bolivia because they don't know Spanish.) The Westerner's ability in this area is not seen as coming from some inherent verbal dexterity, but from the fact, as Cawelti has taught us, that he is the one who bridges the chasm between civilization and savagery, he is the one with knowledge of both camps. "He often functions as an interpreter not only because he understands Spanish or Indian languages, but also because he is better able to 'read' the characterological and gestural language that accompanies speech. He understands not only what people say but what they mean," Virginia Wexman notes.[13]

In general, the accents, dialects, or languages of other characters serve as contrast to the speech of the Western's hero. *They* are from the East, the South, Ireland—but *he* belongs here, *he* is of this land. *They* are Indian or Mexican—but *he* is White. Moreover, he and his fellows speak in a distinct and recognizable idiom of their own.

Although on some occasions, the Western's hero is allowed to be a Southerner, for the most part he speaks "Western." In an area of the vastness of the states and territories west of the Mississippi and a large and blurred time period, the linguist would find many regional variations, but popular culture makes no such careful distinctions, coining an All-Purpose Western Dialect (hereafter APWD). In APWD, all women are addressed as "Ma'am"; all strangers are referred to as "Pardner"; horses are "ponies"; homes are "ranches"; meals are "chow" or "grub"; clothes are "duds"; a gun is a "piece"; employees are "hands" or "boys"; Indians are "Injuns," "bucks" or "squaws"; "hello" is replaced by "howdy"; "think" and "believe" are folded into "reckon"; thank you is covered by "much obliged." Along with a specialized and instantly recognizable vocabulary, Western characters commonly employ an informal pronunciation and syntax: "git" instead of "get," "gonna" instead of "going to," "fella" instead of "fellow," "evenin'" instead of "evening." In 1947,

Lewis Herman published *American Dialects: A Manual for Actors, Directors and Writers.* He counsels actors to drawl their vowel sounds as in "skoowhul" (school), noting that

> These drawled vowels make for a speech that is paced quite slowly, often hesitantly and thoughtfully. It is a calm unhurried speech that takes cognizance of the fact that time is not as fleeting as some may think it to be; that cogitation is a prime virtue; that "shooting off at the mouth" is the sign of a fool.[14]

APWD undoubtedly owes something both to the real use of language in the historical and contemporary West and to literary representations of that language, first by Mark Twain and then by Western writers of both serious literature and penny dreadfuls.[15] Certainly, this dialect shows up in the intertitles of silent Westerns. "The title cards of Broncho Billy films are full of western dialect like 'hog-tied'. Expressions like 'pard' and 'plumb loco' abound in the early film of Tom Mix," Ed Buscombe points out.[16] *The Covered Wagon* includes such titles as: "You two roosters kin get all th'fight ya want when we ferry th'Platte. A fight now would disorganate this hull train."

The coming of sound brought the sound of Western dialect to moviegoers. Victor Fleming's 1929 version of *The Virginian*, famed as the first important sound Western, lays the dialect on thickly. Its opening moments are studded with Westernisms:

"He's a lying polecat"

"Usually I just beat ya by a nose, but this time I am gonna throw ya and hog-tie ya."

"Ain't got a lick of sense."

"Hey ma'am, that steer won't hurt you none."

"Mighty lucky thing I happen'd along. A wild steer is a awful ornery critter."

"You don't need to fret."

The use of Western dialect is an easy method of stressing the story's remove in time and space, of stressing the story's historicity. In writing Westerns, screenwriters might rely upon their memories of previous films or novels, or they could consult handy lexicons of the Western idiom, which appeared throughout the studio era.[17] The degree to which a given film emphasizes APWD varies considerably, as do the artistic ramifications of the stylistic choices. Some screenwriters lay it on perfunctorily and inconsistently; others make dialect an integral part of their characterizations and themes.

In the right hands, the foreignness of the Western idiom can be an extremely expressive tool. In *My Darling Clementine,* Clementine asks Wyatt whether he is going to Sunday services and if he will take her. Wyatt answers, "I'd admire to take you." This antiquated use of the verb "to admire" reawakens the filmgoer to the gap in time between Tombstone and the viewing; moreover, since we know that Wyatt does deeply respect and *admire* Clem, this phrase expresses, as no other could, his solemn pride in being her escort.

Let us examine further the typical patterns of dialogue found in Westerns. Instead of wit or sparkle, Western dialogue features a certain blunt power. In Lawrence Kasden's *Silverado* (1985), when Mel gets the drop on the bad guys beating up his friend, he states flatly: "Now I don't wanna kill you, and you don't wanna be dead." The line's directness and obviousness—the sheer "plain speaking" aspect of it—has surprising force. But its force also stems from its identity as a threat. "Threatening" is a common speech act in Westerns, which is why, when we think of their dialogue, we often think of some cliché on the order of, "This town ain't big enough for the both of us. You'd better be out of town by sunrise."

Because of the tendency to use words as a form of aggression, Westerns frequently turn to "toppers," that form of verbal sparring discussed in chapter 3. In George Cukor's *Heller in Pink Tights* (1960), Maybury, a dangerous gunmen, lusts after the actress Angela Rossini, who is involved in a relationship with Healy, her theatrical director. The two men have a face-off, in which the threats are palpable underneath their rather mild words.

> MAYBURY: I ain't a man to look for trouble, but I don't run from it.
> HEALY: I usually run from it, but not always.

Similarly, at the end of Richard Brooks's *The Professionals* (1960), Rico angers his erstwhile employer:

> GRANT: You bastard!
> RICO: Yes sir. In my case, an accident of birth. But you, sir, you're a self-made man.

Along with threats and toppers, Westerns frequently feature re-peated lines. As discussed in earlier sections, most screenplays get aesthetic mileage out of repetition. Westerns use it to demonstrate a character's fixity, the fact that he has an immutable core. In *The Searchers*, Ethan's "That'll be the day" reveals his superior knowl-edge and his stubbornness, just as Wyatt's "What kind of a town is this?" in *My Darling Clementine* alerts us to his disgust at the Tomb-stone's failure to measure up to his standards. Nathan Brittles's oft-repeated "Never apologize, it's a sign of weakness" in *She Wore a Yel-low Ribbon* represents his credo as an officer.

Another pattern in Westerns (Jane Tompkins also notices this), is the high incidence of commands. Only tenderfoots use polite phrases for requests; no cowboy says to a bartender, "Could I please have a glass of whisky?" Instead, of course, we get the abrupt im-perative: "Whisky." Rather than "I'd like to have a shave," they say "Shave." "Mount up." "Keep your hands in the air." "Deal." "Get out of town." "If they move, kill 'em." This speech pattern conveys the sense of blunt directness, of speakers in a hurry, of men used to commanding, accustomed to imposing their will on others.

This blunt directness also relates to Westerns' tendency to em-ploy dialogue for moral messages. Sooner or later in almost every Western, physical action will pause for discussion of the moral is-sues behind the conflict. Westerns are rarely subtle—the opposing points of view are laid right out on the table. *The Ox-Bow Incident* (1943) and *High Noon* (1952) are both criticized by Robert Warshow in this regard, but their debates about morality are not betrayals of the genre. *Hang 'em High* (1968) dwells on the ambiguities of fron-tier justice; *The Far Country* (1955) discusses the evils of self-centeredness and need to give to the community; *Jesse James* (1939) repeatedly tries to find the line that separates justified rebellion from wild banditry; *Hombre* (1967) includes a moving dispute on the Christian obligation to help others according to their needs, not their merits.

Often the moral messages are couched as dialogue between the male and female leads, and the woman (naturally) speaks for more "civilized" values and at greater length. But the heroes are remark-ably forthright in verbalizing their values. *Ride the High Country* hangs on Steve Judd's, "All I want is to enter my house justified." Even *Unforgiven*, which instead of presenting the Western hero as an ethical model shows him to be a pitiless, brutal, alcoholic destroyer, sums up the film's existential horror in a memorable line—"Deserve's got nothin'to do with it."

The explicitness of Western dialogue is enhanced by the ways in which it is commonly performed, filmed and recorded. Westerns as a genre (with the notable exception of Robert Altman's *McCabe and Mrs. Miller*) stay away from overlapping dialogue or noisy polylogues. For the most part, each line of dialogue—even in the most crowded bar scenes—is rendered clearly, dropped into a well of still water. The most successful Western stars—John Wayne, Henry Fonda, Randolph Scott, Clint Eastwood, Gary Cooper, Lee Marvin, Burt Lancaster—have cultivated performance styles in which they speak slowly, deliberately, and quietly. (The most significant anomaly may be Jimmy Stewart's more expressive performance style; Stewart's quicker pace, his stammering, and his abrupt shifts in volume were used to portray a more "neurotic" hero.) Camera placement and editing are generally designed to capture the dialogue exchanges unobtrusively, showing the face of the speaker or a group of conversationalists in a looser full shot. In short, directors rarely "throw away" dialogue in Westerns; instead, the dialogue explicitly takes center stage.

This chapter has covered many separate aspects of the use of language in Westerns. What is important now is to see how all these different facets of dialogue function, style and structure, and integration work within the dynamics of a given text. I've chosen two examples, John Ford's *Stagecoach* (1939) and John Sturges's *The Magnificent Seven* (1960), both because I presume readers will be familiar with these classics and because their directors' lack of respect for dialogue is on record, so that illustrating the centrality of dialogue in their own movies undercuts their arguments.

Stagecoach combined elements of a Guy de Maupassant story, "Boule de Suif," with its credited source, "Stage to Lordsburg" by Ernest Haycox.[18] The former provided a model for the filmmakers' thematic focus on the issues of social hypocrisy.[19] The latter was the source of several characters and plot elements: Geronimo on the warpath; the stagecoach in peril; the shunned prostitute; the gambler's gallantry toward a female passenger; the hero out to settle a score. But what is notable from my point of view is that Haycox's story contains very little dialogue: the necessary background exposition is given by the narrator, and the characters' thoughts are revealed through free indirect discourse. The stagecoach passengers speak very little (they are, as characters, very meagerly developed), and Haycox makes no attempt to individuate their speech patterns. Thus, although the screenwriter, Dudley Nichols, grabbed a small handful of lines from the original (Ringo's warning about the Apaches picking off strays is one, Lucy Mallory's aborted offer to do something for Dallas is another), 99 percent of the abundant dialogue in *Stagecoach* is original to the film—notwithstanding the fact that Nichols himself once claimed: "The most noticeable feature of a skillful screenplay is its terseness and bareness."[20]

Stagecoach presents an extended study of the complex contrasts between wilderness and civilization. It reveals the savagery in the supposedly settled towns of Tonto and Lordsburg, and, according to Peter Stowell, it illustrates that, ironically, it is "only through confrontation with the hard emptiness and dangerous savagery of Monument Valley that the 'civilized' passengers discover their moral sense."[21] For each of the passengers, the trip represents a physical and personal odyssey, and a movement from solitary isolation into a community.

Stagecoach opens with a scene designed to convey the perilousness of the narrative situation to the viewer. Riders urgently gallop into an army post, but it is the ensuing dialogue that explains the trouble:

> WHITE SCOUT: These hills here are full of Apaches! They've burned every ranch building in sight. He *(indicating a Cheyenne ally)* had a brush with them last night. Says they're being stirred up by Geronimo.

With background narrative information thus conveyed, the film proceeds with the stage's entrance into Tonto. I used the Tonto scene earlier as an example of anchorage of the diegesis and naming of the characters. This scene has a lot of work to do: the viewer is here introduced to Buck, Lucy, Hatfield, Curly, Doc, Dallas, Peacock, and Gatewood in quick succession. In each case, their dialogue reveals their stations in life and their reasons for undertaking the trip; it also provides clues to their personalities. Buck is talkative, and like other Western sidekicks, he has a remarkably colorful voice, a rather cracked falsetto; his dialogue is often used as "verbal wallpaper" for realistic effect (e.g., "Now you kids, get away from that wheel"). Doc Boone, who, like Dallas, is being run out of town by the bigoted ladies of the Law and Order League for his drunkenness, is just as loquacious as Buck, but his extravagant, educated vocabulary sets him up as a debased representative of Eastern culture.

> DOC: (*to landlady*) Is this the face that wrecked a thousand ships and burned the towerless tops of Ilium? . . . (*to Dallas*) Come on, be a proud, glorified dreg like me. . . . Take my arm Madame le Countesse, the tumbrel awaits.

Gatewood, the banker who is escaping with embezzled funds, represents the hypocrisy of the ruling elites. He pontificates: "And remember this, what's good for the banks, is good for the country." Peacock, the effete whiskey salesman, also speaks "too much," in a rapid, high voice:

> PEACOCK: If ever you go East, brother, come out to our house for dinner. No one in all Kansas City, Kansas sets a better table, than my dear wife, Violet.

Hatfield, the doomed Southern gambler, speaks little in this opening scene, although we later hear his accent and his formal politeness to Mrs. Mallory. As for Lucy Mallory, the respected officer's wife, and Dallas, the disgraced prostitute, neither talks at length; the former because of her haughty ladylike reserve, the latter out of bitter resignation to her fate. However, along with the contrast between the two women's appearances and the way they are treated by others, the two have very different voice qualities—Lucy's refined and controlled "Thank you, driver," contrasts with the raw pain that Claire Trevor puts into Dallas's "Doc? Haven't I any right to live? What have I done?"

The Tonto sequence also contains a key scene in Curly's office. This scene is important not because of its introduction of Curly as the marshal (of all the characters in *Stagecoach*, he may be the least individualized and the least interesting) but because this scene gives us all the information we need about the yet-to-be-introduced Ringo. In chapter 1, I discussed the penchant of cinematic characters to talk about the central star; Westerns include a great deal of discussion of their hero:

> BUCK: Well, Marshall, I'm looking for my shotgun guard. Is he here?
> CURLY: Out with a posse, Buck . . . tryin' to ketch the Ringo Kid.
> BUCK: Ringo! I thought Ringo was in the pen.
> CURLY: He was.
> BUCK: Busted out? Well, good for him.

Once the coach leaves Tonto, Ford starts a pattern that, as Tag Gallagher notes, he repeats again and again: "(1) The coach in long shot rolling along the plain (to "Bury Me Not on the Lone Prairie"); (2) Curly and Buck in two-shot conversing on the driver's seat; (3) The passengers inside, always in isolated crosscuts."[22] The long shots of the coach traversing the wilderness of Monument Valley are stunning and evocative, but they do not in and of themselves make a coherent narrative film; Ford intercuts them repeatedly with dialogue. What is notable about the Buck/Curly conversations is that they are classic examples of dialogues of the deaf. Buck is drawn as a comic buffoon, while Curly is seriously engaged in figuring out Gatewood's suspicious behavior. They aren't listening to each other:

> BUCK: My wife's got more relatives than anyone you ever did see! I'll bet I'm feeding half the state of Chihuahua!
> CURLY: It seem funny to you about Gatewood?
> BUCK: Yeah and then what do I get to eat when I get home in Lordsburg? Nothing but frijole beans, that's all. Nothing but beans, beans, beans!

Most of the conversations inside the coach are designed to reveal more about the characters and their interactions with one another. Since they are shot in close quarters, these rely heavily on close-ups, and exchanges of glances assume particular importance (fig. 40).

The traveling sequences are broken up by various interruptions. The first of these is Ringo's stopping the stage—"Hold it!" he commands. Ringo's dialogue here, and throughout, contrasts subtly with that of the other travelers—his speech is less extravagant, less marked than theirs. He talks amiably, but he doesn't rattle on, and his voice is slow and deliberate. Peter Bogdanovich once asked Ford regarding *Stagecoach*: "Someone said you made a star of John Wayne by not letting him talk much. Do you agree?" Ford replied, "No, that isn't true at all—he had a lot to say, plenty of lines. But what he said *meant* something. He didn't do any soliloquies or make any speeches."[23] John Wayne's vocal performance style is a very impor-

40.   *Stagecoach*. Close-ups and conversation inside the coach chart relationships between characters.

tant part of his acting and star persona; Garry Wills argues that Wayne's "calculated and measured phrasing gave his delivery the same air of control, of inevitability, that his motions conveyed."[24] Ringo's command phrases—such as "Sit down, mister" to Hatfield—are polite but authoritative. His vocabulary throughout sticks to "Western" usage; *he* never talks about countesses or tumbrels.

The first major rest stop, at Dry Fork, is dominated by a speech act: the characters vote on whether or not to continue the journey in the face of the danger from the Indians. During the voting scene, as is the case most of the time when the passengers are out of the coach, the camera pulls back to show the characters within their environment. This allows the characters' body gestures to register, quite notably when Hatfield elects to continue with the journey even though (because?) he picks up the ace of spades out of a deck of cards. After the decision, Curly orders the passengers to the table; his phrase, "Set down folks and eat your grub," is a particularly clear example of APWD.

The lunch table sequence, during which Ringo and Dallas are snubbed by the other passengers, has been thoroughly examined by Nick Browne in terms of its use of point-of-view shots and the "position" in which it puts the spectator.[25] Browne, however, pays little attention to the dialogue here. Hatfield's "May I find you another place, Mrs. Mallory? It's cooler by the window" is very polite and gentlemanly, and yet since its intent is to shun Dallas, the very silky smoothness of his words is somehow more reprehensible—the verbal equivalent of the shot in the back that we've been told is Hatfield's signature. When Mrs. Mallory moves, the party regroups itself so that Ringo and Dallas converse together, as do Hatfield and Lucy Mallory. In both cases the quiet privacy of their interactions, and Ford's more intimate two-shots, create romantic overtones; Ford adds in the music of "I Dream of Jeannie" when Hatfield talks, thus winning some of viewer's sympathy back to his side.

Back on the road, Curly's dialogue reveals to Buck and the viewer that he is neither greedy nor heartless—his motive for arresting Ringo is to protect him from the Plummers. However, Gatewood, the one character whom Ford leaves unregenerate and unrepentant throughout, earns the viewer's scorn by hectoring everyone with his pompous speeches: "America for Americans! The government must not interfere with business! Reduce taxes! Our national debt is something shocking. Over one billion dollars a year! What this country needs is a businessman for President." Such dialogue exemplifies what I earlier termed "allegory-lite," in that it mimics the political rhetoric of the Republican opponents of Roosevelt. One of the targets of 1930s legislative reform was corrupt banking practices; Ford's sympathies are all on the side of populism and the New Deal.[26] In direct contrast to Gatewood's overtalkativeness, the romance between Dallas and Ringo proceeds wordlessly, in close-up exchanges of heated glances.

By the second rest station, Apache Wells, the coach has traveled further away from civilization, further into the wilderness. This is emphasized to the viewer by the ethnicity of the landlords: Chris is Mexican and his wife, Yakima, Apache. Chris, a figure of fun, speaks an accented baby talk quoted above, while Yakima is silent and menacing. A short phrase reveals here that Ringo, of all the white characters, is the only one who knows Spanish. Later, Ringo declares his love for Dallas and proposes to her in slow, halting phrases: "It's a nice place . . . a real nice place . . . trees . . . and grass . . . water. . . . There's a cabin half-built . . . a man could live there . . . and a woman." In the kitchen the next morning, Ringo and Dallas again manage to speak alone, and here we find an archetypal statement of the Western hero's resolve to face his enemies, countered by the woman's arguments:

> RINGO: Well, there's some things a man just can't run away from. . . .
> DALLAS: Would it make us any happier if Luke Plummer was dead?

The threat of the Apaches cuts short Ringo's attempted escape and Lucy Mallory's convalescence as the passengers flee in the stagecoach. They need Ringo to help in their defense, but Curly is angry about Ringo's escape attempt. Like so many Westerns, *Stagecoach* goes out of its way to bring up the sanctity of a verbal promise:

> CURLY: Will you give me your word you won't try to escape again?
> RINGO: I give you my word . . . to Lordsburg.

After the stage fords the river at East Ferry, the camera shows us Indians on the hillside watching its progress. This makes the ensuing dialogue in the coach, where the passengers think the danger has passed and start making amends to one another, highly ironical. The irony comes to a head as Doc drinks to his companions' health just as an arrow whistles through the window, striking Peacock. The elaborate Indian attack that follows is mostly devoid of dialogue, with only a few shouts about ammunition and the horses. Hatfield's death, however, must be postponed until he verbally reveals the secret of his identity as the fallen son of Judge Ringfield to Lucy Mallory.

Arriving in Lordsburg, most of the film's subplots are tied up: Lucy's husband is waiting for her, Gatewood is arrested, Peacock will be cared for. This clears the decks for the film to concentrate on Ringo and Dallas. Dallas's own secret, the fact that she is a prostitute, is revealed, but Ford avoids any censorship difficulties by accomplishing this revelation visually as opposed to verbally, by having Ringo walk with her to the seamy side of town in a series of expressionistic dolly shots. Ringo's response to the revelation is quite compressed; he doesn't say, "I don't care what happened in your past. I'm no saint either. Together we can start anew." Instead, Ringo says simply, "I asked you to marry me, didn't I?" and orders Dallas, "Wait here."

Ringo never speaks to the Plummer brothers; he sends Doc and Buck in the role of "seconds" spreading word of his challenge. The Plummers too, are a remarkably terse lot, although it is interesting to notice that Luke, like Ringo, displays his ability to speak Spanish. Yet the showdown itself is surrounded by words: first the newspaper editor's precipitant rewriting of his front page: "Take this down. 'The Ringo Kid was killed on Main Street in Lordsburg tonight and among the additional dead were . . . ' Leave that blank for a spell." And then after the shots ring out, Dallas's anguished cries, "Ringo, Ringo, Ringo," work on the viewer's fears.

At the end, after the shoot-out, Curly and Doc permit Dallas and Ringo to steal away from the corrupt town to Ringo's edenic ranch. Doc's line, "Well, they're saved from the blessings of civilization," and Curly's ambiguous, "Yeah," have been much commented upon, because they so directly encapsulate the film's—and the whole genre's—ambivalence about wilderness versus civilization. Chapter 1 discussed the thematic importance of dialogue placed at a movie's end: these lines are the capstone of *Stagecoach*; the film could not attain the same sense of completeness without them.

In the above discussion, I've tried to show how the dialogue "works" in *Stagecoach,* and how it typifies the generalizations I've been making about the use of dialogue in Westerns, in particular, and in narrative film in general. Let us turn to another example, made more than twenty years later. The source material, Akira Kurosawa's *The Seven Samurai* (1954), may have provided William Roberts, the screenwriter, with many plot points, but since it is in Japanese, it didn't provide him with any ready-made dialogue. According to Joseph Anderson, one of the main differences between Kurosawa's original and John Sturges's remake is that the former uses very little conversation and de-emphasizes what it does employ, so that the words serve primarily as sound effects.[27]

The Magnificent Seven is manifestly a "professional" Western, a film simultaneously celebrating the prowess and elite status of a group of men and stressing their loneliness and sacrifice. Despite its popularity with audiences, it has received little critical attention. One of the few academic analyses is Richard Slotkin's reading of its ideological ramifications: because of the film's condescension to the

Mexican villagers, its emphasis on the mastery, nobility, and honor of their American protectors, and its glorification of violence, Slotkin sees it as a prescient allegory of the cultural attitudes that enabled the Vietnam War.[28]

The Magnificent Seven starts with Calvera's raiding party of bandits entering the Mexican village. Calvera, as played by Eli Wallach, is extremely chatty; he pretends to be engaging in a social call on Sotero, while he actually plunders the village and treats himself to comforts. Calvero dominates the conversation (just as he dominates the village); like Gatewood, he talks too much, and like Gatewood, his words reveal him to be a terrible hypocrite.

> CALVERA: Sotero, my good friend. How are you? You have a drink? I can't tell you what a pleasure it is to see a village like this. Santos! (*Calvera throws a fur to henchman.*) So much restlessness and change in the outside world. People no longer content with their station in life. Women's fashions, shameless. [Give me a] Cigar. Eh, religion! You'd weep if you saw how true religion is now a thing of the past. Last month we were in San Juan—rich town. Sit down. Rich town, much blessed by God. Big church. Not like here. Little church, priest comes twice a year. Big one. You'd think we find gold candlesticks. Poor box filled to overflowing. You know what we found? Brass candlesticks. Almost nothing in the poor box.
>
> HENCHMAN: We took it anyway.
>
> CALVERA: I *know* we took it anyway. I'm trying to show him how little religion some people now have.

Calvera's murder of one of the villagers later in the scene is hardly needed; we already are convinced of what a terrible villain he is by his conversation.

Here and throughout, Wallach's Mexican accent is light; like the rest of the Mexican characters in the film, however, he speaks in syntactically simple sentences: "Not like here. Little church, priest comes twice a year. Big one." Very few Spanish words or phrases used in the film, because to do so would raise questions as to how the American gunfighters and the Mexicans communicate. Instead, the Spanish language is replaced by a lightly accented, slightly singsong style. For instance, after Calvero's group leaves, the villagers discuss how to cope with his attacks:

HILARIO: Even if we had the guns, we know how to plant and grow.
We don't know how to kill.
OLD MAN: Then learn, or die.

This use of language bolsters Richard Slotkin's reading of the film:

> Right from the first we see that the differences between Mexicans and Americans have both a racial and a class aspect: the Americans are a White aristocracy or elite whose caste-mark is their capacity for effective violence; the Mexicans are non-White peasants, technologically and militarily incompetent. Gunfighter professionalism is thus a metonymy of the class and ethnic superiority of Americans to Mexicans.[29]

The villagers decide to travel to an American border town to buy guns. Interestingly, the town is never named (nor, for that matter, is the Mexican village). "Unnamed," "unanchored," the action proceeds in a mythic void.

Into this void steps the Western hero. The camera cuts to an argument in progress between an undertaker and two traveling salesmen. The salesmen want to pay for the burial of an Indian who has died in the street, but the undertaker explains that because the townspeople are prejudiced against Indians, no one will drive the hearse.* All parties are speaking at great length, in a formal "Eastern" style. Off-screen a voice interrupts, "Oh hell!" The camera reframes to show Chris (Yul Brynner), dressed spiffily in black, looking tough. "If that's all that's holding things up, I'll drive the rig." Here is a man who believes in action, not talk.

Chris is joined on top of the hearse by another onlooker, Vin (Steve McQueen), who volunteers to ride shotgun, and their conversation as they drive, expecting trouble, could be the prototype for what I've been called compressed Western speech. Brynner's voice is low, his enunciation crisp; his ambiguous foreign accent almost undetectable. McQueen's voice is slightly higher pitched and more relaxed. (Vin will later prove more talkative; on two occasions he tells parables.) Their bodily gestures convey exaggerated ease, Chris smoking a cigar, Vin adjusting his hat. Here is a excerpt of their conversation on the hearse:

---

* This controversy is implausible. It is another case of allegory-lite, having much more to do with racial prejudice in 1960, than with bigotry on the frontier.

VIN: New in town?
CHRIS: Yeah.
  VIN: Where ya from?
CHRIS: Dodge. You?
  VIN: Tombstone. See any action up there?
CHRIS: Nuh, huh. Tombstone?
  VIN: Same. People all settled down.
CHRIS: Same all over.

The contrast between Chris and Vin and the Eastern traveling sales-men is underlined after they succeed in facing down the town big-ots. One of the salesmen effusively praises Chris and Vin, offers them liquor, brings up his wife: "Wait till Flora hears about this. You know she won't believe one word of it." Chris, on the other hand, de-liberately substitutes gestures for speech:

SALESMAN: Where ya from? (*Chris points behind him.*) Oh yeah, Where ya going? (*Chris points in front.*)

Sturges's emphasis on hand gestures continues throughout the film.

Duly impressed, the Mexican villagers approach Chris and hire him to help them. He accepts because he is touched by their desper-ation: "I have been offered a lot for work, but never everything." Chris seeks additional gunfighters, and scenes follow in which he engages Harry (Brad Dexter), Vin, and Riley (Charles Bronson), turning down Chico (Horst Buchholz), a young Mexican kid who longs for acceptance, but who is too hot-headed and immature, demonstrated throughout the film by his tendency to shoot off his mouth. Each time a new gunfighter joins up, Vin holds up the count on his fingers.

Significantly, the most esteemed gunfighter, the deadliest, Britt (James Coburn), is introduced as the most silent. Britt enters the film in a scene where he is challenged to a duel, his knife-throwing ver-sus his opponent's pistol, yet even before Britt proves his speed, aim, and reflexes superior, he has proven himself to be more macho than his competitor by his marked silence. The other man is driven crazy by Britt's failure to engage verbally; the quieter Britt is, the more his antagonist rages and blusters.

After Lee (Robert Vaughn), another deadly, doomed Southerner, joins the group, they leave for Mexico. The scenes of them riding, like the scenes of the stagecoach cutting across the desert, are visually spectacular and accompanied by stirring music composed here by Elmer Bernstein. Worn down by Chico's persistence, the gunfighters accept him into their group, but they are embarrassed by Chico when, upon arrival in the village, he arrogantly dresses down the inhabitants for the tepidness of their welcome. The Seven begin their preparations for the village's defense, teaching the villagers to shoot, building nets and walls, and so on.

The initial confrontation between Calvera and the Seven is notable for exemplifying the threats, commands, and compression I see as integral to Westerns. Calvera and his men have ridden into the town, and the Seven take turns revealing themselves and the trap they have laid.

CALVERA: I should have guessed. When my men didn't come back I should've guessed. How many of you did they hire?

CHRIS: Enough.

CALVERA: New wall.

CHRIS: There are lots of new walls. All around.

CALVERA: They won't keep me out.

CHRIS: They were built to keep you in.

CALVERA: You hear that?! We're trapped! All forty of us, by these three, or is it four? They couldn't afford to hire more than that.

HARRY: We come cheaper by the bunch.

CALVERA: Five! Even five wouldn't give us too much trouble.

CHRIS: There won't be any trouble . . . if you ride on.

CALVERA: Ride on?! I'm going into the hills for the winter, where am I going to get the food for my men?

CHICO: Buy it or grow it!

RILEY: Or maybe even work for it.

CALVERA: Seven. Somehow I don't think you've solved my problem.

CHRIS: Solving your problems isn't our line.

VIN: We deal in lead, friend.

CALVERA: So do I. We're in the same business, huh?

VIN: Only as competitors.

CALVERA: Why not as partners? Suppose I offer you equal shares?

CHRIS: Of what?

CALVERA: Everything. To the last grain.

CHICO: And the people in the village? What about them?

CALVERA: I leave it to you. Can men of our profession worry about things like that? It may even be sacrilegious. If God didn't want them sheared, he would not have made them sheep. What do you think?

CHRIS: Ride on.

41. *The Magnificent Seven.* CHRIS: Ride on.

Here is the tang of Western dialogue. This bite comes from the use of metaphors, "dealing in lead," "shearing sheep;" it's in the pairing of phrases "keep you out/keep you in," "competitors/partners;" it's in the rhythm of the short phrases, and the alternation of speakers. Perhaps most of all, the power of this dialogue comes from repeated, abrupt commands, ending climactically with Chris's low, authoritative: "Ride on" (fig. 41).

The dialogue leads into the first major battle, a scene of wordless action in which the Seven and the villagers roust Calvera and his men. After the fight, the film proceeds, via dialogue, with scenes primarily designed to reveal the characters of the Seven. Lee talks to the villagers about his nightmares and lost nerve. Harry tries to find out about buried treasure, which he believes will make this job turn out to be more lucrative than the measly twenty dollars he has been promised. Riley is befriended by three young boys and reveals to them that he is half-Mexican. Chico has attracted the regard of a young Mexican girl; he is mostly interested in bragging to her, while she tries to get him to pay attention to her charms. It is during this lull that Vin, in the ledger scene quoted above, voices his doubts about the life of a gunfighter.

The plot now takes complicated turns, all, of course, explained by dialogue. Chico puts on a disguise and penetrates Calvera's camp. When he returns, he informs everyone that Calvera and his men will not leave the village alone, because they are already desperate for food and provisions. The villagers are frightened and despondent; the Seven talk of quitting. Chris reminds them that they took a contract. (Again the emphasis on keeping one's word.) The Seven ride out to "lower the odds" by picking off some of Calvero's men, but Calvero's camp is mysteriously empty; on returning to the village, they discover that Sotero has betrayed them by surrendering it to Calvera. Calvera confiscates the Seven's guns but allows them to leave unharmed.

When their captors free them and return their guns, all of the gunfighters—with the exception of Harry—decide to return to retake the village. They are neither subtle nor quiet about explaining their reasons; their pride and sense of commitment demand a return, even if it may be suicidal. Even Britt is moved to speech: "Nobody throws me my own guns and says run. . . . Nobody!" They return to the village and engage in another pitched battle. Harry (who has belatedly returned to the fray), Riley, Lee, and Britt are killed, but they succeed in vanquishing the bandits.

At the end of the film, the three surviving gunfighters are blessed by a Wise Old Man (played by a Russian actor, not a Mexican) in a rare burst of Spanish: "Via con Dios." Chico, who has now matured, decides to stay with his girlfriend, but he does so with newfound quiet restraint. Chris and Vin "ride on," but not until Chris has bluntly stated the moral of the film, in a line lifted from *The Seven Samurai*, about how the gunfighters have lost, and only the farmers have won.

Joseph Anderson has singled out the dialogue in *The Magnificent Seven* for criticism.

> This explicit, verbal definition of character requires expositional dialogue in the manner of traditional theater. . . . But Sturges and Roberts are not content to leave their people as over-articulate individuals. Each character must also express a capsule philosophy which makes him less of an individual and more of a personification of a familiar point of view. For instance, Harry, the treasure-seeker, becomes the materialistic objection to social conscience.[30]

There *are* lines in *The Magnificent Seven* that make me cringe, such as those where Chico's braggadocio is overstressed and the maudlin interactions between Bernardo Riley and the little boys, which lead into fulsome praises of fatherhood: "You think I'm brave because I carry a gun? Well, your fathers are much braver because they carry responsibility!" But I don't agree with Anderson's main point, that the dialogue is flawed because it is overly explicit.

The straightforward, almost baldness of the dialogue in *The Magnificent Seven* is a characteristic of the genre. Is there a Western with "subtle" dialogue? Certainly not *Stagecoach*, which has been criticized on the same grounds, nor *High Noon*, nor *Shane*, nor *Red River*, nor *The Gunfighter*, nor *The Searchers*, nor *Liberty Valance*, nor *Ride the High Country*. And yet, for that matter, the other signifiers in Westerns are hardly "subtle"—the grand vistas, the rock formations, the expressive costumes, the rousing music are also quite explicit. Like Greek tragedies, like melodramas, Westerns may be quite complicated, and their resolutions fraught or ambiguous, but their characters' moral complexities and the issues involved in the conflict are writ large against the sky. Or, to switch metaphors, they are *spoken loudly into the wind*. Dialogue serves to articulate both what is going on and what is at stake.

FIVE

Word Play

Dialogue in Screwball Comedies

Thirties sound comedy . . . could be defined as the kind of
film where dialogue is most indulged, the most talking kind
of talking picture.

Babington and Evans,
Affairs to Remember (1989)

The importance of dialogue in screwball comedy has long been recognized. Eliot Rubinstein notes, for instance, "The world of screwball
courtship is a world of talk."[1] Which is not to say that dialogue in
such comedies has never been criticized—witness Bosley Crowther's
attack on Preston Sturges's *The Palm Beach Story* (1942): "[The film] is
generally slow and garrulous. . . . [Sturges] is short on action and very
long on trivial talk . . . It should have been a breathless comedy, but
only the actors are breathless—and that from talking so much."[2]

And what is the camera doing during all this talk? The flip answer
would be "not much," and such an assessment is accurate if one defines expert filmmaking only as breathtaking long shots of scenery,
dramatic use of light and shadows, or rapid editing of action sequences—none of which are usually found in American screwball
comedies of the 1930s and 1940s. Instead, these movies feature long
takes that allow the scenes' tension to build, wide shots that permit
us to see the characters in spatial relation to one another, lighting
that flatters the stars and the expensive sets, and subtle reframings to
emphasize a line or a reaction shot. The prominence of "talk" in
screwball comedies leads to an understated, but by no means inartistic, visual style.

Genre definition is a vexing problem for all genres—"screwball comedy" is a particularly difficult term. Recent scholarship bifurcates the broad term "comedy" into two major lines: "comedian comedy," which focuses on the special comic talents of a star (Chaplin, Keaton, Woody Allen, Steve Martin, Whoopi Goldberg), and "romantic comedy," which emphasizes instead a series of narrative conflicts leading to the union of a heterosexual couple.[3] As Northrop Frye has taught us, the union of the young lovers symbolizes the creation of a new vision of society, dominated by youth and freedom from old constraints.[4] "Screwball" comedy is a particular subset of "romantic comedy," a cycle of films that appeared primarily in the 1930s and 1940s. Romantic comedy as a whole is too varied and extensive a field for dialogue analysis; screwball comedies present a more unified and bounded set of texts.

Various explanations have been offered as to why this cycle flourished in those years: the Depression may have engendered a desire for an affirmative, escapist retreat; the enforcement of the Production Code by the studios may have necessitated that sexual energy find covert forms of expression; changes in the status of women and a rising divorce rate may have triggered a cultural reexamination of the relations between the sexes.[5] While not united by a setting as immediately identifiable as in the case of Westerns, screwballs share a particular constellation of features: upper-class settings and characters, generally situated in New York City for at least a portion of the action (with New York portrayed as the apotheosis of modern life); no children (the lovers must be free to act childishly themselves); art deco sets (all those wondrous nightclubs and apartment buildings); glamorous costumes (particularly fanciful hats); and the integration of slapstick physical comedy. The films also share common narrative/thematic threads, in that they generally celebrate play, spontaneity and romance, and revolt against dullness, propriety, and stuffy conventionality. Their courtships are markedly unsentimental and often combative. Moreover, their women protagonists are unusually intelligent and assertive, perhaps, in one way or another "unruly," deliberately flaunting traditional views of feminine behavior and decorum.[6] Concentrating on the films' handling of their female characters, Diane Carson argues that the genre revolves around the taming of the woman who is too threatening.[7] Bruce Babington and Peter Evans take a more affirmative stance in seeing screwball heroines as "redemptresses of a world too long in thrall to the irrationalities/rationalities, largely male-created, of modern life."[8] Stanley Cavell's *Pursuits of Happiness* focuses less on the unique role of the woman in these films, choosing instead to stress that both halves of the couple come to new maturity about the meaning of love; in his eyes these films are linked by a movement—literal or figurative—toward a deep conscious commitment, a "remarriage."[9]

Dialogue is used in screwballs, as it is in Westerns, as a tool of character definition and evaluation, but the rules of the game have changed. Verbal dexterity is as highly prized here as the quick draw is in Westerns. In Frank Capra's *It Happened One Night* (1934), Clark Gable's character, Peter Warne, gets into an argument with a bus driver over moving some newspapers. The bus driver, played by Ward Bond (who soon thereafter became a perennial denizen of John Ford's West), is completely inarticulate; all he can respond is, "Oh yeah?" as Peter verbally runs circles around him. Just as Westerns use dialogue to separate the laconic Westerners from the tenderfoots, screwballs use language to separate the quick-witted stars from the duller clods around them.

Leo McCarey's *The Awful Truth* (1937) is frequently cited as one of the quintessential screwballs; significantly, this film overtly turns Western values upside-down. The sincere Oklahoman, Dan Leeson (Ralph Bellamy), is the fool, and his deficiencies are apparent in such lines as: "Oklahoma's pretty swell," or "Back on my ranch I got a little red rooster and a little brown hen and they fight all the time too. But every once in a while they make up and they're right friendly." By contrast, the urbanites, Jerry (Cary Grant) and Lucy Warriner (Irene Dunne), are clever and sophisticated.

Oklahomans are not the only category selected for ridicule in screwball comedy and specifically ridiculed because of the way they speak. "Hicks" of all stripes, like the mercenary townspeople of Warsaw, Vermont, in *Nothing Sacred* (1937), who are lambasted for their tight-lipped, unfriendly "Yeps" and "Nopes," are figures of fun. So too are immigrants, from Armand in *The Awful Truth*, to Carlo in *My Man Godfrey* (1936), to Mr. Louis Louis in *Easy Living* (1937). Revealingly, in both Mark Sandrich's *Shall We Dance* (1937) and Preston Sturges's *The Lady Eve* (1941), one of the protagonists masquerades as an upper-class foreigner. In *Shall We Dance*, Pete Peters (Astaire) pretends to be a Russian ballet star, "The Great Petrov," a disguise that involves heel clicking and other extravagant gestures; a low, guttural voice; a fake Russian accent; wobbly pronouns, a sprinkling of *nyet*s, and an "Ochi chernye" or two.[10] In *The Lady Eve*, Jean Harrington (Stanwyck) pretends to be a member of the British nobility by donning white gloves, a diamond tiara, a British accent, and a vocabulary featuring such Britishisms as "ripping," "tube," "tram," and "toodle-oo." In both films, the plot revolves around showing the absurdity of the foreign guise and the superiority in all respects of the genuine underlying American identity. Examples such as these support Mark Winokur's argument that under the surface, American films of the time period were an avenue for working out the tensions of emigration and cultural assimilation.[11]

In screwballs, "Western," "hick," and "foreign" accents are all placed in opposition to a speech pattern I'll call "Eastern upper-class, spiced by urban slang." True New York or Boston accents are not found; instead, one notes the crisp articulation of the "transatlantic style" advocated by dialogue coaches of the 1930s as "proper" pronunciation. This dialect is leavened, however, by a certain amount of contemporary slang:[12] Walter Burns calls Hildy "doll face"; Jean Harrington terms Charles a "sap"; Peter Warne says "prize sucker," "spill the beans," "shut your trap." These characters are not moldering old fossils, but rather vibrant participants in modern city life. Howard Hawks's *Ball of Fire* (1941), presents the story of a literary scholar investigating contemporary slang, and its wedding of Bertram Potts's pedantry with Sugarpuss O'Shea's street-smart argot could be taken as a metaphor for the genre's overall verbal strategy.

In Westerns, the romantic couple go horseback riding together; in musicals, they sing a duet. In screwballs, the lovers talk. "Verbal exchanges function mainly to create a sense of attraction, an 'electricity,' " David Shumway notes.[13] Or, as Pauline Kael remarks: "Love became slightly surreal; it became stylized—lovers talked back to each other, and fast. Comedy became the new romance, and trading wisecracks was its courtship rite."[14] Whereas Fred Astaire and Ginger Rogers fall in love when they dance together—each realizes that the other is the perfect partner—in screwball, the lovers learn that the other is the only one he/she can converse with. As Gerald Mast notices regarding Hildy Johnson and Walter Burns: "The two apparent antagonists speak in an identical rhythm, in identical cadences, singing perfect verbal duets—which reveal that the two are spiritually and truly one. Their minds click away at the same pace and in the same rhythm (as opposed to the slow Bruce), just as their words do."[15] *His Girl Friday*'s rhythm happens to be particularly fast. By contrast, in Ernst Lubitsch's *Trouble in Paradise* (1932), Gaston and Mariette speak very slowly, sensuously prolonging their replies:

> MARIETTE: And I wouldn't hesitate one instant to ruin your reputation. (*She snaps her finger*) Like that.
> GASTON: You wouldn't?
> MARIETTE: No, I wouldn't.
> GASTON: (*snaps*) Like that?
> MARIETTE: (*snaps*) Like that.
> GASTON: I know all your tricks.
> MARIETTE: And you're going to fall for them.
> GASTON: So you think you can get me?
> MARIETTE: Any minute I want.
> GASTON: You're conceited.
> MARIETTE: But attractive . . .
> GASTON: Now let me tell you . . .
> MARIETTE: Shut up. Kiss me! (*They kiss.*) Wasting all this marvelous time with arguments.

What is important is not the tempo per se, but the match between the protagonists. In screwballs we are supposed to notice, not only that the central couple are uniquely suited for each other by the way their talk is synchronized, but also that other potential suitors—for instance, Bruce Baldwin in *His Girl Friday*, Francois Filiba in *Trouble in Paradise*—are all wrong.

What makes the dialogue of these comedies so funny? Does screwball depend upon repartee in the same way that the comedies of Shakespeare, Congreve, or Oscar Wilde do? This depends on how one defines "repartee." C. L. Barber argues: "In repartee, each keeps jumping the other's words to take them and make them his own, finding a meaning in them which was not intended."[16] Similarly, M. H. Abrams teaches us that the term was taken from fencing "to signify a contest of wit, in which each person tries to cap the remark of the other, or to turn it to his or her own advantage."[17] For instance, in *The Taming of the Shrew*, Petruchio greets Katherina with an elaborate witticism on "Kate," which is a homonym for *"cate,"* meaning "delicacies," and she answers with puns on "moved" and "moveable," the latter meaning *a piece of furniture.*

> PET.: You lie, in faith, for you are call'd plain Kate,
>   And bonny Kate, and sometimes Kate the curst;
>   But Kate, the prettiest Kate in Christendom,
>   Kate of Kate-Hall, my super-dainty Kate,
>   For dainties are all Kates, and therefore, Kate,
>   Take this of me, Kate of my consolation—
>   Hearing thy mildness prais'd in every town,
>   Thy virtues spoke of, thy beauty sounded,
>   Yet not so deeply as to thee belongs,
>   Myself am mov'd to woo thee for my wife.
> KATE: Mov'd in good time! Let him that mov'd you hither
>   Remove you hence. I knew you at the first
>   You were a moveable. (2.1.185–97)

Kate's implication that Petruchio is a piece of furniture next prompts him to ask her to sit on his lap, leading into puns about asses bearing burdens and women bearing children. Each comment is answered by an elaborate (and perhaps bawdy) retort.

This type of dialogue is not what accounts for the humor of screwball comedy. For all their upper-class trappings, these cinematic characters are not the equal in "wit" to Beatrice and Benedick or Mirabell and Milamant; their lines are shorter and less "clever." Nick and Nora Charles are given to exchanging puns in *The Thin Man* movies, but the puns are silly, not witty. Most of these films were scripted by moderately successful New York playwrights who gave up the theater for Hollywood—Preston Sturges, Sidney Buchman, Frances Goodrich and Albert Hackett, Robert Riskin—or by a gang of irreverent former newspapermen and critics—Ben Hecht, Dudley Nichols, Norman Krasna, Samson Raphaelson, Charles Lederer, Billy Wilder, and Charles Brackett. Their prose style is more offhand, more colloquial, plainer—I'd like to say, more "American." Just as *The Lady Eve* elevates Jean over Eve, and *Shall We Dance* favors plain Pete Peters over Petrov, so these films turn, not to theatrical "repartee," but to wisecracks.

Which is not to say that Shakespearean comedy is not lurking behind screwball comedy, for Cavell has shown the numerous parallels and resonances. Moreover, screwball as a genre is tightly tied to the theatrical tradition, in that many of the films are adaptations of stage plays. But rather than Shakespeare, I believe that the most immediate theatrical model was Noël Coward, whose plays—*Hay Fever* (1925), *Private Lives* (1930), *Design for Living* (1933), *Present Laughter* (1939), *Blithe Spirit* (1941)—were incredibly popular throughout the time period of screwball comedy. John Lahr's discussion of Coward reveals a screwball philosophy:

> Frivolity, as Coward embodies it, was an act of freedom. . . . In all these comedies of bad manners, the characters are grown-up adolescents. There is no family life to speak of, no children, no commitment except to pleasure. The characters do no real work; and money, in a time of world depression, hunger marches and war, is taken for granted.[18]

Three Coward plays were made into movies in the 1930s, and Coward, who starred in Hecht's 1936 *The Scoundrel*, had numerous direct contacts with Hollywood. James Harvey testifies to the specific influence of *Private Lives:* "Probably no romantic couple of the time made more impact than Elyot and Amanda."[19]

What is most striking to me about screwball's debt to Coward is Coward's own analysis of his dialogue:

> To me, the essence of good comedy writing is that perfectly ordinary phrases such as "Just fancy!" should, by virtue of their context, achieve greater laughs than the most literate epigrams. Some of the biggest laughs in *Hay Fever* occur on such lines as "Go on", "No there isn't, is there?" and "This haddock's disgusting." There are many other glittering examples of my sophistication in the same vein. . . . I would add that the sort of lines above mentioned have to be impeccably delivered.[20]

Perfectly ordinary phrases, which are funny because of their context and because of the way in which they are delivered—this may be the best description of the writing in screwball comedy. To go back a moment to *The Awful Truth,* some of the funniest writing is found in the nightclub scene where Jerry runs into Lucy and Dan out on the town and teases her about the prospect of her life after marrying Dan. (Just as "commanding" is a common trope in Westerns, "teasing" is a very common speech act in screwball comedy.)

JERRY: Ah. So you're gonna live in Oklahoma, eh Lucy? How I envy you. Ever since I was a small boy that name has been filled with magic for me. Ok-la-homa.

> DAN: We're gonna live right in Oklahoma City.
> JERRY: Not Oklahoma City itself? Lucy, you lucky girl. No more running around the night spots, no more prowling around in New York shops. I shall think of you every time a new show opens and say to myself, "She's well out of it."
> DAN: New York's all right for a visit but I—
> JERRY: (*Chiming in unison with Dan, who continues*): Wouldn't want to live here.
> LUCY: I know I'll enjoy Oklahoma City.
> JERRY: But of course. And if it should get dull, you can always go over to Tulsa for the weekend.

The scripting of the scene is clever—the buildup (or down) from Oklahoma the state, to Oklahoma City, to Tulsa (!) is a good example of "end position emphasis" discussed earlier. But these lines are not polished epigrams. What makes the scene is the acting: Irene Dunne's pained expression, and the way she uncomfortably shifts her gaze, and Grant's mischievous glee, and the way he delivers the lines, from his stringing out "Ok-la-homa" to his mocking "She's well out of it," to the way he hits the word "Tulsa."[21] Of course, all dialogue needs to be performed skillfully, but the impeccable delivery that Noël Coward expects is particularly crucial in screwball comedy.

The example from *The Awful Truth* illustrates that screwball depends particularly heavily on irony, on the double-layering between what the characters are saying on the surface and what the eavesdropping audience understands. Occasionally, a character like Jerry is consciously being sarcastic. But Dan Leeson's line about not wanting to live in New York is also amusing, not because Leeson is consciously being sarcastic, but because he isn't—he's mouthing this cliché completely sincerely, without even knowing it is a cliché, because he is an Oklahoman who doesn't even know what he's missing by not living in New York. The viewer, however, is "in the know" and our smile is prompted by our feelings of superiority. In short, to a marked degree, the dialogue of screwball operates on two levels, and such dialogue is always pointed toward the audience. In *The Lady Eve*, during the scene at the racetrack when Jean first hatches her plan to impersonate a British lady and get her revenge on Charles, she remarks to her fellow con artists: "I need him [Charles] like the ax needs the turkey." In the background, a racetrack bell sounds, warning the imminent start of another race. Jean continues, "Better go make your bets." On the surface that last warning relates to her companions' racetrack wagering, but in actuality, the remark, which is captured in close-up, is direct address to the viewer, a boast about who is going to win this contest of pride and love.

This double-layeredness of screwball dialogue is also manifest in the high incidence of extratextual references. Many commentators have pointed out the number of times these films refer to themselves, to each other, to Hollywood in general, and to contemporary issues. The joking references range from *Trouble in Paradise*'s wry admission that "beginnings are difficult," to *His Girl Friday*'s repetition of a scene from *The Awful Truth*, to *Sullivan's Travels* satire of movie-making, to *Bringing Up Baby*'s jokes about Cary Grant's real name, Archibald Leach. Similarly, several of the films include reference to Depression-era politics and events, such as comments about prosperity being just around the corner. My students' delight when they catch one of these references emphasizes to me that such lines function both as an inside joke for the filmmakers, and to flatter viewers who are in the know, to make them feel like insiders.*

Sly extratextual references inform a scene in Billy Wilder's *The Major and the Minor* (1942). While dancing at the cadet ball, Susu Applegate (Ginger Rogers) must continually chastise her young escorts for trying to take liberties. Susu begins a litany of "Musts" and "Must Nots" to the cadets—the reference is to the strictures of the Hays Office's Production Code. This rather glib sideswipe shows backhanded recognition of the fact that the Production Code had a major effect on this cycle of films. As Rubinstein argues: "The very style of screwball, the complexity and inventiveness and wit of its detours around certain facts of certain lives, the force of its attack on the very pieties it is pledged to sustain, cannot be explained without recognition of the censors. Screwball comedy is censored comedy."[22]

Exactly how did the pressure of censorship affect the scripting? Richard Maltby believes that the censors "recognized that if the Code

---

* "Self-conscious" dialogue, dialogue that in some way lays bare the film's status as a film, is also very prevalent in contemporary horror films. Thus, in *Scream* (1996), one of the victims argues that she can't be murdered because she must be alive for the sequel. In this genre too such dialogue is both funny and flattering to the viewer's sense of sophistication.

was to remain effective, it had to allow the studios to develop a system of representational conventions 'from which conclusions might be drawn by the sophisticated mind, but which would mean nothing to the unsophisticated and inexperienced.' "[23] Maltby states that screwball in particular worked out methods of "encoding the representation of sexuality in such a way that a pre-existent knowledge was required to gain access to it."[24] Half of *Shall We Dance* is about whether Pete Peters and Linda Keane have been sleeping together, whether she's pregnant, and whether the door between their connecting hotel rooms should be locked or unlocked to allow for nighttime passage, but all of this is conveyed through circumlocutions that children might not understand. The crisis of George Cukor's *The Philadelphia Story* (1940) must be equally mystifying to innocents. Tracy believes that she has committed a terrible lapse by getting drunk and having sex with Mac on the eve of her marriage to Kittridge. In the last scene she goes through a moral reevaluation of herself, apologizes to Dexter, breaks off her engagement to Kittridge, and eventually finds out from Mac that her honor is intact, because, although he was attracted by her, she was "a little worse, or better, for wine and there are rules about that." Note the extreme vagueness of Mac's noun "that"; all of this narrative action proceeds via wording that is perfectly understandable to adults but also deliberately vague, providing a veneer of deniability. In every screwball, a disparity exists between the literal meaning of the sentences and the inferences—ironic, extratextual, sexual—that the sophisticated viewer is supposed to perceive. This disparity works to flatter the viewer's sense of sophistication.

The spirit of fun is also enhanced through the genre's stress on courtship through verbal play, and playacting. James Naremore offers an in-depth discussion of the sequence in Cukor's *Holiday* (1938) in the playroom where Linda Seaton slips proteanly into other "voices"—a cop, a sour patriarch, a society matron, and so on—as she teases Johnny about his upcoming difficulties being accepted as her sister's fiancé by the snobby Seaton family.[25] To me, the more important moment of playacting occurs much earlier in the film, when Linda and Johnny first meet.

LINDA: And of course you've heard about me. I'm the black sheep.
JOHNNY: Baaa.
LINDA: That's a goat.

> JULIA: Johnny, don't pay any attention to her.
> JOHNNY: No, it's too late, the engagement's off. I won't marry into a
> family with a black sheep.
> LINDA: I think I like this man.

From this evidence that Johnny is quick-witted and relaxed enough to *play* with her, the audience knows instantly that Linda and he are meant for each other. A similar moment occurs in *It Happened One Night* when Ellie and Peter are questioned by detectives searching for Ellie. To throw them off the scent, Ellie and Peter playact an argument between a lower-class couple; through combining forces to mislead the opposition, and through finding out how well they can pick up on each other's cues, the two leads discover their bond.*

Above, I was referring to role-playing that is spontaneous and momentary, but calculated masquerades are also endemic to screwball comedy. "By playing fictional characters, the screwball characters freed themselves of their original personalities, expectations and value systems," Tina Olsin Lent remarks.[26] In *My Man Godfrey*, Godfrey feigns being a bum when he's really one of the Parkes of Boston, and John Sullivan in *Sullivan's Travels* pretends to be a hobo to gain experience for his social realist film. In *The Awful Truth*, Lucy Warriner breaks up the romance between Jerry and his rich fiancée by impersonating Jerry's fictitious sister, Lola, as a vulgar alcoholic. Part of the madcap aura of screwballs arises because the masquerading proves infectious and uncontrollable, becoming more and more involved and spreading from one character to another. Susan Applegate, in *The Major and the Minor*, first impersonates a twelve-year-old in order to ride on the train on a half-fare ticket; then she impersonates Kirby's girlfriend, Pamela, and still later she pretends she is Susu's mother. In *Midnight* (1939), Eve Peabody feigns being Baroness Czerny, then her cab-driver suitor pretends to be Baron Czerny, and then her friend gets on the phone and assumes the guise of their fictional baby daughter, Francie! Of the canonic screwballs, only *His Girl Friday* offers no disguise as such, but James Harvey insightfully notes that Walter and Hildy, "are

---

* Similar "bonding through verbal playacting" occurs in films that, while not technically screwball comedies, demonstrate the enduring influence of the genre: look at Philip Marlowe's and Vivian Rutledge's phone call to the police in *The Big Sleep*, or at Joe Gillis's and Betty Schaefer's New Year's Eve flirtation in *Sunset Boulevard*.

both consummate stylists—and conscious self-parodists. And their way of quarreling, as in this case, is to *perform* to each other, their best and most challenging audience. . . . Hildy and Walter are the kind of characters—Hawks's kind of characters—who impersonate themselves."[27]

Masquerades may be abetted by costume changes—Susu Applegate's knee socks and braids, Lola Warriner's fringed dress—but the chief way in which they are enacted is verbally. In each case, the strategy is to co-opt the verbal style of a certain social type and exaggerate it beyond measure. No twelve-year-old ever spoke like Susu: "Oh, what a lovely room! Goldfishes! Look at the ones with the flopsy wopsy tails! That one's sticking his nose up. He wants his din din." The language is exaggerated to foreground for the audience the character's performance, and his or her infectious joy in the role-playing. Masquerading is embraced as a form of freedom and fun; as Maurice Charney notes, "Disguise is a form of play."[28]

Play and disguise are also ways of hiding one's true feelings. Surely it is significant that the era of screwball comedy was also the period in popular music of such songwriters as Cole Porter and the Gershwins, songwriters who characteristically used sophisticated lyrics that both mocked and affirmed romance. Take George and Ira Gershwin's 1931 "Blah-Blah-Blah." It goes in part:

Blah, Blah, Blah, blah moon,
Blah, Blah, Blah above.
Blah, Blah, Blah, blah croon,
Blah, Blah, Blah, blah love.

Or take Cole Porter's more well-known "You're the Top," which compares the beloved to Mona Lisa, the Tower of Pisa, and Mickey Mouse. Like these songs, one of the major hallmarks of this genre is its tendency, as noticed by Bruce Babington and Peter Evans, to sabotage the language of love.[29] These film characters are much too proud, independent, or cynical for romantic mush, and the films go to great lengths—even as they are presenting romances—to distance themselves from sentimentality. In *My Man Godfrey*, Irene's melodramatic moping about when Godfrey refuses her amorous overtures is presented as comic, and in *The Awful Truth*, Dan's love poem is offered for laughs. This eschewal of sentiment infects much of the dialogue; witness the scene in *The Thin Man*, when Nora is unsuccessful in getting Nick to give up some midnight sleuthing and wifely anxiety turns into toppers:

> NORA: All right. Go ahead. Go on. See if I care. But I think it's a dirty trick to bring me all the way to New York just to make a widow out of me.
> NICK: You wouldn't be a widow long.
> NORA: You bet I wouldn't.
> NICK: Not with all your money.

These toppers are a form of teasing, as are the absurd screwball nicknames, nicknames that are simultaneously endearments and taunts—Nicky calls Nora "Sugah," Eve Peabody calls Tibor "Skipper," Dexter calls Tracy "Red," and Jean calls Charles "Hopsie." The names are arch and belittling, but they also suggest affectionate intimacy.

Because of this deep suspicion of corniness—and because of the antagonism between the two principal characters—declarations of love are vexed in screwball comedy; they are more likely to be indirect than plainly spoken. In *Ball of Fire*, Sugarpuss is supposedly returning Bertram's engagement ring, but she sends back Joe Lilac's instead, which is how Bertram knows that she really loves *him*. In *Midnight*, Tibor Czerny has doggedly pursued Eve for days, but he is deeply angered after she humiliates him by telling her hosts that he's crazy; thus at the end of the film when Eve and he are before a divorce judge, he doesn't contest the proceedings at all, but he does behave so eccentrically that the judge believes him to be mentally ill and thus refuses the divorce. In *His Girl Friday*, Walter continually connives to keep Hildy from leaving for Albany, but the closest brush to a declaration is the following exchange:

> HILDY: I thought you didn't love me.
> WALTER: What were you thinking with?

Leigh Bracket, who wrote or co-wrote five of Howard Hawks's later films, provides firsthand testimony regarding his approach to romance. "The word 'love' is not heard, and there is no scene where hero and heroine declare their tender feelings for each other. It's done obliquely."[30]

Given that screwballs foreground verbal play and invention so insistently, one might think that they had left behind the antipathy to language demonstrated by Westerns. However, Diane Carson's analysis, "To Be Seen but Not Heard: *The Awful Truth*," reveals the contrary:

> The primary emphasis is on language, one area in our society in which women have often been credited with "natural" aptitude. To defuse the potential significant threat posed by articulate women, these films perform a deft sleight of hand. They redefine female utterance as something tangential to rational (that is, male) discourse.[31]

The unruliness of the typical screwball heroine is manifested by her "irrational" talk, by her "blathering."

By some reports, the genre took its name "screwball" from descriptions of Carole Lombard's performance as Irene Bullock in *My Man Godfrey*. Irene's conversation is sublimely irrational:

IRENE: Oh, you're more than a butler. You're the first protégé I ever had.
GODFREY: Protégé?
IRENE: You know, like Carlo.
GODFREY: Uh, who is Carlo?
IRENE: He's mother's protégé.
GODFREY: Oh.
IRENE: You know, it's awfully nice Carlo having a sponsor because then he doesn't have to work and he gets more time for his practicing, but then he never does and that makes a difference.
GODFREY: Yes, I imagine it would—
IRENE: Do you play anything, Godfrey? Oh I don't mean games and things like that, I mean the piano and things like that.
GODFREY: Well, I—
IRENE: Oh it doesn't really make any difference, I just thought I'd ask. It's funny how some things make you think of other things.

"Blathering" can thus be defined as not letting one's conversational partner get a word in edgewise, using vague vocabulary and referents, and jumping from one topic to the next in a process of mindless, freewheeling association. Screwball comedies present a large sorority of blatherers, including Irene and her mother, Mary Smith, in *Easy*

Living, Lucy Warriner in *The Awful Truth,* Maude in *The Palm Beach Story,* Klara in Lubitsch's *The Shop around the Corner* (1940), and almost everyone in Cukor's *The Women* (1939), a film that makes its misogyny clear by starting with a credit sequence equating each actress with a different animal. Such characters dominate the conversation by not allowing normal turn-taking. (Perhaps "blathering" gives actresses opportunities for a "star turns," and their talent often makes these moments amusing and impressive, but their dithering and stammering is a far cry from the star turns historically allotted to male actors.) Carson comments, "As screwball comedies inevitably and inexorably pursue conservative agendas, men conquer these verbally adept women by revealing the nonsensical nature of loquacious ramblings, by meeting and topping their verbal aggression, or by co-opting their speech and silencing them."[32]

Carson doesn't discuss that comic "talkativeness" is also shared by numerous secondary male characters in screwballs, characters such as Pettibone in *His Girl Friday,* the professors in *Ball of Fire,* and all the men played by Edward Everett Horton or Cecil Blore. These character actors are often given long turns of very little plot significance to showcase their amusing verbal skills. However this fact does not undermine Carson's argument, because as Winokur observes, in general character actors serve as "projected distortions exorcised from the protagonists."[33] These secondary, talkative men are always presented as figures of fun, and usually subtly or overtly stigmatized as homosexual, differentiating them from the male lead. Thus their loquaciousness further substantiates the genre's association of female = insignificant talk, male = rational talk or action.*

Although I agree with Carson that the genre often mocks women's speech, and worse yet, frequently presents men as right-

---

* Kathleen Rowe's *The Unruly Woman* (Austin: University of Texas Press, 1995) discusses female figures—including Roseanne Barr and Miss Piggy—who transgress social convention in their speech and in their appetites. She offers a psychoanalytic explanation of the fear of women's excessive talk:

> That the unruly woman eats too much and speaks too much is no coincidence; both involve failure to control the mouth. Nor are such connotations of excess innocent when they are attached to the female mouth. They suggest that the voracious and shrewish female mouth, the mouth that both consumes (food) and produces (speech) to excess, is a more generalized version of that other, more ambivalently conceived female orifice, the vagina. Together they imply an intrinsic relation among female fatness, female garrulousness, and female sexuality. (p. 37)

fully regaining the upper hand through physical roughness, there *is* a contradictory strain in screwball. Sometimes the woman is verbally unruly, not because she babbles, but because she dares to speak so frankly. In Jack Conway's *Libeled Lady* (1936), Connie (Myrna Loy) proposes to Bill (William Powell). Ninotchka (Greta Garbo) continually surprises with her straightforwardness: "Must you flirt?" she challenges Leon (Melyvn Douglas) in Lubitsch's *Ninotchka* (1939). "Suppress it." The Girl (Veronica Lake) in Sturges's *Sullivan's Travels* may never be dignified with a name, but she also startles us with her frankness:

SULLIVAN: Mmm, I mean, haven't you got a car?
GIRL: No, have you?
SULLIVAN: No, but . . .
GIRL: Then don't get ritzy. And I'll tell you some other things I haven't got. I haven't got a yacht or a pearl necklace or a fur coat or a country seat or even a winter seat. I could use a new girdle too.

Moments when you'd think that the heroine would be polite, evasive, coy, or blathering, she speaks with complete candor. Such breaking of the constraints of expected decorum is a form of independence—of rebellion—and these heroines' verbal resistance is striking and memorable, even if the films do invariably work around toward domesticating and silencing them.

————

For more detailed analysis of representative texts, I've chosen to concentrate on Howard Hawks's *Bringing Up Baby* (1938) and Preston Sturges's *The Palm Beach Story* (1942), in part because these films are not adaptations of stage plays, so they cannot be charged with presenting "theatrical" dialogue.

Summarizing the absurd plot of *Bringing Up Baby* is challenging. Basically, it is the story of a paleontologist, David Huxley (Cary Grant) who initially has three goals: soliciting a donation for his museum, finishing his brontosaurus skeleton, and marrying his assistant, Miss Swallow, the next day. While golfing with the lawyer of a potential donor to the museum, David accidentally meets Susan Vance (Katharine Hepburn), a young woman who trails chaos in her wake. Susan sabotages David's meeting with Mr. Peabody, and when David coincidentally runs into her that night at a restaurant, she manages to do so again. During their misadventures, Susan develops an interest in David, and she conscripts his help with a tame leopard named Baby that her brother has just sent from Brazil. Susan and David drive the leopard to her aunt's farm in Connecticut for safekeeping, but David's return to New York City is delayed both by Susan's stealing his clothes and by her aunt's terrier, George, burying a bone essential to the brontosaurus skeleton. During dinner that night, Susan makes David masquerade as Mr. Bone, a big-game hunter, because her Aunt Elizabeth is the potential donor to the museum. Baby escapes from his pen in the stable, and Susan and David hunt him in the woods. They are eventually arrested by the town sheriff and confusion ensues because now two leopards are loose, the second being a vicious circus animal that Susan has mistakenly set free. Eventually both leopards are caught; Miss Swallow breaks off her engagement with David; the intercostal clavicle is found; Susan persuades her aunt to give the money to the museum after all; and Susan and David are united.

Bringing Up Baby started as a short story written by Hagar Wilde and published in *Colliers* magazine in 1937. Gerald Mast has studied the film's story development:

> At the core of Wilde's story was the film's central situation. There is a panther (not a leopard) named Baby and a dog named George. There is brother Mark in Brazil and Aunt Elizabeth in Connecticut. Baby responds to the song with his (her? its?) name in the title—"I Can't Give You Anything but Love, Baby." Even some of the film's best lines are in the story: Susan's confusion about whether Baby's liking dogs means that he "eats dogs or is fond of them"; Aunt Elizabeth's describing George as a "perfect little fiend and you know it." On the other hand, David and Susan are already engaged in Wilde's story . . . David is not a scientist. . . . There is no museum, no Swallow, no brontosaurus, no intercostal clavicle, no golf course, no series of adventures on the road to Connecticut, no constable, no drunken gardener, no big-game hunter, and no jail.

When RKO bought the story, it also hired Wilde to come to Hollywood and paired her with Dudley Nichols as screenwriter. (The major differences between Nichols's work on *Stagecoach* and this movie are further evidence of the importance of genre to dialogue.) According to Mast, the two screenwriters began a love affair that lasted for several months, so "the screwball romance of Susan and David on screen was mirrored by the romance of the writers off-screen."[34] By comparing the script with the finished film, however, Mast was also able to uncover the degree to which Hawks departed from the final screenplay by adding on-set improvisation; in addition, Mast highlights significant deletions, the most important of which to me was the excising of three scenes between Susan and David in which their romantic attraction was made more explicit.[35]

Bringing Up Baby is one of the clearest statements of the screwball ethos: it presents a contrast between the world of the natural history museum and the world of the enchanted forest on Midsummer Night's Eve. The former represents work, dedication, seriousness, while the latter stands for playful abandon, vitality, and sexuality. Part of what makes *Bringing Up Baby* so resonant is that the movie itself embodies a wedding between discipline and zaniness. As many have noted, the film is meticulously patterned, with opening and closing scenes in the museum, balanced pairs of characters (Susan versus Alice, George versus Baby), and actions that occur twice (*two* exits on car running boards, *two* sets of evening clothes get ripped); yet simultaneously the film's central plot premise—summarized so memorably by Cavell as "Leopards in Connecticut"—is the epitome of screwball dizziness.

Since David Huxley starts the film as a repressed, workaholic scientist, and Susan Vance as a free spirit, one would think that their dialogue would represent these two contradictory poles. But it is clear from the beginning that each character contains elements of his opposite. As Mast notices, in the very opening scene, David both protests against Miss Swallow's plan for a sexless marriage and uses slang.[36] Moreover, David never uses the elevated professorial vocabulary that one might expect from a man in his position, and he is not above annoying Mr. Peabody with his own overtalkativeness.

As for Susan, one is tempted to put her in the league with other female blatherers, because Hawks includes numerous reaction shots to stress again and again that David cannot get a word in edgewise when Susan is talking. But actually, Susan doesn't talk so terribly much, and she doesn't interrupt. Her technique is to willfully misunderstand. David tells her she's got the wrong golf ball or the wrong car, and she carries on as if he's said quite the opposite. All conversation with her gets tangled, as in this example:

DAVID: (*frightened by the leopard*) Susan, you've got to get out of this apartment.
SUSAN: But David I can't. I have a lease.

Susan is also skilled at encouraging misunderstandings, shading the truth and outright fabrication. She leads David to believe that the leopard has attacked her; she tells Constable Slocum that the car parked at the fire hydrant isn't hers; she tells Aunt Elizabeth that David is a friend of Mark's suffering from a nervous breakdown. As Kathleen Rowe remarks, "Through wordplay, storytelling, misunderstandings and lies Susan entangles David in a script she is authoring, which is also the script of the film—her hunt for David and her demolition of all that stands in her way."[37] One of the ambiguities of *Bringing Up Baby* is that it is never quite clear how much of Susan's dizziness is deliberate; she is perfectly capable of trenchant clear-sightedness, as when she answers David's complaints that she played his golf ball, "What does it matter? It's only a game, anyway." Deliberate or not, as Andrew Britton observes, Susan's daffiness leads to "the breakdown of rational discourse."[38]

Verbal chaos reigns so supreme here that it is possible to overlook the fact that dialogue still fulfills all the usual functions. One of the most crucial is setting the narrative deadline—David's impending wedding—that motivates the story's breakneck pace. And dialogue provides key explanations, such as about where the first leopard came from or where the second leopard's going, that keep the plot functioning.

Moreover, chaos is controlled by the fact that this dialogue is phenomenally marked by repetition. David's "I'll be with you in a minute, Mr. Peabody" recurs as a tag line, so does Susan's, "Everything's gonna be all right." But repetition is much more endemic than just tag lines. Listen to David's reproach to Susan in the woods:

DAVID: *You told her* my name was "Bone" and *you didn't tell me. You told her* I was a big-game hunter and *you didn't tell me. You'd tell* anybody anything that comes into your head and *you don't tell me.* [My emphases.]

Dialogue in *Bringing Up Baby* becomes like music, a play of reiteration and controlled difference. Witness the following passage, which oc-

curs when David and Susan are running around the living room trying to find the dog George:

DAVID: George!
SUSAN: George!
DAVID: George!
SUSAN: George!
DAVID: George!
SUSAN: George!
DAVID: Geor . . .
SUSAN: George!
DAVID: Oh stop it, Susan. You sound like an echo. George!
SUSAN: Nice George!
DAVID: George!
SUSAN: Nice George!
DAVID: Nice George!
SUSAN: George!

We are far away from Shakespearean repartee here—actually verg-
ing on Beckett's blankness—and yet the effect is undeniably comic.

Dialogue in *Bringing Up Baby,* as in so many screwballs, disintegrates into noise. *Bringing Up Baby* relies heavily upon overlapping
dialogue. The strategy of having numerous characters all speak at
once is used whenever several people are trying to straighten out
some tangled mess that Susan has gotten them into, as in the restaurant scene with the mistake over the two purses, or in the country
house when Aunt Elizabeth wants to know why David is wearing a
negligée. Other critics have noticed the frequent use of overlapping
dialogue in Hawk's films in particular, and in screwball in general,
but they have failed to recognize the crucial point: *it is used to show
the characters' confusion, but never to confuse the viewer,* who has a superior understanding of all the events.

The chaos of the overlapping dialogue is intensified in the negligée scene by George's constant yapping. Dogs are part and parcel
of this genre as child substitutes, but Hawks also makes good use of
the dog as sound effect. The leopard, Baby, also participates in the
film's dialogue, through repeated well-placed roars. Rational discourse in *Bringing Up Baby* ultimately disintegrates into animal
noises or—in the singing of "I Can't Give You Anything But Love"—
into four-part animal-human harmony. In its use of the animals, this
film provides a particularly clear example of the genre's habit of

42.   *Bringing Up Baby*. Singing in four-part harmony.

drowning out dialogue with competing noises: the gunshots and yelping dogs of the Ale and Quail Club in *The Palm Beach Story* offer another instance of sonic bedlam. Like overlapping dialogue, overriding sound effects emphasize the difficulties of communication.

Another element of the chaos in *Bringing Up Baby* is the constant confusion over who is being addressed ("addressee confusion" is the guiding principle of *His Girl Friday*). When David is trying to explain the situation to Miss Swallow over the phone and Susan picks up the extension, he tries to split his comments between them, with predictably messy results. During the dinner party sequence, David is being addressed by Major Applegate, but he doesn't respond, because he doesn't know that Susan has told her aunt that he is a big-game hunter. Dr. Lehman mistakes comments that Susan directs to Baby on his rooftop as addressed to him, and takes these as proof that Susan is unbalanced.

The confusion all seems to be designed to flatter the viewer, who sits above the fray, secure in his or her superior knowledge. Our superior knowledge is always enhanced by Hawks's use of the camera, which carefully shows us, for instance, that George has stolen the bone. (Moreover, our sense of preeminence is intensified by the plethora of sexual double entendre throughout the film—Mast and Cavell have both traced the sexual connotations of the repeated references to "bone," "tail," and "puss," connotations that the characters seem too innocent to notice.)

Communication has completely broken down by the end of the film, when all the principal characters have ended up in jail, and none can prove his identity. Inevitably, it is at this point that Susan turns the tables by deliberately assuming a masquerade, taking on the guise of gangster's moll, "Swinging Door Susie," with a nasal accent and a vocabulary including "flatfoot," "copper," "taking the rap," "sucker," "toots," and "cigarette me." At this crisis, the dialogue also becomes extremely self-referential: Susan gives David the name Jerry (Grant's character in *The Awful Truth*), and David complains, "Constable, she's making this all up out of motion pictures she's seen." The film's climax occurs when Susan unknowingly hauls the second, vicious leopard into the jail, and David proves his masculine prowess by fighting off the wild leopard (nature/female sexuality gone too far) and caging it. Yet David's heroic action is immediately undercut by his fainting into Susan's arms.

"Undercutting" is also apparent in the epilogue in the Natural History Museum, where David admits that his madcap day with Susan "was the best day I ever had in my whole life." This leads into an actual declaration of love (fig. 43):

SUSAN: Do you realize what that means? That means that you must like me a little bit.
DAVID: Oh Susan! It's more than that.
SUSAN: Is it?
DAVID: Yes, I love you, I think.
SUSAN: Oh. That's wonderful. Because I love you too.

This rather unromantic declaration—note David's "I think"—is further undercut by Hawks's staging: Susan's swaying on her ladder grows dangerous; she leaps onto the brontosaurus, and her weight causes David's life's work to collapse. Susan apologizes, and for the first time in the film she takes responsibility for her destructiveness. (Compare her "Oh David, look what I've done!" with her earlier "You've torn your coat.") David just stammers; he is virtually

43.   *Bringing Up Baby.* DAVID: I love you, I think.

speechless at the enormity of the disaster. Rational discourse is impossible—what is there to say? David embraces Susan, resigning himself to all the chaos she brings.

Like *Bringing Up Baby, The Palm Beach Story* was not an adaptation of a play. " 'Premise,' [Preston Sturges] wrote in early notes . . . 'that a pretty woman can do anything she wants and go anywhere she wants without money. 2. That a pretty woman can use her appeal for the advancement of her husband.'"[39] Sturges's gradual development of the script from these notes has been traced by Brian Henderson.[40] The story revolves around Gerry Jeffers (Claudette Colbert), who bridles at sitting by in debt as her husband Tom (Joel McCrea) struggles unsuccessfully to make a living through his impractical inventions (such as an airport suspended in the sky). When an eccentric rich old man, the Wienie King, gives Gerry enough money to pay off their debts, she decides that the time has come for her to leave Tom and find a wealthy second husband whom she can finagle into bankrolling Tom's career. Adopted as a mascot by the drunken, raucous Ale and Quail Club, Gerry takes a train to Florida and through a series of misadventures loses her suitcase, ticket, and clothes, only to be rescued by a chance acquaintance, John D. Hackensacker III (Rudy Vallee), who turns out to be one of the richest men in the country. Hackensacker is completely smitten by Gerry and invites her to stay as a guest at his estate. Tom has followed her to Palm Beach, but she persuades him to masquerade as her brother. Tom is pursued by Hackensacker's sister, Maude, Princess Centimilia, who prefers him to her house gigolo, Toto. Although Hackensacker offers Gerry both a life of riches and financial help for her ex-husband, Gerry gives in to her sexual attraction to Tom and returns to her marriage. Hackensacker's and Maude's disappointment over being rejected by Gerry and Tom is assuaged by the last-minute revelation that each has an identical twin sibling; the film ends with a shot of three couples at the altar: Tom with Gerry, Hackensacker with Gerry's twin, and Maude with Tom's twin.

What seems particularly misguided about Crowther's critique of *The Palm Beach Story* is the inference that the film is garrulous. In general the film's visuals demonstrate careful attention and ample budget; it is nicely shot and lit, with a glossy shimmer, and more lushly underscored with music than earlier screwballs. Sturges clearly went out of his way to include extended sequences where there is no dialogue, "silent film" sequences in which all the information is conveyed visually. Such sequences include the film's very beginning, which offers a never-explained frantic montage of a race to a wedding ceremony. The Wienie King's inspection of the Jeffers apartment while Gerry tries to hide from him is all done without dialogue, as is Gerry's writing her farewell note to Tom, and her pivotal decision near the end to ask Tom for help with her stuck zipper. The disintegration of the Ale and Quail Club into drunken revelry is also notable for its lack of dialogue.

Moreover, one of the defining characteristics of screwball comedy is the inclusion of slapstick comedy, such as Bill's struggles to fish in *Libeled Lady*, Jerry Warriner's pratfalls during Lucy's concert in *The Awful Truth*, the acrobatics in *Holiday*. *Bringing Up Baby* has great fun ripping and burning clothes, tossing David and Susan down hills and into streams, bringing dinosaurs crashing down. But Sturges particularly favors slapstick moments—*The Lady Eve* tosses Henry Fonda around on the floor like a flopping fish. Wordless slapstick pervades *The Palm Beach Story*, in such scenes as Tom being pursued by the policeman in Grand Central Station, the hunting dogs on a rampage, or Toto's frequent falls. As Penelope Huston remarks,

"There are moments when Sturges seems to feel that the only thing funnier than a man falling on his face is a man dragging the curtains down with him."[41]

Furthermore, the pace of the dialogue in *The Palm Beach Story* is rather leisurely. Gerry is decidedly not a blatherer—that characterization has been exorcised from the principal female and allotted to a secondary character, Maude, who performs the function with panache. Nor, like Susan Vance, does Gerry misunderstand the statements of others. Her habit, instead, is to oscillate between deliberately stringing along her conversational partner and amazing frankness. Her deceptiveness can be seen when she encourages Tom's jealous suspicions about how she obtained the money from the Wienie King for several long exchanges, or when she lets Hackensacker think that her first husband won't give her a divorce without being paid $99,000. But her unruly frankness and honesty are equally apparent, as when she admits to the cab driver that she hasn't any money but would he please drive her to the train station anyway, and when she openly confesses to J. D. that her plan is to get remarried to a very rich man.

As Gerry oscillates between two rather contradictory strategies (both furthering her aims), so too does she alternate between two different vocal registers, two different "voices." The one I'd call "woman of the world" is lower-pitched and a little throaty; it is the voice in which she says such lines as, "You're thinking of an adven*turer*, dear. An adventur*ess* never goes on anything less that 300 feet, with a crew of eighty" (fig. 44). The other voice is high-pitched, more girlish, the "damsel in distress" voice that she uses at the ticket gate of the train platform when she is trying to get some man to take pity on her: "Oh, I'm sure my ticket will come!" Although Gerry never hides her identity or takes on a masquerade, the viewer always has a clear sense that the "damsel in distress" is playacting, that Gerry is far from weak and helpless.

Colbert's performance highlights how central *voice* is to screwball's manipulation of dialogue. The most successful screwball female stars—Hepburn, Stanwyck, Lombard, Arthur, Russell, Colbert—have distinctive, unforgettable voices, and they can manipulate these instruments to convey the widest variety of expression. Their voices are not conventionally pretty—that is, soft and melodious— they have edginess, perhaps raspiness. As Rubinstein argues, "When comedy needed to be reborn, and needed to be reborn speaking, it

44.   *The Palm Beach Story.* GERRY: You're thinking of an adven*turer,* dear.

was reborn in the female voice and in the voices of certain women. The dazzling heights and cadences of women's voices, the voices of women in the dazzling career of intelligence and independence, these are and have to be the grain itself of romantic comedy."[42]

Male actors' voices in screwball cover a wide range. Some directors selected actors for their smooth urbanity, thus the silkiness of Herbert Marshall in *Trouble in Paradise,* Ronald Coleman in *Talk of the Town,* or Melvyn Douglas in *Ninotchka.* Those films in which the male protagonist is forced into the role of "sap" feature actors such as Gary Cooper (*Ball of Fire*) or Henry Fonda (*The Lady Eve*), whose slower, more stumbling delivery is supposed to be indicative of their sincerity and vulnerability to the woman's machinations.

Joel McCrea as Tom Jeffers falls into the latter category. Like Cooper and Fonda, he has a voice that places him more at home on the range than in an art deco apartment. But Bertram Potts and Charles Pike are both treated with more respect and more tenderness by their films. Tom Jeffers is a thankless role: he is rejected by his wife for his financial failure, has to watch her flirt with another man, gets stuck with the masquerade of being her brother and being called "Captain McGlue," and he gets no witty lines. McCrea utters the lines he is given in a kind of sullen monotone. David Shumway notes that in response to the female's unruliness, "the males in screwball comedy typically scold, lecture or preach."[43] Tom is an particularly stolid example.

This film transfers the vulnerability sometimes allotted to the male lead to the secondary character, J. D. Hackensacker III, whom everyone—in typical screwball style—calls "Snoodles." Hackensacker's riches haven't gone to his head; he rides in a lower berth and finds his grandfather's yacht uncomfortable. Even though he accepts the fact that women will be primarily interested in his money, he has had practically no romantic experience, and he falls so hard, so innocently, for the manipulative Gerry, that the viewer's sympathies are more likely to be engaged by Snoodles than by Tom. This sympathy is deepened by our discovery (although contemporary audiences would have known all along), that Vallee's rather thin, reedy speaking voice is supplanted by a rich, mellifluous singing voice. When Snoodles serenades Gerry outside her window with "Goodnight Sweetheart," the warmth and tenderness of Vallee's voice seduce her, but ironically, this voice leads her not to the slender, less sexy Hackensacker, but back to her broad-shouldered (inarticulate) husband. Like Cyrano de Bergerac, Hackensacker has lent his vocal skill to help a duller, handsomer man.

Hackensacker's sister, Maude, played by Mary Astor, may be the ultimate incarnation of the blathering screwball woman. For an heiress with a European title, she speaks a very informal slang—"What's knittin', kittens?" "What's buzzin', cousins?" She is both sexually rapacious and loquacious. The moment she meets Tom, she gives him the eye and remarks, "How wonderful it is meeting a silent American again. All my husbands were foreigners and such chatterboxes, I could hardly get a word in edgeways." Yet it is clear that she never lets Toto talk at all, and when she's had enough of him, he's sent packing with, "Toto, this is Captain McGlue. I'm going to see more of him and less of you." James Curtis reports that "Sturges spent much time and effort getting the right performance from Mary Astor. 'It was not my thing,' the actress later wrote. 'I couldn't talk in a high fluty voice and run my words together as he thought high-society women did, or at least *mad* high-society women who've had six husbands and six million dollars.' "[44]

With the character Toto, Sturges has taken another screwball trope to extremes. This Foreigner is so "Other" that we are not sure where

45.   *The Palm Beach Story.* Maude and Toto

he's from, and he speaks an incomprehensible, made-up language, composed of strange-sounding words, the most comprehensible being "nitz," "yitz," and "grittinks."But Toto is not the only character whose nonstandard speech is ridiculed. The Wienie King is given an exaggerated Texan diction, including "varmit," "snout," "whoopee" and "hot-diggitty." The black train porter who is ineffectual in controlling the hunting club has been given a broad Uncle Tom persona, complete with elaborate pantomiming and lines such as "I wouldn't do that if I was you, gentlemens. The conductor's apt to get a little arritated."[45]

But it doesn't matter that Toto doesn't speak English, because no one listens to him anyway, just as no one listens to the black porter or the train conductor. For that matter, none of the major characters really seem to listen to one another either, in terms of taking their needs or desires seriously. Peter Brooks's evocative speculation is worth quoting here: "One is tempted to speculate that the different kinds of drama have their corresponding sense deprivations: for tragedy, blindness, since tragedy is about insight and illumination;

for comedy, deafness, since comedy is concerned with problems in communication, misunderstandings and their consequences; and for melodrama, muteness, since melodrama is about expression."[46] Sturges starts the film with the hard-of-hearing Wienie King, because throughout he is playing around varieties of deafness and miscommunication. If this stress on miscommunication reminds us of Susan's willful misinterpretation and the "breakdown of rational discourse" in *Bringing Up Baby*, the similarity is not a coincidence. Comedy relies upon confusion, and in screwball these confusions are engendered by the way characters talk, the way they listen, and the way they (mis)interpret what they've heard.

The Palm Beach Story is perhaps the least romantic of screwballs. Rubinstein is puzzled by how it got by the censors—it is so blatant about sex and greed.[47] Brian Henderson discovered that the Hays Office was slow and contradictory in its handling of the script, perhaps because the bombing of Pearl Harbor that week affected the censors' concentration.[48] Moreover, Sturges, like other filmmakers, is careful to keep his dialogue just on this side of deniability. Thus, Gerry says: "You have no idea what a long-legged gal can do without doing anything." Translation: "You have no idea how a woman can use her sex appeal to her advantage without actually putting out." Sturges's "anti-romanticism" is glaring in the opening caption questioning whether the newly married Tom and Gerry lived happily ever after, which repeats again over the image of the multiple weddings at the end. The very arbitrariness of the device of the twins deliberately satirizes movie conventions of love and courtship. Not surprisingly, this sabotaging of the language of love recurs throughout the dialogue. Witness Maude's discussion with Snoodles about his infatuation with Gerry:

MAUDE: Why don't you marry her? She's lovely.
HACKENSACKER: In the first place, she isn't free yet, in the second place, you don't marry somebody you just met the day before. At least I don't.
MAUDE: But that's the only way, dear. If you get to know too much about them, you'd never marry them. I'd marry Captain McGlue tomorrow, even with that name.
HACKENSACKER: And divorce him next month.
MAUDE: Nothing is permanent in this world except Roosevelt, dear.

Such a frank avowal of the transitory nature of love and marriage is rather astringent.

Like the reference to Roosevelt above, the dialogue of this film is studded with extratextual references, all of which convey the double-layered aspect of screwball, the sense that the eavesdropping viewer knows more than the characters. A host of deliberate parallels are set up between Hackensacker and John D. Rockefeller. And many commentators have remarked upon the resonances of the names that Sturges chose: "Tom and Gerry" referring to the cartoon characters, "Toto" recalling Dorothy's famous dog. More interesting are the ways in which *The Palm Beach Story*, which Sturges deliberately wrote as a vehicle for Claudette Colbert, repeats and inverts the patterns of her 1934 success, *It Happened One Night.* In the earlier film, Colbert also runs away from home pursuing a marriage of which a male family member disapproves. In *It Happened One Night*, she travels from Florida to New York; in *The Palm Beach Story*, the trajectory is exactly reversed. In both cases the woman is progressively shorn of her money and her luggage until she joins forces with a male protector, a man whose social class differs markedly from hers. In both films, the heroine ends up choosing the suitor with less money and standing but more sex appeal. (Another Colbert vehicle, *Midnight,* also presents a similar pattern.) Because of these references, *The Palm Beach Story* is marked by a thoroughgoing double-layeredness.*

Brian Henderson argued in a 1978 article, "Romantic Comedy Today: *Semi-Tough* or Impossible?" that because of the changes in American society, including the rise of feminism and gay rights,

---

* Perhaps the most "inside" of all the inside references in the film are the parallels Sturges includes to his own life; his biographer Diane Jacobs finds it a "treasure trove of personal references" (*Christmas in July: The Life and Art of Preston Sturges* [Berkeley and Los Angeles: University of California Press, 1992], 266–77). Like Tom, Sturges was the designer of impractical and unsaleable inventions, and he could not provide his first wife, Estelle, with a sufficiently luxurious standard of living. Like Gerry, after the disintegration of his first marriage, Sturges met and was smitten by the heir to a grand American fortune—Eleanor Hutton, Sturges's second wife, had family connections to Post Cereals and General Foods. She and Preston once traveled together by train from New York to Palm Beach, where she invited him to stay as a houseguest in the family mansion. I don't want to lay too much stress on the autobiographical layer, in that, unlike the references to American society and to famous films, such references are less widely known and more private. But it is intriguing that Jacobs's access to details of Sturges's life gives her a different reading of many of the film's lines.

women entering the work force, the prevalence of divorce and single parenting, the fall in status of Northeastern cities, and the relaxing of censorship, the contemporary climate is altogether inimical to romantic comedy.[49] The continued production of romantic comedies over the past twenty years proves that such films *are* still possible, but Henderson's attention to cultural shifts alerts us that the factors underlying the cycle of screwball comedies have altered through time. Critics cannot agree whether romantic comedies of later decades, films such as *Some Like it Hot* (1959), *Pillow Talk* (1959), *Tootsie* (1982), *Desperately Seeking Susan* (1985), *Overboard* (1988), *Something to Talk About* (1995), or *One Fine Day* (1996) should be labeled as screwball comedies. Certainly, these later movies depart from the classic screwballs in many respects, and their color cinematography and more contemporary production design give them a completely different "look." Yet concentrating on their dialogue strategies also reveals marked continuities, such as the use of masquerade enacted through verbal exaggeration; sexual double entendres; overlapping speech; unruly women who blather or speak frankly; the casting of actresses with unique, unconventional voices; and the sabotaging of the language of love. Whether or not you classify the more recent films as screwballs, they are obviously the richer for incorporating traditional screwball elements.

My conclusion to the chapter on Westerns pointed out how blatant their dialogue tends to be, how clear those films are about the ethical stakes involved. With the exception of Capra's *Mr. Deeds Goes to Town* (1936) and *Mr. Smith Goes to Washington* (1939), which are so different in tone, aims, and dialogue that I question including them in this classification (perhaps it has been Jean Arthur's voice that confused the issue), screwball comedies are much more oblique. These comedies shy away from bald declarations or moral commentary; everything is conveyed through irony, through inference, through undercutting. Actresses whose intelligence fairly crackles around them masquerade as dizzy dames; actors famed for their stalwart strength play at pratfalls and naiveté. Sex is never mentioned but always inferred. Romance is consistently mocked, but it is the motivation for everything that happens. Like the Gershwin song quoted earlier, these films insist that we are so sophisticated we don't need everything spelled out for us. Screwball comedies invite us to join the game.

SIX

Words as Weapons

Dialogue in Gangster Films

The rest of the time you're just another good-looking, sweet-talking, charm-using, fuck-happy fellow with nothing to offer but some dialogue. Dialogue's cheap in Hollywood, Ben. Why don't you run outside and jerk yourself . . . a soda?

Virginia Hill to Benny Siegel in *Bugsy* (1991)

One of the truisms of film history is that the gangster genre is intimately linked with the birth of sound. This thesis overlooks the significant gangster movies in the silent era, but the mistake is understandable because (a) the very first all-talkie was, in fact, a gangster film, Brian Foy's *Lights of New York* (1928);[1] and (b) the sound of early gangster films was immediately recognized as integral to the genre.

This sound track specifically drew attention because of its sound effects—its squealing tires and roaring machine guns. But critics also noticed the dialogue, which seemed particularly realistic and daring. The very earliest sound gangster films acquainted audiences with a specialized vocabulary: "take him for a ride," "grifter," "cannon," "mug," "on the square," "sucker," "bulls," "cut you in," "lay low," "the heat's on," "bum rap," "mebbe," "cross me," "muscle in," "gat," "rat on one's friends"; just as more contemporary gangster films offer "hitter," "contract," "whacking," "hood," "homeboys," "bustin' my balls," "wiseguys," "made man," and so on. The dialogue of gangster films is blatantly distinct from the language of other kinds of films. In *The Art of Conversation*, the sociolinguist Peter Burke observes:

> The slang of professional beggars and thieves is an extreme case of this creation of a symbolic boundary between a single group and the

rest of society. It has been interpreted as an "antilanguage" which "brings into sharp relief the role of language as a realisation of the power structure of society" and at the same time reflects the organization and values of a "counterculture."[2]

Because many of the scripts of gangster films were written by streetwise newspapermen and/or based on true accounts of criminals' stories, some correlation between this movie dialect and actual usage undoubtedly exists. But the reality-basis of this argot is not actually germane to us here. What is important is that the genre embraces this "anti-language," glorifies it, uses it as a means of "creating a symbolic boundary" between these stories and the rest of American cinema. From the 1930s on, this style of film dialogue has become self-perpetuating, a fact that is spelled out in the beginning of Brian De Palma's 1983 remake of *Scarface:*

IMMIGRATION OFFICIAL: Where'd you learn to speak the English, Tony?

TONY MONTANA: In a school. And my father, he was from United States. Just like you, you know. He was a Yankee. He used to take me a lot to the movies, you know. I learn. I watch the guys like Humphrey Bogart, James Cagney. They teach me to talk. I like those guys.

Bogart and Cagney (and their scriptwriters) have indeed taught later actors how to talk; given the evidence regarding true-life gangsters' fascination with their Hollywood image, Bogart, Cagney, Lee J. Cobb, Rod Steiger, Al Pacino, Robert De Niro et al. may even have taught later gangsters how they should speak.

Gangster films are sometimes classified as an independent genre, sometimes treated as a subset of a larger category of "crime films." Here, as in chapter 5, which concentrated on screwball comedy, as opposed to the larger field of romantic comedy, I shall focus on a comparatively unified subset and leave to the side the more varied, more expansive sphere.

As a working definition, I identify gangster films as those centering on the activities of criminals working in organized groups to attain money and power, generally in an urban setting. (This leaves out films regarding psychotic lone killers, spy stories, and terrorist plots.)[3] These films flourished in the years concurrent with or immediately following the wild gangland days in Chicago; the success of *Little Caesar* (1930), *Public Enemy* (1931), and *Scarface* (1932) led to scores of imitative films quickly being produced. Public uproar over the genre's perceived deleterious effects led to increased pressure from the Hays Office, and the switch of the star from the gangster role to the pursuing policeman (most famously in the 1935 film *"G" Men,* directed by William Keighley, starring Cagney).

During the 1940s, the gangster movie often blended with the film noir, resulting in such amalgams as *The Big Sleep* (1946) and *Out of the Past* (1947), which include gangster figures but center on the solitary detective hero. The gangster film is hard to disentangle from films noirs/detective films, although many critics have sensed a distinction; Foster Hirsch argues that gangster films are shot indoors and noirs on the city streets; Alain Silver maintains that noirs are marked by a darker atmosphere.[4] I notice that the language of noir protagonists' is different, in that these heroes are likely to be more educated and middle-class, they are more cynical and deliberately "hardboiled," and, moreover, they talk less than gangsters because they move through their stories as solitary figures, not in groups of confederates.[5]

Two historical events, the Kefauver Commission's inquiries into Organized Crime in America in 1950–51, and the proof that crime networks were linked provided by the discovery of a large international meeting of leading criminal figures in Apalachia, New York, in 1957, helped spark renewed interest in gangster films throughout the 1950s. *Bonnie and Clyde* (1967), often cited as the start of an American "New Wave," made its criminal anti-heroes extremely glamorous, and the romanticism inherent in this genre reached its apogee with the success of *The Godfather* in 1972. This popularity has continued over the past two decades, leading to movies that are both very self-conscious about the history of their genre and to cycles, such as the "black gangsta films," that lead off in new directions.[6]

Gangster films can be divided into various subcategories. Some critics use visual style as a grid, separating those movies heavily influenced by noir cinematography from those with a semi-documentary look and those filmed in rich color with period art direction. However, I prefer to sort by subject matter. "Biographies" of historical criminals such as Al Capone, Bugsy Siegel, Baby Face Nelson, Legs Diamond, Bonnie and Clyde, and John Dillinger have been popular.

Even more prevalent have been "pseudo-biographies," that is, films loosely modeling a fictitious gangster on real-life counterparts and tracing his rise and fall, as happens in *Little Caesar* (1930), *High Sierra* (1941), and *The Gangster* (1947). Also common are "caper" films focusing on the planning and commission of a major crime—for example, *The Asphalt Jungle* (1950), *The Killing* (1956), and *The Taking of Pelham One Two Three* (1974). "G-men films" (my coinage) detail efforts of a group of law enforcement officials to bring down a gang; examples include *The Street with No Name* (1948), *The Big Heat* (1953), and *The Untouchables* (1987).[7]

Gangster films have thus been a particularly long-lasting genre, maintaining their popularity over the entire history of the sound film. In terms of their dialogue, I believe that while significant continuity can be observed throughout, characteristics that were less developed in earlier films have been elaborated in more recent examples. The turning point between a more restrained "studio style" and the verbal fireworks of contemporary gangster films may have been Martin Scorsese's *Mean Streets* (1973), which blatantly foregrounds a casual, "realistic," and improvisational style.[8]

Returning to Burke's suggestive remark that underworld language reflects the organization and values of a counterculture, we can see how the dialogue meshes with the overarching themes of gangster films. This genre presents a countervision of America, a nightmare inversion of optimistic official ideologies. Edward Mitchell notes the genre's love/hate relationship with ideals drawn from Puritanism, Social Darwinism, and the Horatio Alger myth.[9] Jack Shadoian stresses these films' conflicts over individualism and success, their dark view of the urban landscape, their graphic violence, and their concentration on both the destruction of the family and the corruptibility of the police.[10] All of American society is tainted; as John Baxter argues, "Few gangster films are free of the imputation that criminals are the creation of society rather than rebels against it."[11] Or as J. Hoberman succinctly puts it, "The fact is: The Mafia R Us."[12] Robert Warshow plumbs the depths of audience attraction to these films:

> At bottom, the gangster is doomed because he is under the obligation to succeed, not because the means he employs are unlawful. In the deeper layers of the modern consciousness, *all* means are unlaw-

ful, every attempt to succeed is an act of aggression, leaving one alone and guilty and defenseless among enemies; one is *punished* for success. . . . The effect of the gangster film is to embody this dilemma in the person of the gangster and resolve it by his death. The dilemma is resolved because it is *his* death, not ours. We are safe; for the moment, we can acquiesce in our failure, we can choose to fail.[13]

Gangster films set up something like a parallel universe, portraying their own kind of work, their own quasi-military organization, their own brand of justice and ethics, their own type of families—and all of these are communicated to the viewer by a distinctive use of language.

The specialized vocabulary is intriguing because it revolves around tools of the trade such as guns ("gats") and victims ("suckers") or key activities—"lay low," "cross me," "rat on," "take him for a ride." But the use of a business jargon is only one of the distinguishing features of gangster films—after all, sci-fi films include a great deal of scientific jargon, yet their speech is not at all like that of gangster films. Part of what sets gangster films apart is a constant use of informal slang and constructions that are deliberately marked as "lower-class." As Rocky Sullivan in *Angels with Dirty Faces* (1938), Jimmy Cagney says, "Whadyaknow, whadyasay" as a greeting, not "How do you do?" or "How nice to see you." All characters in gangster films say "yeah" instead of "yes," "hey" instead of "hello," "shaddup" instead of "please be quiet," "get me?" instead of "do you understand?" They speak informally, with a great deal of rambling repetition, and their phrases are less likely to be rhythmically balanced, compressed, or witty. Take these lines from Scorsese's *GoodFellas* (1990), when Paulie, the boss, is warning Henry about his associates:

PAULIE: Don't make a jerk out of me. Just don't do it. Just don't do it. Now, I want to talk to you about Jimmy. You gotta watch out for him. He's a good earner, but he's wild, takes too many chances.

HENRY: No, I know that. I know Jimmy. You think I would take chances like Jimmy?

PAULIE: And Tommy, he's a good kid too, but he's crazy. He's a cowboy. He's got too much to prove.

HENRY: No, I—

PAULIE: You gotta watch out for kids like this.

HENRY: Yeah, I know what they are. I only use them for certain things. Believe me—you don't have to worry—

PAULIE: Listen, I ain't gonna get fucked like Gribbs. You understand? Gribbs is 70 year old and the fuckin'guy's gonna die in prison. I don't need that. So I'm warnin' everybody. Everybody. Could be my son, could be anybody. Gribbs got twenty years just for sayin' hello to some fuck who sneakin' behind his back sellin' junk. I don't need that. Ain't gonna happen to me. You understand?

HENRY: Uh huh.

Compared to the language of other films, the informality and vernacular flavor is striking: "gotta," "gonna," "wanna," "ain't," "kid," "guy," "junk," "some fuck," "uh huh"—this is not the diction of *The Sound of Music*. The short sentences are choppy, not eloquent; the interruptions impatient and rude, the abundant repetition of phrases employed for emotional emphasis, not poetic rhythm. As James Naremore notes, the naturalistic style of acting favored by certain genres calls for actors to

> slop down food and talk with their mouths full. Likewise, they occasionally turn away from the camera, speak softly and rapidly, repeat words, slur or throw away lines, sometimes ask "Huh?" or let dialogue overlap. To achieve the effect of spontaneity, they preface speeches with meaningless intensifiers or qualifiers. . . . Naturalistic actors also cultivate a halting, somewhat groping style of speech: instead of saying "I am very distressed," the actor will say "I am dis- . . . very distressed." By the same logic, he or she will start an action such as drinking from a glass, and then pause to speak before carrying the action through.[14]

This naturalistic style moves to the fore in gangster films.

Equally significant, what sets gangster films apart is the constant use of "accents." When I began my research, I thought that all the accents would be Italian, but this turns out not to be the case. *Public Enemy* and *Barton Fink* use Irish accents; *Scarface* (1983) features Cuban; *The Asphalt Jungle's* chief mastermind is supposed to be German; in *The French Connection*, the archcriminal is French; in *Once Upon a Time in America*, the accent is New York Jewish; in *Menace II Society*, inner-city black. The point is that the characters are all marked by their speech either as immigrants or at least as non-

WASPs, not that they are all Sicilian mafiosi. The accents vary in their thickness (or authenticity), and films vary in choosing whether or not to include snippets of actual Italian, Spanish, or Yiddish for extra spice, but these characters' non-WASPness, their separateness from official American culture, privilege, and power, is continually stressed.

Another motif of gangster dialogue is the characters' lack of education and verbal finesse. In Hawks's *Scarface,* the script goes out of its way to demonstrate that Tony doesn't understand the meaning of "gaudy" or "effeminate"; he refers to a writ of "habeas corpus" as "hocus pocus" (which ironically captures the hoodwinking quality of legal shenanigans). By the same token, the Lucky Luciano character in *Marked Woman* (1937) doesn't know the meaning of the word "intimate." In *On the Waterfront,* Terry Malloy garbles the syntax when he tries a put-down to tell the investigators that he doesn't want to see them again: "Never's gonna be too much soon for me." In *The Untouchables,* Al Capone speaks to reporters with smug assurance and seeming fluidity, but if one listens closely, one hears that Robert De Niro's syllabic stress is consistently just a little "off," giving the impression that Capone is aping a verbal style he doesn't really possess. Gangsters' desire to acquire upper-class speech patterns is highlighted by the opening sequence of Barry Levinson's *Bugsy,* in which Benny Siegel (Warren Beatty) practices nonsensical model sentences to improve his diction:

> BENNY: To speak properly, it is necessary to enunciate every syllable. Example: Twenty dwarves took turns doing handstands on the carpet. Twenty dwarves took turns doing handstands on the carpet. Example: Twenty dwarves took turns doing handstands on the carpet.

The phrase is funny, but the effect of the dialogue is perversely frightening, for Benny repeats it so compulsively and with such intensity that it becomes a mark of his inner drive to succeed.

In most gangster films, what the central figures lack in education or verbal finesse, they make up for in brute verbal power, as if their speech, instead of being a social lubricant and means of sharing information, is to them another weapon against their enemies. This power partially stems from the gangster's use of obscenity. Obscenity indicates strong emotion; employing it also indicates that the speaker is willing or eager to break codes of parental admonishment, polite language, or religious taboo. Early gangster films display an inclination toward obscenity, but the Production Code limited what they could get away with. Instead of saying "horseshit," the cop in the original *Scarface* refers to "the place in the gutter where the horses have been standing." Similarly, every viewer of *Marked Woman* will understand that the female characters work as prostitutes, but the word is studiously avoided. In *Key Largo* (1948), Rocco presumably whispers sexual obscenities in Nora's ear, but the viewer's point of audition is placed so that these are inaudible. As late as 1959, the dominant epithet in *Al Capone* is "louse." However, pushed by the boundary-testing of authors such as Norman Mailer, obscenity became more and more acceptable in postwar literature, and rigid censorship of the screen became more and more untenable. More than any other genre, gangster films may have benefited from the demise of the Production Code, and since the 1970s they have made obscenity a major tool.

In *Cursing in America*, Timothy Jay makes us realize that cursing is culturally based, so that, for instance, the decline over time of blasphemy and the increase in scatological and sexual cursing reflect the diminished role of religion in our cultural life. Jay discusses the development of cursing in childhood as a means of expressing discomfort, frustration, and anger, on the one hand, and of playing with humorous incongruity, on the other. In adolescents and adults, Jay notes the use of dirty words to express anger and cites data supporting the general belief that males curse much more than females. In his section, "A Study of Cursing in American Films, 1939–1989," Jay presents statistics on the frequency of curse words in 120 films, ranging from 0 in *Casablanca, High Noon,** *It's a Wonderful Life,* and *North by Northwest* to 58 in *Alien,* 92 in *M*A*S*H,* 105 in *Blazing Saddles,* and 234 in *North Dallas Forty* (a film about football players). The highest scorer among Jay's samples is—no surprise—De Palma's *Scarface,* in which Jay's researchers counted 299 instances of cursing.[15]

---

* Real cowboys apparently raised cursing to a high art, but obscenity is not really a major component of Westerns—neither in the form of indirect (censored) curses in Production Code era nor in more contemporary films.

Thus, in gangster films the heavy reliance on obscenity emphasizes the characters' crudeness, their hypermasculinity, and the power of their emotions. In *The Untouchables*, Al Capone's fury upon hearing that Eliot Ness has succeeded in capturing a major shipment of booze leads him into this tantrum:

> CAPONE: I want that son of a bitch *dead*. . . . I want you to get this fuck where he breathes. I want you find this fancy boy Eliot Ness. I want him *dead*. I want his family *dead*. I want his house burnt to the ground. I wanna go in the middle of the night, I want to piss on his ashes.

"Piss on his ashes" is a vivid image, and "son of a bitch" and "this fuck" serve to testify to Capone's rage.

In many of the gangster films of the 1980s and 1990s, "fucking" occurs in nearly every sentence, to the point where the moll, Elmira, in the remake of *Scarface*, deliberately calls audience attention to this pattern: "Can't you stop saying 'fuck' all the time?" she complains. "Can't you stop talking about money? It's boring, Tony." Elmira's comment points out that obscenity can be used so often that it loses its power to shock or emphasize. The gangster's overdependence upon cursing eventually calls to mind a child's boring insistence on goading its parents with toilet language—it becomes a sign of his childishness, his limitation.

Capone's lines quoted above illustrate another characteristic of gangster dialogue and another aspect of that dialogue's power—the frequency of threats, implicit or explicit. If "commanding" is the salient speech act in Westerns, and "teasing" is the corollary in screwball comedies, "threatening" moves to fore in gangster films. Major plot activities include pressuring speakeasies to buy only this mob's bootleg whisky (*The Public Enemy*), strong-arming bettors to pay their gambling debts (*Mean Streets*), and menacing anyone who wants to bow out of the gang (*Force of Evil*). Threats may take many forms, from explicit crudeness to the arch "I'll make him an offer he can't refuse," but they are always completely serious; we know they will be carried out if the person does not knuckle under. Thus, threats often embody the deadline (discussed in chapter 1) that dominates the film's action, and they are responsible for creating an atmosphere of dread. Recall Hitchcock's famous distinction between "surprise" and "suspense," and his belief in superiority of the latter for audience manipulation—gangster threats make explicit to the viewers the jeopardy involved, and then leave us to watch helplessly as violent events unfold.

However, gangster films also punctuate their suspense with surprise. To my knowledge it is only in gangster films that one finds the following archetypal scene: character X begins a long monologue in a public, sometimes formal setting, seemingly amiable and rational. After a few lulling moments, however, he suddenly slips into frothing fury and erupts into horrendous violence, beating an associate with a testimonial pool stick in *Party Girl* (1958), slamming a coke bottle in his mistress's face in *The Long Goodbye* (1973), smashing someone's brains out with a baseball bat in *The St. Valentine's Day Massacre* (1967) and *The Untouchables,* stabbing someone through the hand in *New Jack City* (1991). The public-speech-turned-nightmare scene may derive from the fact that the real Al Capone reportedly killed two associates at a banquet.

Related to the public-speech-turned-nightmare scene are those scenes in which a manageable altercation goes ballistic because of intemperate speech. In such scenes, characters are involved in a trivial dispute or may seem to be joking. However, because character Z crosses some invisible verbal line, character Y suddenly snaps— brutally attacking, kicking, stabbing, or shooting the other. Scenes of mob rubouts played silently are not as frightening as the opening of *Menace II Society,* which starts as two black teenagers enter a Korean convenience store, chatting to each other about girls and parties. As they go over to the beer refrigerator, they notice that the female store owner is eyeing them suspiciously:

> O DOG: Let's see what's up in this motherfucker. *(To female store owner)* Hey. You ain't got to be creepin'. I don't know why you tryin' to act like you cleanin' up? Damn. Always think we gonna steal somethin'.
> CAINE: Hey, what you want Dog?
> O DOG: Um, go ahead and give me that Ol' E. Yeah.
> CAINE: I'm gonna fuck with some of this.
> O DOG: Oh no, boy. Oh man, I'm from the old school, brother. *(They start to drink.)*
> MALE OWNER: You not drink beer in store!
> CAINE: Hey man, I'm a pay you.

Woman grocer is following the boys, pretending to dust as they move around the store.

> O DOG: Hey, look, bitch, stop followin' me around this motherfucker! You gettin' on my nerves.
>
> FEMALE OWNER: Hurry up and buy.
>
> O DOG: Shut the fuck up, man.
>
> MALE OWNER: Just pay and leave.
>
> CAINE: Hey man, I said I'm a pay you. Why don't you calm your motherfuckin' nerves? Damn!
>
> MALE OWNER: Hurry up and go.
>
> O DOG: *(To Caine)* Hey man, why don't you go 'head and get it [inaudible].
>
> CAINE: I got your back.
>
> O DOG: Shit.
>
> CAINE: *(To O Dog)* You get my change.
>
> O DOG: Yeah. Hey, why don't you give my homeboy his change?
>
> MALE OWNER: I don't want any trouble. Just get out!
>
> O DOG: I can't stand y'all motherfuckers!
>
> MALE OWNER: I feel sorry for your mother.

Whereas up to this point, it seemed possible that the boys would buy their beer and leave without trouble, the grocer's mention of O Dog's mother immediately electrifies the atmosphere.

> O DOG: What you say about my momma? You feel sorry for who?
>
> MALE OWNER: I don't want any trouble! Just get out!
>
> O DOG: The fuck you say about my momma?
>
> MALE OWNER: I don't want any trouble. Just get out! [inaudible]
>
> O DOG: You talkin' shit. [inaudible]

O Dog shoots male grocer, as his wife screams.

In a fury, O Dog proceeds to murder the female grocer too, rip out the store security tape, loot the cash register, and search the man's body for more money. As Caine comments in voice-over: "Went into the store just to get a beer. Came out an accessory to murder and armed robbery. It was funny like that in the ['hood] sometimes. You never knew what was gonna happen or when." In gangster films, you never know when the wrong comment is going to be your death warrant.

Robert Warshow argues that one of the most important qualities of the Western hero is his restraint, the fact that he never goes looking for a fight, and tries to avoid it as much as he can. The gangster, on the contrary, is totally unrestrained; his power comes from the fact that his hair-trigger temper could snap at any moment. This contrast is also manifest in the different quantities of speech associated with the gangster and the Westerner. We saw before that the popular impression of the Western hero is of his taciturnity. But as Warshow has noticed:

> Like other tycoons, the gangster is crude in conceiving his ends but by no means inarticulate; on the contrary, he is usually expansive and noisy (the introspective gangster is a fairly recent development), and can state definitely what he wants: to take over the North Side, to own a hundred suits, to be Number One.[16]

In other words, just as the gangster is unrestrained in his approach to violence, so is he promiscuous in his approach to words. He boasts, swears, threatens; he lies, jokes, teases. The talkative gangster can be quite humorous, and much of the dialogue in these films is quite funny. Johnny Friendly in *On the Waterfront*, Johnny Boy in *Mean Streets*, Tommy in *GoodFellas* are the life of the room, spinning tales, amusing their gangs. The talkative gangster even philosophizes:

> RICO: When I get in a tight spot, I shoot my way out of it. Like tonight . . . sure, shoot first—argue afterwards. If you don't the other guy gets you. This game ain't for guys that's soft.
>
> TONY CAMONTE: There is only one law, do it first, do it yourself, and keep doing it.
>
> TERRY MALLOY: Hey, you wanna hear my philosophy of life? Do it to him before he does it to you.
>
> EDDIE BARTLETT: While the gravy's flowin' I'm gonna be right there with my kisser under the faucet.

But always there seems to be a connection between unrestrained words and unrestrained violence, a connection made explicit in *Bugsy* in the scene where Virginia Hill first comes to Benny Siegel's house for sex:

> VIRGINIA: Do you always talk this much before you do it?
>
> BENNY: I only talk this much before I wanna kill someone.

If the gangster talks so much, is he in any way associated with femininity? On the surface, no. The gangster protagonist as embodied by Cagney, Robinson, Muni, De Niro, and Pacino corresponds to all the social tropes of masculinity: aggressive, ambitious, powerful, tough, brave. His talk is not the scatterbrained blathering of screwball heroines, but showboating, obscenity, intimidation, or self-justification. And yet I would argue that, on another level, gangsters are clearly marked with traits stereotyped as feminine; after all, they are always presented as vain and bedazzled by gaudy clothing, they are irrational and ruled by their emotions. Perhaps their talkativeness cuts both ways—it is both a weapon and a sign of their weakness. The gangster's death in the gutter at the film's end is payback for breaking, not only the laws of capitalism, but also the strictures of masculinity.

Westerns generally feature a deliberate contrast between East and West, between educated Eastern speech and Western dialect. What is striking about gangster films is how hermetically sealed they are. With a few exceptions, such as Jean in *The Roaring Twenties,* Doris in *Force of Evil,* Edie in *On the Waterfront,* and Kay in *The Godfather,* there are no schoolmarms from New England here, no one to contrast with the closed group of the gang. Many gangster films contain no significant women characters at all, and thus "declarations of love," which are so momentous in so many American films, play a negligible role in this genre.

Those gangster films that do include women portray them as part of the corrupt system, part of this anti-society. Poppy in *Scarface,* Candy in *Pickup on South Street* (1953), Debby in *The Big Heat* (1953), Sheila in *The Killers* (1964), Irene in *Prizzi's Honor* (1985), and Ginger in *Casino* (1995) share many qualities: they are sexually available, tough, and able to dish it out. Their interchanges with their lovers have some of the same edge as the interactions among the male gangsters—threats, obscenity, and one-upmanship are common. Such conversations seem to highlight the degree to which sex and violence are intertwined in this world, leading to exchanges that might best be described as "smoldering." Take, for example, this segment of the scene when Benny first meets Virginia on a movie set in *Bugsy:*

BEN: May I . . .

VIRGINIA: If you want a simple yes or no you're gonna have to finish the question.

BEN: ... light your cigarette?
VIRGINIA: Sure. *(laughs)* The way you were staring at me I thought you
were gonna ask me for something a little more exciting.
BEN: Like what?
VIRGINIA: Use your imagination.
BEN: I'm using it.
VIRGINIA: Let me know when you're finished.

If the women characters fail to serve as a counterpoint to the gangster anti-society, so too do representatives of the law. Gangster films can be divided into those whose central character is a criminal and those whose star is the policeman trying to bring the mob to justice. One would think that the policeman would serve as a contrast to the gangsters in terms of his moral probity, his values, and his speech. In *The Untouchables*, Eliot Ness is a straightlaced prig who ludicrously embarks on a raid shouting, "Let's do some good!" But even in this instance, Ness's status as contrast is compromised by his gradual education in street fighting under the tutelage of the much savvier Irish cop played by Sean Connery. In the majority of gangster films, the G-man walks the walk and talks the talk of the men he is pursuing; like the cowboy hero who speaks Navaho, these policemen speak Gangsterese. "Infiltration" plots, where a policeman goes undercover in order to get evidence for future court cases, as in *Street with No Name* (1948), *White Heat* (1949), *New Jack City* (1991), and *Donnie Brasco* (1997), hinge upon the policeman's ability to blend in seamlessly with his underworld pals.

Neither women nor legal authority figures thus serve as "representatives of civilization" in the gangster world. On rare occasions, a priest appears, but his rhetoric sounds as if it comes from another universe—which it does. For the most part, the filmic underworld is hermetically sealed off from contrasting characters, contrasting values, contrasting speech. The conventions of the gangster milieu become the norm. As Karen Hill says in voice-over in *GoodFellas*, "And we were also very close. I mean, there were never any outsiders around. Absolutely never! And being together all the time made everything seem even more normal." Unlike Westerns, these films evince almost no intertexuality in terms of outside discourses being incorporated into the gangster world, no quoted poetry, no performances of Shakespeare (although gangland figures sometimes attend or listen to recordings of Italian opera). What I have found is a high incidence of internal references, of later gangster films literally poaching lines from earlier works (*New Jack City*'s Nino Brown quotes *Scarface*'s, "The world is mine" while watching De Palma's version in his screening room). I see such intra-genre repetition as further indication of this world's self-enclosure. Without the benefit of contrasting styles, their "anti-language" becomes language itself.

The viewer has a conflicted relationship to the gangster universe. We are both attracted and repelled by the gangster's energy and acquisitiveness, both in awe of and disgusted by his violence. The dynamics of the dialogue only further this conflict. Some of the dialogue relies so heavily on crime jargon, foreign accents, or even foreign languages that it may be more or less incomprehensible to the eavesdropping moviegoer. These audibility frustrations are exacerbated by the genre's penchant for polylogues—in gangster films there are countless scenes of overlapping conversations between gang members horsing around, playing cards, having drinks. These polylogues are designed to show group solidarity and to create an informal and realistic atmosphere. But because so much of this dialogue is quick and overlapping, the viewer will not catch every word. Mark Winokur points out the particularly noticeable difficulties with contemporary black films: "Some black inflections are so difficult for white audiences to understand that . . . minutes can go by in *Boyz 'N the Hood* and *New Jack City* that are difficult for white audience to follow. . . . Linguistic opacity redefines the gangster film as the 'gangsta' film."[17] But "struggling to understand" is confined neither to any one gangster ethnic group nor to any one time period; segments of *Dead End* (1936) and *Angels with Dirty Faces* (1937) featuring a gang of white slum kids are very hard to follow, so are exchanges in *Pickup on South Street* (white urban hoods), the 1983 *Scarface* (Cuban immigrants), and *GoodFellas* (Italian-Americans). Some degree of linguistic opacity may define the gangster film in toto, although the extent to which an individual viewer will struggle depends upon the viewer's own linguistic proficiencies: a black moviegoer may have less trouble with *Boyz N the Hood* and more trouble with De Palma's *Scarface,* while the opposite might hold true for a Hispanic viewer.

These audibility problems don't represent technical flaws in gangster films; this frustration is part of their aesthetic. Whatever our own ethnic background, no filmgoers are supposed to catch every word of every gangster film; we are not expected to understand every inside reference. Our failure to hear or comprehend continually throws in our face that we are outside this gang; the characters are pals and equals, and we are not included. Unlike the case with screwball comedies, where the dialogue winks at us and includes the viewer in the fun, in gangster films the characters are hip and cool and oh so tough; we are merely weak-kneed tourists. Whereas almost all other film dialogue is designed for the comfort of the eavesdropper, these films pretend not to give a flying fuck about our comfort, and we admire them the more for their disdain.

A difficulty arises here. If, as chapter 1 argued, dialogue serves major narrative functions such as anchoring the diegesis or explaining causality, how can these films get away with slighting the audience's ability to hear or understand? The answer is multifaceted. Numerous gangster films don't try very hard to surmount the dilemma, as if narrative clarity (and all that such clarity implies about a stable, ordered world and society), were not important to these texts—their complicated plots and entangled relationships remain somewhat cloudy to the audience, at least without numerous viewings. Other films carefully relegate their inaudible conversations to fulfilling the functions of character revelation or realism; when moments of key plot information arrive, the filmmakers make sure such lines are clearly telegraphed. Still other films design methods of compensating for their dialogue's expositional weakness. One of the benefits of studying dialogue is that these choices ricochet to affect other cinematic signifiers. A major reason why gangster films rely upon *so many* shots of newspaper headlines, *so many* montage sequences of silent action, and *so much* voice-over narration, is to fulfill the functions that the dialogue is abdicating.

––––––––

Once one starts analyzing dialogue, it is easy to fall into the mindset of some contemporary literary theorists to whom Language becomes the all-important force. Instead of gangster films being "about" the American Dream, crime, greed, hubris, or sadism, one might claim that their real subject is language per se. And such a claim is only moderately absurd, because the shift to studying gangster dialogue, as opposed to the visual elements so often cited (trenchcoats, cars, guns, and so on), leads us to see that this genre is virtually obsessed with the issue of talk.

Not "talk," in terms of conversation, but "talk" in terms of *talking*, squealing, squawking, ratting on one's friends. In these films, the criminals form a social group, a clan. In *GoodFellas*, Jimmy Conway overtly explains to Henry Hill the two cardinal rules of their world, and the issue is so vital to them that no one realizes that the "two" rules virtually overlap: "Never rat on your friends and always keep your mouth shut." Many characters make it clear that informing is the absolute worst sin; like Eddie in *The Roaring Twenties* (1939), they believe that killing their enemy is more moral than informing on him. The abhorrence of verbal betrayal obviously owes something to the historical existence of the code of *omerta*, a Sicilian word that literally translates as "manliness" and figuratively means "the belief that it is dishonorable to tell anything about a fellow countryman which could get him into trouble."[18] Informing or testifying is so terrible, partly because of the legal consequences, but also because going to the authorities sunders the quasi-family emotional ties among the group. Moreover, talking to the authorities is a betrayal, because it punctures the airtight seal of the underworld, forcing the realization that the gang's mode of life and values are aberrant, not dominant. Within their world, gang leaders are obsequiously pandered to as caesars; out in the glare of the wider society, they are shown up to be vermin. The gravest jeopardy portrayed in gangster films is thus not physical violence but a speech act.

Furthermore, "squealing" is involved in the majority of gangster films; nearly every plot includes the potentiality or the actuality of some gang member going to the police. In *GoodFellas*, Henry Hill accepts Jimmy's maxims unquestioningly . . . until the time comes when it is more expedient for him to turn state's evidence and rat on all his erstwhile buddies. (As J. Hoberman notes: "The emphasis on gangster codes of loyalty to friends or family is an inoculation against the realization that, out in the marketplace, the only valid ideology is a paranoid loyalty to the self.")[19] In doing so, Henry joins a long line of informers, stretching from Joe Massara in *Little Caesar*, to Jean Collins in *"G" Men*, to Moe in *Pickup on South Street*, to Terry in *On the Waterfront*, to Thomas Farrell in *Party Girl*, to C. J. Moss in *Bonnie and Clyde*, to Joe Valachi in *The Valachi Papers*, to Pentangeli in

Godfather II, to Danny in *Prince of the City*, to the title character in *Donnie Brasco*.

In 1936, at Lucky Luciano's trial, Thelma Jordan, a prostitute testifying against the mob boss, said: "I knew what happened to girls who talked about the combination. The soles of their feet and their stomachs were burned with cigar butts for talking too much. . . . I heard Ralph say that their tongues were cut when girls talked."[20] And Victor Navasky notes: "The castration with a blowtorch of James Ragen, a Chicago racketeer and suspected government informer, by three syndicate executioners in 1947 is testimony both to the violence that the informer provokes and to the power his information has over the corrupt."[21] American movie screens are littered with the bodies of characters who have informed, threatened to inform, or merely possessed information that they might conceivably tell somebody sometime. Incredible amounts of energy and sadistic, sexualized violence are thus expended in *silencing*. The overall impression that one gets is that this genre presents an extensive cautionary tale concerning male speech, a lesson on when it is all right to talk. Within the tribe, with your buddies, verbosity may be a sign of wit and skill—*but don't ever talk to strangers*.

Attentive study reveals, however, that even within the clan, words can be treacherous. Whereas in Westerns, the hero believes in the utter sanctity of his word as bond, in gangster films, the characters continually profess such integrity and then immediately break their vows. These people *lie* to one another incessantly. They betray one another continually—making alliances they plan to break, double-crossing one another on the take, pledging fealty to leaders they intend to murder. In the Introduction, we looked at the cultural prejudices against speech, including the charge that words can be used to mislead. Gangster films provide an object lesson in that paranoia.

"Informing" and "lying" both affect the positioning of viewers, but in contradictory ways. When a character informs to the cops or investigators, he is telling this story to some (often unseen) authority outside of the world of the mob. Usually, the means by which he gathers evidence is by wearing a wire, so that the removed authorities can themselves eavesdrop on the gangsters' conversations. Because he acts as the bridge between the crime world and normal society, the informer is symbolically telling the story to us, the audience. What the films rub our noses in, again and again, is the extent to which, in telling us the story, the informer is violating a code of ethics and betraying deep emotional ties, and the extent to which he puts himself in dire jeopardy. The audience suffers terrible suspense waiting for the infiltrator/informer to be "found out," because when he is, it is almost as if the viewer too had been discovered listening outside a closed door.

The constant lying in gangster films has an opposite effect on the eavesdropping viewer, usually working to enhance our feelings of superiority. When we know more than any of the characters, when we are able to see how they are deceiving one another, we are conscious of our privileged, omniscient overview.

———————

Because the gangster genre has such prominence in contemporary cinema, I have chosen two relatively recent examples for closer analysis, Francis Ford Coppola's *The Godfather* (1972), and Quentin Tarantino's *Reservoir Dogs* (1992). These will illustrate many of the topics discussed above and lead us off in new directions.

As is well known, Coppola's *The Godfather* is an adaptation of the phenomenally popular novel of that title by Mario Puzo, with a screenplay crafted by both Puzo and Coppola. Puzo denies that he had any mafioso friends or direct contact with that world; he researched his story through reference works, through transcripts of congressional hearings on drugs and crime, and by watching the Valachi hearings on television. He freely acknowledges that the story is "romanticized myth" as opposed to having documentary pretensions.[22] Much of the dialogue in the movie is lifted intact from the novel (including the famous line about making an offer that can't be refused). However, in the book, the characters' speech is embedded in the flow of a rather unappealing, hackneyed narrative voice. For example, the opening scene between Don Corleone and Bonasera, the undertaker, when Bonasera comes to ask the Don to kill the men who have assaulted his daughter, was originally interlaced with the following explanatory comments: "He [Bonasera] was trembling, his sallow face flushed an ugly dark red"; "But when he [Don Corleone] spoke, the words were cold with offended dignity"; and "The cruel and contemptuous irony with which all this was said, the controlled anger of the Don, reduced the poor undertaker to a quivering jelly."[23]

Transposing the novel's lines to film involved replacing the novel's narrator with Coppola's mise-en-scène and giving the words to skilled actors; thus the same dialogue sounds much better in the film than in the novel.

Coppola was granted the job of directing partly on the basis of his ethnicity, because Italian-American groups were offended by the novel and the producers believed that hiring a director of Italian-American descent would blunt their criticisms. Interestingly, it was not the Production Code, which had so affected screwball comedy, but was now defunct, but lobbying by the Italian-American League that led to very specific verbal strictures. "In place of the words 'Mafia' and 'Cosa Nostra' the crime syndicate will be referred to in the film as 'the five families' and other non-Italian phrases," conceded the producer, Al Ruddy.[24] I also suspect that Italian-American pressure was responsible for the film's striking compensatory stress on the discrimination suffered by this ethnic group, as in the movie producer Woltz's line: "I don't care how many dago, guinea, wop, greaseball goombahs come out of the woodwork." By including such dialogue, Coppola exposes filmgoers to the virulence of anti-Italian prejudice, and thus, as Todd Boyd argues, the film implies that "oppression forced these Italian immigrants into a subversive lifestyle."[25]

The Godfather is the story of the Corleone family: the father, Don Corleone (Marlon Brando), who heads his mafioso clan with dignity and warmth; his three sons, Sonny (James Caan), Fredo (John Cazale), and Michael (Al Pacino); his adopted son, Tom Hagen (Robert Duvall); and his daughter Connie (Talia Shire). The movie begins at the lavish wedding of Connie Corleone to Carlo Rizzi, during which we meet the family and see how the family business is organized. Don Corleone faces challenges: first he has to get Woltz to hire his godson, and then he has to deal with a business proposition put forward by another mobster, Sollozzo, involving drug trafficking. When the Don turns down the drug deal, Sollozzo and his associates make an attempt on his life, which leads to a bloody gang war. Michael Corleone, who has hitherto stayed above the criminal fray, gets revenge by murdering Sollozzo and his protector, Police Captain McClusky (Sterling Hayden), and then hides out in Sicily. In Sicily, Michael is briefly married to a young Sicilian girl, but she is killed by a bomb meant for Michael. His father recovers from his wounds, but his brother Sonny is gunned down. Michael returns to America, marries his former girlfriend, Kay (Diane Keaton), takes over the reins of power from his aging father, and eliminates his family's enemies, even though this includes killing his brother-in-law. The film, which began with Connie's wedding, thus ends with her becoming a widow.

The Godfather is famous for the artistry of its visual style, enhanced by cinematographer Gordon Willis's careful control of light and dark, the period art direction, and the sophisticated editing. Of all the films I've analyzed closely, this contains the most and longest sequences relying solely on visual appeal: the dancing at Connie's wedding, the scenes of the Sicilian countryside, the montage sequences of the gangland battles, Sonny's murder, and Michael's wedding to Apollonia literally exclude conversation. (In view of the general preference for visual filmmaking, I find it refreshing that, instead of praising these sequences as the epitome of pure cinema, Jack Shadoian criticizes the film's "prolonged silences" and "stupefying grandeur and glutted glamorousness," which he finds antithetical to the genre's energetic tradition.)[26]

The Godfather, released the year before *Mean Streets*, features dialogue that is more restrained, less freewheeling, than later examples of the genre. Most of the polylogue scenes are "pseudo," in that while numerous people are present, only the dominant figure, Don Corleone, or, later, Michael, speaks to the guest. Even in the family scenes, which contain some overlapping dialogue, all the speakers' contributions are fully audible. Obscenity is noticeable ("goddamn," "piece of ass," "son of a bitch"), but not as incessant or as crude as in more recent gangster films.

The dialogue may be restrained (in comparison to *Reservoir Dogs*), but two verbal factors nonetheless stress the separation of this clan from the rest of society—the use of special euphemisms and the use of Italian.

Gangster films appear so rough and blunt that it is odd to realize how much they resort to evasive wording, how they cover up ugliness with cleaner phrasing. But *The Godfather* makes us recognize the degree to which movie gangsters' protect themselves from (self-?) castigation by verbal evasion. Just as 1930s gangsters "take someone for a ride" rather than murder him, so Don Corleone "makes someone an offer he can't refuse" rather than extort or strong-arm him.

The mobsters "go to the mattresses" instead of barricading themselves in a hideout; they "hit" Bruno Tattaglia, as opposed to assassinating him.

In the opening scene Don Corleone admonishes Bonasera who has come to him asking for retribution after the courts have failed him:

> DON CORLEONE: We've known each other many years but this is the first time you ever came to me for counsel or for help. . . . But let's be frank here. You never wanted my friendship—and—you were afraid to be in my debt.[27]

Corleone is actually being anything but frank—Bonasera is not asking for "counsel" or for "help" or "friendship," but for the Don to arrange to murder two men. But Bonasera's crudeness (he even openly offers to pay for the deed) offends the Don, and the conversation proceeds as a lesson to Bonasera in the proper euphemistic language and attitude of respect. Finally, Bonasera submits: "Be my friend . . . Godfather," he says, and kisses the Don's hand.

The habit of phrasing everything in the best possible light saturates this film. The cloak of respectability covers all. The term "Godfather," with all its overtones of patriarchal and religious benevolence, is used instead of "Boss"; instead of a bald statement that Sollozzo has killed Luca, we are told, "Luca Brasi sleeps with the fishes." Most insistently, the rhetoric of business replaces the rhetoric of crime. The Corleones are involved in "the family business," rather than racketeering. When Michael joins the mob, he "is working for [his] father now"; "narcotics is the thing of the future"; staking Sollozzo's drug operation is called "finance"; fellow mobsters are labeled "associates." (*Grosse Point Blank* [1997] takes the substitution of business jargon for the language of crime to amusing lengths. In general, "gangsterese" is easy to parody.)

In chapter 2, we considered the importance of the repetition of key words. The most important two words in *The Godfather* are "business" and "personal," which recur as a leitmotif throughout, ostensibly referring to contrasting value systems, but inevitably getting everything tangled up. Consider the scene where Sonny is trying to coordinate the family's response to the attempted murder of Don Corleone:

HAGEN: Your father wouldn't want to hear this! This is business, not personal.
SONNY: They shot my father, it's business your ass!
HAGEN: Even the shooting of your father was business, not personal, Sonny!

The conversation continues, and Michael volunteers to shoot Sollozzo and Police Captain McClusky.

SONNY: *(teasing his brother)* You're taking this very personal. Tom, this is business and this man is taking it very, very personal. . . .

More talk, making it clear that Michael is prepared to do this and that he has calculated the risk.

MICHAEL: It's not personal, Sonny. It's strictly business.

In his discussion of the mythologies of the *Godfather* sagas, Thomas Ferraro notes that the appeal of Puzo's novel has often been ascribed to its nostalgic image of ethnic family life and its critique of modern capitalism, but he argues that the book's "cultural significance lies not in the simultaneous appeals of 'family' and 'business' imagery but rather in the appeal of an actual structural simultaneity: *the business of family.*"[28] Ferraro's thesis is borne out by dialogue like that above, which shows the characters' *conflation* of their emotional responses and financial interests.

The second strategy by which the film creates a separate linguistic space is its heavy reliance on Italian. The characters do not have broad Italian accents, but they speak Italian frequently, both peppering the dialogue with Italian words or phrases—"grazie," "prego," "consigliere," "salud," "Sue bequero Scotch?" "Come si diche"—and using it in more extended exchanges. Each time they slip into Italian, the audience is reminded of their foreignness, their otherness, and the fact that they all share this background (while we may not). Coppola and Puzo are very clever in their utilization of Italian (the scenes in Sicily offer a mixture of Italian and Sicilian dialect); the words chosen often have close cognates in English, or the context makes their import clear. But certain scenes include extended passages in Italian, and then we are provided with subtitles. (Interestingly, no Italian words are employed in the novel. The multiple, overlapping signifiers of film are needed to integrate a foreign language.) Italian surrounds the most violent scenes in the film, such as the murders of Luca, Sollozzo and McClusky, and Apollonia. The language of the "Old Country" is seen as fitting for the language of blood.

Along with its creation of a separate linguistic sphere, this film further substantiates our earlier discussion in terms of presenting object lessons of what happens when the sphere is breached. The gang war ostensibly starts because of a verbal lapse. During the meeting with Sollozzo to discuss his drug proposition, Sonny breaks in and speaks when he's not supposed to. (Throughout, Sonny is the typical hot-headed gangster, unable to control his sexual desires, his temper, his flying fists, or his mouth; Michael is much quieter and restrained, more in the mold of the Western hero.) The mere fact that Sonny breaks protocol by speaking indicates to Sollozzo that there is division in the family, and that the Don is not firmly in control. Coppola underscores the gravity of the situation with cutaways to Tom's and Clemenza's shocked faces. The Don himself is aware of the damage that has been done; he rebukes Sonny: "What's the matter with you? . . . Never tell anybody outside the Family what you're thinking again."

There are four outsiders in the film, who break down into two groups. Woltz and McClusky, who are enemies of the Family, are given dialogue that economically reveals their personalities in the most disreputable light, mitigating the viewer's shock at their eventual punishment. Tom Hagen and Kay Adams, however, are sympathetic figures who are both shown as desiring to blend into the Family. Tom is only moderately successful, loved and appreciated by the Corleones but never quite accepted to the degree that he would be if he were Sicilian.

Kay plays a crucial role in the film, a role that continues in *The Godfather,* Part II (1974), as the representative of the outside world. Tall and fair, instead of dark and petite, an educated WASP from New Hampshire, she is originally important to Michael because she is untainted by the family business. At the opening wedding, she serves as audience-surrogate when Michael introduces the other characters to her and fills her in on the family's past. However, Michael abandons Kay when his father is shot, instantly and instinctively closing her out of the phone booth where he goes to call Sonny.

Michael marries her after Apollonia's death in order to start a family of his own, but their marriage is much less happy and more inequitable than their initial romance.

With all its violent and showy action, the film is essentially a dual character study, or rather a presentation of two intersecting arches—Don Corleone's decline and death, and Michael's gradual embrace of the mafioso lifestyle and his assumption of his father's place. As with all character studies, the viewer's knowledge of these characters depends upon the dialogue. Marlon Brando's performance as Don Corleone earned special attention. "Brando's acting has mellowed in recent years," wrote Pauline Kael in her review. "His effects are subtler, less showy, and he gives himself over to the material. . . . He has not acquired the polish of most famous actors; just the opposite—less mannered as he grows older, he seems to draw directly from life, and from himself."[29] Don Corleone starts at the apogee of power, giving orders, granting favors, receiving tribute, deciding business deals, but the attempts on his life leave him injured, diminished, marginalized. He is kept in the dark about events, sheltered from the news of Sonny's death—in a memorable moment he approaches Tom Hagen and says: "My wife is crying upstairs. I hear cars coming to the house. Consigliere of mine, I think you should tell your Don what everyone seems to know." Later in the film, he is aging and enfeebled, repeating advice to Michael, but still capable of wry irony: "I like to drink wine more than I used to—Anyway, I'm drinking more." Throughout, Brando's delivery is noteworthy. His Don Corleone speaks slowly, with quiet dignity, and yet the voice is flavored by a raspy texture, a cracked quality, conveying a melange of ethnicity, earthiness, and naturalism.

Michael starts as a clean-cut college boy, the patriotic war hero, the son who is ashamed of and has rejected his family's criminality. "That is my family, Kay; it's not me," he claims. However, when his family is threatened, Michael returns to the fold. He first proves his mettle by taking charge of the situation at the hospital when a second attempt is made to kill his father. Subsequently, it is Michael who comes up with the daring strategy to kill Sollozzo and McClusky: "We can't wait. I don't care what Sollozzo says about a deal, he's gonna kill Pop, that's it. That's the key for him. Gotta get Sollozzo. . . . [I]f Clemenza can figure a way—to have a weapon planted there for me—then I'll kill 'em both." Michael's acceptance of his heritage is furthered by his sojourn in Sicily, and he returns to America after Sonny's death completely reconciled to following in his father's footsteps. Kay confronts him:

> KAY: I thought you weren't going to become a man like your father. That's what you told me.
> MICHAEL: My father's no different than any other powerful man.
> KAY: Hah.
> MICHAEL: Any man who's responsible for other people. Like a senator or president.

Whereas in the early part of the film, Michael saw and rejected his family's brutal criminality, by this point he seems to believe the euphemistic language of respectability with which the family cloaks itself. Michael's degeneration becomes further apparent in the "baptism scene" (discussed in chapter 3), in which the filmmakers edit together Michael's claim to renounce evil with the murders he has ordered. Michael's embrace of power and hypocrisy and the coldness of his heart become even more apparent as the film moves toward its conclusion.

The last scenes present two instances of Michael lying, and lying with such cold-blooded aplomb that the viewer is left gaping. In the first, Michael gets Carlo to admit that he set up Sonny's assassination by reassuring his terrified brother-in-law that no harm will come to him: "Come on. Don't be afraid, Carlo. Come on, do you think I'd make my sister a widow? I'm Godfather to your son, Carlo." While viewing this scene, the spectator has no information as to Michael's heart or intention; like Carlo, we fear his wrath, yet we trust his words and reassuring, paternal demeanor. Carlo's brutal murder in the car moments later is shocking both in its gory particulars, and in the fact that it reveals that Michael, who seemed so sincere and trustworthy, tricked his brother-in-law into confessing and sealing his own doom.

But the second instance is in some ways the climax of the film, because it hinges on the viewer knowing in advance that Michael is lying. In front of Kay, Connie accuses Michael of Carlo's murder, and although Michael passes his hysterical sister off to a lieutenant, he has to face Kay's accusation and doubt. Michael, who, like his father, is generally so quiet, responds with noisy (feigned? diversion-

46.   *The Godfather.* Michael's lie to Kay

ary? sincere?) anger that she would dare to ask him about his business. Then:

> MICHAEL: Enough! All right. This one time—this one time I'll let you ask me about my affairs.
> KAY: Is it true?
> MICHAEL: *(completely convincingly)* No.

Michael's bald-faced lie to his wife is somehow his most shocking action in the film. Yes, he's murdered, or had others murder for him, nearly a dozen people, but they were enemies and generally low-life criminals. Kay, on the other hand, is his wife, she is a civilian, she is innocent. Most important, she is "us," the non-mafioso tag-along who has been seduced by his power and glamour. When, conscienceless, he lies to her and then closes her out of his study, it is as if he had kicked the viewer in the face.

———

Reservoir Dogs was written and directed by Quentin Tarantino, the first film of a young man who reportedly has an IQ of 150 but never graduated high school. An independent production, it was eventually financed for $1.5 million dollars once Harvey Keitel agreed to star. The relatively low budget led to certain decisions, such as confining more than half of the screen time to one location, an abandoned warehouse. Perhaps it was the budget that led the film to prioritize its talk over photographic beauty or special effects (there are no scenes here of visual spectacle à la *The Godfather*); however Tarantino's later *Pulp Fiction* (1994), made with much more generous funding, shows the same verbal audacity, as do the scripts he wrote for *True Romance* (1993) and *Natural Born Killers* (1994). Tarantino has claimed that never showing the central action of the heist was integral to his vision from the start.[30]

A "caper film," *Reservoir Dogs* tells the story of a gang of thieves who are hired by a gangster, Joe Cabot (Lawrence Tierney), to heist a shipment from a diamond wholesaler. The robbery goes terribly wrong, because the police have been forewarned. Mr. Blonde (Michael Madsen), one of the gang, begins murdering employees; the others flee from police pursuit. Those remaining alive—Mr. White (Harvey Keitel), Mr. Orange (Tim Roth), who is shot in the belly, Mr. Pink (Steve Buscemi), and later Mr. Blonde—rendezvous as directed at a warehouse, where they argue over how to care for Mr. Orange, about who might be the traitor, and about what to do next. Flashback scenes provide information about the initial hiring of the criminal gang and furnish evidence of the robbers' messy escape from the scene of the crime. The waiting gang members are joined by Nice Guy Eddie (Chris Penn), Cabot's son, and while Eddie, Mr. White, and Mr. Pink are dumping their stolen cars, Mr. Blonde tortures a policeman he has kidnapped from the robbery. Just as Mr. Blonde is about to burn the policeman alive, the wounded Mr. Orange gathers up his strength and shoots Mr. Blonde, revealing that he is the undercover agent. Cabot, Eddie, Pink, and White return to the warehouse, where Eddie kills the policeman, and Cabot realizes that Orange is the traitor. White defends his friend Orange, killing Cabot and Eddie, and getting shot in the process. As sounds off-screen indicate that the police have caught the fleeing Pink, Orange confesses his identity to White. White kills him and then is himself blown away by the cops.

Reservoir Dogs has attracted a great deal of controversy, and it was banned on video in the United Kingdom for two years. First, there's the explicit violence, especially the torture scene where Mr. Blonde slices off the cop's ear while dancing to a 1970s rock song, "Stuck in the Middle with You." Then there's the overall quantity of blood, which pours out of Mr. Orange all over the car, his clothes, the floor. Then there are the film's misogynistic, racist, and homophobic over-tones,[31] which are blatant in such lines as Nice Guy Eddie's, "Ain't that a sad sight, Daddy. Man walks into prison a white man, walks out talkin' like a fuckin' nigger. You know what? I think it's all that black semen been pumped up your ass so far. Now it's backed up into your fuckin' brain, and it's comin' out your mouth."

All of the dialogue is unrelentingly obscene, generally over the top, and decidedly relentless. "Having created the characters and fashioned the outline," Roger Ebert observes, "Tarantino doesn't do much with his characters except to let them talk too much, especially when they should probably be unconscious from shock and loss of blood."[32] And yet other critics have specifically admired the film for its dialogue: Owen Gleiberman wrote in *Entertainment Weekly,*

> Some of the most enthralling movies of our time have come down to the spectacle of raging macho blowhards hurling profanities and hell-raising wisecracks at each other. . . . In a civilized world where people have to watch their tongues on the job, in the classroom, even perhaps when speaking to their loved ones, there's something primal and liberating about characters who can let it all hang out, whose ids come bursting forth in white hot chunks of verbal shrapnel.[33]

"White hot chunks of verbal shrapnel" is perhaps too poetic a de-scription, but it does capture the film's quality of verbal aggression. That breaking all the rules of movie dialogue is the film's guiding principle is made clear in the opening scene, where all the characters are finishing breakfast in a pancake house. The dialogue in this se-quence is aberrant on many levels. First, it is not completely audible, because the sound is muffled to a degree, characters don't articulate clearly, and often their dialogue is overlapping. Secondly, the cam-era, which is restlessly moving around the table, doesn't initially iso-late speakers, so it is hard to know who is speaking to whom and where they are sitting.

Thirdly, the content of the conversation is like nothing ever before heard on film. As Tarantino told an interviewer, "So you've got these movie guys, they look like genre characters but they're talking about things that genre characters don't normally talk about."[34] Mr. Brown, played by Tarantino himself, starts by giving a pseudo-academic in-terpretation of Madonna's song "Like a Virgin." (" 'Like a Virgin' is

47.   The opening scene of *Reservoir Dogs.*

all about a girl who digs a guy with a big dick. The whole song is a
metaphor for big dicks.") Joe Cabot is looking at an old address
book, and Mr. White teasingly takes it away. ("For the past fifteen
minutes now, you've been droning on about names. 'Toby . . . Toby
. . . Toby . . . Toby Wong . . . Toby Wong . . . Toby Wong . . . Toby
Chung . . . fuckin' Charlie Chan.' I've got Madonna's big dick outta
my left ear, and Toby the Jap I-don't-know-what, comin' outta my
right [fig. 47]") Mr. Pink explains that he is opposed to the practice of
tipping, and the others argue with him. None of these conversations
have anything whatsoever to do with the narrative, and especially
here at the opening, when the viewer will be anticipating anchorage
and exposition, our expectations are completely frustrated.

Which is not to say that the sequence actually escapes the functions outlined in chapter 1, for it is serving a crucial job in terms of
character development. Mr. Brown, the director, shows himself to be
smug and arrogant; Nice Guy Eddie is somewhat stupid; Mr. White
is relaxed, teasing Joe Cabot, and stands up for waitresses; Mr. Orange is relatively silent throughout; Mr. Pink comes across as being
stingy and unempathetic, which affects the viewer's later understanding of the story. Tarantino, who has become such a cult figure
and given so many interviews that he has glossed almost every moment of his films (here might be a genuine case of someone talking
too much), explains that "People write off Mr. Pink as being this
weasely kind of guy who just cares about himself, but that's actually
not the case. Mr. Pink is right throughout the whole fucking movie.
Everything he says is right, he just doesn't have the courage of his

own convictions."[35] Mr. Pink's capitulation to the group's pressure to cough up his share of the tip thus foreshadows his later inability to act to forestall the gang's disintegration.

Indeed, dialogue is used throughout as the major tool for character revelation. Orange, who will later become so emotionally involved with White, early on demonstrates his tendency toward overly identifying with the criminals whom he is supposed to be spying on when he tells his police superior, Holdaway, how grateful he is for Long Beach Mike's bogus reference. White reveals his compassionate nature when he comforts the injured Orange in quasi-maternal terms, teasing him about hurting the floor by banging his head on it, reassuring Orange that he'll be right back. And White is the one who expresses sorrow over the death of women employees at the holdup. Yet at the same time, White's dialogue illustrates extreme cold-bloodedness, as when he instructs Orange on how to get a manager to cooperate by cutting off his fingers. The underlying tension of the film—is White a "good guy" or a "bad guy"? to whom will Orange be loyal, his gangster friend or the claims of the outside world?—are constructed for the viewer by the characters' talk.

Indeed, dialogue does most of its usual jobs throughout the film: explaining causality, enacting narrative events, representing macho banter (which Tarantino apparently intends as "realistic"). However, part of the unique flavor of the talk in *Reservoir Dogs* stems from the fact that Tarantino strenuously eschews using dialogue to anchor time and place. From the film's nonsensical title to the characters' anti-names, the text evinces a certain opacity. No one mentions what city we are in. Viewers don't know how much time separates the meal at the diner from the heist. We don't know the temporal or spatial relationships between the flashback scenes and the "present" in the warehouse. We jump from one moment in the flashback past to another without preparation, explanation, or re-anchorage. The viewer is thus jolted from one moment of the diegesis to another with only visual clues and suppositions concerning causality as guidelines. Part of the fun of the film is solving the puzzle, figuring out how each scene relates to others.

Equally unusual is the role given to talk that seemingly has nothing to do with the story at hand. Digressive conversations recur throughout, often about pop culture touchstones such as 1970s television shows. However, what is particularly striking is the extent to which *Reservoir Dogs* foregrounds the act of storytelling, substituting verbal storytelling for more conventional movie events. Some of these stories are plot-related. Yet as the film progresses, the stories become more and more tangential to narrative causality: Mr. White tells Mr. Pink about his last job, Nice Guy Eddie tells the guys a story about a woman he knows named Elois who superglued her husband's penis. Finally, a long section of the film, Mr. Orange's flashback, centers on his learning to tell "the commode story," a fictitious tale about marijuana trafficking designed to ingratiate Orange with his new associates. Most strikingly, yet another story—a highway patrolman telling his buddies about how he almost shot a civilian—is embedded inside of the commode story. *Reservoir Dogs* glories in storytelling.

All this emphasis on verbal storytelling foregrounds the constructed nature of the film we are watching. "Instead of developing characters who form a kind of alternate society, *Reservoir Dogs* investigates the very nature of character," J. P. Telotte observes.[36] This theme is overtly stressed by Holdaway's instructions to Orange, "An undercover cop's gotta be Marlon Brando. To do this job you gotta be a great actor. You gotta be naturalistic; you gotta be naturalistic as hell." The reference to Brando and acting is part of a pattern of movie references, to Lee Marvin, Doris Day, Charles Bronson, and so on. All of these serve to ironize the text and foreground its hip knowingness.

Reservoir Dogs is an "infiltration story," revolving around the danger faced by a member of the outside society who infiltrates the gang to gather evidence. Mr. Orange is in terrible jeopardy throughout, and his survival rests upon his being able to participate in gangster life, particularly the verbal milieu, without a slipup. At the same time, he is torn because of the emotional bonds that develop between himself and Mr. White. These bonds are demonstrated by physical action, such as White's tenderly combing Orange's hair, and by the fact that White has violated the strictures against verbal self-revelation, by telling Orange his first name and hometown.

Thus, like other gangster films, *Reservoir Dogs* stresses both the dangers of talking and the deeply felt need to do so. The showy torture scene further focuses our attention on the pressures surrounding speech and explicitly discloses the fact that in gangster films, eliciting or suppressing speech is suffused with sexual tension. Mr. Blonde reveals that actually getting information from the policeman is the last of his priorities—he's more interested in the sadism. "Now I'm not gonna bullshit you. I don't really care about what you know or don't know. I'm gonna torture you for a while regardless. Not to get information, but because torturing a cop amuses me." After he slices off his victim's ear, he quips, "Was that as good for you as it was for me?" Given the lengths to which Mr. Blonde goes, one of genuine surprises of the film is that the cop, Marvin Nash, holds out and maintains his utter ignorance.

Marvin Nash and Orange are both good liars. They fool the other gangsters and they fool the viewer for many scenes. Interestingly, the viewer's reaction to finding out the truth is diametrically opposed to one's experience with *The Godfather:* instead of feeling betrayed when we find out the truth, we admire Nash and Orange for their skillful performances, and admire their stoicism in standing up to pain. (It is intriguing that the most important thing that Orange and Nash feel the need to communicate to each other while they are both suffering and in terrible danger is their real names.)

However, like *The Godfather,* the climax of the film is a speech act. Out of friendship and loyalty, White defends Orange against Joe and Nice Guy Eddie, to the point of a preposterous Mexican standoff in which Joe and Eddie are killed and White seriously wounded. In the wake of such loyalty, Orange feels compelled to admit that he is an infiltrator. "I'm a cop," he groans, hoarsely. "Larry. I'm so sorry. I'm a cop." Orange's confession is a move toward genuine connection. But White's identification with his criminal community and anger at being misled are stronger than his love for his friend. He kills the infiltrator.

Along with its other similarities to *The Godfather, Reservoir Dogs* uses verbal repetition to highlight a key contrast. Here, however, the dichotomy is not "family" versus "business," but "professional" behavior versus childish behavior, the latter referred to by a variety of phrases including references to "infants," "kids," a "first-year thief," and "playgrounds." Under the stress of the heist gone wrong, the conspirators try to fall back on some internal code of professional gangster rules, as when Mr. Pink yells at Mr. White, "Fuck you, White! I didn't create this situation, I'm dealin' with it. You're acting like a first-year fuckin' thief. I'm actin' like a professional." At the same time, the whole group of them, complete with their silly pseudonyms, frequently lapse into words and behavior that reminds one of children. Immature behavior is blatantly apparent during the scene where Joe, at the blackboard, like a teacher, is assigning their names and instructing them on the plan, while they bicker and talk back. Joe castigates them, "You guys like to tell jokes and giggle and kid around, huh? Giggling like a bunch of young broads in a school yard."

"Childishness" ultimately seems an important touchstone to understanding *Reservoir Dogs*. Gavin Smith argues that "Tarantino ultimately redeems genre morally; even in *Reservoir Dogs*'s world of simulation and identity-projection, betrayal is still betrayal." I believe that the film withdraws from any serious thematic statement about betrayal or anything else when it plays the absurd song "Coconut," about limes, coconuts, and bellyaches, immediately after White kills Orange. Notwithstanding its intricate narrative structure, and notwithstanding this subtext dealing with loyalty and betrayal, *Reservoir Dogs* is a completely "childish" film, from its title to its little in-jokes (the woman whom Mr. Orange shoots is Tim Roth's real-life dialogue coach), to its stoned-out radio announcer, to its relentless obscenity. Instead of showing gangsters as tragic heroes of a hermetic subculture that serves as a negative comment on official America, *Reservoir Dogs* shows its gangsters as squabbling children afloat in the jetsam of pop culture. Instead of eating authentic Italian cuisine in private restaurants, they eat fast food; instead of listening to opera, they listen to K-Billy's Sounds of the Seventies. Instead of being bonded together by ethnicity, community, and family ties, these gangsters don't even know each others' names, and they end up killing each other off even before the police arrive. As Sharon Willis has remarked, "Tarantino's films offer a masculinity whose worst enemy is itself."[37]

Yet far from being a betrayal of the gangster genre, *Reservoir Dogs* may be its fulfillment. Robin Wood once argued that because of Tony's immaturity, because of the film's mingling of farce and horror, and because of its fascination with irresponsibility, the original *Scarface* should be analyzed along with Hawks's *comedies*.[38] Wood's insights are obviously pertinent to all the films discussed in this chapter. *Reservoir Dogs* merely takes these elements two steps further, hurling its "verbal shrapnel" with anarchic glee.

SEVEN

Misunderstandings

Dialogue in Melodramas

> We parted and I threw my life away because I didn't care to
> bargain for love with words.
>
> Shanghai Lily to Captain Harvey
> in *Shanghai Express* (1932)

Like screwball comedies, melodramas have long been associated
with excessive talk. But whereas the comedies have somewhat pro-
tected themselves from criticism by their slapstick antics, irreverence, and irony, melodramas—which by their very nature aim at
emotional revelation and sincerity—have no such armor. Screwball
comedy is seen as appealing to audiences of both genders; melodrama has traditionally been associated with women viewers.
Screwballs "sabotage the language of love," but melodramas dare to
play it straight. Whether because of their association with female
viewers, their privileging of emotion, or their emphasis on dialogue
as opposed to physical action, melodramas have long met with great
disdain, still apparent in the capsule reviews in the *New York Times*
television guide, which frequently refer to melodramas as "sudsy"
or "weepie."

Since the 1970s, however, film academics have been fascinated by
melodrama and what it illuminates about the pressures and contradictions of gender roles and family life in American society. *Imitations of Life*, edited by Marcia Landy, and *Home Is Where the Heart Is*,
edited by Christine Gledhill, illustrate the large variety of analyses
that have been applied to this genre, including historical, feminist,
psychoanalytic, and Marxist approaches.[1] Although the genre's special variety of dialogue sometimes comes up, few film scholars have

given the topic their full attention. This may be because so much of their emphasis, following the lead of Thomas Elsaesser, has been focused on illustrating the ways in which the genre covertly formulates a "devastating critique of the ideology that supports it."[2] "Reading against the grain" of the films, exploring the texts' freighted contradictions in terms of their portrayals of social class, sexuality, and gender roles, results in scholars themselves sabotaging the language of love—that is, questioning and ironizing the sentiments so baldly expressed in these texts. Peter Brooks's study of theatrical melodramas and their influence on the novel, *The Melodramatic Imagination: Balzac, Henry James, Melodrama and the Mode of Excess* is the only source I have found that takes dialogue in melodrama seriously.[3]

"Melodrama" has been used both to describe a style or mode of artistic expression and as a term for a somewhat loosely connected group of texts. As a style, "melodramatic" is opposed to "realist"; it is marked by a disdain for probability, a polarization of good and evil, and a serious, heightened, expressivity. As a genre, melodramas are identifiable by the wedding of such a style to a story centering on romantic and familial relationships, a story that privileges the private life over the public.* (Thus a Western such as *Shane* may be melodramatic, but since the love story is secondary to its emphasis on "settling the West," it is not a melodrama; by the same token, *When Harry Met Sally* may center on a love story, but its comic tone is the reverse of the melodramatic.)

Melodrama began as a form of drama in France in the years immediately following the French Revolution. Silent films, such as Griffith's *Way Down East* were often adaptations of stage melodramas,[4] and stage melodrama's conventions of expressive gesture and

---

* The definition of melodrama as genre is quite contested. I am following along the lines of the Gledhill and Landy anthologies, and the work of other critics of the 1980s. Thus my definition corresponds very closely with that offered by Robert Lang in *American Film Melodrama: Griffith, Vidor, Minnelli* (Princeton, N.J.: Princeton University Press, 1989), 49: "Courtship, marriage and family as major preoccupations of bourgeois society, found their way into almost every film made, and when they were the main subject of a movie, the movie was (and is) generally and simply called a melodrama." This use of the term, however, has been criticized by Russell Merritt in "Melodrama: Post-Mortem for a Phantom Genre," *Wide Angle* 5.3 (1983): 24–31, and by Rick Altman in "Reusable Packaging: Generic Product and the Recycling Process," in *Refiguring American Film Genres*, ed. Nick Browne (Berkeley and Los Angeles: University of California Press, 1998), 24–33.

tableau, of stereotyped characters representing good and evil, and of plots marked by improbable swings from one climatic incident to the next influenced the general tenor of the silent era. (Linda Williams convincingly argues that the melodramatic mode has actually deeply influenced all of American cinema.)[5] After the coming of sound, one notes certain cycles of plot and setting: "the fallen woman" subgenre represented by *Blonde Venus* (1932) or *Baby Face* (1933); "the maternal melodrama," such as *Stella Dallas* (1937) or *To Each His Own* (1946); "illness melodramas," such as, for example, *Camille* (1935) or *Dark Victory* (1939); "the costume/historical melodrama," such as *Letter From an Unknown Woman* (1948); and its close relation "the exotic-locale melodrama," such as *Morocco* (1930). While the melodramas of the 1930s and 1940s often featured a female star and were told from her perspective, the 1950s were an era of "family melodramas" that focused on a larger group of characters, including males, such as Nicholas Ray's *Rebel without a Cause* (1955), Douglas Sirk's *Written on the Wind* (1956), and Vincente Minnelli's *Some Came Running* (1958).

Melodrama's development after 1960 has not been thoroughly studied. My belief is that during the past four decades, melodramas have varied widely, but the challenge of the illness or death of a loved one has remained a particularly popular formula, as in *Love Story* (1970), *Beaches* (1988), and *Longtime Companion* (1990). So too has the costume/historical setting, often in the guise of an adaptation of a prestigious novel, witness *The Color Purple* (1985) and *Out of Africa* (1985). The border between the costume melodrama and the historical epic is fuzzy; classification may depend upon how much emphasis is given to private lives, how much to the sweep of historical events and social forces.[6]

Nevertheless, melodrama's thematic concerns cut across the surface variations of its prevailing subsets. Screwball comedies are about playacting and spontaneity and fun; melodramas, of whatever subcategory, are about the persecution of innocence, self-sacrifice, the contest between duty and desire. Thomas Schatz observes:

> Whereas the characters of romantic or screwball comedies scoff at social decorum and propriety, in melodrama they are at the mercy of social conventions; whereas the comedies integrated the anarchic

lovers into a self-sufficient marital unit distinct from their social milieu, the melodrama traces the ultimate *resignation* of the principals to
the strictures of social and familial tradition.[7]

The dominant emotion these films evoke in a viewer is pathos.

What dialogue conventions could be shared by such a large and
diffuse group of films? First, this genre privileges one possible function of film dialogue, a particular variety of character revelation—
the open discussion of emotions. As Peter Brooks has noted, "Nothing is *under*stood, all is *over*stated."[8]

> The desire to express all seems a fundamental characteristic of the
> melodramatic mode. Nothing is spared because nothing is left un-
> said; the characters stand on stage and utter the unspeakable, give
> voice to their deepest feelings, dramatize through their heightened
> and polarized words and gestures the whole lesson of their relation-
> ship.[9]

In screwball comedies, characters will go to any lengths *not* to say "I
love you," but in George Cukor's *Camille*, after witnessing the wedding of their friends, Armand and Marguerite have the following exchange:

> ARMAND: You mean you'd give up everything for me?
> MARGUERITE: Everything in the world. Everything. Never be jealous
> again. Never doubt that I love you more than the
> world, more than myself.
> ARMAND: Then marry me.
> MARGUERITE: What?
> ARMAND: I married you today. Every word the priest said was
> meant for us. In my heart I made all the vows. To you—
> MARGUERITE: —and I to you.
> ARMAND: Then . . .
> MARGUERITE: No, no, that isn't fitting. Let me love you, let me live for
> you, but don't let me ask any more from heaven than
> that. God might get angry.

And it is not just love that is so boldly spoken. In *Leave Her to Heaven*
(1945), Ellen directly admits her feelings toward her unborn child: "I
hate the little beast. I wish it would die." In *Shanghai Express* (1932),
Madeline talks openly to Captain Harvey about her own trustwor-

thiness: "When I needed your faith, you withheld it. And now, when I don't need it and don't deserve it, you give it to me."

Cathy's blatant avowal of identity with Heathcliff, in the excerpt from *Wuthering Heights* analyzed at the start of this study, is thus not unique to that film but characteristic of the whole genre. Characters in these films are not embarrassed to declare their love, their devotion, or their reasons for living. According to Brooks, melodramas portray a victory over psychological repression: "The melodramatic utterance breaks through everything that constitutes the 'reality principle,' all its censorships, accommodations, tonings-down."[10]

Dialogue in melodramas functions to reveal feelings, and it does so through a heightened, even overblown, rhetorical style. Marguerite cannot say, as Gershwin's lover does, "I'm stuck on you, sweetie pie"; she has to say, "Never doubt that I love you more than the world, more than myself." Doctor Steele in Edmund Golding's *Dark Victory* tells Judith Treherne, "I want you to find peace. Tragic difference is that you know when [you are going to die] and we don't. But the important thing is the same for all of us: to live our lives so that we can meet death, whenever it comes. Beautifully, finely." In Anthony Minghella's *The English Patient* (1996), Count Almásy, claims that because of the death of his lover, "You can't kill me. I died years ago." No wonder Peter Brooks finds that melodramatic rhetoric "tends toward the inflated and the sententious. Its typical figures are hyperbole, antithesis, and oxymoron: those figures, precisely, that evidence a refusal of nuance and the insistence on dealing in pure, integral concepts."[11]

Dialogue in film melodramas is ornate, literary, charged with metaphor. In King Vidor's *Stella Dallas,* trying to describe Helen's upper-class grace to her mother, Laurel calls her "a flower in Maine." In Leo McCarey's *An Affair to Remember* (1957), Terry and Nickie realize that this may be their last chance for love. "Winter must be cold for those with no warm memories," Terry tells him. "We've already missed the spring." They decide to reunite on the top of the Empire State Building, because the skyscraper "is the nearest thing to Heaven we have in New York."

Melodramatic rhetoric is so distinctive that one can recognize it easily when it migrates to other genres. Sidney Lumet's *Network* (1976) is a black social satire, yet the famous scene in which Louise

Scumacher, a cast-aside wife, lambastes her husband's selfishness gains its power from its resort to the language of melodrama. Listen to its direct revelation of emotional states, coupled with its charged metaphors:

> LOUISE: This is your great winter romance, isn't it? Your last roar of passion before you settle into your emeritus years. Is that what's left for me? Is that my share? She gets the winter passion, and I get the dotage? What am I supposed to do? Am I supposed to sit home knitting and purling while you slink back like some penitent drunk? I'm your wife, damn it! And if you can't work up a winter passion for me, the least I require is respect and allegiance! I hurt! Don't you understand that? I hurt badly!

Beatrice Straight won an Academy Award for this scene because its revelation of anger and pain resonated so strongly with viewers.

We must recognize too that the inflated rhetoric of melodrama is wedded to a particular performance style—the use of melodramatic gesture. The archetypal image of stage melodrama that I hold is of the stern patriarch thunderously ordering the erring child from his house, with a broad arm gesture pointing outside. The actors in film melodramas similarly "embody" their emotions. To return to *Camille*, when Marguerite discusses giving up Armand with his father, she sinks to her knees. In Douglas Sirk's *Imitation of Life* (1959), when Sarah Jane shows up at her mother's funeral, she tries to throw herself on the coffin. In *All That Heaven Allows* (1955), the weeping Kay throws herself into her mother's arms when she talks about the cruel town gossip about her mother's love affair. This is the genre of tears and fainting, of hands being wrung or clutched around the stomach, of words so hurtful that they provoke a slap, of kisses so passionate that the woman is bent over backward, of illness or accident so dire that the victim must be cradled in someone's arms. The large gestures are an inheritance from the stage tradition; in film, thanks to close-ups, even smaller movements can resonate with the same expressiveness. Barbara Stanwyck's biting of her handkerchief at the end of *Stella Dallas* is exceedingly evocative, and Marlene Dietrich manages to telegraph her characters' deep distress merely by wildly darting her enormous eyes around.

During the 1930s and 1940s, upper-class, "transatlantic" diction and phraseology held sway. Most of the characters are supposed to be well-off, socially prominent, perhaps even foreign aristocrats. British actors and British accents are legion: Clive Brooks stars in *Shanghai Express* (1932), Herbert Marshall in *Blonde Venus* (1932), Leslie Howard in *Intermezzo* (1939), Joan Fontaine in *Rebecca* (1940), Greer Garson in *Random Harvest* (1942), James Mason in *The Seventh Veil* (1945). And unlike the upper-crust characters in screwballs, these characters rarely resort to slang or informal speech.* Rather than representing contemporary urban vibrancy, their roles are deliberately set in past eras; formal or antiquated speech patterns predominate. The fact that many of these films are adaptations of nineteenth-century novels and plays intensifies their tendency to use "dated," as opposed to contemporary, phraseology.

In later decades, ethnic and lower-class accents become more common, as in Elia Kazan's *A Streetcar Named Desire* (1951), but upper-class speech is still notable in melodramas, as are British performers, witness *Shadowlands* (1993). Moreover, since the 1950s, numerous melodramas have been set in the South and Texas. Perhaps oil money gave the South an aura of money and power that allowed it to substitute for the traditional Northeastern and European settings. Perhaps it was the model of Tennessee Williams, whose plays connected Southern settings with grand passion. At any rate, Southern accents can be heard to varying degrees in *Written on the Wind* (1956), *Cat on a Hot Tin Roof* (1958), *The Long Hot Summer* (1958), *Home from the Hill* (1960), and *Steel Magnolias* (1989). I believe, however, that the Southern accents operate similarly to "transatlantic" and British diction, in that they have a "dated" aura and bring to mind a past of landed aristocracy.

Melodramas are marked not only by a certain style of dialogue, but by talkativeness. The drama of melodramas lies primarily in the development of interpersonal relationships—there are few, if any, scenes of silent physical action. On-screen time is devoted to discussing the characters' feelings or decisions—melodramas convey the sense of a "debating society" where the action lies in the thrashing out of contesting viewpoints, or even in philosophical discussions of the nature of love or duty. And since physical movement—

---

* *The Ghost and Mrs. Muir* (1947) is an interesting exception in that it features the clash between formal Edwardian speech, and "raw" lingo of seafarers. However, the curses and rough talk of Captain Griggs are themselves antiquated and quaint.

in the sense of chases on horseback, machine-gun shoot-outs, and even slapstick pratfalls—is generally denied, these films' excitement lies in their dialogue exchanges, which recurrently enact a suspenseful jockeying for power.

So far this chapter has concentrated on illustrating the degree to which speech is allotted free rein in melodramas. Yet this is only half the story. The paradox of dialogue's position in Westerns (which ostensibly devalue speech, while actually glorying in it) is reversed here: melodramas—which seem so verbally overexplicit—actually hinge around *the not said, the words that cannot be spoken.*

In most melodramas, the driving tension of the plot stems from one character keeping some secret, a secret that the viewer knows.[12] We know that Marguerite is lying when she breaks up with Armand, that she is sacrificing her heart and health for his future and social respectability, so the remainder of the film is agonizing until he finds out the truth. We know that Stella Dallas is playacting when she chases Laurel away, that she is giving up her reason for living for the sake of her daughter's well-being. In *Shanghai Express,* we know that Madeline has agreed to become the mistress of the Chinese warlord only to save Donald Harvey from being blinded. In *Magnificent Obsession* (1954), we know that Robbie Robinson, Cary's new love, is actually Bob Merrick, the playboy responsible for her husband's death. We know that Tina is actually "Aunt Charlotte's" illegitimate daughter in *The Old Maid* (1939), just as Griggsie is Jody Norris's illegitimate son in *To Each His Own* (1946), just as Rafe is Wade Hunnicutt's illegitimate son in *Home from the Hill* (1959). We know that Judith Treherne in *Dark Victory* is blind and on the verge of death when she cheerfully sends her unaware husband off to his scientific meeting. And we know that the reason that Terry seems to have thrown over Nickie in *An Affair to Remember* is that she's been crippled in a car accident. We always know who really loves whom—that Cathy loves Heathcliff, not Linton.

But the characters don't have the benefit of our wise perspective. Sometimes they find out at the story's end; sometimes they never know. In the absence of such crucial information, the characters blunder around in the dark, doing and *saying* the most terrible things. In no other genre is the viewer's superior knowledge of the narrative so influential in our understanding of the double-layering behind individual speeches. When Tina in *The Old Maid* fawns over her mother's rival, Delia, who is lax and spoiling, and criticizes her stern "Aunt Charlotte," we cringe at the pain she is unwittingly causing. When Nickie vents his bitter broken heart on Terry, who sits quietly accepting the abuse with a quilt hiding her crippled legs, we can hardly stand it. Melodramatic dialogue is suffused with the tension and pathos of dramatic irony.

Why should this be so? Why is it, that in these films, as Jeanine Basinger so pithily puts it, "A little sensible talk is never allowed to sort things out"?[13] Generally the need for secrecy is explained by (a) the impossibility/undesirability of going against social mores regarding illegitimacy, sexuality, divorce, or social class; or (b) the willingness of the secret holder to sacrifice herself for another's good, or (c) the secret holder's belief that love or recognition has to come completely unbidden, granted without prompting. Frequently, the pressures are conflated, so that in *Camille,* Marguerite gives up Armand *because* it would be better for him, *because* of the pressures of bourgeois respectability. These films thus clearly lend themselves to interpretations seeing them as supporters of conventional morality, as parables of self-sacrifice and self-abnegation for women.

From different perspectives, Peter Brooks and Tania Modleski help us further understand the role of secrets and silence in this genre. Throughout *The Melodramatic Imagination,* Brooks stresses the importance of physical gestures in a theatrical genre that began as pantomime set to music; he lays great stress on what he calls "the text of muteness," which includes extravagant gestures and tableaus, and on the surprising frequency with which these stories include a character who is literally mute. Brooks points to the genre's persistent fascination with what cannot be expressed verbally, with "the ineffable." Ultimately, he believes that the genre is about the drive toward recognition of the hidden moral significance of our lives and actions; he maintains that "melodrama becomes the principal mode of uncovering, demonstrating, and making operative the essential moral universe in a post-sacred era."[14]

Brooks underscores his narratives' drive toward an explicit recognition of the persecuted heroine's innocence and virtue. Discussing the "vows of silence" permeating the stage plays, he notes that

> Virtue, expulsed, eclipsed, apparently fallen, cannot effectively articulate the cause of the right. Its tongue is in fact often tied by the

structure of familial relationships: virtue cannot call into question the judgments and the actions of a father or an uncle or a guardian, for to do so would be to violate its nature as innocence.[15]

Although the heroines of the classic Hollywood melodramas often differ from the virtuous young girls Brooks discusses, they too must wait with humility, patience, and passivity until others spontaneously recognize the truth. Her ability to endure—and to hold her tongue—is what makes the central character heroic. Her silence is simultaneously a mark of her martyrdom and of her power.

But Tania Modleski demonstrates how strongly the genre empathizes with the cost and pain of such silence to the woman.[16] Modleski concentrates on Max Ophuls's *Letter from an Unknown Woman*, in which Lisa Brendl worships Stefan Brand for two decades, and has a child by him, without ever telling him her name. Modleski quotes Hélène Cixous: "Silence is the mark of hysteria. . . . The great hysterics have lost speech, they are aphonic, and at times they have lost more than speech. They are pushed to the point of choking, nothing gets through." Modleski continues: "It seems fair to say that many of classic film melodramas from the 30s through the 50s are peopled by great, or near-great, hysterics—women possessed by an overwhelming desire to express themselves, to make themselves known, but continually confronting the difficulty, if not the impossibility of realizing this desire."[17] Indeed, the metaphor of "choking" is a brilliantly apt description of the silencing that goes on in melodramas. Insofar as these films demand viewers' recognition of the extent to which women are mistreated and silenced by patriarchal strictures, they can—paradoxically—also be viewed as conveying feminist perspectives.

Thus melodramas, which are so logo-philic, so unrepressed in terms of their extravagant and naked rhetoric, actually continually dramatize the repression of speech, the impossibility of using words to gain one's desire or to win recognition. The implications for the eavesdropper-viewer are complex. Our superior knowledge about the secret, and our identification with the characters, creates great suspense and an almost physical release from the sensation of choking as when, at the very last second of *To Each His Own*, the light dawns on Jody's (somewhat dense) son and he approaches her, "I think this is our dance, *Mother*." Yet in a significant number of texts, the silence is never broken on-screen. In *Stella Dallas,* melodrama's thematic work is actually completed off-screen—that is, *we viewers* are the ones called upon to recognize and admire the heroine's quiet virtue and self-sacrifice; we complete Brooks's "drama of recognition."

Modleski argues that one of the basic pleasures of melodrama lies in the fact that it is "fundamentally about events that do not happen: the wedding that did not occur; the meeting in the park that was missed; and above all, the word that was not spoken." These missed opportunities and misunderstandings create much of the pathos of melodrama. I find it telling that this genre, the one most closely associated with women, is, in a convoluted way, about the superiority of silence. If recognition comes, it must come unprompted, given freely by the child or lover, or granted by the hand of fate. Above all, the woman may not articulate her own needs or desires. Shanghai Lily's "We parted and I threw my life away because I didn't care to bargain for love with words" brilliantly captures the genre's paradox, *because it is a nakedly revelatory statement about not talking.*

The struggle between expression and repression has had numerous effects on the filmic texts. One is the heightened expressivity of nonverbal elements, a quality much commented on by melodrama scholars. Noting that "[i]n this group of films, little is left to language," Mary Ann Doane directs us to pay attention to how they habitually deflect "signifying material onto other, nonlinguistic registers of the sign." She points out the extreme importance of mise-en-scène, of the glances that the characters exchange with one another, of their gestures, and of the music.[18]

That music would play a particularly large role in supplementing dialogue in melodramas seems inevitable. Many of the scores were written by Hollywood's most renowned studio composers, including Max Steiner, Franz Waxman, Alfred Newman, and Bernard Herrmann. In this genre, scoring is particularly likely to be used *under* conversation. Alfred Newman's score for *Wuthering Heights,* which covers 75 minutes of the film's 103-minute running time, is famous for its integration with the dialogue.[19] Besides, as Claudia Gorbman's puts it: "Music appears in classical cinema as a signifier of emotion. . . . Music is seen as augmenting the external representation, the objectivity of the image-track, with its inner truth."[20] Music speaks the love the characters cannot express, or the pain they are trying to hide. In *All That Heaven Allows,* when Cary (Jane Wyman) gives in to the pressure exerted by her children and goes to break off with her lover, Ron (Rock Hudson), the sound track sadly plays a D flat minor Schumann melody from the Opus 12 *Fantasiestücke* titled "Warum?" ("Why?").

Moreover, just as public-speech-turned-slaughter scenes are only found in gangster films, melodramas have their own hallmark "sotto voce" scenes where the character's real meaning is spoken only under his or her breath, illustrating the extent to which speech is rendered impossible in certain situations. Perhaps the clearest and most heartrending example is the moment in *Imitation of Life* (1959) when Annie has traced her runaway daughter, Sarah Jane, to her hotel room. Sarah Jane's showgirl friend bursts in, and, because Annie is black and Sarah Jane has been passing for white, the showgirl mistakes Annie for the hotel maid.

> SHOWGIRL: Say, listen—if you're the new maid, I want to report that my shower is full of ants!
> ANNIE: Oh, I'm sorry Miss. That must be very uncomfortable. But I just happened to be in town and I—dropped in to see Miss Linda. I used to take care of her. Well—I guess I'll be running along. My plane's leaving in a little while—Miss Linda. Good-bye honey. You take good care of yourself.
> SARAH JANE: Good-bye. *(whispering)* Mama.

Annie leaves.

> SHOWGIRL: Well—get you! So honey chil', you had a Mammy!
> SARAH JANE: Yes—all my life.

Sarah Jane *does* love her mother and *does* want to acknowledge her, but she is in full flight from a society that immediately assumes that any black woman must be a maid or a Mammy. To maintain her ability to pass as white among her acquaintances and co-workers she must cooperate with the fiction that her mother was her servant. These irreconcilable pressures lead to the sotto voce "Mama," a word that has to be spoken but cannot be spoken out loud.

The pressures against speech lead also to another hallmark of melodramatic films—the breakdown into weeping. Whereas when the gangster's emotions get the best of him, he erupts into violence, in melodrama, the female characters dissolve into tears.

Moreover, I realize now, it is partially because of the pressure between speech and silence that women's films are so particularly prone to use voice-over narration. As *Letter from an Unknown Woman* so clearly illuminates, the pressure to make oneself known, which may be blocked on the level of inter-character conversation, may surface at the level of voice-over speech to the eavesdropper-viewer. Stefan Brand does not "know" Lisa until the film's final moments, but the viewers have "recognized" her all along.

The integration of dialogue with the rest of the filmic text will be more apparent as we study extended examples. I have chosen to focus initially on a classic women's film, *Now, Voyager*, directed by Irving Rapper for Warner Brothers in 1942. As Jeanne Allen, who has detailed the film's production history, observes, this is Rapper's most renowned film; he was originally a theater director in New York. When he came to Hollywood, he worked as an assistant director and a dialogue coach, before becoming a dialogue director in 1936. Rapper has never enjoyed a very high reputation. "Some critics regard his work as betraying the staginess and talky direction of his theater work," Allen notes,[21] and he usually gets very little credit for this film's widespread appeal. Close examination reveals, however, that it *is* very well directed—all the performances are strong, and decisions about camerawork and editing are extraordinarily effective.

The film is an adaptation of a popular novel of the same title by Olive Higgins Prouty, who had also written *Stella Dallas*. The first treatment was written by Edmund Golding, and the screenplay by Casey Robinson, both of whom had previously scored major successes for the star, Bette Davis. *Now, Voyager* was well received and won an Academy Award for its score by Max Steiner.

In the absence of a director with a strong reputation as auteur, minor squabbling has erupted over who deserves credit for the script of *Now, Voyager*. Bette Davis claims to have had a large hand in it; Casey Robinson flatly denies this.[22] Allen argues that Prouty has been insufficiently recognized for her contribution to the film, specifically in the realm of the dialogue:

In some respects Prouty's novel lent itself easily to film script adaptation. It is a remarkably talky novel without the intricate and subtle governance of a narrating intelligence that provides insight, interpretations, and innuendo. Prouty claimed that her task was to allow her characters to speak and act plausibly. Easily three-quarters of the novel is conversation . . . much of it is transposed directly into dialogue. Indeed critics who tend to praise Davis and Robinson for their wit knew little of how much of that was supplied by Prouty's pen. . . . [T]he scenes between Charlotte and her mother are taken virtually intact from the novel.[23]

Allen is correct; most of the film's lines come directly from the novel, as do specific instances of stage business, including Jerry's method of lighting cigarettes.*

Now, Voyager is the story of Charlotte Vale (Bette Davis), of the Vales of Boston, whom we meet as a dowdy, overweight spinster, under the thumb of a dominating mother who demands her daughter's devotion and explicitly squelches any expression of Charlotte's sexuality. Charlotte has a nervous breakdown and is treated by the kind Dr. Jaquith (Claude Rains) at his sanitarium in the country. Continuing her recovery by taking an ocean cruise, the now beautiful and fashionable but still emotionally vulnerable Charlotte meets Jerry Durrance (Paul Henreid), who is trapped in a loveless marriage and unhappy household, a home life that is especially detrimental to his youngest daughter, Tina, who was unwanted by her mother. Charlotte and Jerry fall in love and have a brief romantic affair. When Charlotte returns to Boston, she is newly able to stand up to her mother's tyranny, and she becomes engaged to a local socialite, Elliot Livingston. Accidentally meeting Jerry again at a party prompts Charlotte to break her engagement to a man she doesn't love. Her mother reacts badly to the news and dies of a heart attack; Charlotte flees back to Jaquith's sanitarium, where she coinciden-

---

* Ironically, Prouty herself must be lumped with the anti-dialogue crowd. Prouty once wrote to her literary agent about the potential adaptation of her novel, urging the expansive use of silent flashbacks. "I am one of those who believe the silent picture had artistic potentialities which the talking picture lacks. The acting, facial expressions, every move and gesture is more significant, and far more closely observed by an audience waiting for the explanatory caption or voice [-over]." Quoted in Rudy Behlmer, ed., *Inside Warner Brothers (1935–1951)* (New York: Simon & Schuster, 1985), 167.

tally finds Jerry's very unhappy daughter, Tina, also under treatment. Charlotte takes Tina under her wing and nurses her back to emotional health. At the end of the film, Tina is living with Charlotte, and Jerry may visit them, under the watchful eyes of Dr. Jaquith, who will only allow Charlotte to serve as Tina's foster mother so long as the relationship between Jerry and herself remains platonic.

Regardless of who deserves credit for it, the dialogue in *Now, Voyager* serves to illustrate many of this chapter's major points. The characters are upper-class, and their speech observes the diction expected of Boston Brahmins—one of the first lines is Mrs. Vale's, "We'll be pouring tea in the drawing room this afternoon." Gladys Cooper, who plays Mrs. Vale, and Claude Rains were both British-born actors, and Paul Henreid, raised in Italy and of Viennese descent, speaks with a vague Continental accent. Bette Davis, who proved in other films that she could easily go slumming diction-wise, here speaks in her most proper, clipped New England tones, pronouncing "mother" as "mutha." One of the small grace notes of the film, however, is the casting of Mary Wickes as Dora Pickford, Mrs. Vale's nurse. Wickes's fast-paced delivery, scratchy voice, and more earthy vocabulary—she calls the formidable Mrs. Vale "Granny dear"—provide a nice contrast.

The use of dialogue for speaking explicitly about feelings among the characters is equally marked. Dr. Jaquith boldly tells Charlotte's mother: "My dear Mrs. Vale, if you had deliberately and maliciously planned to destroy your daughter's life, you couldn't have done it more completely." Charlotte tells Jerry about her past: "I'm the fat lady with the heavy brows and all of the hair. I'm poor Aunt Charlotte. And I've been ill. I have been in a sanitarium for three months. And I'm not well yet." Later, when they are parting in the Boston train station, Jerry tells Charlotte, "I'll look for you around every corner." In one of their confrontations, Mrs. Vale accuses Charlotte, "You've never done anything to make your mother proud." Tina blurts out, "I'm ugly and mean and nobody likes me." Part of the strength of the acting of *Now, Voyager* is that although all the characters participate in this style of revelatory explicitness, in every case we get a sense of how hard it is for them to speak their hearts (and indeed, as Lea Jacobs points out, in the first scene of the film, Charlotte has been rendered nearly mute by her mother's domination);[24] through small hesitations and then rushed delivery, we hear these characters bursting through "the censorships, accommodations, tonings down" identified by Brooks.

More than just revelatory, the dialogue in *Now, Voyager* is often blatantly ornate. There is a purposeful and explicit pattern of reference to nineteenth-century literary models: first in the quotation from Walt Whitman, "Now, Voyager, sail thou forth to seek and find," and in the explicit echoes of *Camille,* such as Jerry using the name as a nickname for Charlotte and later sending her camellias. Jaquith, in particular, often speaks metaphorically, alluding to patients growing and blossoming, wandering in the woods, going through tunnels, and becoming fledglings. When Jerry discusses the love he and Charlotte share, he turns their connection into something living: "It won't die—what's between us. Do what we will—ignore it, neglect it, starve it—it's stronger than both of us together."

The film's use of melodramatic gesture is equally noticeable. Charlotte breaks down in the drawing room; Mrs. Vale throws herself down the stairs; Tina cries hysterically on several occasions. Most memorably, several times during the film Jerry turns giving Charlotte a cigarette into a passionate moment, by first lighting two in his own mouth, and then passing one to her.

The sexual passion that suffuses *Now, Voyager* has been brilliantly analyzed by Maria LaPlace, who writes:

> Female sexuality is a key term throughout the film. The beginning posits repression of female sexuality as a major cause of Charlotte's neurotic misery and ties this repression to her lack of independence from her mother. . . . A major project of the first sequence of the film is to establish that Charlotte *is* sexual, that she is merely "inhibited" rather than frigid or asexual. . . . The one relationship that is socially acceptable, that promises to lead to marriage and children, is between Charlotte and Elliot Livingston and it is dull and passionless. Any reference to sex, no matter how indirect, shocks him; Charlotte feels "depraved" at her own sexuality in his presence. . . . The impossibility of the heroine's marriage to the hero in the woman's film is not necessarily a renunciation of sexuality on the woman's part; rather it is the prolongation of passion and desire. Emotional intensity is substituted for genital sexuality.[25]

The one perspective I can add to LaPlace's discussion is that sexuality is not only repressed by the characters; the topic is repressed on the level of the film's dialogue, owing both to the prevailing social mores and to the explicit interference of the Hays Office enforcing the Production Code. Joe Breen wrote to Warner Brothers in March 1942: "We have received and read the final script dated March 15, 1942 . . . and regret to advise that the present version contains one element that seems to be in violation of the provisions of the Production Code and which could not be approved in the finished picture. This unacceptable element is an indication of an adulterous affair between the leads Charlotte and Jerry."[26] Thus, all discussion of sex is handled through inference and circumlocution.[27] Charlotte's sexual desire is coded in her "cigarettes and medicated sherry and books [her] mother would never allow [her] to read."[28] Jerry and Charlotte talk about "the night on the mountain" and "that"; Charlotte rather vaguely mumbles to Elliot about "losing inhibitions." There is a certain ambiguity about the sex in *Now, Voyager* (which is characteristic of Hollywood films of this era). Is Charlotte so passionate with her first boyfriend Leslie because she desires him or because she believes that this is a strategy to make him want her? Do Charlotte and Jerry have sex the night in the mountain cabin, or after the balcony scene in Buenos Aires, or both times? Does she break up with Elliot because she senses that he won't satisfy her sexually or because he makes her feel inhibited? The dialogue (and the images) give us contradictory guidance through these issues. Brooks's theory regarding the openness of melodramatic speech fails to account for this evasion. The conclusion to draw is that *classical Hollywood melodramas are explicit about every feeling, except the ones that count most,* the sexual desires that traditionally prompt personal and cultural repression.

The "secret" of this film lies in the fact that Jerry and Charlotte have had an illicit passionate affair, and that their enduring love for one another affects many of their subsequent actions. The love affair completes Charlotte's ability to stand up to her mother, and it helps Jerry return to the architectural career he loves. Furthermore, Charlotte's devotion to Jerry underlies her rejection of Elliot and her adoption of Tina. However, Charlotte cannot explain any of this to anyone, and the script purposely leads her into tricky situations where she can't reveal where the camellias have come from, or can't clarify why she believes that Elliot and she are incompatible, or justify how she knows Tina's nickname. The viewer is continually called upon to witness Charlotte's evasions and avoidances, and the isolation she suffers from her inability to speak the truth.

One of the consequences of Charlotte's repression is the film's re-sorting to what Michel Chion terms "subjective-internal sound,"[29] a rendering of Charlotte's unspoken thoughts. Traveling in a car with Elliot, Charlotte notes that his deceased first wife left him her sons, "And I have only a dried corsage and an empty bottle of perfume. And I can't even say his name." In addition, while she is comforting the distraught Tina, we hear her thoughts: "This is Jerry's child in my arms. This is Jerry's child clinging to me."

The pressures of *not speaking* also account for the fact that *Now, Voyager* contains two sotto voce scenes. The first is at the dinner party where Charlotte and Jerry meet unexpectedly, where they are surrounded by the very society that must never know about their love affair, and yet their passionate attachment keeps bursting through (fig. 48).

> CHARLOTTE: George tells me you've been in Boston very often this winter, Mr. Durrance. *(Sotto voce)* And I didn't know.
> JERRY: Yes, several times. *(Sotto voce)* You look simply glorious.
> CHARLOTTE: An architect. *(Sotto voce)* I could cry with pride.
> JERRY: Yes, its an interesting job I'm doing for George. *(Sotto voce)* I wanted horribly to call you up.
> CHARLOTTE: The medical center, isn't it?
> JERRY: Yes. *(Sotto voce)* I walk by your house on Marlborough Street. Once I almost rang the bell. . . .
> CHARLOTTE: How is Tina?

Jerry hands her a lit cigarette. They stare at each other for a few seconds.

> JERRY: Well, Tina. We're having quite a bad time with Tina.
> CHARLOTTE: Tell me about it.
> JERRY: I'm afraid we've got to send her away somewhere. The doctor thinks she shouldn't be with her mother. I took her to see Dr. Jaquith. He was highly recommended to me by this Camille Beauchamp I mistook you for. *(Sotto voce)* Camille, I am still horribly in love.

The second sotto voce scene is briefer: at the end of the film, when Jerry comes to visit Tina at Charlotte's house, he embraces his daughter and tells her that he loves her, but the direction of his glance makes it clear that he means the words for Charlotte too.

The expressive power of the sotto voce scenes in *Now, Voyager* is aided and abetted by Max Steiner's score. At the dinner party

48. *Now, Voyager.* The sotto voce scene.

when Charlotte and Jerry start to speak to each other, an off-screen piano "coincidentally" starts to play Cole Porter's "Night and Day." The lyrics of that song, which would have been completely familiar to 1942 audiences ("Night and day, you are the one. Only you beneath the moon and under the sun. Whether near to me or far, it's no matter, darling, where you are, I think of you, night and day"), thus underlie the two lovers' conversation. By the same token, on the Vales' staircase at the end of the film, when Jerry avows his love, Max Steiner's famous *Now, Voyager* love theme swells on the sound track. This love theme—a sultry melody carried by strings redolent of unfulfilled longing—accompanies all of the most romantic moments, including the Buenos Aires balcony scene where Charlotte surrenders to Jerry and the film's finale.[30] This theme is elaborately developed, rising, falling, modulating with the back and forth of the characters' talk. But the music throughout the film seems tied to Charlotte's heart, rising in agitation when she rails against her mother, light-hearted when she goes camping with Tina.

The music also plays a key role in one of the confrontation scenes between Charlotte and her mother, a scene that I'd like to pause over. After the welcome home dinner party, Charlotte visits her mother's sickbed and Mrs. Vale threatens to punish Charlotte's new independence by cutting her off financially.

> MRS. VALE: I guess you'll be laughing out of the other side of your face if I actually did carry out my suggestion.
> CHARLOTTE: I don't think I would. I'm not afraid, Mother. *(To herself)* I'm not afraid. *(To her mother)* I'm not afraid, Mother.

Charlotte's new courage is a key discovery for her—actually a moment of self-revelation. Casey Robinson's script remarks, "The wonder of it fills her with a sort of radiance."[31] The problem is that in translating this moment of epiphany to the screen, Rapper chooses to emphasize its meaning through a tight close-up of Bette Davis, lit with "radiant" light, and a surge of the music track. The result is an awkward overemphasis—a moment that has striking parallels with *Wuthering Heights*'s "I *am* Heathcliff." The flaw, I've come to believe, lies in directors not trusting enough in the communicative power of their dialogue, so that they goose up the visual track. Perhaps I'll propose a new filmmaking rule: "Keep lighting, close-ups, and music in their places during psychological epiphanies!"

With the exception of "I'm not afraid," *Now, Voyager* carries its visual and verbal excess with assurance. Consider the film's ending. The scene begins as a quarrel between Jerry and Charlotte in the library of her house over her keeping Tina. Like earlier standoffs between Charlotte and her mother, like so many similar scenes in melodramas, the argument is exciting because two strong-willed characters care deeply about their positions and so much seems to be at stake. Jerry's pride is hurt, since he believes that Charlotte is sacrificing herself for him, and Charlotte gets angry in return because she had assumed that Jerry would understand how raising his child made her feel as if they were a family. Jerry tries to kiss her, but she resists him in order to be true to Dr. Jaquith's prohibition; the sexual energy is sublimated into the ritual sharing of cigarettes. Jerry asks: "And will you be happy, Charlotte? Will it be enough?" And Charlotte answers, "Oh Jerry, don't let's ask for the moon. We have the stars." The camera pans up into the starry sky as the music swells.

Her line, and its integration with the music and the starry scenic backdrop, is over the top, and unabashed.

———————

More than with any of my other extended examples, I have debated over selecting James Brooks's *Terms of Endearment* (1983). As a more contemporary text than the 1940s women's films, or even 1950s family melodramas, this choice would expand our discussion, adding historical perspective. Moreover, despite its temporal remove, *Terms* offers interesting connections with *Now, Voyager* in that it, too, is an adaptation of a popular novel, focuses on a woman's relationship with both her own mother and children, and foregrounds illness. The film is well known and popular, having won five Academy Awards, including Best Picture. Yet the problem with using *Terms of Endearment* is that, although at least one critic sees it as "a classical weepie,"[32] this text is a generic hybrid. The first thirty minutes are completely comedic, the next hour a mixture of comedy with darker scenes, and the last half hour powerful melodrama.

The genre confusion is present in Larry McMurtry's original novel, published in 1975. Seven-eighths of the novel is a satire of Aurora Greenway's foibles and her troubles with men (with contrast provided by a look at the marital problems of Rosie, Aurora's maid). McMurtry's portrait of Aurora's controlling, selfish, indolent behavior, which is principally ascribed to her lack of sex and her needing a man who can put her in her place, is both sexist and empathetic. Although McMurtry is very enamored of Emma, who also appears in his earlier novels *Moving On* and *All My Friends Are Going to Be Strangers* (he once commented, "Emma is what women are at their best"),[33] her marital problems and her illness are relegated to a short epilogue at the end of the book, an epilogue that is an abrupt departure from the preceding comedy.

James L. Brooks, the writer-producer-director of the adaptation, is at home with comedy—his background has primarily been in television shows such as *Mary Tyler Moore, Lou Grant,* and *Taxi.* His later films, such as *Broadcast News* (1987) and *As Good As It Gets* (1997), are unequivocally categorizable as comedies (although they too contain quite painful moments, where the pain is caused by cruel words). Yet in *Terms,* Brooks chose to readjust the balance of McMurty's original, cutting out nearly all the subplots with Aurora's suitors, vastly min-imizing Rosie's role, inventing a new character for Jack Nicholson to play, gradually darkening the light tone, and doubling the amount of time devoted to Emma's illness and death.

The film starts with a scene of Aurora Greenway (Shirley Mac-Laine) as a young mother worrying about her daughter, Emma, in her crib—she pinches the baby and makes her cry to prove she's still breathing. The film briefly indicates that Aurora is widowed while Emma is a young girl, but the central events begin when the grown-up Emma, played by Debra Winger, insists on marrying Flap Horton (Jeff Daniels), a young academic, despite her mother's objections. Aurora, reassessing her middle-aged loneliness, starts a relationship with her neighbor, Garrett Breedlove (Jack Nicholson), a drunken, raucous ex-astronaut. Emma and Flap, who have moved from Texas to Des Moines, are beset by the stress of three young children and money problems. Their marriage begins to disintegrate—Flap is un-faithful with a graduate student, and Emma starts an affair with a shy local banker. When Emma discovers Flap's affair she takes the kids back to her mother's, but Flap persuades her to return to him and moves the family to Nebraska, where he takes a new job as chair of an English department. Meanwhile, Garrett, feeling too obligated, breaks off his relationship with Aurora. Just as Emma discovers that Flap is still carrying on with his girlfriend, Janice, Emma's doctor finds a lump in Emma's armpit. Emma has a brief period of health, during which time she visits her best friend, Patsy, in New York, but then she is hospitalized. Aurora and Rosie come to Nebraska to nurse Emma and help take care of the children, and Garrett makes a surprise visit to comfort Aurora. The custody of the children after Emma's death must be decided, and there are several farewell scenes. Emma dies. The film ends with family and friends grieving after Emma's funeral at a gathering in Aurora's backyard.

The most salient point of contrast between *Terms* and 1940s women's films is the openness about sex.* As we have seen, in *Now, Voyager*, the lovers' desire for each other is what cannot be known, cannot be shown, and cannot be spoken, although it may be hinted at by numerous indirect means. By contrast, during an early scene of

---

* Comparing the 1990 remake of *Stella* to the 1937 *Stella Dallas* reveals a similar striking contrast in the explicitness of the sexual situations and the sexual language.

Terms, Emma plays a recording of "Anything Goes," and anything does go in this film, from moving men looking up Emma's skirt, to Aurora tightening Emma's bra straps in public, to Garrett getting his hand stuck in Aurora's cleavage. The language is equally uninhibited, from Flap's calling Emma his "sweet-ass gal," to Emma's discussion of how wet Flap makes her, to Garrett's reference to Aurora curtseying on his face. Much of the film's comedy stems from its sexual references and scenes; Jack Nicholson's trademark wolfishness is heavily exploited.

And yet this bawdy frankness is not initially universal. Aurora—who is from the East, we are told—is a throwback to traditional mores and hates Garrett's coarseness. She is a Mrs. Vale transplanted to modern Houston. Her most treasured possession is a Renoir painting, she is generally overdressed and overcoiffed, and she talks with ornate, literary formality. (Although Shirley MacLaine had been practicing a Texas accent for two years, on the first day of shooting Brooks forbade her to use it.)[34] Aurora says things like: "I'm totally convinced if you marry Flap Horton tomorrow, it will be a mistake of such gigantic proportions it will ruin your life and make wretched your destiny"; "Grown women are prepared for life's little emergencies"; "I think that is extremely rude, noticing other women when you're with me"; "A moth to flame. This affair is going to kill me."

Whereas we accept such rhetoric in classic women's films because it is the norm there (in *Now, Voyager,* everyone except Dora speaks this way), here, because Aurora is shown to be out of step with everyone else, the elevated diction sparks laughs. As the film progresses, Aurora is brought down off her verbal high horse, to the point where she adopts a phrase of Garrett's about how "fan-fucking-tastic" sex can be.

Other melodramatic elements are also modified in this more contemporary text. The music, by Michael Gore, is much more restrained than that of Max Steiner, never lush or passionate. Early scenes actually use very little scoring aside from miscellaneous source music. As the film progresses, however, we periodically hear the theme, carried by a piano, orchestrated with a small group of instruments and a synthesizer. This theme, in C major, has a simple melody and simple harmony; it sounds somewhat like "folk" or "feel good" music. It is too lively for pathos; instead, it conveys a sense of "life goes on."

Clothing and appearance are as important here, as in any melodrama, but again with a twist. Whereas *Now, Voyager* is famous for the way it "makes over" Bette Davis, turning her from an ugly duckling into a glamorous swan, *Terms* moves its women characters in the opposite direction. Neither Aurora nor Emma start as sartorial role models, since the mother overdresses in outfits that are too youthful and frilly, and the daughter's clothes are casual and cheap, yet they both look worse and worse as the film progresses. Emma is ravaged by illness, Aurora by exhaustion and distress. Their suffering is made visually manifest.

Gestures are important in *Terms* but they are equally likely to be used for comic slapstick or melodramatic effect, depending upon the circumstances. Garrett is prone to drunken falls, and Aurora has a funny habit of taking off her high heels at odd moments, which shows the free spirit lurking underneath her formal pretensions. Yet, when Emma is hospitalized and Aurora asks the nurse to give her daughter her pain medicine, the nurse's lack of urgency throws Aurora into a screaming fit of desperation, and her wild dance around the nurses' station (enhanced by a 360-degree camera movement), is anything but funny. Similarly, when Tommy criticizes his dying mother, Aurora slaps the boy, and they engage in an awkward tussle as he tries to run away while she attempts to embrace him. In such cases, gesture is working to heighten the emotional impact of speech.

Even when one focuses on the film's more serious second half, *Terms* departs from key elements of melodrama discussed earlier in this chapter. This film presents no major plot secrets, no mistaken identities, no illegitimate children, no amnesia—in short, no major plot twist about which the viewer can feel that his/her knowledge is superior to that of the characters. Even out-of-wedlock sex is shorn of great secrecy or moral disapprobation. Illness is not kept secret to ennoble a masochistic sufferer, but discussed openly.

And yet, when closely attended to, this film does feature characters who are struggling over how to express their deepest secrets: they are wrestling with finding the "terms"—in the sense of negotiated settlement of conflicting needs, but also literally, in the sense of *the words*—"of endearment." In this effort to push through repression and speak feelings out loud, *Terms* is indeed a classic melodrama.

Scene after scene foregrounds the problem of communication of love, particularly Aurora's problems speaking to Emma. Theirs is the most important relationship in the film, and it yet it is always vexed. ("The intense love between mother and daughter, not mother and son, stands as our culture's primary taboo," Kathleen Rowe argues. "Patriarchy is deeply threatened by this bond, whether it takes the form of the connections between mothers and daughters, or, more generally, the solidarity among women.")[35] We see the snarls in their relationship at the film's very beginning, with Aurora pinching her baby out of her exaggerated fears for its safety. All the phone calls between Aurora and Emma further demonstrate how close they are and how often they talk, and yet knots are manifest in the occasions when Emma won't answer the phone, the time that Aurora interrupts Emma's other call, the way they hang up on each other or are too busy when the other really needs to talk. Mary Ann Doane teaches us to pay particular attention to characters' glances at one another. Throughout this film, the exchange of looks between mother and daughter—not between any of the heterosexual couples—assumes center stage. Significantly, Emma dies neither in Flap's arms (à la *Camille*) nor alone (à la *Dark Victory*), but looking toward her mother, while Aurora questioningly returns her gaze.

The film's male characters also have difficulty finding the terms of endearment. Garrett (like a director of melodramas who siphons off repressed speech into his overwrought mise-en-scène) overdecorates his house with astronaut paraphernalia to impress young girls. He enjoys his affair with Aurora but feels compelled to break it off when he starts to feel too tied to her. And yet he displays surprising loyalty and compassion by coming to visit Aurora when she is most distraught, watching her daughter die. In their farewell on the airport sidewalk, Aurora casually tells Garrett she loves him, and he departs into the terminal, but Aurora calls him back for an answer to her declaration.

> AURORA: I was curious. Do you have any reaction at all to my telling you I love you?
> GARRETT: (*A sardonic aside*) I was just inches from a clean getaway.
> AURORA: Well, you're stuck. So face it.
> GARRETT: I don't know what else to say except my stock answer.
> AURORA: Which is?
> GARRETT: I love you too, kid.

The fact that he claims this is his "stock" response takes away from the declaration any sense of Exclusive, Lifelong, Grand Passion, and viewers are likely to laugh at his aside. But the warmth conveyed by Garrett's voice, smile, and embrace, indicate that love, of some sort, is really there.

Garrett's reluctance to express his feelings is shared by two other central male characters, Flap and Tommy. Flap tries to compensate for his failures and get revenge on Emma for her closeness to her mother through infidelity. Tommy reacts to his parents' financial, marital, and health crises with embarrassment and anger. But Emma's strategy for dealing with them is different from Aurora's. Aurora is always conversationally combative, and what is most striking about Emma is her verbal generosity. Compare the ways each character deals with double-talk from doctors. When the cancer specialist tells Aurora sententiously, "I always tell my patients to hope for the best and expect the worst," Aurora snaps back, "And they let you get away with that?" Things are different when Emma's doctor evasively breaks bad news (as he rather pathetically plucks at Emma's quilt):

DOCTOR: The response to the drugs we tried isn't what we hoped. But there are investigatory drugs which we're willing to utilize. However, if you become incapacitated, or it becomes unreasonable for you to handle your affairs for a block of time, it might be wise to make some decisions now. Any questions?

Emma responds, "No. I know what you're saying. I have to figure out what to do with my kids." What Emma has done here is to take the burden from a man who can't handle it—she does the plain speaking for him.

This is precisely what happens in the dialogue in the film's concluding hospital scenes, much of which has been lifted straight from the novel.

Flap spends his last scene with Emma apologizing for his cheating on her and for his general inadequacies. Their conversation is friendly and affectionate—he has gone to great trouble to wear a tie that she once gave him. (Ah! the importance of props in melodrama.) "I'm so glad we're talking," Emma sighs with great relief. But then the topic turns to custody of the children after her death. Although Flap has indirectly admitted he is not prepared to raise them, he cannot say the words; Emma takes the burden on herself, she speaks the

49–50.*Terms of Endearment*

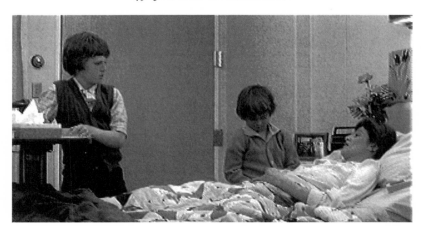

49.   Emma's farewell to her boys.

decision out loud for him: "I really don't think you should have them, Flap."

Her generosity about verbalizing difficult feelings is most strikingly apparent in the next scene, her farewell to her boys. While Teddy is tearful and huggy, Tommy is sullen and withdrawn. Emma tells him:

EMMA: I know you like me. I know it. For the last year or two you've been pretending like ya hate me. I love you very much. I love you as much as I love anybody. As much as I love myself. And in a few years, when I haven't been around to be on your tail about something or irritating you, you're gonna remember. You're gonna remember that time that I bought you the base-ball glove when you thought we were too broke. You know? Or when I—I read you those stories. Or when I—I let you goof off instead of mowing the lawn. Lots of things like that. And you're gonna realize that you love me. And maybe you're gonna feel badly because you never told me. But don't. I know that you love me. So don't ever do that to yourself, all right?
TOMMY: Okay.
EMMA: Okay?
TOMMY: I said okay.

Emma here has not only told Tommy how she feels; she has also articulated his feelings for him.

50.   Emma's speech to Tommy.

Terms of Endearment thus refuses to be about the words-that-were-never-spoken. Its women suffer, but they do not suffer in silence. The words that need to be spoken *are* spoken, even if Aurora has to pry them out, even if Emma has to speak them herself. This film, like *Now, Voyager,* is about accepting the arbitrary cruelties of life, about accepting one's own limitations and the limitations of loved ones. At the ending, Aurora asks neither for the moon, nor the stars, but merely for her granddaughter to sit beside her.

———————

Terms of Endearment is hardly the only film of recent decades to mix melodrama and comedy. *Steel Magnolias* (1989) presents a similar mélange, as does *Postcards from the Edge* (1990). Kathleen Rowe argues that romantic comedy and melodrama are shadow genres to one another: a few more obstacles and the lovers in the comedies might end up bereft and lonely; a little more strength and unconventionality and the melodrama heroine might slide into the role of the unruly woman of comedies.[36] To use the concepts focused on in this study, connections surely can be drawn between the "masquerades" of screwball and the "secrets" of melodrama, between the "complicity" that screwball asks of its eavesdropping viewer and the "recognition" that melodrama entreats.

Notwithstanding this study's orientation toward formalism, I am very aware that what makes genres fascinating is the way they change. The alterations in the status of women, the relative acceptability of divorce and single parenting, have made the plots of the women's films of the 1930s and 1940s impossible nowadays, and the overall trends toward informality, explicit sexuality, and cynicism have rendered the emotional dialogue of *Camille* or *Now, Voyager* problematic. As Barbara Klinger points out, because of their romanticism and their stylistic excess, older melodramas have become fodder for camp readings,[37] and a camp sensibility finds it impossible to take such dialogue straight.

But I don't think this style of dialogue has truly been put behind us—it is hiding in plain sight. It's still allowed to surface in costume films and adaptations, such as *The Age of Innocence* (1993), where the time period requires that a grand passion suffer barriers and repression. Or listen to *The English Patient,* in which Hannah tells Almásy: "I always wear it [the thimble]. I've always worn it. I've always loved you." And melodramatic dialogue gives *Titanic* (1997) the over-the-top romanticism that made the blockbuster so satisfying to young girls.

I'd like to close by looking at Norman Jewison's *Moonstruck* (1987), a film that is very important to Kathleen Rowe, for her major goal is to condemn melodrama's model of female self-sacrifice in favor of what she sees as the more progressive approach of comedy. Thus Rowe is attracted to this film's blatant alternation of the two modes, with the triumph here not of the melodramatic, as in *Terms,* but of the comic. Yet the scene to which Rowe herself is particularly drawn is *Moonstruck*'s most emotionally charged moment.

It takes place after Ronny, played by Nicholas Cage, has taken Loretta (Cher) to see *La Bohème* at the Metropolitan Opera. Ronny asks Loretta to come up to his apartment, to commit to their relationship, to give up her scruples and hesitations. Jewison uses the occasion to deliberately restage *La Bohème* on the streets of Brooklyn.

The dark street is empty, a light snow falls. Midway through Ronny's speech, tender music from act 1 starts to play. The selection has been carefully chosen: in the opera, Rudolpho has just met Mimi when her candle has gone out on the staircase. Mimi has dropped her key, and they are feeling around on the dark floor to find it. His hand accidentally touches hers, and he sings (in Italian):

How cold your little hand is.
Let me warm it up in mine . . .
What's the use of searching?
We'll never find it in the dark.
But luckily,
There's a moon,
And she's our neighbor here.[38]

Ronny argues with complete seriousness and sincerity—Cage's performance is without the slightest hint of irony or condescension. At the end of his speech, he holds out his hand to Loretta in a dramatic gesture (figs. 51–53).

> RONNY: Everything seems like nothin' to me now against that I want you in my bed. I don't care if I burn in hell. I don't care if you burn in hell. The past and the future is a . . . a joke to me now. I see that they're nothin'. I see they ain't here. The only thing that's here is you and me. Loretta, I love you. Not like they told you love is and I didn't know this either but love don't make things nice. It ruins everything. It breaks your heart, it makes things a mess. We, we aren't here to make things perfect. Snowflakes are perfect. (*Music starts*) The stars are perfect. Not us. Not us. We are here to ruin ourselves, and, and to break our hearts, and love the wrong people, and, and die. I mean, the storybooks are bullshit. Now I want you to come upstairs with me and get in my bed.

Rowe quotes this speech to assert that "Ronny is arguing for the position of comedy, for an acceptance of the totality of life and the imperfection of experience."[39] I'm not sure I agree. First of all, his argument reminds me of the ending lines of *Now, Voyager,* where acquiescence to limitations is proposed as high melodrama, not comedy.* Secondly, although Ronny claims that romantic stories are misleading, he is also asserting the preeminence of love over religion, over time, over human imperfection. Ronny's diction may be insistently lower-class, but the "all for love" sentiment is as exalted

---

* There are additional echoes of *Now, Voyager* in *Moonstruck.* Loretta, like Charlotte, has been repressing her sexuality into middle age. As the story progresses, her psychological changes are written on her body; like Charlotte, she reinvents herself over as a fashionable woman. Jewison even mimics *Now, Voyager'*s camerawork with a shot of the made-over Loretta that starts on her elegant shoes and ankles, the same composition that is used to reintroduce the newly fashionable Charlotte Vale.

51–53. *MOONSTRUCK*

51.   Ronny reaching out to Loretta.

52.   Loretta reacting to Ronny's impassioned argument.

as that found in Shakespeare's *Anthony and Cleopatra* or Marlowe's *Dr. Faustus.* And the staging, the music, Cage's performance, the dialogue's references to stars and snowflakes, its emotional openness, and its explicit debate about the meaning of life are the rhetoric of melodrama. The film as a whole may very well come down on the

53.   Joining hands (like Mimi and Rudolpho).

side of comedy, but this scene demonstrates the unique power of melodrama.

Those who have faith in the power of words to make a genuine connection between people, may believe there will always be a need for cinematic words that reveal what is in their hearts.

Conclusion

> Dialogue is not uncinematic. . . . The point is that there's no
> war between the visual and the aural. Why not the best of
> both?
>
> Sidney Lumet, *Making Movies* (1995)

The more I examined the dialogue conventions of Westerns, screwball comedies, gangster films, and melodramas, the more I felt I was
penetrating to the core of each genre's dynamics. Perhaps this is because our understanding of these films has always been heavily influenced by what the characters say—most genre description is,
after all, a distillation and analysis of information about narrative,
themes, and character gleaned from the dialogue. What this study
has done is merely to become self-conscious about the source of our
information.

Covering four genres is enough, but others beckon; I hear them as
faint rhythms and melodies. Films noirs use short sentences, urban
slang, unusual metaphors, toppers, and questions. All war films feature the collision of national languages, and they constantly use dialogue to discuss the meaning and rectitude of the military conflict,
but a seismic change in the incorporation of obscenity separates Vietnam films from those about earlier wars. Sports films regularly build
up to climax in a coach's motivational locker-room speech; this
speech act is nearly as important as the final championship game.
Contemporary horror films, as Philip Brophy has shown, rely upon
a unique kind of punning, a gross kind of tongue in cheek, that
forges a sense of complicity with the viewer.[1] I look forward to the
day when analysis of verbal conventions is an expected part of genre
study.

The genre chapters picked up on the feminist argument articulated
early on. The more I examine American films, the more I am convinced

that, although they are fictional works, made for commercial gain by a predominantly elite, male workforce, they bear traces of the cultural struggles of the twentieth century. Each of the genres displays an almost agonized division over how to talk and when to talk, over what to reveal and what to keep in, over how women (should) speak and how men (should) speak. Certainly, the films I have examined in this study show women being silenced or ridiculed for blathering and illustrate male dominance either through impenetrable taciturnity or verbal bludgeoning. But I also think they bear traces of women's efforts to find voices that will be heard and respected, and of men to forge a language less constricting than the models to which they've been relegated.

In the preceding pages I have sidestepped one of the major topics of film theory—auteurism.[2] I have done so because I am convinced that in terms of dialogue, genre and source material (which itself is determined by genre) trump individual style. *Twentieth Century* does not sound like *Wuthering Heights*, even though Hecht and McArthur wrote both; *Ball of Fire* sounds nothing like *Sunset Boulevard*, even though Billy Wilder co-wrote each; *Spartacus* sounds very different from *Lonely Are the Brave*, even though both were written by Dalton Trumbo. Perhaps minute textual analysis would find recurring patterns of vocabulary and sentence structure, but these don't rise to a noticeable level. Only in the case of screenwriters who repeatedly work in one genre—Preston Sturges's comedies, Bordon Chase's Westerns, Comden and Green's musicals, Casey Robinson's melodramas—would one be likely to find a consistent style of dialogue. And as for directors, given the prevailing prejudices against film speech, we know little about their characteristic approaches. The same small handful of insights are repeated endlessly: Capra is corny, Hawks favors overlapping sound, Welles manipulates sound perspective, Altman uses radio mikes, Joseph Mankiewicz lets everyone talk too much. Perhaps this study can be of some use to auteurist-oriented critics wishing to refine our understanding of directors' approach to their sound tracks.

One summer morning, while completing the final revisions of this study, I was driving to campus to work in the library. When my car overheated and broke down, I was forced to get off the highway in an unfamiliar area. At a service station pay phone, calling for help, I needed to describe my exact location. I addressed another motorist:

> M E: Where *am* I?
> MOTORIST: *(friendly, with just a touch of flippancy)* You're not in Kansas anymore.

And of course he was right, being in a new place, being forced to deal with an unforeseen emergency, getting help from strangers, is something like an adventurous trip to Oz.

The point is: the words that automatically sprang to his lips, and that captured (as nothing else could) my exact predicament, come from a movie made sixty years ago. That these words reverberate so is a testimony to how important they were in their original context, and to how important all film dialogue has become in American culture.

Earlier I spoke of the prejudices against film dialogue—despite the efforts of earlier advocates—lingering like the undead. Movies have taught me that there are two ways of finally vanquishing a vampire: driving a stake through his heart or tricking him into tarrying until touched by the light of day. What I've tried to do here is the latter, and my chief ploy has been seduction by quotation: *Wait! Don't leave! There's more for you to hear, to hear again.* And with each example, from *Wuthering Heights* to *Moonstruck,* my hope is that the sky has grown a little brighter.

Notes

INTRODUCTION: THE STUDY OF FILMIC SPEECH

1. From Bill Libby, "The Old Wrangler Rides Again," *Cosmopolitan*, March 1964, 14–21, reprinted in *My Darling Clementine*, ed. Robert Lyons (New Brunswick, N.J.: Rutgers University Press, 1984), 136.

2. A. Scott Berg, *Goldwyn: A Biography* (New York: Knopf, 1989), 324–25.

3. See, e.g., Philip Brophy, "Read My Lips: Notes on the Writing and Speaking of Film Dialogue," *Continuum* 5.2 (1992): 247–66; Mary Devereaux, "In Defense of Talking Film," *Persistence of Vision* 5 (1987): 17–27; id., "Of 'Talk and Brown Furniture': The Aesthetics of Film Dialogue," *Post Script* 6.1 (1986): 32–52; Christopher Faulkner, "René Clair, Marcel Pagnol and the Social Dimension of Speech," *Screen* 35.2 (Summer 1994): 157–70; John Fawell, "The Musicality of the Filmscript," *Literature/Film Quarterly* 17.1 (1989): 44–49; John Simon, "The Word on Film," *Hudson Review* 30.4 (1977–78): 501–21.

4. For fuller discussion of the anti-sound bias of classical film theory, see Sarah Kozloff, *Invisible Storytellers: Voice-Over Narration in American Fiction Film* (Berkeley and Los Angeles: University of California Press, 1988), 8–22; Rick Altman, "Introduction," in *Cinema/Sound*, ed. id., *Yale French Studies* 60 (1980): 3–15; and Devereaux, "Of 'Talk and Brown Furniture.' "

5. Susan Sontag, "Theater and Film," in *Film and/as Literature*, ed. John Harrington (Englewood Cliffs, N.J.: Prentice-Hall, 1977), 78.

6. Noël Carroll, "The Specificity Thesis," in *Film Theory and Criticism: Introductory Readings*, ed. Gerald Mast, Marshall Cohen, and Leo Braudy, 4th ed. (New York: Oxford University Press, 1992), 282.

7. David Mamet, *On Directing Film* (New York: Penguin Books, 1991), 72.

8. Ephraim Katz, *The Film Encyclopedia*, 3d ed., rev. Fred Klein and Ronald Dean Nolean (New York: Harper Perennial, 1998), 366.

9. Rachel Crothers, "The Construction of a Play," in *The Art of Playwriting: Lectures Delivered at the University of Pennsylvania on the Mask and Wig Foundation, by Jesse Lynch Williams, Langdon Mitchell, Lord Dunsany, [and] Gilbert Emery [pseud.] Rachel Crothers* (Philadelphia: University of Pennsylvania Press, 1928), 129.

10. Sam Smiley, *Playwriting: The Structure of Action* (Englewood Cliffs, N.J.: Prentice-Hall, 1971), 139.

11. Stanley Vincent Longman, *Composing Drama for Stage and Screen* (Newton, Mass.: Allyn & Bacon, 1986), 145.

12. Peter Schwenger, *Phallic Critiques: Masculinity and Twentieth Century Literature* (London: Routledge & Kegan Paul, 1984).

13. Benjamin Franklin, *Poor Richard's Almanack*, quoted in *The Harper Book of American Quotations*, ed. Gorton Carruth and Eugene Ehrlich (New York: Harper & Row, 1988), 531.

14. Ambrose Bierce, *The Devil's Dictionary*, quoted in *The Harper Book of American Quotations*, 530.

15. Søren Kierkegaard, *The Last Years: Journals, 1853–55*, ed. and trans. Ronald Smith (New York: Harper & Row, 1965), 262.

16. Elizabeth Closs Traugott and Mary Louise Pratt, *Linguistics for Students of Literature* (New York: Harcourt Brace Jovanovich, 1980), 228.

17. Wayne C. Booth, *The Rhetoric of Fiction* (Chicago: University of Chicago Press, 1961).

18. Sandra M. Gilbert and Susan Gubar, "Sexual Linguistics: Gender, Language, Sexuality," in *The Feminist Reader: Essays in Gender and Politics of Literary Criticism*, ed. Catherine Belsey and Jane Moore (New York: Basil Blackwell, 1989), 91.

19. Patricia Parker, *Literary Fat Ladies: Rhetoric, Gender, Property* (New York: Methuen, 1987), 26, 180.

20. Patricia Meyer Spacks, *Gossip* (New York: Knopf, 1985), 38–42, 150–53.

21. Elaine Chaika, *Language: The Social Mirror* (Rowley, Mass.: Newbury House, 1982), 204.

22. Dale Spender, *Man Made Language* (London: Routledge & Kegan Paul, 1980), 41–42. For more contemporary research on how women and men use language, see Camille Roman, Suzanne Juhasz, and Christanne Miller, *The Women and Language Debate: A Sourcebook* (New Brunswick, N.J.: Rutgers University Press, 1994).

23. Quoted in Donald Spoto, *The Dark Side of Genius: The Life of Alfred Hitchcock* (New York: Ballantine Books, 1983), 431.

24. Penelope Huston, "Scripting," *Sight and Sound* 19 (January 1951): 376.

25. Elisabeth Weis, "The Narrative Functions of the Ecouteur," in *Cinesonic: The World of Sound in Film*, ed. Philip Brophy (Sydney, Australia: AFTRS, 1999), 79–107.

26. Herbert H. Clark and Thomas B. Carlson, "Hearers and Speech Acts," *Language* 58.2 (1982): 344–45.

27. Jean Chothia, *Forging a Language: A Study of Plays of Eugene O'Neill* (Cambridge: Cambridge University Press, 1979), 7–8.

28. See David Bordwell, *Narration in the Fiction Film* (Madison: University of Wisconsin Press, 1985), 57–61.

29. Michel Chion, *Audio-Vision: Sound on Screen*, ed. and trans. Claudia Gorbman (New York: Columbia University Press, 1994), 6–7.

30. Chaika, *Language*, 91.

31. Norman Page, *Speech in the English Novel* (London: Longman, 1973), 6.

32. See Robin Tolmach Lakoff and Deborah Tannen, "Conversational Strategy and Metastrategy in a Pragmatic Theory: The Example of *Scenes from a Marriage*," *Semiotica* 49.3–4 (1984): 323–46.

33. Tom Shachtman, *The Inarticulate Society: Eloquence and Culture in America* (New York: Free Press, 1995), 46.

34. Faulkner, "René Clair, Marcel Pagnol and the Social Dimension of Speech," 165.

35. Barbara Klinger, *Melodrama and Meaning: History, Culture, and the Films of Douglas Sirk* (Bloomington: Indiana University Press, 1994), 151.

36. Barry Salt, "Film Form 1900–1906," in *Early Cinema: Space, Frame, Narrative*, ed. Thomas Elsaesser (London: BFI, 1990), 40.

37. Eileen Bowser, *The History of American Cinema*, vol. 2: *The Transformation of Cinema, 1907–1915* (Berkeley and Los Angeles: University of California Press, 1990), 143–45.

38. Alan Williams, "The Raw and the Coded: Sound Conventions and the Transition of the Talkies," in *Cinesonic: The World of Sound in Film*, ed. Philip Brophy (Sydney, Australia: AFTRS, 1999), 229–43.

39. See Douglas Gomery, "The Coming of Sound: Technological Change in the American Film Industry," in *Film Sound: Theory and Practice*, ed. Elisabeth Weis and John Belton (New York: Columbia University Press, 1985), 5–24 and Donald Crafton, *The Talkies: American Cinema's Transition to Sound 1926–1931* (New York: Scribner, 1997).

40. Pauline Kael, "Raising Kane," in id., *The Citizen Kane Book* (New York: Limelight Editions, 1984), 19.

41. Motion Picture Producers and Distributors of America, "The Motion Picture Production Code of 1930," reprinted in *The Movies in Our Midst: Documents in the Cultural History of Film in America*, ed. Gerald Mast (Chicago: University of Chicago Press, 1982), 329.

42. Pat McGilligan, *Backstory: Interviews with Screenwriters of Hollywood's Golden Age* (Berkeley and Los Angeles: University of California Press, 1986), 148.

43. See Todd Berliner, "Hollywood Movie Dialogue and the 'Real Realism' of John Cassavetes," *Film Quarterly* 52:3 (Spring 1999): 2–16. Unfortunately this article appeared just as this book was going to press.

44. See Charles Shreger's discussion in "Altman, Dolby and the Second Sound Revolution," in *Film Sound: Theory and Practice*, ed. Elisabeth Weis and John Belton, 348–55 (New York: Columbia University Press, 1985), and Helen Keysser, *Robert Altman's America* (New York: Oxford University Press, 1991).

45. David Kipen, *World Policy Journal*, quoted in Fareed Zakaria, "Peace Is Hell," *New York Times Magazine*, 16 November 1997, 132.

46. Erich Auerbach, *Mimesis: The Representation of Reality in Western Literature*, trans. Willard R. Trask (Princeton: Princeton University Press, 1953).

47. Nan Withers-Wilson, *Vocal Direction for the Theatre: From Script Analysis to Opening Night* (New York: Drama Book, 1993), 9. See also Crafton, *Talkies*, 445–63.

48. Mark Winokur, "Marginal Marginalia: The African-American Voice in the Nouvelle Gangster Film," *Velvet Light Trap*, no. 35 (Spring 1995): 21.

49. Tom McArthur, *The Oxford Companion to the English Language* (New York: Oxford University Press, 1992), 672; and Jon Auerbach, "They Can't Spell It, Can't Pronounce It and Don't Get It," *Wall Street Journal*, 2 June 1998, A1.

50. Peter Biskind, *Seeing Is Believing: How Hollywood Taught Us to Stop Worrying and Love the Fifties* (New York: Pantheon Books, 1983), 2.

51. Patricia Davis, "The Curious Case of the College, a Jade Piece and a $6 Million Fax," *Wall Street Journal*, 25 July 1997, B1.

52. Hannah Arendt, "On Humanity in Dark Times," in id., *Men in Dark Times* (New York: Harcourt, Brace & World, 1968), 25. I am indebted to Patricia Sparks's *Gossip* for knowledge of Arendt's statement.

CHAPTER 1. THE FUNCTIONS OF DIALOGUE IN NARRATIVE FILM

1. For screenwriting manuals that also offer discussions of the functions of dialogue, see Stanley Longman, *Composing Drama for Stage and Screen* (Newton, Mass.: Allyn & Bacon, 1986), 145–46, and Alan Armer, *Writing the Screenplay: TV and Film* (Belmont, Calif.: Wadsworth, 1988).

2. Erika Fisher-Lichte, *The Semiotics of Theater*, trans. Jeremy Gaines and Dorothy L. Jones (Bloomington: Indiana University Press, 1992), 20–21.

3. Roland Barthes, "Rhetoric of the Image," in id., *Image/Music/Text*, trans. Stephen Heath (New York: Hill & Wang, 1977), 32–51.

4. Julie Salamon, *The Devil's Candy: "The Bonfire of the Vanities" Goes to Hollywood* (Boston: Houghton Mifflin, 1991), 117.

5. David Bordwell, Janet Staiger, and Kristin Thompson, *The Classical Hollywood Cinema* (New York: Columbia University Press, 1985), 33.

6. Tzvetan Todorov, "Speech According to Constant," in id., *The Poetics of Prose*, trans. Richard Howard (Ithaca, N.Y.: Cornell University Press, 1977), 93–94.

7. Bordwell et al., *Classical Hollywood Cinema*, 31.

8. Roland Barthes, *S/Z*, trans. Richard Miller (New York: Hill & Wang, 1974).

9. Bordwell et al., *Classical Hollywood Cinema*, 31.

10. Pat McGilligan, *Backstory: Interviews with Screenwriters of Hollywood's Golden Age* (Berkeley and Los Angeles: University of California Press, 1986), 32.

11. Seymour Chatman, *Story and Discourse: Narrative Structure in Fiction and Film* (Ithaca, N.Y.: Cornell University Press, 1978), 53.

12. Bordwell et al., *Classical Hollywood Cinema*, 16.

13. Virginia Wright Wexman focuses on the kiss as the privileged element associated with romantic attraction in *Creating the Couple: Love, Marriage and Hollywood Performance* (Princeton, N.J.: Princeton University Press, 1993), 18.

14. Richard Dyer, *Stars* new ed. (London: BFI, 1998), 106.

15. Rachel Crothers, "The Construction of a Play," in *The Art of Playwriting: Lectures Delivered at the University of Pennsylvania on the Mask and Wig Foundation, by Jesse Lynch Williams, Langdon Mitchell, Lord Dunsany, [and] Gilbert Emery [pseud.] Rachel Crothers* (Philadelphia: University of Pennsylvania Press, 1928), 129.

16. Norman Page, *Speech in the English Novel* (London: Longman, 1973), 15.

17. Ibid., 90.

18. Sidney Lumet, *Making Movies* (New York: Knopf, 1995), 37.

19. Syd Field, *The Screenwriter's Workbook* (New York: Dell, 1984), 72.

20. Elizabeth Closs Traugott and Mary Louise Pratt, *Linguistics for Students of Literature* (New York: Harcourt Brace Jovanovich, 1980), 229.

21. Mary Devereaux, "In Defense of Talking Film," *Persistence of Vision* 5 (Spring 1987): 24.

22. Myra Forsberg, "Lean Mean Lines," *New York Times,* Sunday 15 November 1987, 25.

23. Anne Dean, *David Mamet: Language as Dramatic Action* (Rutherford, N.J.: Farleigh Dickinson University Press, 1990), 18.

24. "That was the thing we changed most about [Fleming's] books as far as the pictures were concerned," the screenwriter Richard Maibaum is quoted as saying. "We made Bond more humorous, throwing away those one-liners that are now obligatory in Bond films" (McGilligan, *Backstory,* 286).

25. See Philip Brophy, "Read My Lips: Notes on the Writing and Speaking of Film Dialogue," *Continuum* 5.2 (1992): 247–266.

26. Jackie Byars, *All That Hollywood Allows: Re-reading Gender in 1950s Melodrama* (Chapel Hill: University of North Carolina Press, 1991), 111–12.

27. M. H. Abrams, *A Glossary of Literary Terms,* 6th ed. (Fort Worth, Tex.: Harcourt Brace Jovanovich College Publishers, 1993), 4.

28. See Al LaValley, "*Invasion of the Body Snatchers:* Politics, Psychology, and Sociology," in id., ed., *Invasion of the Body Snatchers* (New Brunswick, N.J.: Rutgers University Press, 1989), 3–17.

29. James Naremore, *Acting in the Cinema* (Berkeley and Los Angeles: University of California Press, 1988), 47.

30. Ibid.

CHAPTER 2. STRUCTURAL AND STYLISTIC VARIABLES

1. Michel Chion, *Audio-Vision: Sound on Screen,* ed. and trans. Claudia Gorbman (New York: Columbia University Press, 1994), 57.

2. Jack Shadoian, "Writing for the Screen—Some Thoughts on Dialogue," *Literature/Film Quarterly* 9.2 (1981): 86.

3. Chion, *Audio-Vision,* 57.

4. Quoted in Elisabeth Weis, *The Silent Scream: Alfred Hitchcock's Sound Track* (Rutherford, N.J.: Fairleigh Dickinson University Press), 142.

5. Stuart Rumens, "Carte Blanche: Button Up That Lip," *Movie-Maker* 19 (May 1985): 12.

6. Sidney Howard, "The Story Gets a Treatment," in *We Make the Movies,* ed. Nancy Naumberg (New York: W. W. Norton, 1937), 40.

7. Hank Poster, "The Film Writer: Solving the Dilemma of Dialogue," *Today's Film Maker* 3.3 (1974): 47.

8. Gerald Mast, *Howard Hawks, Storyteller* (New York: Oxford University Press, 1982), 48.

9. Ibid., 48.

10. John Fawell, "The Musicality of the Filmscript," *Film/Literature Quarterly* 17.1 (1989): 44.

11. See Marisa Smith and Amy Schewel, eds., *The Actor's Book of Movie Monologues* (New York: Penguin Books, 1986), and Marisa Smith and Joceyln Beard, eds., *Contemporary Movie Monologues: A Sourcebook for Actors* (New York: Fawcett Columbine, 1991).

12. Sam Smiley, *Playwriting: The Structure of Action* (Englewood Cliffs, N.J.: Prentice-Hall, 1971), 137.

13. "Noël Coward started the vogue for brief speeches, almost none more than a line long, in the mid-twenties," says John Van Druten, *Playwright at Work* (New York: Harper Brothers, 1953), 144.

14. Manfred Pfister, in *The Theory and Analysis of Drama,* trans. John Halliday (Cambridge: Cambridge University Press, 1988), argues that in Anglo-American criticism, the term "soliloquies" is more likely to be used for one-character speech, while "monologues" refer to any long, self-contained speeches (127). However, I shall maintain my terminology for the sake of parallelism.

15. See ibid., 131–34, on monologues in the theater and the distinction between "conventional" and "motivated" monologues.

16. John Ellis, "Stars as Cinematic Phenomenon," in *Film Theory and Criticism,* ed. Gerald Mast, Marshall Cohen, and Leo Braudy, 4th ed. (New York: Oxford University Press, 1992), 619.

17. Bernard M. Dupriez, *A Dictionary of Literary Devices, Gradus, A–Z,* trans. and adapted Albert W. Halsall (Toronto: University of Toronto Press, 1991), 132.

18. Dennis Ira Aig, "Jules Furthman and the Popular Aesthetics of Screenwriting" (diss. Ohio State Univ., 1983), 96.

19. Robin Lakoff, *Language and Woman's Place* (New York: Harper & Row, 1975), 14.

20. Dennis Ira Aig, "Jules Furthman and the Popular Aesthetics of Screenwriting," 98.

21. Deborah Tannen, *Talking Voices: Repetition, Dialogue and Imagery in Conversational Discourse* (Cambridge: Cambridge University Press, 1989), 192.

22. Robert T. Self, "The Sounds of *M*A*S*H,*" in *Close Viewings,* ed. Peter Lehman (Tallahassee: Florida State University Press, 1990), 152. See also Helene Keyssar, *Robert Altman's America* (New York: Oxford University Press, 1991), 36–37.

23. See Michel Chion, "Le Dernier Mot du muet," in id., *La Voix au Cinéma* (Paris: *Cahiers du Cinéma*/Editions de L'Etoile, 1982), 81–89.

24. Peter Brooks, *The Melodramatic Imagination: Balzac, Henry James, Melodrama and the Mode of Excess* (New York: Columbia University Press, 1985).

25. Edward Dmytryk, *On Screen Writing* (Boston: Focal Press, 1985), 31.

26. Anne Dean, *David Mamet: Language as Dramatic Action* (Rutherford, N.J.: Fairleigh Dickinson University Press, 1990), 24.

27. Will G. Moore, "Speech," in *Molière: A Collection of Critical Essays,* ed. Jacques Guicharnaud (Englewood Cliffs, N.J.: Prentice-Hall, 1964), 47.

28. For information on distribution of American films abroad, see Nataša Ďurovičová, "Translating America: The Hollywood Mutlilinguals, 1929–1933,"

in *Sound Theory/Sound Practice,* (New York: Routledge, 1992), ed. Rick Altman, 138–53, and Ruth Vasey, "Foreign Parts: Hollywood's Global Distribution and the Representation of Ethnicity," *American Quarterly* 44.4 (December 1992): 617–42.

29. Lewis Herman, "The Gift of Tongues," *Screen Writer* 1 (March 1946): 26–32.

30. Ella Shohat and Robert Stam, *Unthinking Eurocentrism: Multiculturalism and the Media* (New York: Routledge, 1994), 191. It is interesting that sensitivity to this ventriloquising was expressed as early as the late 1920s. See Donald Crafton, "The Voice Squad," in *The Talkies: American Cinema's Transition to Sound, 1926–1931* (New York: Scribner, 1997), 462.

31. Elaine Chaika, *Language: The Social Mirror* (Rowley, Mass.: Newbury House, 1982) 139.

32. Lewis Herman, "Dialect Dialectics," *Screen Writer* 1 (April 1946): 5.

33. Donald Bogle, *Toms, Coons, Mulattoes, Mammies, and Bucks: An Interpretive History of Blacks in American Films,* 2d ed. (New York: Continuum, 1990), 93.

34. Robert Scholes, *Structuralism in Literature: An Introduction* (New Haven: Yale University Press, 1974), 83–85.

35. Deborah Tannen, *Talking Voices: Repetition, Dialogue and Imagery in Conversational Discourse* (Cambridge: Cambridge University Press, 1989), and Ronald Wardhaugh, *How Conversation Works* (Oxford: Basil Blackwell, 1985), 20.

36. See Elizabeth Closs Traugott and Mary Louise Pratt, *Linguistics for Students of Literature* (New York: Harcourt Brace Jovanovich, 1980), 21; Jonathan Culler, *Structuralist Poetics: Structuralism, Linguistics and the Study of Literature* (Ithaca, N.Y.: Cornell University Press, 1975), 55–74.

37. Smiley, *Playwriting,* 56.

38. Fawell, "Musicality of the Filmscript," 45.

CHAPTER 3. INTEGRATION

1. Edward Sapir, "Speech as a Personality Trait," in *Selected Writings of Edward Sapir in Language, Culture and Personality,* ed. David Mandelbaum (Berkeley and Los Angeles: University of California Press, 1949), 536.

2. Jean Renoir, *My Life and My Films: From Silent Films to Talkies,* trans. Norman Denny (New York: Atheneum, 1974), 103.

3. Amy Lawrence, *Echo and Narcissus: Women's Voices in Classical Hollywood Cinema* (Berkeley and Los Angeles: University of California Press, 1990), 125.

4. Roland Barthes, *The Pleasure of the Text,* trans. Richard Miller (New York: Hill & Wang, 1975), 67.

5. Gavin Lambert, "Studies in Scarlett," in *Gone with the Wind as Book and Film,* ed. Richard Harwell (Columbia: University of South Carolina Press, 1992), 132–37.

6. Elizabeth Kendall, *The Runaway Bride: Hollywood Romantic Comedy of the 1930s* (New York: Knopf, 1990), 165.

7. J. L. Styan, *The Elements of Drama* (Cambridge: Cambridge University Press, 1960), 86.

8. Mary Deveraux, "In Defense of Talking Film," *Persistence of Vision* 5 (Spring 1987): 23.

9. Styan, *Elements of Drama*, 89.

10. Gary Collier, *Emotional Expression* (Hillsdale, N.J.: Lawrence Earlbaum, 1985), 141.

11. Ronald Wardhaugh, *How Conversation Works* (London: Basil Blackwell, 1985), 78.

12. James Naremore, *Acting in the Cinema* (Berkeley and Los Angeles: University of California Press, 1988), 42.

13. See Elisabeth Weis and John Belton, eds., *Film Sound: Theory and Practice* (New York: Columbia University Press, 1985), for excerpts of the classic debate, and modern discussions such as Mary Ann Doane's "Ideology and the Practice of Sound Editing and Mixing," in ibid. 54–62.

14. Michel Chion, *Audio-Vision: Sound on Screen*, ed. and trans. Claudia Gorbman (New York: Columbia University Press, 1994), 67–94.

15. Rick Altman "Moving Lips: Cinema as Ventriloquism," in *Cinema/Sound*, ed. id., *Yale French Studies* 60 (1980): 69.

16. Doane, "Ideology and the Practice of Sound Editing and Mixing," 61.

17. Amy Lawrence, "Women's Voices in Third World Cinema," in *Sound Theory/Sound Practice*, ed. Rick Altman (New York: Routledge, 1992), 179.

18. Joseph D. Anderson, "Sound and Image Together: Cross-Modal Confirmation," *Wide Angle* 15.1 (Jan 1993): 30–43.

19. Wardhaugh, *How Conversation Works*, 90. See also Collier, *Emotional Expression*, 49.

20. Murray Smith, "The Logic and Legacy of Brechtianism," in *Post-Theory: Reconstructing Film Studies*, ed. David Bordwell and Noël Carroll (Madison: University of Wisconsin Press, 1996), 130–48. See also Vance Kepley, "Whose Apparatus? Problems of Film Exhibition and History," in ibid., 533–49.

21. Richard Dyer, *Stars*, new ed. (London: BFI, 1998), 112.

22. William Rothman, *Hitchcock: The Murderous Gaze* (Cambridge, Mass.: Harvard University Press, 1982), 276–88.

23. Karel Reisz and Gavin Millar, *The Technique of Film Editing* (New York: Hastings House, 1968), 86.

24. David Bordwell and Kristin Thompson, *Film Art*, 4th ed. (New York: McGraw-Hill, 1993), 305.

25. See Doane, "Ideology and the Practice of Sound Editing and Mixing."

26. Barry Salt, "Film Style and Technology in the Forties," *Film Quarterly* 31.1 (Fall 1977): 46–47.

27. Phillip Lopate, "It's Not Heroes Who Have Bad Grammar; It's Films," *New York Times*, 18 June 1995, 28.

28. Claudia Gorbman, *Unheard Melodies: Narrative Film Music* (Bloomington: Indiana University Press, 1987), 77.

29. See *"Terminator 2: Judgment Day,"* in *Sound For Picture*, ed. Jeff Forlenza and Terri Stone (Emeryville, Calif.: Mix Books, 1993), 30–35.

30. Vincent LoBrutto, *Sound on Film: Interviews with Creators of Film Sound* (Westport, Conn.: Praeger, 1994), 54.

31. Stephen Handzo, "Appendix: A Narrative Glossary of Film Sound Technology," in *Film Sound: Theory and Practice*, ed. Elisabeth Weis and John Belton (New York: Columbia University Press, 1985), 383–426.

32. See "James G. Stewart," in *Sound For Picture*, ed. Jeff Forlenza and Terri Stone (Emeryville, Calif.: Mix Books, 1993), 12–17.

33. Chion, *Audio-Vision*, 6

34. Rick Altman, "Sound Space," in *Sound Theory/Sound Practice* (New York: Routledge, 1992), 60.

35. Ibid., 61.

36. See Clayton Koppes and Gregory Black, *Hollywood Goes to War* (Berkeley and Los Angeles: University of California Press, 1990), 98–104. See also, Pat McGilligan ed., *Backstory: Interviews with Screenwriters of Hollywood's Golden Age* (Berkeley and Los Angeles: University of California Press, 1986) 330, and Jeanine Basinger, *The World War II Combat Film: Anatomy of a Genre* (New York: Columbia University Press, 1986), 228–35.

37. Axel Madsen, *William Wyler* (New York: Crowell, 1973), 217. See also Jan Herman, *A Talent for Trouble: The Life of Hollywood's Most Acclaimed Director, William Wyler* (New York: Da Capo Press, 1997), 235–37.

PART II. DIALOGUE AND GENRE

1. Harry Purvis, "Sure Fire Dialogue: Please Feel Free to Help Yourself," *Films in Review* 6.6 (June–July 1955): 278–83.

2. Susan Sontag, "The Imagination of Disaster," in *Film Theory and Criticism*, ed. Gerald Mast and Marshall Cohen (New York: Oxford University Press, 1974), 437.

3. Vivian Sobchack, *Screening Space: The American Science Fiction Film* (New York: Ungar, 1988), 146–222.

4. Steve Neale, "Questions of Genre," *Screen* 31.1 (Spring 1990), 46–47.

5. Ibid., 56.

6. See, e.g., Andrew Tudor, "Genre," Edward Buscombe, "The Idea of Genre in American Cinema," and Rick Altman, "A Semantic/Syntactic Approach to Film Genre," in *Film Genre Reader II*, ed. Barry Keith Grant (Austin: University of Texas Press, 1995), 3–40; Tom Ryall, "Genre and Hollywood," in *The Oxford Guide to Film Studies*, ed. John Hill and Pamela Church Gibson (London: Oxford University Press, 1998) 327–38; and Rick Altman, "Reusable Packaging: Generic Products and the Recycling Process," in *Refiguring American Film Genres*, ed. Nick Browne (Berkeley and Los Angeles: University of California Press, 1998), 1–41.

CHAPTER 4. VERBAL FRONTIERS: DIALOGUE IN THE WESTERN

1. Jane Tompkins, *West of Everything: The Secret Life of Westerns* (New York: Oxford University Press, 1992), 49.

2. Tag Gallagher argues against this simplification in "Shoot Out at the Genre Corral: Problems in the 'Evolution' of the Western," in *Film Genre Reader II*, ed. Barry Keith Grant (Austin: University of Texas Press, 1995), 246–60.

3. Will Wright, *Sixguns and Society: A Structural Analysis of the Western* (Berkeley and Los Angeles: University of California Press, 1975).

4. John Cawelti, *The Six-Gun Mystique*, 2d ed. (Bowling Green, Ohio: Bowling Green Popular Press, 1984), 73.

5. Ibid., 89.

6. Tompkins, *West of Everything*, 52, 60, 64, 54.

7. Edward Buscombe, *Stagecoach* (London: BFI Film Classics, 1992), 75.

8. Robert Warshow, "Movie Chronicle: The Westerner," in *Film Theory and Criticism*, ed. Gerald Mast and Marshall Cohen, 2d ed. (New York: Oxford University Press, 1979), 474.

9. Philip French, *Westerns* (London: Oxford University Press, 1973), 10.

10. Robert Lyons, "Introduction: *My Darling Clementine* as History and Romance," in *My Darling Clementine*, ed. Robert Lyons (New Brunswick, N.J.: Rutgers University Press, 1984), 13.

11. John Price, "The Stereotyping of North American Indians in Motion Pictures," in *The Pretend Indians: Images of Native Americans in the Movies*, ed. Gretchen M. Bataille and Charles L. P. Silet (Ames: Iowa State University Press, 1980), 80.

12. Virginia Wright Wexman, *Creating the Couple: Love, Marriage and Hollywood Performance* (Princeton, N.J.: Princeton University Press, 1993), 97.

13. Ibid., 99.

14. Lewis Herman, *American Dialects: A Manual for Actors, Directors and Writers* (New York: Theatre Art Books, 1947), 299.

15. T. J. Ross in "Western Approaches: A Note on Dialogue," in *Focus on the Western*, ed. Jack Nachbar (Englewood Cliffs, N.J.: Prentice-Hall, 1974), 78–80, complains that speech in Western films is often anachronistic. I don't find this very surprising.

16. Edward Buscombe, ed., *The BFI Companion to the Western* (New York: De Capo Press, 1988), 170.

17. See, e.g., Ramon Adams, *Cowboy Lingo* (Boston: Houghton Mifflin, 1936); *Western Words: A Dictionary of the Range, Cow Camp and Trail* (Norman: University of Oklahoma Press, 1944; 2nd ed., 1968).

18. Ernest Haycox, "Stage to Lordsburg," reprinted in Andrew Sinclair, ed., *Stagecoach: A Film by John Ford and Dudley Nichols* (New York: Lorrimer, 1971), 5–19. Nichols's screenplay is included in this text.

19. Gary Wills, *John Wayne's America* (New York: Touchstone, 1998), 82–83.

20. Dudley Nichols, "The Writer and the Film," in *Film: A Montage of Theories*, ed. Richard Dyer MacCann (New York: Dutton, 1966), 82.

21. Peter Stowell, *John Ford* (Boston: Twayne, 1986), 27.

22. Tag Gallagher, *John Ford: The Man and His Films* (Berkeley and Los Angeles: University of California Press, 1986), 148.

23. Peter Bogdanovich, *John Ford*, new revised and enlarged ed. (Berkeley and Los Angeles: University of California Press, 1978), 70.

24. Garry Wills, "John Wayne's Body," *New Yorker*, 19 August 1996, 44.

25. Nick Browne, "The Spectator-in-the-Text: The Rhetoric of *Stagecoach*," in *Narrative/Apparatus/Ideology*, ed. Philip Rosen (New York: Columbia University Press, 1986), 102–19.

26. Edward Buscombe, *Stagecoach* (London: British Film Institute, 1992), 30–31.

27. Joseph Anderson, "When the Twain Meet: Hollywood's Remake of *The Seven Samurai*," *Film Quarterly* 15.3 (Spring 1962): 57.

28. Richard Slotkin, *Gunfighter Nation: The Myth of the Frontier in Twentieth-Century America* (New York: Harper, 1993), 474–86.

29. Ibid., 476.

30. Anderson, "When the Twain Meet," 56.

CHAPTER 5. WORD PLAY: DIALOGUE IN SCREWBALL COMEDIES

1. Eliot Rubinstein, "The End of Screwball Comedy: *The Lady Eve* and *The Palm Beach Story*," *Post Script* 1.3 (Spring–Summer 1982): 45.

2. Bosley Crowther, review of *The Palm Beach Story*, *New York Times*, 11 December 1942, 33.

3. See, e.g., Kathleen Rowe, "Comedy, Melodrama and Gender: Theorizing the Genres of Laughter," in *Classical Hollywood Comedy*, ed. Kristine Branovska Karnick and Henry Jenkins (New York: Routledge, 1995), 39–62.

4. Northrop Frye, *Anatomy of Criticism: Four Essays* (Princeton, N.J.: Princeton University Press, 1957).

5. On the issue of divorce, see David R. Shumway, "Screwball Comedies: Constructing Romance, Mystifying Marriage," in *Film Genre Reader II*, ed. Barry Keith Grant (Austin: University of Texas Press, 1995), 381–401.

6. See also Wes D. Gehring, "Screwball Comedy: An Overview," *Journal of Popular Film and Television*, Winter 1986, 178–85; Elizabeth Kendall, *The Runaway Bride: Hollywood Romantic Comedy of the 1930s* (New York: Knopf, 1990), and Gerald Weales, *Canned Goods as Caviar: American Film Comedy of the 1930s* (Chicago: University of Chicago Press, 1985).

7. Diane Carson, "To Be Seen but Not Heard: *The Awful Truth*," in *Multiple Voices in Feminist Film Criticism*, ed. Diane Carson, Linda Dittmar, and Janice Welsch (Minneapolis: University of Minnesota Press, 1994), 213–25.

8. Bruce Babington and Peter Evans, *Affairs to Remember: The Hollywood Comedy of the Sexes* (Manchester University Press, 1989), 3.

9. Stanley Cavell, *Pursuits of Happiness: The Hollywood Comedy of Remarriage* (Cambridge, Mass.: Harvard University Press, 1981).

10. "Ochi chernye" ("Dark Eyes") is the title of a famous Russian gypsy song.

11. Mark Winokur, *American Laughter: Immigrants, Ethnicity and 1930s Hollywood Film Comedy* (New York: St. Martin's Press, 1996).

12. I am indebted to James Gordon, "The Comic Structures of Preston Sturges" (Ph.D. diss., Northwestern University, 1980), for his recognition of the importance of slang in Sturges's films.

13. Shumway, "Screwball Comedies," 388.

14. Pauline Kael, "The Man from Dream City," in *When the Lights Go Down* (New York: Holt, Rinehart & Winston, 1975), 16.

15. Gerald Mast, *Howard Hawks, Storyteller* (New York: Oxford University Press, 1982), 215.

16. C. L. Barber, *Shakespeare's Festive Comedy: A Study of Dramatic Form and Its Relation to Social Custom* (Princeton, N.J.: Princeton University Press, 1959), 100.

17. M. H. Abrams, *A Glossary of Literary Terms,* 6th ed. (New York: Holt, Rinehart & Winston, 1993), 220.

18. John Lahr, *Coward the Playwright* (London: Methuen, 1982), 3, 5.

19. James Harvey, *Romantic Comedy in Hollywood from Lubitsch to Sturges* (New York: Knopf, 1987), 61.

20. Quoted in Cole Lesley, *Remembered Laughter: The Life of Noël Coward* (New York: Knopf, 1976), 434.

21. Of all the scholars who have studied screwball, James Harvey gives the most attention to acting, and, as in his discussion of this sequence, sensitively verbalizes the results of small nuances. See his *Romantic Comedy in Hollywood,* 240.

22. Rubinstein, "End of Screwball Comedy," 43.

23. Richard Maltby, "The Production Code and the Hays Office," in *Grand Design: Hollywood as a Modern Business Enterprise, 1930–1939,* ed. Tino Balio (New York: Scribner, 1993), 40.

24. Ibid., 64.

25. James Naremore, *Acting in the Cinema* (Berkeley and Los Angeles: University of California Press, 1988), 186–87.

26. Tina Olsin Lent, "Romantic Love and Friendship: The Redefinition of Gender Relations in Screwball Comedy," in *Classical Hollywood Comedy,* ed. Kristine Branovska Karnick and Henry Jenkins (New York: Routledge, 1995), 323.

27. Harvey, *Romantic Comedy in Hollywood,* 437–38.

28. Maurice Charney, *Comedy High and Low: An Introduction to the Experience of Comedy* (New York: Oxford University Press, 1978), 55.

29. Babington and Evans, *Affairs to Remember,* 27.

30. Leigh Brackett, "A Comment on the Hawksian Woman," *Take One* 3.6 (July–August 71): 19.

31. Carson,"To Be Seen but Not Heard," 215.

32. Ibid., 214.

33. Winokur, *American Laughter,* 190.

34. Gerald Mast, "Everything's Gonna Be All Right: The Making of *Bringing Up Baby,*" in *Bringing Up Baby,* ed. id. (New Brunswick, N.J.: Rutgers University Press, 1988), 4–5. This volume contains a continuity script.

35. Ibid. 8, 13.

36. Mast, *Bringing Up Baby,* 298.

37. Kathleen Rowe, *The Unruly Woman: Gender and Genres of Laughter* (Austin: University of Texas Press, 1995), 151.

38. Andrew Britton, *Cary Grant: Comedy and Male Desire* (Newcastle: Tyneside Cinema, 1983), unpaginated.

39. Diane Jacobs, *Christmas in July: The Life and Art of Preston Sturges* (Berkeley and Los Angeles: University of California Press, 1992), 266–77.

40. Brian Henderson, "Introduction" to *The Palm Beach Story*, in Preston Sturges, *Four More Screenplays* (Berkeley and Los Angeles: University of California Press, 1995), 19–82.

41. Penelope Houston, "Preston Sturges," *Sight and Sound* 34.3 (Summer 1965): 133.

42. Rubinstein, "End of Screwball Comedy," 44.

43. Shumway, "Screwball Comedies," 389.

44. James Curtis, *Between Flops: A Biography of Preston Sturges* (New York: Harcourt Brace Jovanovich, 1982), 161.

45. For more on the racism of Sturges's films, see John Pym, *The Palm Beach Story* (London: British Film Institute, 1998), 38–48.

46. Peter Brooks, *The Melodramatic Imagination: Balzac, Henry James, Melodrama and the Mode of Excess* (New York: Columbia University Press, 1985), 56–57.

47. Rubinstein, "End of Screwball Comedy," 38.

48. Henderson, "Introduction," in Sturges, *Four More Screenplays*, 56.

49. Brian Henderson, "Romantic Comedy Today: *Semi-Tough* or Impossible?" in *Film Genre Reader*, ed. Barry Keith Grant (Austin: University of Texas Press, 1986), 309–28.

CHAPTER 6. WORDS AS WEAPONS: DIALOGUE IN GANGSTER FILMS

1. Harry Geduld has an interesting discussion of this film in *The Birth of the Talkies: From Edison to Jolson* (Bloomington: Indiana University Press, 1975), 201–9.

2. Peter Burke, *The Art of Conversation* (Ithaca, N.Y.: Cornell University Press, 1993), 25–26.

3. This definition corresponds closely with the one offered by Marilyn Yaquinto, *Pump 'em Full of Lead: A Look at Gangsters on Film* (New York: Twayne, 1998), xii.

4. Foster Hirsch, *Film Noir: the Dark Side of the Screen* (New York: Da Capo Press, 1981), 58–65; "Appendix A," in *Film Noir: An Encyclopedic Reference to the American Style*, ed. Alain Silver and Elizabeth Ward (Woodstock, N.Y.: Overlook Press, 1979), 323–25.

5. Examples are collected in Peggy Thompson and Saeko Usukawa, *Hard-Boiled: Great Lines from Classic Noir Films* (San Francisco: Chronicle Books, 1995).

6. Mark Reid shows that the popular 1990s films are part of a long tradition of black filmmakers' treatment of organized crime, starting as early as Oscar Micheaux's *Spider Web* (1926); see Reid, "The Black Gangster Film," in *Film Genre Reader II*, ed. Barry Keith Grant (Austin: University of Texas Press, 1995), 456–73. For a longer, more detailed discussion of the gangster genre's development, see Colin McArthur, *Underworld U.S.A.* (New York: Viking, 1972), 34–58.

7. John McCarty, *Hollywood Gangland: The Movies' Love Affair with the Mob* (New York: St. Martin's Press, 1993), includes other plot categories such as "murder for hire" and "yakusas." Prison films, boxing films, and "communist infiltration" films are also sometimes treated as subsets of the gangster genre.

8. See Robert Phillip Kolker, *A Cinema of Loneliness: Penn, Kubrick, Coppola, Scorsese, Altman* (New York: Oxford University Press, 1980), 218–21, and Marion W. Weiss, "Linguistic Coding in the Films of Martin Scorsese," *Semiotica* 55.3–4 (1985): 185–94.

9. Edward Mitchell, "Apes and Essences: Some Sources of Significance in the American Gangster Film," in *Film Genre Reader*, ed. Barry Keith Grant (Austin: University of Texas Press, 1986), 159–68.

10. Jack Shadoian, *Dreams and Dead Ends: The American Gangster/Crime Film* (Cambridge, Mass.: MIT Press, 1977), 5–9.

11. John Baxter, *The Gangster Film* (London: Zwemmer, 1970), 7.

12. J. Hoberman, "Believe It or Not," *Artforum*, January 1991, 20.

13. Robert Warshow, "The Gangster as Tragic Hero," in *The Immediate Experience* (New York: Doubleday, 1962), 133.

14. James Naremore, *Acting in the Cinema* (Berkeley and Los Angeles: University of California Press, 1988), 44.

15. Timothy Jay, *Cursing in America: A Psycholinguistic Study of Dirty Language in the Courts, in the Movies, in the Schoolyards and on the Streets* (Philadelphia: John Benjamins, 1992).

16. Robert Warshow, "Movie Chronicle: The Westerner," in *The Immediate Experience* (New York: Doubleday, 1962), 136.

17. Mark Winokur, "Marginal Marginalia: The African-American Voice in the Nouvelle Gangster Film," *Velvet Light Trap* 35 (Spring 1995): 26.

18. *Funk and Wagnalls New Standard Dictionary of the English Language* (New York: Funk & Wagnalls, 1943), 1722, quoting from *The Evening Sun* (New York), 13 May 1909.

19. Hoberman, "Believe It or Not," 20.

20. *New York Times*, 26 May 1936, 2, quoted in Charles Eckert, "The Anatomy of a Proletarian Film: Warner's *Marked Woman*," in *Movies and Methods*, ed. Bill Nichols (Berkeley and Los Angeles: University of California Press, 1985), 2: 410.

21. Victor S. Navasky, *Naming Names* (New York: Viking, 1980), xiv.

22. "Dialogue on Film: Mario Puzo," *American Film* 4 (May 1979): 38.

23. Mario Puzo, *The Godfather* (New York: Putnam, 1969), 30, 32.

24. Peter Cowie, *Coppola: A Biography* (New York: Scribner, 1990), 66.

25. Todd Boyd, *Am I Black Enough For You? Popular Culture from the 'Hood and Beyond* (Bloomington: Indiana University Press, 1997), 84.

26. Shadoian, *Dreams and Dead Ends*, 329.

27. Transcriptions from *The Godfather* were aided by the script published in Sam Thomas, ed. *Best American Screenplays*. Vol. 3 (New York: Crown, 1995).

28. Thomas J. Ferraro, "Blood in the Marketplace: The Business of Family in the *Godfather* Narratives," in *The Invention of Ethnicity*, ed. Werner Sollors (New York: Oxford University Press, 1989), 178.

29. Pauline Kael, "Alchemy," in *Deeper into Movies* (Boston: Little, Brown, 1973), 423.

30. "Quentin Tarantino: Answers First, Questions Later: An Interview with Graham Fuller," in *Reservoir Dogs and True Romance: Screenplays by Quentin Tarantino* (New York: Grove Press, 1994), xiii.

31. See Sharon Willis, "The Fathers Watch the Boys' Room," *Camera Obscura* 32 (June 1995): 40–73, and Gary Indiana et al., "Pulp the Hype on the Q.T.," *Artforum* 33.7 (March 1995): 62 –67.

32. Roger Ebert, *"Reservoir Dogs," Chicago Sun Times,* 26 October 1992. Reprinted at www.suntimes.com/ebert_reviews/1992/10/785503.html.

33. Quoted in Jeff Dawson, *Quentin Tarantino: The Cinema of Cool* (New York: Applause Books, 1995), 73–74.

34. "Quentin Tarantino interviewed by Gavin Smith," *Film Comment* 30.4 (July–August 1994): 34

35. Ibid., 38.

36. J. P. Telotte, "Fatal Capers: Strategy and Enigma in Film Noir," *Journal of Popular Film and Television* 23.4 (Winter 1996): 163–70.

37. Willis, "Fathers Watch the Boys' Room," 58.

38. Robin Wood, *Howard Hawks* (London: British Film Institute, 1983), 58–68.

CHAPTER 7. MISUNDERSTANDINGS: DIALOGUE IN MELODRAMAS

1. Marcia Landy, ed., *Imitations of Life: A Reader on Film and Television Melodrama* (Detroit: Wayne State University Press, 1991); Christine Gledhill, ed., *Home Is Where the Heart Is: Studies in Melodrama and the Woman's Film* (London: British Film Institute, 1987).

2. Thomas Elsaesser, "Tales of Sound and Fury: Observations on the Family Melodrama," in *Imitations of Life,* ed. Landy, 85.

3. Peter Brooks, *The Melodramatic Imagination: Balzac, Henry James, Melodrama and the Mode of Excess* (New York: Columbia University Press, 1985).

4. See Sarah Kozloff, "Where Wessex Meets New England: Griffith's *Way Down East* and Hardy's *Tess of the d'Urbervilles*," *Literature/Film Quarterly* 13.1 (1985): 35–41.

5. Linda Williams, "Melodrama Revised," in *Refiguring American Film Genres,* ed. Nick Browne (Berkeley and Los Angeles: University of California Press, 1998), 42–88.

6. Leger Grindon discusses the function of romance in the historical film in *Shadows on the Past: Studies in the Historical Fiction Film* (Philadelphia: Temple University Press, 1994).

7. Thomas Schatz, "The Family Melodrama," in *Imitations of Life,* ed. Landy, 149.

8. Brooks, *Melodramatic Imagination,* 41.

9. Ibid., 4.

10. Ibid., 41.

11. Ibid., 40.

12. See Edward Branigan, *Narrative Comprehension and Film* (New York: Routledge, 1992), 66–76, on disparities and hierarchies of knowledge in film.

13. Jeanine Basinger, *A Woman's View: How Hollywood Spoke to Women, 1930–1960* (New York: Knopf, 1993), 5.

14. Brooks, *Melodramatic Imagination*, 15.

15. Ibid., 31.

16. Tania Modleski, "Time and Desire in the Woman's Film," in *Home Is Where the Heart Is*, ed. Gledhill, 326–38.

17. Ibid., 327.

18. Mary Ann Doane, *The Desire to Desire: The Woman's Film of the 1940s* (Bloomington: Indiana University Press), 85.

19. A. Scott Berg, *Goldwyn: A Biography* (New York: Knopf, 1989), 328.

20. Claudia Gorbman, *Unheard Melodies: Narrative Film Music* (Bloomington: Indiana University Press, 1987), 79.

21. Jeanne Thomas Allen, "Introduction: *Now, Voyager* as Women's Film: Coming of Age Hollywood Style," in *Now, Voyager*, ed. id. (Madison: University of Wisconsin Press, 1984), 31.

22. Pat McGilligan, ed., *Backstory: Interviews with Screenwriters of Hollywood's Golden Age* (Berkeley and Los Angeles: University of California Press, 1986), 303–4.

23. Allen, "Introduction: *Now, Voyager* as Women's Film," 22–23.

24. Lea Jacobs, "*Now, Voyager*: Some Problems of Enunciation and Sexual Difference," *Camera Obscura* 7 (Spring 1981): 93.

25. Maria LaPlace, "Producing and Consuming the Women's Film: Discursive Strategies in *Now, Voyager*," in *Home Is Where the Heart Is*, ed. Gledhill, 156–61.

26. Quoted in Gerald Gardner, *The Censorship Papers: Movie Censorship Letters from the Hays Office, 1934–1968* (New York: Dodd, Mead, 1987), 76–77.

27. For more on this kind of ambiguity, see Lea Jacobs, *The Wages of Sin: Censorship and the Fallen Woman Film, 1928–1942* (Madison: University of Wisconsin Press, 1991), 111–15.

28. See Jacobs, "*Now, Voyager*," 92.

29. Michel Chion, *Audio-Vision: Sound on Screen*, ed. and trans. Claudia Gorbman (New York: Columbia University Press, 1990), 76.

30. Discussed by Claudia Gorbman, *Unheard Melodies: Narrative Film Music* (Bloomington: Indiana University Press, 1987), 65–66.

31. Allen, ed. *Now, Voyager*, 160.

32. Karen Jaehne, "*Terms of Endearment*" (film review) *Cineaste* 13.4 (1984): 49.

33. Larry McMurtry, "Preface," in *Terms of Endearment* (New York: Pocket Books, 1989), xi.

34. James L. Brooks interviewed by Kenneth Turan, "On His Own 'Terms,' " *Film Comment* 20.2 (1984): 21–22.

35. Kathleen Rowe, *The Unruly Woman: Gender and the Genres of Laughter* (Austin: University of Texas Press, 1995), 112.

36. Ibid., 110.

37. Barbara Klinger, *Melodrama and Meaning: History, Culture, and the Films of Douglas Sirk* (Bloomington: Indiana University Press, 1994), 132–56.

38. Giacomo Puccini, *La Bohème*, librettists Giuseppe Gialosa and Luigi Illica, reprinted in *The Book of 101 Opera Librettos*, ed. Jessica M. MacMurray (New York: Black Dog & Leventhal, 1996), 790.

39. Rowe, *Unruly Woman*, 208.

CONCLUSION

1. Philip Brophy, "Read My Lips: Notes on the Writing and Speaking of Film Dialogue," *Continuum* 5.2 (1992): 247–66.

2. See Richard Corliss, *Talking Pictures: Screenwriters in the American Cinema* (New York: Penguin Books, 1974).

Select Filmography

Airplane! 1980. Paramount. Directed by Jim Abrahams, David Zucker, and Jerry Zucker. Screenplay by Jim Abrahams, David Zucker, and Jerry Zucker.

Al Capone. 1959. Allied Artists. Directed by Richard Wilson. Screenplay by Malvin Wald and Henry F. Greenberg.

Alien. 1979. 20th Century Fox. Directed by Ridley Scott. Screenplay by Dan O'Bannon, based on the story by Dan O'Bannon and Ronald Shusett.

All about Eve. 1950. 20th Century Fox. Directed by Joseph L. Mankiewicz. Screenplay by Joseph L. Mankiewicz, based on a story by Mary Orr.

An Affair to Remember. 1957. 20th Century Fox. Directed by Leo McCarey. Screenplay by Leo McCarey and Delmer Daves, from the story by Delmer Daves, Mildred Cram, and Leo McCarey.

Angel and the Badman. 1947. Republic. Directed by James Edward Grant. Screenplay by James Edward Grant.

Angels with Dirty Faces. 1938. Warner Brothers. Directed by Michael Curtiz. Screenplay by John Wexley and Warren Duff, from the story by Rowland Brown.

The Awful Truth. 1937. Columbia. Directed by Leo McCarey. Screenplay by Viña Delmar, from a play by Arthur Richman.

The Big Sleep. 1946. Warner Brothers. Directed by Howard Hawks. Screenplay by William Faulkner, Leigh Brackett, and Jules Furthman, based on the novel by Raymond Chandler.

Blade Runner. 1982. The Ladd Company. Directed by Ridley Scott. Screenplay by Hampton Fancher and David Webb Peoples, based on the novel by Philip K. Dick.

Bringing Up Baby. 1938. RKO. Directed by Howard Hawks.Screenplay by Dudley Nichols and Hagar Wilde, from the story by Hagar Wilde.

Bugsy. 1991. Tri-Star. Directed by Barry Levinson. Screenplay by James Toback, based on a book by Dean Jennings.

Butch Cassidy and the Sundance Kid. 1969. 20th Century Fox. Directed by George Roy Hill. Screenplay by William Goldman.

Cabaret. 1972. ABC Circle Films. Directed by Bob Fosse. Screenplay by Jay Presson Allen, based on the musical by Joe Masteroff, play by John Van Druten, and stories by Christopher Isherwood.

Camille. 1937. MGM. Directed by George Cukor. Screenplay by Zoë Akins, James Hilton, and Frances Marion, based on the novel and play by Alexandre Dumas *fils*.

Casablanca. 1942. Warner Brothers. Directed by Michael Curtiz. Screenplay by Julius J. Epstein, Philip G. Epstein, and Howard Koch, based on a play by Murray Burnett and Joan Alison.

Chinatown. 1974. Paramount. Directed by Roman Polanski. Screenplay by Robert Towne.

Citizen Kane. 1941. RKO. Directed by Orson Welles. Screenplay by Herman J. Mankiewicz and Orson Welles.

The Comancheros. 1961. 20th Century Fox. Directed by Michael Curtiz. Screenplay by James Edward Grant and Clair Hutfaker, based on a novel by Paul Wellman.

The Conversation. 1974. Paramount. Directed by Francis Ford Coppola. Screenplay by Francis Ford Coppola.

Cool Hand Luke. 1967. Warner Brothers. Directed by Stuart Rosenberg. Screenplay by Donn Pearce and Frank Pierson, based on the novel by Donn Pearce.

The Covered Wagon. 1923. Paramount. Directed by James Cruze. Screenplay by Jack Cunningham and Emerson Hough.

Dance, Girl, Dance. 1940. RKO. Directed by Dorothy Arzner. Screenplay by Frank Davis and Tess Slesinger, based on the story by Vicki Baum.

Dark Victory. 1939. Warner Brothers. Directed by Edmund Goulding. Screenplay by Casey Robinson, based on the play by George Emerson Brewer Jr. and Bertam Bloch.

Dirty Harry. 1971. Warner Brothers. Directed by Don Siegel. Screenplay by Harry Julian Fink, Rita M. Fink, and Dean Riesner, based on the story by Rita M. Fink and Dean Riesner.

Dr. Strangelove. 1963. Hawk Films. Directed by Stanley Kubrick. Screenplay by Stanley Kubrick, Terry Southern, and Peter George, based on the novel by Peter George.

Duck Soup. 1933. Paramount. Directed by Leo McCarey. Screenplay by Bert Kalmar, Harry Ruby, Nat Perrin, and Arthur Sheekman.

The English Patient. 1996. Miramax. Directed by Anthony Minghella. Screenplay by Anthony Minghella, based on the novel by Michael Ondaatje.

Escape from Alcatraz. 1979. The Malpaso Company and Paramount. Directed by Don Siegel. Screenplay by Campbell Bruce and Richard Tuggle, based on a novel by Campbell Bruce.

E. T.: The Extra-Terrestrial. 1982. Universal, Amblin Entertainment. Directed by Steven Spielberg. Screenplay by Melissa Mathison.

Field of Dreams. 1989. Gordon Company. Directed by Phil Alden Robinson. Screenplay by Phil Alden Robinson, based on the novel by W. P. Kinsella.

Force of Evil. 1948. Enterprise, MGM. Directed by Abraham Polonsky. Screenplay by Abraham Polonsky and Ira Wolfert, based on the novel by Ira Wolfert.

Foreign Correspondent. 1940. United Artists. Directed by Alfred Hitchcock. Screenplay by Charles Bennett, Richard Maibaum, and Joan Harrison, with additional dialogue by James Hilton and Robert Benchley.

Fort Apache. 1948. Argosy Pictures. Directed by John Ford. Screenplay by
Frank S. Nugent, from the story by James Warner Bellah.

Four Weddings and a Funeral. 1994. PolyGram. Directed by Mike Newell.
Screenplay by Richard Curtis.

The Fugitive. 1993. Warner Brothers. Directed by Andrew Davis. Screenplay
by David N. Twohy and Jeb Stuart, based on characters created by Roy
Huggins.

The Gay Divorcee. 1934. RKO. Directed by Mark Sandrich. Screenplay by
Edward Kaufman, George Marion Jr., Dorothy Yost, and Dwight Taylor.

The Godfather. 1972. Paramount. Directed by Francis Ford Coppola. Screenplay by Mario Puzo and Francis Ford Coppola, from the novel by Mario
Puzo.

Gone With the Wind. 1939. Selznick International. Directed by Victor Fleming. Screenplay by Sidney Howard, from the novel by Margaret
Mitchell.

Good Will Hunting. 1997. Miramax. Directed by Gus Van Sant. Screenplay
by Ben Affleck and Matt Damon.

GoodFellas. 1990. Warner Brothers. Directed by Martin Scorsese. Screenplay
by Nicholas Pileggi and Martin Scorsese, from the novel by Nicholas Pileggi.

Heller in Pink Tights. 1960. Paramount. Directed by George Cukor. Screenplay by Walter Bernstein and Dudley Nichols, from the novel by Louis
L'Amour.

High Noon. 1952. Stanley Kramer Productions. Directed by Fred Zinne-
mann. Screenplay by Carl Foreman, based on the story by John W. Cunningham.

High Sierra. 1941. Warner Brothers. Directed by Raoul Walsh. Screenplay by
John Huston and W. R. Burnett, based on the novel by W. R. Burnett.

His Girl Friday. 1940. Columbia. Directed by Howard Hawks. Screenplay by
Charles Lederer and Ben Hecht, based on the play by Ben Hecht and
Charles MacArthur.

Holiday. 1938. Columbia. Directed by George Cukor. Screenplay by Donald
Ogden Stewart and Sidney Buchman, from the play by Philip Barry.

How Green Was My Valley. 1941. 20th Century Fox. Directed by John Ford.
Screenplay by Philip Dunne, from the book by Richard Llewellyn.

Imitation of Life. 1959. Universal International. Directed by Douglas Sirk.
Screenplay by Eleanore Griffin and Allan Scott, from the novel by Fan-
nie Hurst.

It Happened One Night. 1934. Columbia. Directed by Frank Capra. Screenplay by Robert Riskin, from the story by Samuel Hopkins Adams.

Jaws. 1975. Universal. Directed by Steven Spielberg. Screenplay by Peter
Benchley and Carl Gottlieb, from the novel by Peter Benchley.

Kramer vs. Kramer. 1979. Columbia. Directed by Robert Benton. Screenplay
by Robert Benton, based on the book by Avery Corman.

The Lady Eve. 1941. Paramount. Directed by Preston Sturges. Screenplay by
Preston Sturges, from a story by Monckton Hoffe.

Leave Her to Heaven. 1945. 20th Century Fox. Directed by John M. Stahl. Screenplay by Jo Swerling, based on the novel by Ben Ames Williams.

Little Caesar. 1930. Warner Brothers. Directed by Mervyn LeRoy. Screenplay by Francis Edward Faragoh, Robert N. Lee, and Robert Lord, from the novel by W. R. Burnett.

The Magnificent Seven. 1960. Mirisch Company. Directed by John Sturges. Screenplay by William Roberts, based on the film *The Seven Samurai* by Akira Kurosawa.

The Major and the Minor. 1942. Paramount. Directed by Billy Wilder. Screenplay by Charles Brackett and Billy Wilder, based on the story by Fanny Kilbourne and the play by Edward Childs Carpenter.

The Man Who Shot Liberty Valance. 1962. John Ford Productions, Paramount. Directed by John Ford. Screenplay by James Warner Bellah and Willis Goldbeck, from the story by Dorothy M. Johnson.

Marathon Man. 1976. Paramount. Directed by John Schlesinger. Screenplay by William Goldman, based on his novel.

M*A*S*H. 1970. 20th Century Fox. Directed by Robert Altman. Screenplay by Ring Lardner Jr., based on the novel by Richard Hooker.

Menace II Society. 1993. New Line Cinema. Directed by Allen Hughes and Albert Hughes. Screenplay by Allen Hughes, Albert Hughes, and Tyger Williams.

Mission: Impossible. 1996. Paramount. Directed by Brian De Palma. Screenplay by Robert Towne and David Koepp, based on the story by David Koepp and Steven Zaillian.

Moonstruck. 1987. MGM. Directed by Norman Jewison. Screenplay by John Patrick Shanley.

Morocco. 1930. Paramount. Directed by Josef von Sternberg. Screenplay by Jules Furthman, from the novel by Benno Vigny.

Mr. Smith Goes to Washington. 1939. Columbia. Directed by Frank Capra. Screenplay by Sidney Buchman, from the story by Lewis Foster.

Mrs. Miniver. 1942. MGM. Directed by William Wyler. Screenplay by Arthur Wimperis, George Froeschel, James Hilton, and Claudine West, based on the book by Jan Struther.

The Music Man. 1962. Warner Brothers. Directed by Morton DaCosta. Screenplay by Marion Hargrove, based on the play by Meredith Wilson and Franklin Lacey.

My Darling Clementine. 1946. 20th Century Fox. Directed by John Ford. Screenplay by Samuel G. Engel, Winston Miller, and Sam Hellman, based on a book by Stuart N. Lake.

My Man Godfrey. 1936. Universal. Directed by Gregory La Cava. Screenplay by Morrie Ryskind and Eric Hatch, based on the novel by Eric Hatch.

Network. 1976. United Artists, MGM. Directed by Sidney Lumet. Screenplay by Paddy Chayefsky.

Ninotchka. 1939. MGM. Directed by Ernst Lubitsch. Screenplay by Charles Brackett, Billy Wilder, and Walter Reisch, based on the story by Melchior Lengyel.

North by Northwest. 1959. MGM. Directed by Alfred Hitchcock. Screenplay by Ernest Lehman.

Notorious. 1946. RKO, Selznick International. Directed by Alfred Hitchcock. Screenplay by Ben Hecht.

Now, Voyager. 1942. Warner Brothers. Directed by Irving Rapper. Screenplay by Casey Robinson, based on the novel by Olive Higgins Prouty.

On the Waterfront. 1954. Columbia, Horizon Pictures. Directed by Elia Kazan. Screenplay by Budd Schulberg, based on stories by Malcolm Johnson.

Only Angels Have Wings. 1939. Columbia. Directed by Howard Hawks. Screenplay by Jules Furthman and Howard Hawks, based on a story by Jules Furthman and Howard Hawks.

The Palm Beach Story. 1942. Paramount. Directed by Preston Sturges. Screenplay by Preston Sturges.

Paths of Glory. 1957. United Artists, Bryna Productions. Directed by Stanley Kubrick. Screenplay by Stanley Kubrick, Calder Willingham, and Jim Thompson, based on the novel by Humphrey Cobb.

Philadelphia. 1993. Tri-Star. Directed by Jonathan Demme. Screenplay by Ron Nyswaner.

The Philadelphia Story. 1940. MGM. Directed by George Cukor. Screenplay by Donald Ogden Stewart, based on the play by Philip Barry.

The Professionals. 1966. Pax Enterprises. Directed by Richard Brooks. Screenplay by Richard Brooks, based on the novel by Frank O'Rourke.

Psycho. 1960. Shamley Productions, Paramount. Directed by Alfred Hitchcock. Screenplay by Joseph Stefano, based on the novel by Robert Bloch.

Public Enemy. 1931. Warner Brothers. Directed by William Wellman. Screenplay by John Bright, Harvey F. Thew, and Kubec Glasmon.

Rear Window. 1954. Paramount. Directed by Alfred Hitchcock. Screenplay by John Michael Hayes, based on the story by Cornell Woolrich.

Red River. 1948. United Artists/Monterey Productions. Directed by Howard Hawks. Screenplay by Borden Chase and Charles Schnee, based on the story by Borden Chase.

Reservoir Dogs. 1992. Dog Eat Dog Productions. Directed by Quentin Tarantino. Screenplay by Quentin Tarantino.

Ride the High Country. 1962. MGM. Directed by Sam Peckinpah. Screenplay by N. B. Stone Jr.

Roman Holiday. 1953. Paramount. Directed by William Wyler. Screenplay by Ian McLellan Hunter and John Dighton, based on the story by Ian McLellan Hunter (fronting for Dalton Trumbo).

The Roaring Twenties. 1939. Warner Brothers. Directed by Raoul Walsh. Screenplay by Jerry Wald, Richard Macaulay, and Robert Rossen, based on the story by Mark Hellinger.

Scarface. 1983. Universal. Directed by Brian De Palma. Screenplay by Oliver Stone.

Scarface: The Shame of a Nation. 1932. United Artists. Directed by Howard Hawks and Richard Rosson. Screenplay by Seton I. Miller, John Lee

Mahin, W. R. Burnett, and Ben Hecht, based on the novel by Armitage Trail.

The Searchers. 1956. Warner Brothers. Directed by John Ford. Screenplay by Frank S. Nugent, based on the novel by Alan Le May.

Sense and Sensibility. 1995. Columbia. Directed by Ang Lee. Screenplay by Emma Thompson, based on the novel by Jane Austen.

Shadow of a Doubt. 1943. Universal. Directed by Alfred Hitchcock. Screenplay by Thorton Wilder, Sally Benson, and Alma Reville, based on the story by Gordon McDonnell.

Shane. 1953. Paramount. Directed by George Stevens. Screenplay by A. B. Guthrie Jr. and Jack Sher (additional dialogue), from a story by Jack Schaefer.

Shanghai Express. 1932. Paramount. Directed by Josef von Sternberg. Screenplay by Jules Furthman, based on the story by Harry Hervey.

She Wore a Yellow Ribbon. 1949. Argosy Pictures, RKO. Directed by John Ford. Screenplay by Frank S. Nugent and Laurence Stallings, from the story by James Warner Bellah.

Silverado. 1985. Columbia. Directed by Lawrence Kasdan. Screenplay by Lawrence Kasdan and Mark Kasdan.

Singin' in the Rain. 1952. MGM. Directed by Stanley Donen and Gene Kelly. Screenplay by Betty Comden and Adolph Green.

So Proudly We Hail! 1943. Paramount. Directed by Mark Sandrich. Screenplay by Allan Scott.

Stagecoach. 1939. Walter Wanger Pictures. Directed by John Ford. Screenplay by Dudley Nichols, based on the story by Ernest Haycox.

Stella Dallas. 1937. Goldwyn. Directed by King Vidor. Screenplay by Joe Bigelow, Harry Wagstaff Gribble, Victor Heerman, Sarah Y. Mason, and Gertrude Purcell, from the novel by Olive Higgins Prouty.

Sullivan's Travels. 1941. Paramount. Directed by Preston Sturges. Screenplay by Preston Sturges.

Terms of Endearment. 1983. Paramount. Directed by James L. Brooks. Screenplay by James L. Brooks, from the novel by Larry McMurtry.

The Terminator. 1984. Cinema '84. Directed by James Cameron. Screenplay by James Cameron and Gale Anne Hurd, with additional dialogue by William Wisher Jr.

The Thin Man. 1934. MGM. Directed by W. S. Van Dyke. Screenplay by Albert Hackett and Frances Goodrich, based on the novel by Dashiell Hammett.

To Each His Own. 1946. Paramount. Directed by Mitchell Leisen. Screenplay by Jacques Thery, from the story by Charles Brackett.

Tombstone. 1993. Cinergi Productions, Hollywood Pictures. Directed by George P. Cosmatos. Screenplay by Kevin Jarre.

Tootsie. 1982. Columbia. Directed by Sydney Pollack. Screenplay by Larry Gelbart and Murray Schisgal, based on the story by Don McGuire.

Trouble in Paradise. 1932. Paramount. Directed by Ernst Lubitsch. Screenplay by Samson Raphaelson and Grover Jones, from a play by Aladar Laszlo.

Unforgiven. 1992. Warner Brothers. Directed by Clint Eastwood. Screenplay by David Webb Peoples.

The Untouchables. 1987. Paramount. Directed by Brian De Palma. Screenplay by David Mamet, based on books by Oscar Fraley, Eliot Ness, and Paul Robsky.

The Virginian. 1929. Paramount. Directed by Victor Fleming. Screenplay by Howard Estabrook, Grover Jones, Kirk LaShelle, Keene Thompson, and Edward E. Paramore Jr., from the novel by Owen Wister.

The Wild Bunch. 1969. Warner Brothers. Directed by Sam Peckinpah. Screenplay by Walon Green and Sam Peckinpah, from the story by Walon Green and Roy N. Sickner.

Wizard of Oz. 1939. MGM. Directed by Victor Fleming. Screenplay by Noel Langley, Florence Ryerson, and Edgar Allan Woolf, based on the book by L. Frank Baum.

Wuthering Heights. 1939. Goldwyn. Directed by William Wyler. Screenplay by Charles MacArthur and Ben Hecht, based on the novel by Emily Brontë.

Young Mr. Lincoln. 1939. 20th Century Fox. Directed by John Ford. Screenplay by Lamar Trotti.

Bibliography

Abrams, M. H. *A Glossary of Literary Terms.* 1957. 6th ed. Fort Worth, Tex.: Harcourt Brace Jovanovich College Publishers, 1993.

Adams, Ramon F. *Cowboy Lingo.* Boston, Houghton Mifflin, 1936.

———. *Western Words.* Norman: University of Oklahoma Press, 1944.

Aig, Dennis Ira. "Jules Furthman and the Popular Aesthetics of Screenwriting," Diss., Ohio State University, 1983.

Allen, Jeanne Thomas, ed. *Now, Voyager.* Madison: University of Wisconsin Press, 1984.

Altman, Rick. "Introduction." In *Cinema/Sound,* ed. Rick Altman. *Yale French Studies* 60 (1980): 3–15.

———. "Moving Lips: Cinema as Ventriloquism." In *Cinema/Sound,* ed. Rick Altman. *Yale French Studies* 60 (1980): 67–79.

———. "Reusable Packaging: Generic Product and the Recycling Process." In *Refiguring American Film Genres,* ed. Nick Browne, 24–33. Berkeley and Los Angeles: University of California Press, 1998.

———. "A Semantic/Syntactic Approach to Film Genre." In *Film Genre Reader II.,* ed. Barry Keith Grant, 26–40. Austin: University of Texas Press, 1995.

———. "Sound Space." In *Sound Theory/Sound Practice,* ed. Rick Altman, 46–64. New York: Routledge, 1992.

———, ed. *Sound Theory/Sound Practice.* New York: Routledge, 1992.

Anderson, Joseph D. "Sound and Image Together: Cross-Modal Confirmation." *Wide Angle* 15.1 (January 1993): 30–43.

———. "When the Twain Meet: Hollywood's Remake of *The Seven Samurai.*" *Film Quarterly* 15.3 (Spring 1962): 55–58.

Archer, William. *Playmaking: A Manual of Craftsmanship.* New York: Dover, 1912. Reprint, 1960.

Arendt, Hannah. *Men in Dark Times.* New York: Harcourt, Brace & World, 1968.

Armer, Alan. *Writing the Screenplay: TV and Film.* Belmont, Calif.: Wadsworth, 1988.

Auerbach, Erich. *Mimesis: The Representation of Reality in Western Literature.* Translated by Willard R. Trask. Princeton, N.J.: Princeton University Press, 1953.

Auerbach, Jon. "They Can't Spell It, Can't Pronounce It and Don't Get It." *Wall Street Journal,* 2 June 1998, A1.

Babington, Bruce, and Peter William Evans. *Affairs to Remember: The Holly-wood Comedy of the Sexes*. New York: Manchester University Press, 1989.

Bakhtin, M. M. *The Dialogic Imagination*. Edited by Michael Holquist. Trans-lated by Caryle Emerson and Michael Holquist. Austin: University of Texas Press, 1981.

Barber, C. L. *Shakespeare's Festive Comedy: A Study of Dramatic Form and its Re-lation to Social Custom*. Princeton, N.J.: Princeton University Press, 1959.

Barthes, Roland. *Image/Music/Text*. Translated by Stephen Heath. New York: Hill & Wang, 1977.

———. *S/Z*. Translated by Richard Miller. New York: Hill & Wang, 1974.

———. *The Pleasure of the Text*. Translated by Richard Miller. New York: Hill & Wang, 1975.

Basinger, Jeanine. *A Woman's View: How Hollywood Spoke to Women, 1930–1960*. New York: Knopf, 1993.

———. *The World War II Combat Film: Anatomy of a Genre*. New York: Co-lumbia University Press, 1986.

Baxter, John. *The Gangster Film*. London: Zwemmer, 1970.

Behlmer, Rudy, ed. *Inside Warner Brothers (1935–1951)*. New York: Simon & Schuster, 1985.

Bentley, Eric. *The Playwright as Thinker: A Study of Drama in Modern Times*. New York: Meridian, 1955.

Berg, A. Scott. *Goldwyn: A Biography*. New York: Knopf, 1989.

Berliner, Todd. "Hollywood Movie Dialogue and the 'Real Realism' of John Cassavetes." *Film Quarterly* 52:3 (Spring 1999): 2–16.

Biskind, Peter. *Seeing is Believing: How Hollywood Taught Us to Stop Worrying and Love the Fifties*. New York: Pantheon Books, 1983.

Bogdanovich, Peter. *John Ford*. London: Studio Vista, 1967. New revised and enlarged ed. Berkeley and Los Angeles: University of California Press, 1978.

Bogle, Donald. *Toms, Coons, Mulattoes, Mammies, and Bucks: An Interpretative History of Blacks in American Films*. 2d ed. New York: Continuum, 1990.

Bold, Alan, ed. *Harold Pinter: You Never Heard Such Silence*. London: Vision; Totowa, N.J.: Barnes & Noble, 1984.

Booth, Wayne C. *The Rhetoric of Fiction*. Chicago: University of Chicago Press, 1961.

Bordwell, David. *Narration in the Fiction Film*. Madison: University of Wis-consin Press, 1985.

Bordwell, David, Janet Staiger, and Kristin Thompson. *The Classical Holly-wood Cinema*. New York: Columbia University Press, 1985.

Bordwell, David, and Kristin Thompson. *Film Art*. 4th ed. New York: Mc-Graw-Hill, 1993.

Bordwell, David, and Noël Carroll, eds. *Post-Theory: Reconstructing Film Studies*. Madison: University of Wisconsin Press, 1996

Bowser, Eileen. *The History of American Cinema*. Volume 2: *The Transforma-tion of Cinema, 1907–1915*. Berkeley and Los Angeles: University of Cali-fornia Press, 1990.

Boyd, Todd. *Am I Black Enough For You? Popular Culture from the 'Hood and Beyond.* Bloomington: Indiana University Press, 1997.

Brackett, Leigh. "A Comment on the Hawksian Woman." *Take One* 3.6 (July–August 1971): 19–20.

Branigan, Edward. *Narrative Comprehension and Film.* New York: Routledge, 1992.

Britton, Andrew. *Cary Grant: Comedy and Male Desire.* Newcastle: Tyneside Cinema, 1983.

Brooks, Peter. *The Melodramatic Imagination: Balzac, Henry James, Melodrama and the Mode of Excess.* New York: Columbia University Press, 1985.

Brophy, Philip. "Read My Lips: Notes on the Writing and Speaking of Film Dialogue." *Continuum* 5.2 (1992): 247–66.

Browne, Nick. "The Spectator-in-the-Text: The Rhetoric of *Stagecoach.*" In *Narrative / Apparatus / Ideology,* ed. Philip Rosen, 102–19. New York: Columbia University Press, 1986.

Burke, Peter. *The Art of Conversation.* Ithaca, N.Y.: Cornell University Press, 1993.

Buscombe, Edward. "The Idea of Genre in American Cinema." In *Film Genre Reader II,* ed. Barry Keith Grant, 11–25. Austin: University of Texas Press, 1995.

———. *Stagecoach.* London: British Film Institute, 1992.

———, ed. *The BFI Companion to the Western.* New York: Da Capo Press, 1988.

Byars, Jackie. *All That Hollywood Allows: Re-reading Gender in 1950s Melodrama.* Chapel Hill: University of North Carolina Press, 1991.

Camille Roman, Suzanne Juhasz, and Christanne Miller. *The Women and Language Debate: A Sourcebook.* New Brunswick, N.J.: Rutgers University Press, 1994.

Carroll, Noël. "The Specificity Thesis." In *Film Theory and Criticism: Introductory Readings,* ed. Gerald Mast, Marshall Cohen, and Leo Braudy, 278–85. 4th ed. New York: Oxford University Press, 1992.

Carson, Diane. "To Be Seen and Not Heard: *The Awful Truth.*" In *Multiple Voices in Feminist Film Criticism,* ed. Diane Carson, Linda Dittmar, and Janice Welsch, 213–25. Minneapolis: University of Minnesota Press, 1994.

Cavell, Stanley. *Pursuits of Happiness: The Hollywood Comedy of Remarriage.* Cambridge, Mass.: Harvard University Press, 1981.

Cawelti, John. *The Six-Gun Mystique.* 2d ed. Bowling Green, Ohio: Bowling Green State University Popular Press, 1984.

Chaika, Elaine. *Language: The Social Mirror.* Rowley, Mass.: Newbury House, 1982.

Chapman, Raymond. *Forms of Speech in Victorian Fiction.* London: Longman, 1994.

Charney, Maurice. *Comedy High and Low: An Introduction to the Experience of Comedy.* New York: Oxford University Press, 1978.

Chatman, Seymour. *Story and Discourse: Narrative Structure in Fiction and Film*. Ithaca, N.Y.: Cornell University Press, 1978.

Chion, Michel. *Audio-Vision: Sound on Screen*. Translated and edited by Claudia Gorbman. New York: Columbia University Press, 1994.

———. *La Voix au cinéma*. Paris: *Cahiers du Cinéma*/Editions de l'Etoile, 1982.

Chothia, Jean. *Forging a Language: A Study of Plays of Eugene O'Neill*. Cambridge: Cambridge University Press, 1979.

Clark, Herbert H., and Thomas B. Carlson. "Hearers and Speech Acts." *Language* 58.2 (1982): 344–45.

Cohn, Ruby. *Dialogue in American Drama*. Bloomington: Indiana University Press, 1971.

———. *Just Play: Beckett's Theater*. Princeton, N.J.: Princeton University Press, 1980.

Collier, Gary. *Emotional Expression*. Hillsdale, N.J.: Lawrence Earlbaum, 1985.

Corey, Melinda, ed. *The Dictionary of Film Quotations*. New York: Crown, 1995.

Corliss, Richard. "Still Talking." *Film Comment* 28.6 (Nov.–Dec. 1992): 11–23.

———. *Talking Pictures: Screenwriters in the American Cinema*. New York: Penguin Books, 1974.

Cowie, Peter. *Coppola: A Biography*. New York: Scribner, 1990.

Crafton, Donald. *The Talkies: American Cinema's Transition to Sound, 1926–1931*. New York: Scribner, 1997.

Crawley, Tony, ed. *Chambers Film Quotes*. Edinburgh: W & R Chambers, 1991.

Crothers, Rachel. "The Construction of a Play." In *The Art of Playwriting: Lectures Delivered at the University of Pennsylvania on the Mask and Wig Foundation, by Jesse Lynch Williams, Langdon Mitchell, Lord Dunsany, [and] Gilbert Emery [pseud.] Rachel Crothers*, 115–34. Philadelphia: University of Pennsylvania Press, 1928.

Crowther, Bosley. Review of *The Palm Beach Story*, by Preston Sturges. *New York Times*, 11 January 1942, 33.

Culler, Jonathan. *Structuralist Poetics: Structuralism, Linguistics and the Study of Literature*. Ithaca, N.Y.: Cornell University Press, 1975.

Curtis, James. *Between Flops: A Biography of Preston Sturges*. New York: Harcourt Brace Jovanovich, 1982.

Dawson, Jeff. *Quentin Tarantino: The Cinema of Cool*. New York: Applause Books, 1995.

Dean, Anne. *David Mamet: Language as Dramatic Action*. Rutherford, N.J.: Fairleigh Dickenson University Press, 1990.

Devereaux, Mary. "In Defense of Talking Film." *Persistence of Vision* 5 (Spring 1987): 17–27.

———. " 'Of Talk and Brown Furniture': The Aesthetics of Film Dialogue." *Post Script* 6.1 (Fall 1986): 32–52.

Dixon, Peter. *Rhetoric*. London: Methuen, 1971.

Dmytryk, Edward. *On Screen Writing*. Boston: Focal Press, 1985.

Doane, Mary Ann. *The Desire to Desire: The Woman's Film of the 1940s*. Bloomington: Indiana University Press, 1987.

———. "Ideology and the Practice of Sound Editing and Mixing." In *Film Sound: Theory and Practice,* ed. Elisabeth Weis and John Belton, 54–62. New York: Columbia University Press, 1985.

Dupriez, Bernard M. *A Dictionary of Literary Devices, Gradus, A–Z.* Translated and adapted by Albert W. Halsall. Toronto: University of Toronto Press, 1991.

Ďurovičová, Nataša. "Translating America: The Hollywood Multilinguals, 1929–1933." In *Sound Theory/Sound Practice,* ed. Rick Altman, 138–53. New York: Routledge, 1992.

Dyer, Richard. *Stars.* London: British Film Institute, 1979. New ed., 1998.

Ebert, Roger. *"Reservoir Dogs." Chicago Sun Times.* 26 October 1992. Reprinted www.suntimes.com/ebert_reviews/1992/10/785503.html.

Eckert, Charles, "The Anatomy of a Proletarian Film: Warner's *Marked Woman.*" In *Movies and Methods,* vol. 2, ed. Bill Nichols, 407–28. Berkeley and Los Angeles: University of California Press, 1985.

Ellis, John. "Stars as Cinematic Phenomenon." In *Film Theory and Criticism,* ed. Gerald Mast, Marshall Cohen, and Leo Braudy, 614–21. 4th ed. New York: Oxford University Press, 1992.

Elsaesser, Thomas. "Tales of Sound and Fury: Observations on the Family Melodrama." In *Imitations of Life: A Reader on Film and Television Melodrama,* ed. Marcia Landy, 68–92. Detroit: Wayne State University Press, 1991.

Faulkner, Christopher. "René Clair, Marcel Pagnol and the Social Dimension of Speech." *Screen* 35.2 (Summer 1994): 157–70.

Fawell, John. "The Musicality of the Filmscript." *Literature/Film Quarterly* 17.1 (1989): 44–49.

Ferraro, Thomas J. "Blood in the Marketplace: The Business of Family in the *Godfather* Narratives." In *The Invention of Ethnicity,* ed. Werner Sollors, 176–207. New York: Oxford University Press, 1989.

Field, Syd. *The Screenwriter's Workbook.* New York: Dell, 1984.

Fischer, Lucy, ed. *Imitation of Life: Douglas Sirk, Director.* New Brunswick, N.J.: Rutgers University Press.

Fisher-Lichte, Erika. *The Semiotics of Theater.* Translated by Jeremy Gaines and Doris L. Jones. Bloomington: Indiana University Press, 1992.

Forlenza, Jeff, and Terri Stone, ed. *Sound for Picture.* Emeryville, Calif.: Mix Books, 1993.

Forsberg, Myra. "Lean Mean Lines." *New York Times,* 15 November 1987, 25.

French, Philip. *Westerns: Aspects of a Movie Genre.* 1973. Rev. ed. New York: Oxford University Press, 1977.

Frye, Northop. *Anatomy of Criticism: Four Essays.* Princeton, N.J.: Princeton University Press, 1957.

Fuller, Graham. "Quentin Tarantino: Answers First, Questions Later: An Interview with Graham Fuller." In *Reservoir Dogs and True Romance: Screenplays by Quentin Tarantino,* ix–xviii. New York: Grove Press, 1994.

Gaggi, Silvio. "Pinter's Betrayal: Problems of Language or Grand Metatheatre?" *Theatre Journal* 33.4 (December 1981): 504–16.

Gallagher, Tag. *John Ford: The Man and His Films.* Berkeley and Los Angeles: University of California Press, 1986.

————. "Shoot Out at the Genre Corral: Problems in the 'Evolution' of the Western." In *Film Genre Reader II*, ed. Barry Keith Grant, 246–60. Austin: University of Texas Press, 1995.

Gardner, Gerald. *The Censorship Papers: Movie Censorship Letters from the Hays Office, 1934–1968*. New York: Dodd, Mead, 1987.

Garrand, Timothy Paul. "The Comedy Screenwriting of Preston Sturges: An Analysis of Seven Paramount Auteurist Screenplays." Diss., University of Southern California, 1984.

Geduld, Harry. *The Birth of the Talkies: From Edison to Jolson*. Bloomington: Indiana University Press, 1975.

Gehring, Wes D. "Screwball Comedy: An Overview." *Journal of Popular Film and Television* (Winter 1986): 178–85.

Genette, Gérard. *Narrative Discourse: An Essay in Method*. Translated by Jane E. Lewin. Foreword by Jonathan Culler. Ithaca, N.Y.: Cornell University Press, 1980.

Giannetti, Louis D. *Understanding Movies*. 1972. 8th ed. Upper Saddle River, N.J. : Prentice-Hall, 1998.

Gilbert, Sandra M., and Gubar, Susan. "Sexual Linguistics: Gender, Language, Sexuality." In *The Feminist Reader: Essays in Gender and Politics of Literary Criticism*, ed. Catherine Belsey and Jane Moore, 81–99. New York: Basil Blackwell, 1989.

Gledhill, Christine, ed. *Home Is Where Heart Is: Studies in Melodrama and the Woman's Film*. London: British Film Institute, 1987.

Goldman, William. *Adventures in the Screen Trade: A Personal View of Hollywood and Screenwriting*. New York: Warner Books, 1983.

Gomery, Douglas. "The Coming of Sound: Technological Change in the American Film Industry." In *Film Sound: Theory and Practice*, ed. Elisabeth Weis and John Belton, 5–24. New York: Columbia University Press, 1985.

Gorbman, Claudia. *Unheard Melodies: Narrative Film Music*. Bloomington: Indiana University Press, 1987.

Gordon, James. "The Comic Structures of Preston Sturges." Diss., Northwestern University, 1980.

Grant, Barry, ed. *Film Genre Reader*. Austin: University of Texas, 1986.

————, ed. *Film Genre Reader II*. Austin: University of Texas Press, 1995.

Gray, Frances. *Noël Coward*. New York: St. Martin's Press, 1987.

Grindon, Leger. *Shadows on the Past: Studies in the Historical Fiction Film*. Philadelphia: Temple University Press, 1994.

Hammond, Carol. "Sound and Image." *Wide Angle* 6.2 (1984): 24–33.

Handzo, Stephen. "Appendix: A Narrative Glossary of Film Sound Technology." In *Film Sound: Theory and Practice*, ed. Elisabeth Weis and John Belton, 383–426. New York: Columbia University Press, 1985.

Harmetz, Aljean. *Round up the Usual Suspects: The Making of Casablanca*. New York: Hyperion, 1992.

Harvey, James. *Romantic Comedy in Hollywood from Lubitsch to Sturges*. New York: Knopf, 1987.

Haycox, Ernest. "Stage to Lordsburg." Reprinted in *Stagecoach*, ed. Andrew Sinclair, 5–19. New York: Lorrimer, 1971.

Henderson, Brian. "Romantic Comedy Today: *Semi-Tough* or Impossible?" in *Film Genre Reader,* ed. Barry Keith Grant, 309–28. Austin: University of Texas Press, 1986.

Herman, Jan. *A Talent for Trouble: The Life of Hollywood's Most Acclaimed Director, William Wyler.* New York: Da Capo Press, 1997.

Herman, Lewis. *American Dialects: A Manual of Actors, Directors and Writers.* New York: Theatre Art Books, 1947.

———. "Dialect Dialectics." *Screen Writer* 1 (April 1946): 1–8.

———. "The Gift of Tongues." *Screen Writer* 1 (April 1946): 27–32.

Hirsch, Foster. *Film Noir: The Dark Side of the Screen.* New York: Da Capo, 1981.

Hoberman, J. "Believe It or Not." *Artforum,* January 1991, 19–20.

Houston, Penelope. "Preston Sturges." *Sight and Sound* 34.3 (Summer 1965): 130–34.

———. "Scripting." *Sight and Sound* 19 (January 1951): 376.

Howard, Sidney. "The Story Gets a Treatment." In *We Make the Movies,* ed. Nancy Naumberg. New York: W. W. Norton, 1937.

Indiana, Gary, Bell Hooks, Jeanne Silverthorne, Dennis Cooper, and Robin Wood. "Pulp the Hype on the Q.T." *Artforum* 33.7 (March 1995): 62–67.

Ingarden, Roman. "Functions of Language in the Theater." Appendix to id., *The Literary Work of Art: An Investigation on the Borderlines of Ontology, Logic, and Theory of Literature,* trans. George G. Grabowicz, 377–96. Evanston, Ill.: Northwestern University Press, 1973.

Jacobs, Diane. *Christmas in July: The Life and Art of Preston Sturges.* Berkeley and Los Angeles: University of California Press, 1992.

Jacobs, Lea. "*Now, Voyager:* Some Problems of Enunciation and Sexual Difference." *Camera Obscura* 7 (Spring 1981): 89–109.

———. *The Wages of Sin: Censorship and the Fallen Woman Film, 1928–1942.* Madison: University of Wisconsin Press, 1991.

Jaehne, Karen. Review of *Terms of Endearment* by James L. Brooks. *Cineaste* 13.4 (1984): 49.

Jakobson, Roman. "Closing Statement: Linguistics and Poetics." In *Style in Language,* ed. Thomas A. Sebeok, 350–77. Cambridge, Mass.: Technology Press of Massachusetts Institute of Technology; New York: John Wiley & Sons, 1960. Reprint. Cambridge, Mass.: MIT Press, 1971.

Jay, Timothy. *Cursing in America: A Psycholinguistic Study of Dirty Language in the Courts, in the Movies, in the Schoolyards and on the Streets.* Philadelphia: John Benjamins, 1992.

Kael, Pauline. "Alchemy." In id., *Deeper Into Movies,* 420–26. Boston: Little, Brown, 1973.

———. "The Man from Dream City." In id., *When the Lights Go Down,* 3–32. New York: Holt, Rinehart & Winston, 1975.

———. "Raising Kane." In id., *The Citizen Kane Book,* 1–84. New York: Limelight Editions, 1984.

Katz, Ephraim. *The Film Encyclopedia.* 1979. 3d ed. Revised by Fred Klein and Ronald Dean Nolean. New York: Harper Perennial, 1998.

Kawin, Bruce. *Telling It Again and Again: Repetition in Literature and Film.* Boulder: University Press of Colorado, 1989.

Kendall, Elizabeth. *The Runaway Bride: Hollywood Romantic Comedy of the 1930s.* New York: Knopf, 1990.

Kennedy, Andrew. *Six Dramatists in Search of a Language.* Cambridge: Cambridge University Press, 1975.

Kepley, Vance. "Whose Apparatus? Problems of Film Exhibition and History." In *Post Theory: Reconstructing Film Studies,* ed. David Bordwell and Noël Carroll, 533–49. Madison: University of Wisconsin Press, 1996.

Kernan, Alvin B., ed. *The Modern American Theater: A Collection of Critical Essays,* Englewood Cliffs, N.J.: Prentice-Hall, 1967.

Kerr, Walter. *How Not to Write A Play.* New York: Simon & Schuster, 1955.

Keyssar, Helene. *Robert Altman's America.* New York: Oxford University Press, 1991.

Klinger, Barbara. *Melodrama and Meaning: History, Culture and the Films of Douglas Sirk.* Bloomington: Indiana University Press, 1994.

Kolker, Robert Phillip. *A Cinema of Loneliness: Penn, Kubrick, Coppola, Scorsese, Altman.* New York: Oxford University Press, 1980.

Koppes, Clayton, and Gregory Black. *Hollywood Goes To War.* Berkeley and Los Angeles: University of California Press, 1990.

Kozloff, Sarah. *Invisible Storytellers: Voice-over Narration in American Fiction Film.* Berkeley and Los Angeles: University of California Press, 1988.

———— "Narrative Theory and Television." In *Channels of Discourse, Reassembled,* ed. Robert C. Allen, 67–100. Chapel Hill: University of North Carolina Press, 1992.

————. "Where Wessex Meets New England: Griffith's *Way Down East* and Hardy's *Tess of the d'Urbervilles." Literature/Film Quarterly* 13.1 (1985): 35–41.

Lahr, John. *Coward the Playwright.* London: Methuen, 1982.

Lakoff, Robin. *Language and Woman's Place.* New York: Harper & Row, 1975.

Lakoff, Robin Tolmach, and Deborah Tannen. "Conversational Strategy and Metastrategy in a Pragmatic Theory: The Example of *Scenes from a Marriage." Semiotica* 49.3–4 (1984): 323–46.

Lambert, Gavin. "Studies in Scarlett." In *Gone With the Wind as Book and Film,* ed. Richard Harwell, 132–37. Columbia, S.C.: University of South Carolina Press, 1992.

Landy, Marcia, ed. *Imitations of Life: A Reader on Film and Television Melodrama.* Detroit: Wayne State University Press, 1991.

Lang, Robert. *American Film Melodrama: Griffith, Vidor, Minnelli.* Princeton, N.J.: Princeton University Press, 1989.

Langman, Larry, and Paul Gold, eds. *Comedy Quotes from the Movies: Over 4000 Bits of Humorous Dialogue from All Film Genres, Topically Arranged and Indexed.* Jefferson, N.C.: McFarland, 1993.

Lanham, Richard A. *A Handlist of Rhetorical Terms: A Guide for Students of English Literature.* Berkeley and Los Angeles: University of California Press, 1968.

LaPlace, Maria. "Producing and Consuming the Women's Film: Discursive Strategies in *Now, Voyager."* In *Home Is Where Heart Is: Studies in Melodrama and the Woman's Film,* ed. Christine Gledhill, 156–61. London: British Film Institute, 1987.

LaValley, Al. "*Invasion of the Body Snatchers:* Politics, Psychology, and Sociology." In *Invasion of the Body Snatchers,* ed. Al LaValley, 3–17. New Brunswick, N.J.: Rutgers University Press, 1989.

Lawrence, Amy. *Echo and Narcissus: Women's Voices in Classical Hollywood Cinema.* Berkeley and Los Angeles: University of California Press, 1990.

———. "Women's Voices in Third World Cinema." In *Sound Theory/Sound Practice,* ed. Rick Altman, 178–90. New York: Routledge, 1992.

Lawson, John Howard. *Theory and Technique of Playwriting.* New York: Putnam, 1936.

Lent, Tina Olsin. "Romantic Love and Friendship: The Redefinition of Gender Relations in Screwball Comedy." In *Classical Hollywood Comedy,* ed. Kristine Branovska Karnick and Henry Jenkins, 314–31. New York: Routledge, 1995.

Lesley, Cole. *Remembered Laughter: The Life of Noël Coward.* New York: Knopf, 1976.

Libby, Bill. "The Old Wrangler Rides Again." Reprinted in *My Darling Clementine,* ed. Robert Lyons, 136–40. New Brunswick, N.J.: Rutgers University Press, 1984.

LoBrutto, Vincent. *Sound on Film: Interviews with Creators of Film Sound.* Westport, Conn.: Praeger, 1994.

Longman, Stanley Vincent. *Composing Drama for Stage and Screen.* Newton, Mass.: Allyn & Bacon, 1986.

Lopate, Phillip. "It's Not Heroes Who Have Bad Grammar; It's Films." *New York Times,* 18 June 1995, 28.

Lumet, Sidney. *Making Movies.* New York: Knopf, 1995.

Lyons, Robert. "*My Darling Clementine* as History and Romance." In *My Darling Clementine,* ed. Robert Lyons, 3–18. New Brunswick, N.J.: Rutgers University Press, 1984.

Madsen, Axel. *William Wyler.* New York: Crowell, 1973.

Maltby, Richard. "The Production Code and the Hays Office." In *Grand Design: Hollywood as a Modern Business Enterprise, 1930–1939,* ed. Tino Balio, 37–92. New York: Scribner, 1993.

Mamet, David. *On Directing Film.* New York: Penguin Books, 1991.

Marie, Michel. "The Poacher's Aged Mother: On Speech in *La Chienne* by Jean Renoir." In *Cinema/Sound,* ed. Rick Altman. *Yale French Studies* 60 (1980): 219–32.

Mast, Gerald. "Everything's Gonna Be All Right: The Making of *Bringing Up Baby.*" In *Bringing Up Baby,* ed. Gerald Mast, 3–16. New Brunswick: Rutgers University Press, 1988.

———. *The Comic Mind: Comedy and the Movies.* Indianapolis: Bobbs-Merrill, 1973.

———. *Film/Cinema/Movie.* New York: Harper & Row, 1977. Reprint. University of Chicago Press, 1983.

———. *Howard Hawks, Storyteller.* New York: Oxford University Press, 1982.

McArthur, Colin. *Underworld U.S.A.* New York: Viking, 1972.

McArthur, Tom, ed. *The Oxford Companion to the English Language.* New York: Oxford University Press, 1992.

McCarty, John. *Hollywood Gangland: The Movies' Love Affair with the Mob*
New York: St. Martin's Press, 1993.

McGilligan, Pat, ed. *Backstory: Interviews with Screenwriters of Hollywood's Golden Age*. Berkeley and Los Angeles: University of California Press, 1986.

McMurtry, Larry. *Terms of Endearment*. New York: Simon & Schuster, 1975. Reprint. New York: Pocket Books, 1989.

Merritt, Russell. "Melodrama: Post-Mortem for a Phantom Genre." *Wide Angle* 5.3 (1983): 24–31.

Mitchell, Edward. "Apes and Essences: Some Sources of Significance in the American Gangster Film." In *Film Genre Reader*, ed. Barry Keith Grant, 159–68. Austin: University of Texas Press, 1986.

Modleski, Tania. "Time and Desire in the Woman's Film." In *Home Is Where Heart Is: Studies in Melodrama and the Woman's Film*, ed. Christine Gledhill, 326–38. London: British Film Institute, 1987.

Moore, Will G. "Speech." In *Molière: A Collection of Critical Essays*, ed. Jacques Guicharnaud, 40–49. Englewood Cliffs, N.J.: Prentice-Hall, 1964.

Motion Picture Producers and Distributors of America. "The Motion Picture Production Code of 1930." Reprinted in *The Movies in Our Midst: Documents in the Cultural History of Film in America*, ed. Gerald Mast, 321–33. Chicago: University of Chicago Press, 1982.

Mukarovsky, Jan. *The Word and Verbal Art: Selected Essays by Jan Mukarovsky.* Translated and edited by John Burbank and Peter Steiner. New Haven, Conn.: Yale University Press, 1977.

Naremore, James. *Acting in the Cinema*. Berkeley and Los Angeles: University of California Press, 1988.

Navasky, Victor S. *Naming Names*. New York: Viking Press, 1980.

Neale, Steve. "Questions of Genre," *Screen* 31.1 (Spring 1990): 45–66.

Nichols, Dudley. "The Writer and the Films." In *Film: A Montage of Theories*, ed. Richard Dyer MacCann, 73–87. New York: Dutton, 1966.

Nicoll, Allardyce. *Film and Theater*. New York: Crowell, 1936.

Nowlan, Robert A. and Gwendolyn W. Nolan, eds. *"We'll Always Have Paris": The Definition Guide to Great Lines in Movies*. New York: Harper-Collins, 1995.

Olson, Elder. *Tragedy and the Theory of Drama*. Detroit: Wayne State University Press, 1961.

Page, Norman. *Speech in the English Novel*. London: Longman, 1973.

Pagnol, Marcel. "The Talking Film." In *Rediscovering French Film*, ed. Mary Lea Braudy, 91. New York: Museum of Modern Art, 1983.

Parker, Patricia. *Literary Fat Ladies: Rhetoric, Gender, Property*. New York: Methuen, 1987.

Pfister, Manfred. *The Theory and Analysis of Drama*, Translated by John Halliday. Cambridge: Cambridge University Press, 1988.

Poster, Hank. "The Film Writer: Solving the Dilemma of Dialogue." *Today's Film Maker* 3.3 (1974): 8, 47.

Price, John. "The Stereotyping of North American Indians in Motion Pictures." In *The Pretend Indians: Images of Native Americans in the Movies,* eds. Gretchen M. Bataille and Charles L. P. Silet, 75–91. Ames, Iowa: Iowa State University Press, 1980.

Purvis, Harry. "Sure Fire Dialogue." *Films in Review* 6:6 (June/July 1955): 278–283.

Puzo, Mario. "Dialogue on Film: Mario Puzo." *American Film* 4 (May 1979): 33–44.

———. *The Godfather.* New York: Putnam, 1969.

Pym, John, *The Palm Beach Story.* London: British Film Institute, 1998.

Reid, Mark A. "The Black Gangster Film." In *Film Genre Reader II,* ed. Barry Keith Grant, 456–73. Austin: University of Texas Press, 1995.

Reisz, Karel and Millar, Gavin. *The Technique of Film Editing.* New York: Hastings House, 1968.

Renoir, Jean. *My Life and My Films: From Silent Films to Talkies.* Translated by Norman Denny. New York: Atheneum, 1974.

Robinson, David. "Bad Language and Big Bucks," *Verbatim,* 17:4 Spring 1991: 16–17.

Ross, T. J. "Western Approaches: A Note on Dialogue." In *Focus on the Western,* ed. Jack Nachbar, 78–80. Englewood Cliffs, N.J.: Prentice-Hall, 1974.

Rothman, William. *Hitchcock: The Murderous Gaze.* Cambridge, Mass.: Harvard University Press, 1982.

Rowe, Kathleen. "Comedy, Melodrama and Gender: Theorizing the Genres of Laughter." In *Classical Hollywood Comedy,* ed. Kristine Branovska Karnick and Henry Jenkins, 39–62. New York: Routledge, 1995.

———. *The Unruly Woman: Gender and Genres of Laughter.* Austin: University of Texas Press, 1995.

Rubenstein, Eliot. "The End of Screwball Comedy: *The Lady Eve* and *The Palm Beach Story.*" *Post Script.* 1:3 (Spring/Summer 1982): 33–47.

Rumens, Stuart. "Carte Blanche: Button Up That Lip," *Movie-Maker,* 19 (May 1985): 11–14.

Ryall, Tom. "Genre and Hollywood" In *The Oxford Guide to Film Studies.* ed. John Hill and Pamela Church Gibson, 327–338. London: Oxford University Press, 1998.

Safire, William. "Worth a Thousand Words." *New York Times Magazine,* 7 April 1996, 16.

Salamon, Julie. *The Devil's Candy: "The Bonfire of the Vanities" Goes to Hollywood.* Boston: Houghton Mifflin, 1991.

Salt, Barry. "Film Forum 1900–1906." In *Early Cinema: Space, Frame, Narrative,* ed. Thomas Elsaesser, 31–44. London: British Film Institute, 1990.

———. "Film Style and Technology in the Forties," *Film Quarterly* 31.3 (Fall 1977): 46–57.

Sapir, Edward. *Selected Writings of Edward Sapir in Language, Culture and Personality.* Edited by David Mandelbaum. Berkeley and Los Angeles: University of California Press, 1949.

Schatz, Thomas. "The Family Melodrama." In *Imitations of Life: A Reader on Film and Television Melodrama,* ed. Marcia Landy, 148–67. Detroit: Wayne State University Press, 1991.

Scholes, Robert. *Structuralism in Literature: An Introduction.* New Haven: Yale University Press, 1974.

Schwenger, Peter. *Phallic Critiques: Masculinity and Twentieth Century Literature.* London: Routledge & Kegan Paul, 1984.

Self, Robert T. "The Sounds of M*A*S*H." In *Close Viewings,* ed. Peter Lehman, 141–57. Tallahassee: Florida State University Press, 1990.

Shachtman, Tom. *The Inarticulate Society: Eloquence and Culture in America.* New York: Free Press, 1995.

Shadioan, Jack. *Dreams and Dead Ends: The American Gangster/Crime Film.* Cambridge, Mass.: MIT Press, 1977.

———. "Writing for the Screen—Some Thoughts on Dialogue," *Literature/Film Quarterly* 9.2 (1981): 85–91.

Shohat, Ella, and Robert Stam. *Unthinking Eurocentrism: Multiculturalism and the Media.* New York: Routledge, 1994.

Shreger, Charles. "Altman, Dolby and the Second Sound Revolution." In *Film Sound: Theory and Practice,* ed. Elisabeth Weis and John Belton, 348–55. New York: Columbia University Press, 1985.

Shulevitz, Judith. "Tongues on Wry Lend Special Flavor to Movies." *New York Times,* 9 February 1992, 13, 16.

Shumway, David, "Screwball Comedies: Constructing Romance, Mystifying Marriage." In *Film Genre Reader II,* ed. Barry Keith Grant, 381–401. Austin: University of Texas Press, 1995.

Silver, Alain, and Elizabeth Ward, eds. *Film Noir: An Encyclopedic Reference to the American Style.* Woodstock, N.Y.: Overlook Press, 1979.

Silverman, Kaja. *The Acoustic Mirror: The Female Voice in Psychoanalysis and Cinema.* Bloomington: Indiana University Press, 1988.

Simon, John. "The Word on Film." *Hudson Review* 30.4 (1977–78): 501–21.

Sinclair, Andrew, ed. *Stagecoach: A Film by John Ford and Dudley Nichols.* London: Lorrimer, 1971.

Slotkin, Richard. *Gunfighter Nation: The Myth of the Frontier in Twentieth-Century America.* New York: Harper, 1993.

Smiley, Sam. *Playwriting: The Structure of Action.* Englewood Cliffs, N.J.: Prentice-Hall, 1971.

Smith, Gavin. "Quentin Tarantino Interviewed by Gavin Smith." *Film Comment* 30.4 (July–August 1994): 32–37.

Smith, Marisa, and Amy Schewel, eds. *The Actor's Book of Movie Monologues.* New York: Penguin Books, 1986.

Smith, Marisa, and Jocelyn Beard, eds. *Contemporary Movie Monologues: A Sourcebook for Actors.* New York: Fawcett Columbine, 1991.

Smith, Murray. "The Logic and Legacy of Brechtianism." In *Post Theory: Reconstructing Film Studies,* ed. David Bordwell and Noël Carroll, 130–48. Madison: University of Wisconsin Press, 1996.

Sobchack, Vivian. *Screening Space: The American Science Fiction Film.* 2d ed. New York: Ungar, 1988.

Sontag, Susan. "The Imagination of Disaster." In *Film Theory and Criticism,* ed. Gerald Mast and Marshall Cohen, 488–504. 2d ed. New York: Oxford University Press, 1979.

———. "Theater and Film." In *Film and/as Literature,* ed. John Harrington, 76–92. Englewood Cliffs, N.J.: Prentice-Hall, 1977.

Spacks, Patricia Meyer. *Gossip.* New York: Knopf, 1985. Reprint. Chicago: University of Chicago Press, 1986.

Spender, Dale. *Man Made Language.* London: Routledge & Kegan Paul, 1980.

Spoto, Donald. *The Dark Side of Genius: The Life of Alfred Hitchcock.* New York: Ballantine Books, 1983.

Statta, Richard W. *The Cowboy Encyclopedia.* Santa Barbara, Calif.: ABC–Clio, 1994.

Stowell, Peter. *John Ford.* Boston: Twayne, 1986.

Sturges, John. Interview by Sasha Alpert. *American Cinema, Part 4: The Western.* New York Center for Visual History–KCCT-TV–BBC, 1994.

Sturges, Preston. *Four More Screenplays.* Introduction by Brian Henderson. Foreword by Tom Sturges. Berkeley and Los Angeles: University of California Press, 1995.

Styan, J. L. *The Elements of Drama.* Cambridge: Cambridge University Press, 1960.

Tannen, Deborah. *Talking Voices: Repetition, Dialogue and Imagery in Conversational Discourse.* Cambridge: Cambridge University Press, 1989.

———. *You Just Don't Understand: Women and Men in Conversation.* New York: Morrow, 1990.

Telotte, J. P. "Fatal Capers: Strategy and Enigma in Film Noir." *Journal of Popular Film and Television* 23.4 (Winter 1996): 163–71.

———. *Voices in the Dark: The Narrative Patterns of Film Noir.* Urbana: University of Illinois Press, 1989.

Thompson, Peggy, and Saeko Usukawa, *Hard-Boiled: Great Lines from Classic Noir Films.* San Francisco: Chronicle Books, 1995.

Todorov, Tzvetan. "Speech According to Constant." In id., *The Poetics of Prose,* trans. Richard Howard, 89–107. Ithaca, N.Y.: Cornell University Press, 1977.

Thomas, Sam, ed. *Best American Screenplays,* vol. 3. New York: Crown, 1995.

Tompkins, Jane. *West of Everything: The Inner Life of Westerns.* New York: Oxford University Press, 1992.

Traugott, Elizabeth Closs, and Mary Louise Pratt. *Linguistics for Students of Literature.* New York: Harcourt Brace Jovanovich, 1980.

Tudor, Andrew. "Genre." In *Film Genre Reader II,* ed. Barry Keith Grant, 3–10. Austin: University of Texas Press, 1995.

Turan, Kenneth. "On His Own 'Terms.' " James L. Brooks interviewed by Kenneth Turan, *Film Comment,* 20:2 (1984): 21–22.

Vale, Eugene. *The Technique of Screenplay Writing.* Rev. ed. New York: Grosset & Dunlap, 1972.

Van Druten, John. *Playwright at Work.* New York: Harper Brothers, 1953. Reprint. Westport, Conn.: Greenwood Press, 1971.

Van Lann, Thomas F. *The Idiom of Drama.* Ithaca, N.Y.: Cornell University Press, 1970.

Vanoye, Francis. "Conversations Publiques." *Iris* 3.1 (1985): 99–117.

Vasey, Ruth. "Foreign Parts: Hollywood's Global Distribution and the Representation of Ethnicity." *American Quarterly* 44.4 (December 1992): 617–42.

Wardhaugh, Ronald. *How Conversation Works.* London: Basil Blackwell, 1985.

Warshow, Robert. "The Gangster as Tragic Hero." In id., *The Immediate Experience,* 127–33. Garden City, N.Y.: Doubleday, 1962.

———. *The Immediate Experience: Movies, Comics, Theatre & Other Aspects of Popular Culture.* Garden City, N.Y.: Doubleday, 1962. Reprint. New York: Atheneum, 1979.

———. "Movie Chronicle: The Westerner." In id., *The Immediate Experience,* 35–54. Garden City, N.Y.: Doubleday, 1962.

Weales, Gerald. *Canned Goods as Caviar: American Film Comedy of the 1930s.* Chicago: University of Chicago Press, 1985.

Weintrub, Walter. *Verbal Behavior in Everyday Life.* New York: Springer, 1989.

Weis, Elisabeth. "The Narrative Functions of the Ecouteur." In *Cinesonic: The World of Sound in Film,* ed. Philip Brophy, 79–107. Sydney, Australia: AFTRS, 1999.

———. *The Silent Scream: Alfred Hitchcock's Sound Track.* Rutherford, N.J.: Fairleigh Dickinson University Press, 1982.

Weis, Elisabeth, and John Belton, eds. *Film Sound: Theory and Practice.* New York: Columbia University Press, 1985.

Weiss, Marion W. "Linguistic Coding in the Films of Martin Scorsese," *Semiotica* 55.3–4 (1985): 185–94.

Wexman, Virginia Wright. *Creating the Couple: Love, Marriage and Hollywood Performance.* Princeton, N.J.: Princeton University Press, 1993.

Williams, Alan. "The Raw and the Coded: Technological Change in the American Film Industry." In *Cinesonic: The World of Sound in Film,* ed. Philip Brophy, 229–43. Sydney, Australia: AFTRS, 1999.

Williams, Linda. "Melodrama Revised." In *Refiguring American Film Genres,* ed. Nick Browne, 42–88. Berkeley and Los Angeles: University of California Press, 1998.

Willis, Sharon. "The Fathers Watch the Boys' Room." *Camera Obscura* 32 (June 1995): 40–73.

Wills, Gary. *John Wayne's America.* New York: Touchstone, 1998.

———. "John Wayne's Body." *New Yorker,* 19 August 1996, 38–49.

Winokur, Mark. *American Laughter: Immigrants, Ethnicity and 1930s Hollywood Film Comedy.* New York: St. Martin's Press, 1996.

———. "Marginal Marginalia: The African-American Voice in the Nouvelle Gangster Film." *Velvet Light Trap* 35 (Spring 1995): 19–32.

Withers-Wilson, Nan. *Vocal Direction for the Theatre: From Script Analysis to Opening Night.* New York: Drama Book, 1993.

Wood, Robin. *Howard Hawks.* London: British Film Institute, 1981.

Wright, Will. *Six Guns and Society: A Structural Study of the Western.* Berkeley and Los Angeles: University of California Press, 1975.

Wyman, Walker, and Clifton Kroeber, eds. *The Frontier in Perspective.* Madison: University of Wisconsin Press, 1957.

Yaquinto, Marilyn. *Pump 'Em Full of Lead: A Look at Gangsters on Film.* New York: Twayne, 1998.

Zinman, Toby Silverman. "Jewish Aporia: The Rhythm of Talking in Mamet." *Theatre Journal* 44.2 (May 1992): 207–15.

Index

Abrahams, Jim, 5
Abrams, M. H., 59, 174
Academy Awards, 119, 240, 247, 255
accents: 83; character revelation through, 43; foreign. *See* foreign languages and accents; in melodramas, 241, 257; in Westerns, 149–53
acting. *See* casting; performance; stars
acting style, changes in, 23, 25; in gangster films, 206
Adam's Rib, 74
"added value," 17
Addicted to Love, 15
Affair to Remember, An, 239, 242
African-Americans, 26, 27, 82; "gangsta" films of, 203, 210–11, 215
Age of Innocence, The, 263
Aig, Dennis, 74, 75
Airplane!, 54
Al Capone, 208
Alice Doesn't Live Here Anymore, 24, 47
Alien, 51, 103–4, 208
All About Eve, 14, 44, 55
All I Desire, 53
All My Friends Are Going to Be Strangers, 255
All-Purpose Western Dialect (APWD), 151–53, 159
All That Heaven Allows, 240, 246
All That Jazz, 121–22
allegory, 34, 59–61; in Westerns, 163
allegory-lite, 60, 164n
Allen, Jeanne, 247
Allen, Woody, 78, 171
Altman, Rick, 97, 120–21, 236n
Altman, Robert, 23, 70–71, 96, 155, 268
American culture: anti-intellectualism in, 77; code of realism in, 47, 48; face-to-face conversation in, 98; influence of dialogue on, 27–28, 268–69; role of language in, 81; shift to naturalism in, 25
anchorage, 33–37, 47, 61, 62, 156, 216; lack of, 164, 230, 231
art direction: of gangster films, 203, 221; interaction of dialogue and, 133; of

melodramas, 259; of screwball comedies, 171; of westerns, 169
Anderson, Joseph, 98, 162, 168–69
Angel and the Bad Man, 149
Angels with Dirty Faces, 205, 215
Anna Christie, 23
Anthony and Cleopatra, 265
Apollo 13, 41
Applause, 66
Arden, Eve, 92
Arendt, Hannah, 29
Arnheim, Rudolf, 6, 62
Arthur, Jean, 61, 91, 194, 200
Arzner, Dorothy, 35
As Good As It Gets, 255
As You Like It, 34
Ashby, Hal, 23
Asian-Americans, 26, 82
Asphalt Jungle, The, 204, 206
Astaire, Fred, 74, 173
Astor, Mary, 196
asynchronous sound, 97, 101
Auden, W. H., 53
Auerbach, Erich, 24
auteur theory, 66, 268
authorial commentary, 34, 56–59, 61, 122–34, 154–55
Austin, J. L., 41
Awful Truth, The, 172, 176–78, 180, 181, 183, 184, 191, 193

Babington, Bruce, 170–72, 181
Baby Face, 237
background dialogue, 73, 88
backstories, 39–40
Badham, John, 72
Ball, Lucille, 92
Ball of Fire, 66, 173, 182, 184, 195, 268
Barber, C. L., 174
Barnard, Fred, 10n
Barr, Roseanne, 184n
Barrow, Clyde, 203
Barry, Philip, 21
Barthes, Roland, 34n, 35, 37, 91
Barton Fink, 206

311

Text:	10/13 Palatino
Display:	Palatino
Composition:	Impressions Book and Journal Services, Inc.
Printing and binding:	Thomson-Shore, Inc.

DATE DUE		
OCT 2 0 2006		